GLOBAL STUDIES

CHINA

THIRTEENTH EDITION

Dr. Zhiqun Zhu
Bucknell University

OTHER BOOKS IN THE GLOBAL STUDIES SERIES
- Africa
- Europe
- Islam and the Muslim World
- India and South Asia
- Japan and the Pacific Rim
- Latin America
- The Middle East
- Russia, the Baltics and Eurasian Republics, and Central/Eastern Europe

 **Higher Education**

Boston   Burr Ridge, IL   Dubuque, IA   New York   San Francisco   St. Louis
Bangkok   Bogotá   Caracas   Kuala Lumpur   Lisbon   London   Madrid   Mexico City
Milan   Montreal   New Delhi   Santiago   Seoul   Singapore   Sydney   Taipei   Toronto

The McGraw·Hill Companies

Mc Graw Hill Higher Education

GLOBAL STUDIES: CHINA, THIRTEENTH EDITION

Global Studies® is a registered trademark of the McGraw-Hill Companies, Inc.
Global Studies is published by the **Contemporary Learning Series** group within the McGraw-Hill Higher Education division.

1 2 3 4 5 6 7 8 9 0 QPD/QPD 0 9

ISBN 978–0–07–337987–6
MHID 0–07–337987–5
ISSN 1050–2025

Managing Editor: *Larry Loeppke*
Senior Managing Editor: *Faye Schilling*
Senior Developmental Editor: *Jill Peter*
Editorial Coordinator: *Mary Foust*
Editorial Assistant: *Nancy Meissner*
Production Service Assistant: *Rita Hingtgen*
Permissions Coordinator: *Shirley Lanners*
Senior Marketing Manager: *Julie Keck*
Marketing Communications Specialist: *Mary Klein*
Marketing Coordinator: *Alice Link*
Senior Project Manager: *Jane Mohr*
Design Specialist: *Tara McDermott*
Cover Graphics: *Rick D. Noel*

Compositor: Laserwords
Cover Image: © Getty Images/RF (background); Courtesy of Markus Raab (inset)

Library in Congress Cataloging-in-Publication Data
Main entry under title: Global Studies: China, 13th ed.
      1. Africa—History—1976–. 2. Taiwan—History—1945–.
I. Title: China. II. Zhu, Zhiqun, *comp.*

www.mhhe.com

CHINA

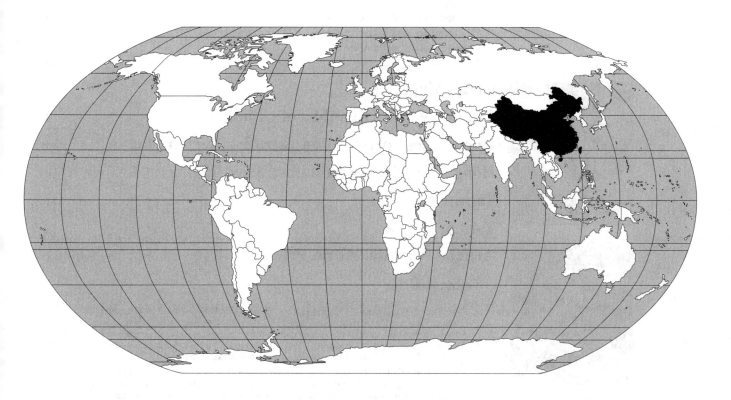

AUTHOR/EDITOR

Dr. Zhiqun Zhu

Dr. Zhiqun Zhu is an associate professor of political science and international relations and John D. and Catherine T. MacArthur Chair in East Asian Politics at Bucknell University in Pennsylvania. He writes primarily about Chinese politics, Chinese foreign policy, and East Asian political economy. His recent publications include *US-China Relations in the 21st Century: Power Transition and Peace* (London and New York: Routledge, 2006), and *Understanding East Asia's Economic Miracles* (Ann Arbor, MI: Association for Asian Studies, 2009). He is writing a new book about China's efforts to seek energy and promote "soft power" globally.

Contents

Articles from the World Press

China Articles

Using *Global Studies*: *China*

THE GLOBAL STUDIES SERIES

The Global Studies series was created to help readers acquire a basic knowledge and understanding of the regions and countries in the world. Each volume provides a foundation of information—geographic, cultural, economic, political, historical, artistic, and religious—that will allow readers to better assess the current and future problems within these countries and regions and to comprehend how events there might affect their own well-being. In short, these volumes present the background information necessary to respond to the realities of our global age.

Each of the volumes in the Global Studies series is crafted under the careful direction of an author/editor—an expert in the area under study. The author/editors teach and conduct research and have traveled extensively through the regions about which they are writing.

MAJOR FEATURES OF THE GLOBAL STUDIES SERIES

The Global Studies volumes are organized to provide concise information on the regions and countries within those areas under study. The major sections and features of the books are described here.

Country Reports

Concise reports are written for each of the countries within the region under study. These reports are the heart of each Global Studies volume. *Global Studies: China, Thirteenth Edition,* contains three country reports: People's Republic of China, Hong Kong, and Taiwan.

The country reports are composed of five standard elements. Each report contains a detailed map that visually positions the country among its neighboring states; a summary of statistical information; a current essay providing important historical, geographical, political, cultural, and economic information; a historical timeline, offering a convenient visual survey of a few key historical events; and four "graphic indicators," with summary statements about the country in terms of development, freedom, health/welfare, and achievements.

A Note on the Statistical Reports

The statistical information provided for each country has been drawn from a wide range of sources. (The most frequently referenced are listed on page 200.) Every effort has been made to provide the most current and accurate information available. However, sometimes the information cited by these sources differs to some extent; and, all too often, the most current information available for some countries is somewhat dated. Aside from these occasional difficulties, the statistical summary of each country is generally quite complete and up to date. Care should be taken, however, in using these statistics (or, for that matter, any published statistics) in making hard comparisons among countries. We have also provided comparable statistics for the United States and Canada, which can be found on pages x and xi.

World Press Articles

Within each Global Studies volume is reprinted a number of articles carefully selected by our editorial staff and the author/editor from a broad range of international periodicals and newspapers The articles have been chosen for currency, interest, and their differing perspectives on the subject countries. There are 37 articles in *Global Studies: China, Thirteenth Edition.*

The articles section is preceded by an annotated table of contents. This resource offers a brief summary of each article.

WWW Sites

An extensive annotated list of selected World Wide Web sites can be found on pages viii–ix in this edition of *Global Studies: China.* In addition, the URL addresses for country-specific Web sites are provided on the statistics page of most countries. All of the Web site addresses were correct and operational at press time. Instructors and students alike are urged to refer to those sites often to enhance their understanding of the region and to keep up with current events.

Glossary, Bibliography, Index

At the back of each Global Studies volume, readers will find a glossary of terms and abbreviations, which provides a quick reference to the specialized vocabulary of the area under study and to the standard abbreviations used throughout the volume.

Following the glossary is a bibliography that lists general works, national histories, and current-events publications and periodicals that provide regular coverage on China.

The index at the end of the volume is an accurate reference to the contents of the volume. Readers seeking specific information and citations should consult this standard index.

Currency and Usefulness

Global Studies: China, like the other Global Studies volumes, is intended to provide the most current and useful information available necessary to understand the events that are shaping the cultures of the region today.

This volume is revised on a regular basis. The statistics are updated, regional essays and country reports revised, and world press articles replaced. In order to accomplish this task, we turn to our author/editor, our advisory boards, and—hopefully—to you, the users of this volume. Your comments are more than welcome. If you have an idea that you think will make the next edition more useful, an article or bit of information that will make it more current, or a general comment on its organization, content, or features that you would like to share with us, please send it in for serious consideration.

Selected World Wide Web Sites for *Global Studies: China*

Some websites continually change their structure and content, so the information listed here may not always be available.

GENERAL SITES

Access Asia
http://www.accessasia.org

Asia Intelligence Home Page
http://www.asiaint.com/

Asia News
http://www.asianews.it/view.php?l=en&art=537

Asia Resources on the World Wide Web
http://www.aasianst.org/wwwchina.htm

Asia Source (Asia Society)
http://www.asiasource.org

Asia Times
http://www.atimes.com/

BBC News, China
http://news.bbc.co.uk/1/hi/in_depth/asia_pacific/2004/china/default.stm

Brookings Institution, Center for Northeast Asian Studies
http://www.brookings.edu/fp/cnaps/center_hp.htm

Center for Strategic & International Studies
http://www.csis.org/China

PEOPLE'S REPUBLIC OF CHINA

Beijing International
http://www.ebeijing.gov.cn/Tour/default.htm

Beijing Review
http://www.bjreview.com.cn

Carnegie Endowment for International Peace: China Program
http://www.ceip.org/files/events/events.asp?pr=16&EventID=674

Center for US-China Policy Studies
http://cuscps.sfsu.edu/

China Business Information Center
http://www.cbiz.cn/

The China Daily
http://www.chinadaily.com.cn

China Development Brief: Index of International NGOS in China
http://www.chinadevelopmentbrief.com/dingo/index.asp

China Digital News
http://www.ceip.org/files/events/events.asp?pr=16&EventID=674

China Elections and Governance
http://chinaelections.org/en/default.asp

Chinese Embassy in the U.S.
http://www.china-embassy.org/eng

China Law and Governance Review
http://chinareview.info/

China's Ministry of Foreign Affairs
http://www.fmprc.gov.cn/eng/

China Online
http://www.chinaonline.com

China Related Web Sites
http://orpheus.ucsd.edu/chinesehistory/othersites.html

China's Official Gateway to News & Information
http://www.china.org.cn

Chinese Human Rights Web
http://www.chinesehumanrightsreader.org

Chinese Military Power Research Sites
http://www.comw.org/cmp/links.html

Cold War International History Project
http://wwics.si.edu/index.cfm?topic_id=1409&fuseaction=topics.home

Congressional-Executive Commission on China
http://www.cecc.gov/

CSIS International Security Program
http://www.chinatopnews.com/MainNews/English/

East Turkestan Information Center
http://www.uygur.org/enorg/h_rights/human_r.htm

Foreign Policy in Focus
http://www.fpif.org/index.html

Foreign Policy in Focus Policy Brief Missile Defense & China
http://www.fpif.org/briefs/vol6/v6n03taiwan.html
http://www.uschinaedu.org-Program.asp

Inside China Today—Groups Urge EU to Censure China at UN Over Rights Learn Chinese with Homestay in China
http://www.lotusstudy.com/

Jamestown Foundation
http://www.jamestown.org/

Mainland Affairs Council Malaysia News Center—China News
http://news.newmalaysia.com/world/china/

Modern East-West Encounters
http://www.thescotties.pwp.blueyonder.co.uk/ew-asiapacific.htm

National Committee on U.S. China Relations
http://www.ncuscr.org/

Needham Research Institute, Cambridge, England
http://www.nri.org.uk/

People's Daily Online
http://english.peopledaily.com.cn/

SCMP.com - Asia's leading English news channel
http://www.scmp.com/

Sinologisches Seminar, Heidelberg University
http://www.sino.uni-heidelberg.de/

Status of Population and Family Planning Programme in China by Province
http://www.unescap.org/esid/psis/population/database/chinadata/intro.htm

Tiananmen Square, 1989, The Declassified Story: A National Security Archive Briefing Book
http://www.gwu.edu/ nsarchiv/NSAEBB/NSAEBB16/documents/index.html

The Chairman Smiles - Chinese Posters 1966–1976
http://www.iisg.nl/exhibitions/chairman/chnintro2.html

The China Journal
http://rspas.anu.edu.au/ccc/journal.htm

The Chinese Military Power Page–The Commonwealth Institute
http://www.comw.org/cmp/

U.S. China Education Programs
http://www.fpif.org/briefs/vol6/v6n03taiwan.html

U.S. Embassy
http://www.usembasy-china.org.cn

U.S. International Trade Commission
http://www.usitc.gov/

UCSD Modern Chinese History Site
http://www.usitc.gov/

United Nations: China's Millennium Goals, Progress
http://www.unchina.org/MDGConf/html/reporten.pdf

United Nations Human Development Reports, China
http://hdr.undp.org/

US-China Education and Culture Exchange Center
www.uschinaedu.edu

World Link Education's China Programs
http://www.worldlinkedu.com/?source=overture&OVRAW=List% 20of %20Chinese%20language%20television%20channels&OVKEY= chinese%20language&OVMTC=advanced

Xinhua Net
http://news.xinhuanet.com/english/

Yahoo! News and Media Newspapers by Region Countries China
http://dir.yahoo.com/News_and_Media/Newspapers/By_Region/ Countries/China/

HONG KONG

Chinese University of Hong Kong
http://www.usc.cuhk.edu.hk/uscen.asp

CIA
http://www.cia.gov/cia/publications/factbook/geos/hk.html

Civic Exchange, Christine Loh's Newsletter
http://www.civic-exchange.org/n_home.htm

Clean the Air
http://www.cleartheair.org.hk/

Hong Kong Special Administrative Region Government Information
http://www.info.gov.hk/eindex.htm

Hong Kong Transition Project, 1982–2007
http://www.hkbu.edu.hk/ hktp/

Shenzhen Government Online
http://english.sz.gov.cn/

South China Morning Post
http://www.scmp.com/

TAIWAN
The China Post
http://www.chinapost.com.tw

Mainland Affairs Council
http://www.mac.gov.tw/

My Egov
http://english.www.gov.tw/e-Gov/index.jsp

Taipei Times
http://www.taipeitimes.com/News/

Taipei Yearbook
http://english.taipei.gov.tw/yearbook/index.jsp?recordid=7345

Taiwan Economic and Cultural Representative Office in the U.S.
http://www.tecro.org/

Taiwan Headlines
http://www.taiwanheadlines.gov.tw/mp.asp

Taiwan News
http://www.etaiwannews.com/Taiwan/

See individual country report pages for additional Web sites.

The United States

GEOGRAPHY

Area in Square Miles (Kilometers): 3,793,079 (9,826,630) about ½ the size of Russia

Capital (Population): Washington, D.C. (581,530, 2006 est.)

Environmental Concerns: air and water pollution; limited natural fresh water resources; desertification; loss of habitat; waste disposal; acid rain

Geographical Features: vast central plain, mountains in west, hills and low mountains in east; rugged mountains and broad river valleys in Alaska; rugged, volcanic topography in Hawaii

Climate: mostly temperate, but ranging from tropical to arctic

PEOPLE
Population

Total: 303,824,640 (July, 2008 est.)

Annual Growth Rate: 0.883% (2008 est.)

Rural/Urban Population Ratio: 19/81 (WHO 2006)

Major Languages: 82.1% English; 10.7% Spanish; 7.1% other (2000 census)

Ethnic Makeup: 81.7% white; 12.9% black; 4.2% Asian; 1% Amerindian (2003 est.)

Religions: 51.3% Protestant; 23.9% Roman Catholic; 16.1% none or unaffiliated; 8.8% others (2007 est.)

Health

Life Expectancy at Birth: 75.29 years (male); 81.13 years (female) (2008 est.)

Infant Mortality: 6.3/1000 live births (2008 est.)

Per Capita total expenditure on Health: $6,347 (WHO 2005)

HIV/AIDS Rate in Adults: 0.6% (WHO 2005 est.)

Education

Adult Literacy Rate: 99% (2003 est.)

Compulsory (Ages): 7–16; free

COMMUNICATION

Telephones: 172,000,000 (2006)

Cell Phones: 255,000,000 (2007)

Internet Users: 223,000,000 (2008)

TRANSPORTATION

Highways in Miles (Kilometers): (6,430,366 km) (2005)

Railroads in Miles (Kilometers): (226,612 km) (2005)

Usable Airfields: 14,947 (2007)

GOVERNMENT

Type: federal republic

Independence Date: July 4, 1776

Head of State/Government: Barack Obama

Political Parties: Democratic Party; Republican Party; others of relatively minor political significance

Suffrage: 18 years of age; universal

MILITARY

Military Expenditures (% of GDP): $583.283 billion (FY 2008); 4.06% (FY 2006) (SIPRI)

Current Disputes: Wars in Afghanistan and Iraq

ECONOMY

Per Capita Income/GDP: $45,800/$13.84 trillion (2007 est.)

GDP Growth Rate: 2.2% (2007 est.)

Inflation Rate: 2.9% (2007 est.)

Unemployment Rate: 4.6% (2007 est.)

Population Below Poverty Line: 12% (2004 est.)

Natural Resources: many minerals and metals; petroleum; natural gas; timber; arable land.

Agriculture: wheat, corn, other grains, fruits, vegetables, cotton; beef, pork, poultry, dairy products; fish; forest products

Industry: leading industrial power in the world, highly diversified and technologically advanced; petroleum, steel, motor vehicles, aerospace, telecommunications, chemicals, electronics, food processing, consumer goods, lumber, mining

Exports: $1,149 trillion (2007 est.) (primary partners Canada, Mexico, China, Japan, UK)

Imports: $1,965 trillion (2007 est.) (primary partners China, Canada, Mexico, Japan, Germany) (2006)

Human Development Index (ranking): 12 (UNDP 2008)

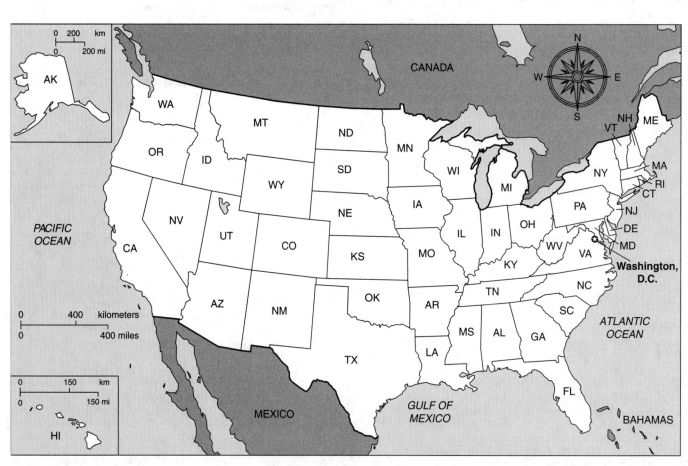

Canada

GEOGRAPHY

Area in Square Miles (Kilometers): 3,854,083 (9,984,670)

Capital (Population): Ottawa (812,129) (2006)

Environmental Concerns: air and water pollution; acid rain; industrial damage to agricultural and forest productivity

Geographical Features: permafrost in the north; mostly plains with mountains in west and lowlands in southeast

Climate: varies from temperate in south to subarctic and arctic in north

PEOPLE

Population

Total: 33,212,696 (July, 2008 est.)

Annual Growth Rate: 0.83% (2008 est.)

Rural/Urban Population Ratio: 20/80 (WHO 2006)

Major Languages: English (Official) 59.3%; French (Official) 23.2%; Other 17.5%

Ethnic Makeup: British Isles origin 28%, French origin 23%, other European 15%, Amerindian 2%, other, mostly Asian, African, Arab 6%, mixed background 26%

Religions: 42.6% Roman Catholic; 23.3% Protestant; 4.4% Other Christian; 1.9% Muslim; 11.8% other; 16% none (2001 Census)

Health

Life Expectancy at Birth: 78.65 years (male); 83.81 (female). (2008 est.)

Infant Mortality: 5.08/1000 live births (2008 est.)

Per Capita expenditure on Health: $3,452 (WHO 2005)

HIV/AIDS Rate in Adults: 0.3% (WHO 2005 est.)

Education

Adult Literacy Rate: 99%

Compulsory (Ages): primary school

COMMUNICATION

Telephones: 21,000,000 main lines (2006)

Cell Phones: 18,749,000 (2006)

Internet Users: 22 million (2005)

TRANSPORTATION

Highways in Miles (Kilometers): (1,042,300 km.)

Railroads in Miles (Kilometers): (48,467 km.)

Usable Airfields: 1,343 (2007)

GOVERNMENT

Type: constitutional monarchy that is also a parliamentary democracy and a federation

Independence Date: July 1, 1867

Head of State/Government: Queen Elizabeth II/Prime Minister Stephen Harper

Political Parties: Conservative Party of Canada, Liberal Party, Green Party, New Democratic Party, Bloc Quebecois.

Suffrage: universal at 18

MILITARY

Military Expenditures (% of GDP): $18,695 million (2008); (1.2%) (2006) (SIPRI)

Current Disputes: with NATO forces in Afghanistan

ECONOMY

Currency (US equivalent): 1.0724 Canadian dollars to $1 US (2007)

Per Capita Income/GDP: $38,400 (2007 est.)/$1.266 trillion (2007 est.)

GDP Growth Rate: 2.7%

Inflation Rate: 2.1% (2007 est.)

Unemployment Rate: 6% (2007 est.)

Population Below Poverty Line: 10.8% (2005)

Labor Force by Occupation: 75% Services, 13% Manufacturing, 6% Construction, 2% Agriculture, 2% other (2006)

Natural Resources: petroleum; natural gas, fish; minerals; cement; forestry products; wildlife; hydropower

Agriculture: wheat, barley, oilseed, tobacco, fruits, vegetables; dairy products; forest products; fish

Industry: transportation equipment, chemicals, processed and unprocessed minerals, food products, wood and paper products, fish products, petroleum and natural gas

Exports: $433.1 billion f.o.b. (2007 est.) (primary partners United States, UK, China) (2006)

Imports: $386.9 billion f.o.b. (2007 est.) (primary partners United States, China, Mexico) (2006)

Human Development Index (ranking): 4 (UNDP 2008)

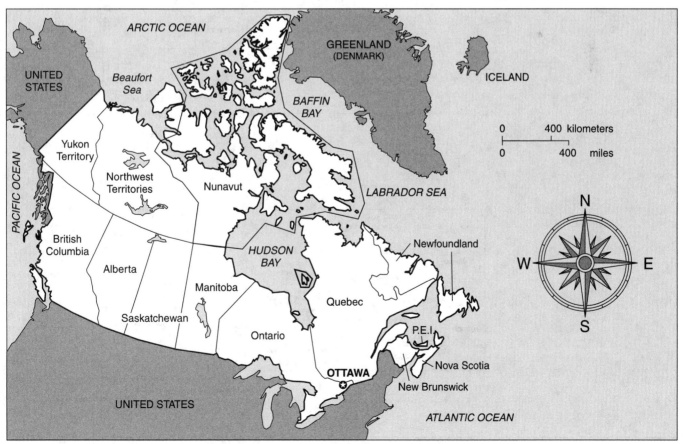

GLOBAL ● STUDIES

This map is provided to give you a graphic picture of where the countries of the world are located, the relationship they have with their region and neighbors, and their positions relative to major trade and power blocs. We have focused on certain areas to illustrate these crowded regions more clearly. China is shaded for emphasis.

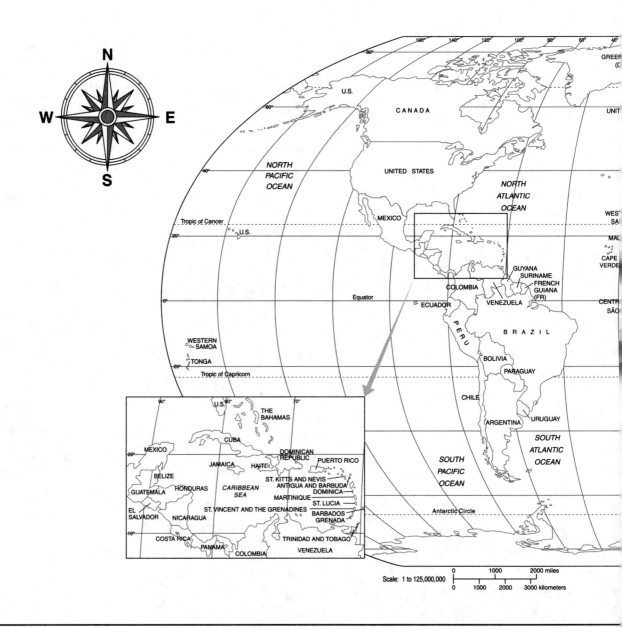

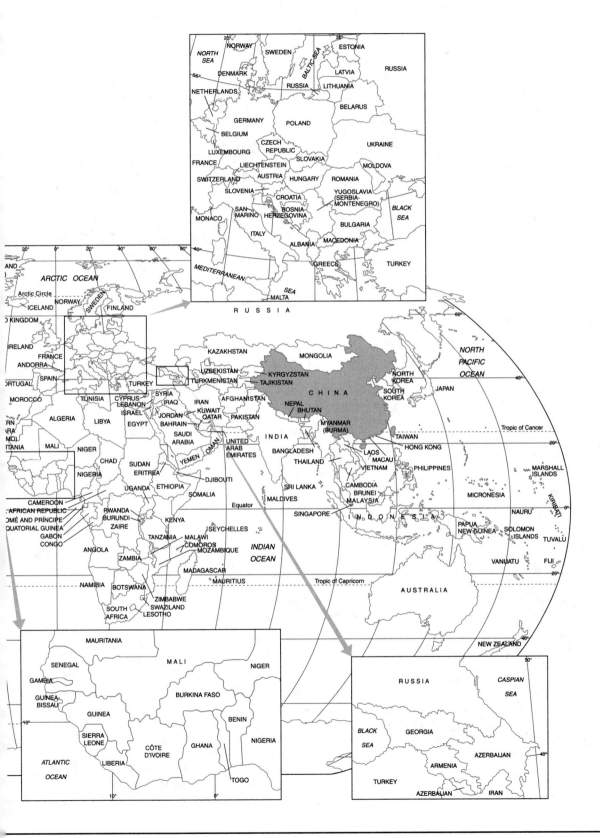

China Map

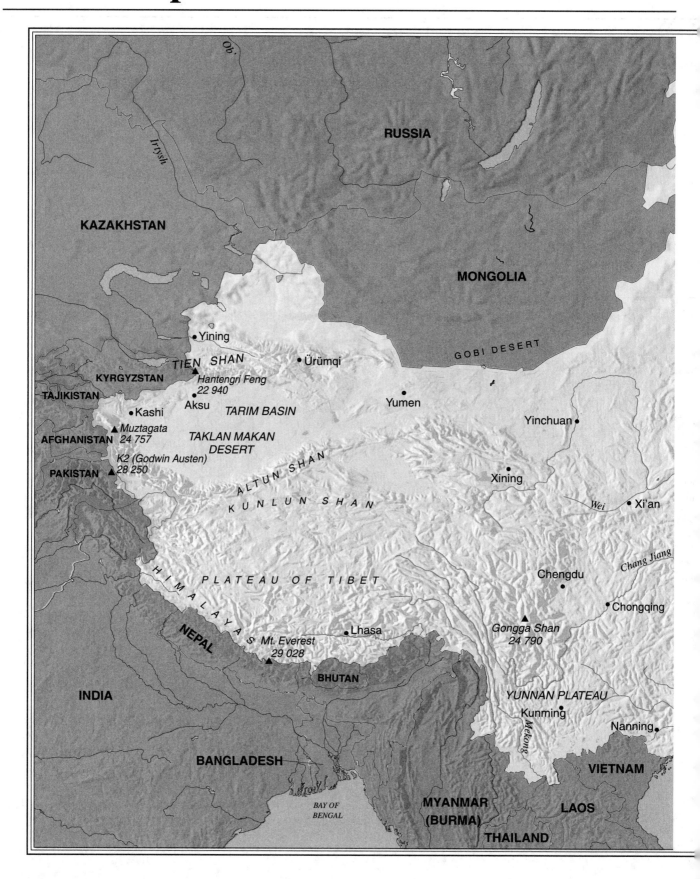

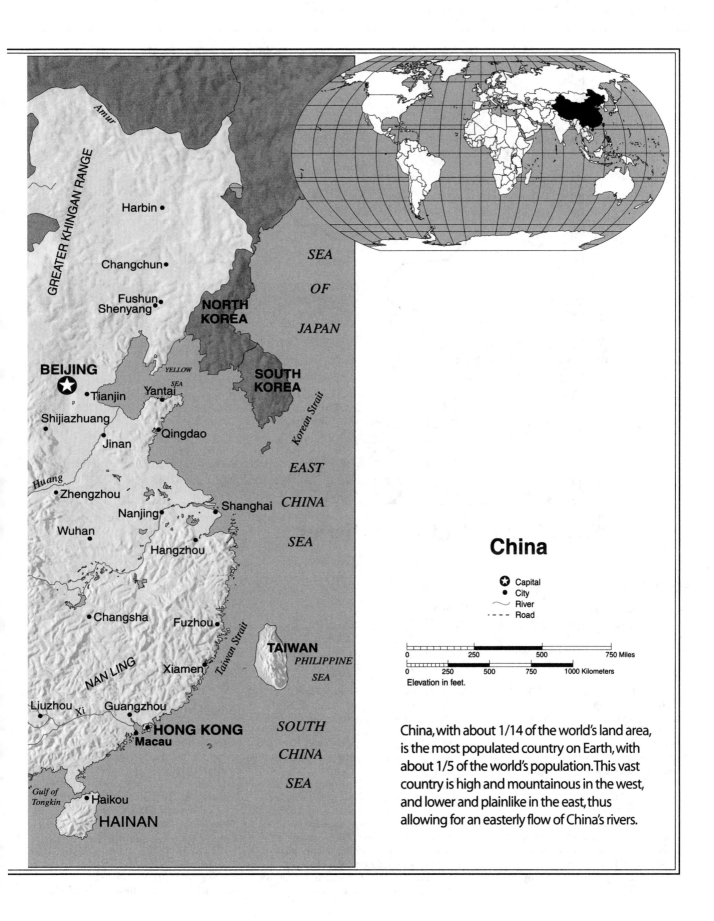

China

★ Capital
● City
〜 River
- - - Road

| 0 | 250 | 500 | 750 Miles |
| 0 | 250 | 500 | 750 | 1000 Kilometers |

Elevation in feet.

China, with about 1/14 of the world's land area, is the most populated country on Earth, with about 1/5 of the world's population. This vast country is high and mountainous in the west, and lower and plainlike in the east, thus allowing for an easterly flow of China's rivers.

China (People's Republic of China)

People's Republic of China Statistics

GEOGRAPHY

Area in Square Miles (Kilometers):
3,705,386 (9,596,960) (about the same size as the United States)
Capital (Population): Beijing, 8.7 million (city proper), 17.4 million (metro area)
Other Large Cities: Shanghai, Chongqing (Chungking), Tianjin, Wuhan, Shenyang (Mukden), Guangzhou, Harbin, Xi'an, Chengdu, and Nanjing (Nanking)
Environmental Concerns: air and water pollution; water shortages; desertification; trade in endangered species; acid rain; loss of agricultural land; deforestation
Geographical Features: mostly mountains, high plateaus, and deserts in the west and northwest; plains, deltas, and hills in the east
Climate: extremely diverse, from tropical to subarctic

PEOPLE

Population

Total: 1,330,044,544 (July 2008 est.)
Annual Growth Rate: 0.629% (2008 est.)
Rural/Urban Population Ratio: 61/39
Sex Ratio of Total Population: 1.04 male(s)/1.0 female (2008 est.)
Major Languages: Standard Chinese or Mandarin (Putonghua, based on the Beijing dialect), Yue (Cantonese), Wu (Shanghainese), Minbei (Fuzhou), Minnan (Hokkien-Taiwanese), Xiang, Gan, Hakka dialects, minority languages
Ethnic Makeup: Han Chinese 91.5%, Zhuang, Manchu, Hui, Miao, Uyghur, Tujia, Yi, Mongolian, Tibetan, Buyi, Dong, Yao, Korean, and other nationalities 8.5% (2000 census)
Religions: officially atheist; but popular religions include Daoism (Taoism), Buddhism, Islam, Christianity, ancestor worship, and animism

Health

Life Expectancy at Birth: 73.18 years (male: 71.37 years, female: 75.18 years) (2008 est.)
Infant Mortality Rate: 21.16 deaths/1,000 live births (2008 est.)
Number of Physicians Per 1000 People: 1.65
HIV/AIDS Rate in Adults: 0.1% (2003 est.)

Education

Adult Literacy Rate: 91%
Compulsory Years of Schooling: 9

COMMUNICATION

Telephones: Landlines: 368 million (2007); Cell phones: 548 million (2007)
Newspapers: 2,081
Daily Newspaper Circulation: 93.5 million
Journals and Magazines: 9,363
Publishing Houses: 600
Internet Users: 253 million (2008)

TRANSPORTATION

Airports: 467 (2007)
Major Ports: Shanghai, Dalian, Guangzhou, Ningbo, Qingdao, Qinhuangdao, Shenzhen, Tianjin
Railways: 75,438 km (20,151 km electrified) (2005)
Roadways: 1,930,544 km, 1,575,571 km paved (includes 41,005 km of expressways) (2005)
Waterways: 124,000 km navigable (2006)
Motor Vehicles in Use: 160 million, including over 30 million privately owned cars (2007)

GOVERNMENT

Type: one-party state ruled by the Communist Party
Independence Date: unification in 221 B.C. The People's Republic of China was established on October 1, 1949
Head of State/Government: President Hu Jintao; Premier Wen Jiabao
Political Parties: Chinese Communist Party; eight registered small parties under the leadership of the CCP
Suffrage: universal at 18 in village and urban district elections

MILITARY

Military Expenditures (% of GDP): 4.3% (2006)
People's Liberation Army (PLA): Ground Forces, Navy, Air Force, and Second Artillery Corps (strategic missile force); People's Armed Police (PAP)
Current Disputes: territorial disputes with a few countries, especially India, Japan, and Russia, and potentially serious disputes over Spratly and Paracel Islands with several countries

ECONOMY

Currency: yuan
Exchange Rate: US$1 = 6.845 yuan (December 2008)
GDP (purchasing power parity): $6.991 trillion (2007 est.)
GDP (official exchange rate): $3.251 trillion (2007 est.)
Per Capita Income (purchasing power parity): $5,300 (2007 est.)
Labor Force: 803.3 million (2007 est.)
Unemployment Rate: 4% unemployment in urban areas; substantial unemployment and underemployment in rural areas (2007 est.)
Distribution of Family Income — Gini index: 47 (2007)
Inflation Rate (consumer prices): 4.8% (2007 est.)
Investment (gross fixed): 40.4% of GDP (2007 est.)
Agricultural Products: rice, wheat, potatoes, corn, peanuts, tea, millet, barley, apples, cotton, oilseed, pork, fish
Industries: mining and ore processing; iron, steel, aluminum, and other metals, coal; machine building; armaments; textiles and apparel; petroleum; cement; chemicals; fertilizers; consumer products, including footwear, toys, and electronics; food processing; transportation equipment; telecommunications equipment, commercial space launch vehicles, satellites
Industrial Production Growth Rate: 13.4% (2007 est.)
Exports: $1.217 trillion f.o.b. (2007 est.)
Exports Commodities: machinery, electrical products, data processing equipment, apparel, textiles, steel, mobile phones
Exports Partners: US 19.4%, Hong Kong 15.2%, Japan 8.4%, South Korea 4.6%, Germany 4.1% (2006)
Imports: $901.3 billion f.o.b. (2007 est.)
Imports Commodities: machinery and equipment, oil and mineral fuels, plastics, LED screens, data processing equipment, optical and medical equipment, organic chemicals, steel, copper
Imports Partners: Japan 13.9%, South Korea 11%, Taiwan 10.6%, US 7.5%, Germany 4.7% (2006)

SUGGESTED WEB SITES

https://www.cia.gov/library/publications/the-world-factbook/geos/ch.html
http://www.DemographicsNowChina.com
http://www.infoplease.com/ipa/A0107411.html
http://www.chinatoday.com/data/data.htm

People's Republic of China Country Report

Chinese civilization originated in the Neolithic Period, which began around 5000 B.C., but scholars know little about it until the Shang Dynasty, which dates from about 2000 B.C. By that time, the Chinese had already developed the technology and art of bronze casting to a high standard; and they had a sophisticated system of writing with ideographs, in which words are portrayed by picturelike characters. From the fifth to the third centuries B.C., the level of literature and the arts was comparable to that of Greece in the Classical Period, which flourished at the same time. Stunning breakthroughs occurred in science, a civil service evolved, and the philosopher Confucius developed a highly sophisticated system of ethics for government and moral codes for society. Confucian values were dominant until the collapse of the Chinese imperial system in 1911, but even today they influence Chinese thought and behavior in China, and in Chinese communities throughout the world.

From several hundred years B.C. until the 15th century, China was the world's leader in technology, had the largest economy, and enjoyed the highest GDP per capita income in the world. By 1500, however, the government had closed China's doors to broad international trade, and Europe's GDP per capita surpassed China's. Still, it remained the world's largest economy, accounting for some 30 percent of the world's GDP in 1820. Over the next 130 years, war, revolution, and invasions ate away at China's productive capabilities. By the time the Chinese Communist Party came to power in October 1949, China's share of the world's GDP had dropped to 5 percent.[1] The historical baggage that China carried into the period of the People's Republic of China in 1949 was, then, substantial. China had fallen from being one of the world's greatest empires—not just from an economic perspective, but also from cultural and scientific perspectives—before 1500, to one of the poorest countries in the world. When the Chinese Communists interpreted that history through the lens of Marxism and Leninism, they saw feudalism, capitalism, and imperialism as the cause of China's problem. They saw China as a victim both of exploitation within their own society, and from abroad.

The Chinese Empire

By 221 B.C., the many feudal states ruled by independent princes had been conquered by Qin Shi Huang Di, the first ruler of a unified Chinese Empire. He established a system of governmental institutions and a concept of empire that continued in China until A.D. 1911. Although China was unified from the Qin Dynasty onward, it was far less concrete than the term *empire* might indicate.

China's borders really reached only as far as its cultural influence did. Thus China contracted and expanded according to whether or not other groups of people accepted the Chinese ruler and culture as their own.

Those peoples outside "China" who refused to acknowledge the Chinese ruler as the "Son of Heaven" or pay tribute to him were called "barbarians." In part, the Great Wall, which stretches more than 2,000 miles across north China and was built in stages between the third century B.C. and the seventeenth century A.D., was constructed in order to keep marauding "barbarians" out of China. Nevertheless, they frequently invaded China and occasionally even succeeded in subduing the Chinese—as in the Yuan (Mongol) Dynasty (1279–1368) and, later, the Qing (Manchu) Dynasty (1644–1911).

However, the customs and institutions of the invaders eventually yielded to the powerful cultural influence of the Chinese. Indeed, in the case of the Manchus, who seized control of the Chinese Empire in 1644 and ruled until 1911, their success in holding onto the throne for so long may be due in part to their willingness to assimilate Chinese ways and to rule through existing Chinese institutions, such as the Confucian-ordered bureaucracy. By the time of their overthrow, the Manchu were hardly distinguishable from the ethnic Han Chinese in their customs, habits, and beliefs. When considering today's policies toward the numerous minorities who inhabit such a large expanse of the People's Republic of China, it should be remembered that the central Chinese government's ability to absorb minorities was key to its success in maintaining a unified entity called China (*Zhongguo*—"the Central Kingdom") for more than 2,000 years.

The Imperial Bureaucracy

A distinguishing feature of the political system of imperial China was the civil service examinations through which government officials were chosen. These examinations tested knowledge of the moral principles embodied in the classical Confucian texts. Although the exams were, in theory, open to all males in the Chinese Empire, the lengthy and rigorous preparation required meant that, in practice, the sons of the wealthy and powerful with access to a good education had an enormous advantage. Only a small percentage of those who began the process actually passed the examinations and received an appointment in the imperial bureaucracy. Some of those who were successful resided in the capital to advise the emperor, while others were sent as the emperor's agents to govern throughout the far-flung realm.

The Decline of the Manchus

The vitality of Chinese institutions and their ability to respond creatively to new problems came to an end during the Manchu Dynasty (1644–1911). A stagnant agricultural system incapable of supporting the burgeoning population and the increasing exploitation of the peasantry who comprised the vast majority of Chinese people led to massive internal rebellions and the rise of warlords. As the imperial bureaucracy became increasingly corrupt and incompetent, the Manchu Dynasty gradually lost the ability to govern effectively.

China's decline in the nineteenth century was exacerbated by a social class structure that rewarded those who could pass the archaic, morality-based civil service examinations rather than those who had expertise in science and technology and could thereby contribute to China's development. An inward-looking culture contributed to the malaise by preventing the Chinese from understanding the dynamism of the Industrial Revolution then occurring in the West. Gradually, the barriers erected by the Manchu rulers to prevent Western culture and technology from polluting the ancient beauty of Chinese civilization crumbled, but too late to strengthen China to resist the West's military onslaughts.

The Opium War (1839–1842)

In the early nineteenth century, the British traded with China, but it was primarily a one-way trade. The British nearly drained their coffers buying Chinese silk, tea, and porcelain; China's self-satisfied rulers found little of interest to purchase from the rapidly industrializing British. The British were also frustrated by China's refusal to recognize the British Empire as an equal of the Chinese Empire, and to open up ports to trade with them along China's extensive coastline and rivers.

Opium, produced in the British Empire's colony India, proved to be the one product that the Chinese were willing to purchase, and it reversed the trade balance in favor of the British. Eventually they used the Chinese attack on British ships carrying opium as an excuse for declaring war on the decrepit Chinese Empire. The Opium War ended with defeat for the Chinese and the signing of the Treaty of Nanjing (sometimes called Nanking). This treaty ceded the island of Hong Kong to the British as a colony and allowed them to establish trading posts.

Subsequent wars with the British and other European powers brought further concessions—the most important of which was the Chinese granting of additional "treaty ports" to Europeans. The Chinese had hoped that they could contain and

Public Domain (PD01-Confucius)
Confucius.

CONFUCIUS: CHINA'S FIRST "TEACHER"

Confucius (551–479 B.C.), whose efforts to teach China's rulers how to govern well were spurned, spent most of his life teaching his own disciples. Yet 300 years later, Confucianism, as taught by descendants of his disciples, was adopted as the official state philosophy. The basic principles of Confucianism include hierarchical principles of obedience and loyalty to one's superiors, respect for one's elders, and filial piety; and principles and practices for maintaining social order and harmony; and the responsibility of rulers to exercise their power benevolently.

control Europeans within these ports. Although that was true to a degree, this penetration of China led to the spread of Western values that challenged the stagnant, and by then collapsing, Chinese Empire. As the West and, by the late nineteenth century, Japan, nibbled away at China, the Manchu rulers made a last-ditch effort at reform to strengthen and enrich China. But it was too late, and the combination of internal decay, warlordism, revolution, and foreign imperialism finally toppled the Manchu Dynasty. Thus ended more than 2,000 years of imperial rule in China.

REPUBLICAN CHINA

The 1911 Revolution, which led to the overthrow of Manchu rule and derived its greatest inspiration from Chinese nationalist Sun Yat-sen, resulted in the establishment of the Republic of China (R.O.C.).

OPIUM AS A PRETEXT FOR WAR

Although the opium poppy is native to China, large amounts of opium were shipped to China by the English-owned East India Company, from the British colony of India. Eventually India exported so much opium to China that 5 to 10 percent of its revenues derived from its sale.

By the late 1700s, the Chinese government had officially prohibited first the smoking and selling of opium, and later its importation or domestic production. But because the sale of opium was so profitable—and also because so many Chinese officials were addicted to it—the Chinese officials themselves illegally engaged in the opium trade. As the number of addicts grew and the Chinese government became more corrupted by its own unacknowledged participation in opium smuggling, so grew the interest of enterprising Englishmen in smuggling it into China for financial gain.

The British government was primarily interested in expanding trade with China. But it also wanted to establish a diplomatic relationship based on equality to supplant the existing one, in which the Chinese court demanded that the English kowtow to the Chinese emperor. In addition, it wanted to secure legal jurisdiction over its nationals residing in China to protect them against Chinese practices of torture of those suspected of having committed a crime.

China's efforts to curb the smuggling of opium and the Chinese refusal to recognize the British as equals reached a climax in 1839, when the Chinese destroyed thousands of chests of opium aboard a British ship. This served as an ideal pretext for the British to attack China with their sophisticated gunboats (pictured below destroying a junk in Canton's (Guangzhou's) harbor). Ultimately their superior firepower gave victory to the British.

Thus the so-called Opium War (1839–1842) ended with defeat for the Chinese Empire and the signing of the Treaty of Nanjing, which ceded the island of Hong Kong to the British and allowed them to establish trading posts on the Chinese mainland.

Library of Congress Prints and Photographs Division/LC-USZ62-86300
Opium War (1839–1842). British attack on junks in Canton / Guangzhou Harbor.

It was, however, a "republic" only in name, for China was unable to successfully transfer Western forms of democratic governance to China. This was in no small part because of China's inability to remain united and to maintain law and order. China had been briefly united under the control of the dominant warlord of the time, Yuan Shikai; but with his death in 1916, China was again torn apart by the resurgence of contending warlords, internal political decay, and further Japanese territorial expansion in China. Efforts at reform failed in the context of China's weakness and internal division.

Chinese intellectuals searched for new ideas from abroad to strengthen their nation during the vibrant May Fourth period and New Culture Movement (spanning the period from roughly 1917 through the mid-1920s). In the process, the Chinese invited influential foreigners such as the English mathematician, philosopher, and socialist Bertrand Russell, and the American philosopher and educator John Dewey, to lecture in China. Thousands of Chinese traveled, worked, and studied abroad. It was during this period that ideas such as liberal democracy, syndicalism, guild socialism, and communism were put forth as possible solutions to China's many problems.

The Founding of the Chinese Communist Party

It was during that period, in 1921, that a small Marxist study group in Shanghai founded the Chinese Communist Party (CCP). The Moscow-based Comintern (Communist International) advised this highly intellectual but politically and militarily powerless group to join with the more militarily powerful Kuomintang (KMT or Nationalist Party, led first by Sun Yat-sen and, after his death in 1925, by Chiang Kai-shek) until it could gain strength and break away to establish themselves as an independent party. Thus it was with the support of the Communists in a "united front" with the Nationalists that Chiang Kai-shek conquered the warlords and reunified China under one central government. Chiang felt threatened by the Communists' ambitions to gain political power, however, so in 1927 he executed all but the few Communists who managed to escape.

Members of the CCP continued to take their advice from Moscow; and they tried to organize an orthodox Marxist, urban-based movement of industrial workers. Because the cities were completely controlled by the KMT, the CCP found it difficult to organize the workers, and ultimately the KMT's police and military forces decimated the ranks of the Communists. It is a testimony to the appeal of communism in that era that the CCP managed to recover its strength each time. Indeed, the growing power of the CCP was such that Chiang Kai-shek considered the CCP, rather than the invading Japanese, to be the main threat to his complete control of China.

Eventually the Chinese Communist leaders agreed that an urban strategy could not succeed. Lacking adequate military power to confront the Nationalists, however, they retreated. In what became known as the Long March (1934–1935), they traveled more than 6,000 miles from the southeast, through the rugged interior and onto the windswept, desolate plains of Yan'an in northern China.

It was during this retreat, in which as many as 100,000 followers perished, that Mao Zedong staged his contest for power within the CCP. With his victory, the CCP reoriented itself toward a rural strategy and attempted to capture the loyalty of China's peasants, then comprising some 85 percent of China's total population. Mao saw the downtrodden peasantry as the major source of support for the revolutionary overthrow of Chiang Kai-shek's government. Suffering from an oppressive and exploitative system of landlord control, disillusioned with the government's unwillingness to carry out land reform, and desirous of owning their own land, the peasantry looked to the CCP for leadership. Slowly the CCP started to gain control over China's vast countryside.

United against the Japanese

In 1931, Japan invaded China and occupied Manchuria, the three northeastern provinces. In 1937, Japan attacked again, advancing southward to occupy China's heartland. Although the CCP and KMT were determined to destroy each other, Japan's threat to spread its control over the rest of China caused them to agree to

MAO ZEDONG: CHINA'S REVOLUTIONARY LEADER

Mao Zedong (1893–1976) came from a moderately well-to-do peasant family and, as a result, received a very good education, as compared to the vast majority of the Chinese of his time. Mao was one of the founders of the Chinese Communist Party in 1921, but his views on the need to switch from an orthodox Marxist strategy, which called for the party to seek roots among the urban working class, to a rural strategy centered on the exploited peasantry were spurned by the leadership of the CCP and its sponsors in Moscow.

Later, it became evident that the CCP could not flourish in the Nationalist-controlled cities, as time and again the KMT quashed the idealistic but militarily weak CCP. Mao appeared to be right: "Political power grows out of the barrel of a gun."

The Communists' retreat to Yan'an in northern China at the end of the Long March was not only for the purpose of survival but also for regrouping and forming a stronger Red Army. There the followers of the Chinese Communist Party were taught Mao's ideas about guerrilla warfare, the importance of winning the support of the people, principles of party leadership, and socialist values. Mao consolidated his control over the leadership of the CCP during the Yan'an period and led it to victory over the Nationalists in 1949.

From that time onward, Mao became a symbol of the new Chinese government, of national unity, and of the strength of China against foreign humiliation. In later years, although his real power was eclipsed, the party maintained the public illusion that Mao was the undisputed leader of China.

In his declining years, Mao waged a struggle, in the form of the "Cultural Revolution," against those who followed policies antagonistic to his own—a struggle that brought the country to the brink of civil war and turned the Chinese against one another. The symbol of Mao as China's "great leader" and "great mentor" was used by those who hoped to seize power after him: first the minister of defense, Lin Biao, and then the "Gang of Four," which included Mao's wife.

Mao's death in 1976 ended the control of policy by the Gang of Four. Within a few years, questions were being raised about the legacy that Mao had left China. By the 1980s, it was broadly accepted throughout China that Mao had been responsible for a full 20 years of misguided policies. Since the Tiananmen Square protests of 1989, however, there has been a resurgence of nostalgia for Mao. This nostalgia is reflected in such aspects of popular culture as a tape of songs about Mao entitled "The Red Sun"—a best-selling tape in China, at over 5 million copies—that captures the Mao cult and Mao

Mao Zedong.

mania of the Cultural Revolution; and in a small portrait of Mao that virtually all car owners and taxi drivers hang over their rear-view mirrors for "good luck." Many Chinese long for the "good old days" of Mao's rule, when crime and corruption were at far lower levels than today and when there was a sense of collective commitment to China's future. But they do not long for a return to the mass terror of the Cultural Revolution, for which Mao also bears responsibility. In the commercialized twenty-first century China, attaching the name of Mao to a product is a good way to sell it.

a second "united front," this time for the purpose of halting the Japanese advance. Both the KMT and the CCP had ulterior motives, but according to most accounts, the Communists contributed more to the national wartime efforts. The Communists organized guerrilla efforts to peck away at the fringes of Japanese-controlled areas while Chiang Kai-shek, head of the KMT, retreated to the wartime capital of Chongqing (Chungking). His elite corps of troops and officers kept the best of the newly arriving American supplies for themselves, leaving the rank-and-file Chinese to fight against the Japanese in cloth boots and with inferior equipment. It was not the Nationalist Army but, rather, largely the unstinting efforts and sacrifices of the Chinese people and the American victory over

Japan that brought World War II to an end in 1945. With the demobilization of the Japanese, however, Chiang Kai-shek was free once again to focus on defeating the Communists.

The Communists Oust the KMT

It seemed as if the Communists' Red Army had actually been strengthened through its hard fighting during World War II, turning itself into a formidable force. Meanwhile, the relatively soft life of the KMT military elite during the war did not leave it well prepared for civil war against the Red Army. Chiang Kai-shek relied on his old strategy of capturing China's cities, but the Communists, who had gained control over the countryside by winning the support of

the vast peasantry, surrounded the cities. Like besieged fortresses, the cities eventually fell to Communist control. By October 1949, the CCP could claim control over all of China, except for the island of Taiwan. It was there that the Nationalists' political, economic, and military elites, with American support, had fled.

Scholars still dispute why the Red Army ultimately defeated the Nationalist Army. They cite as probable reasons the CCP's promises to undertake land reform; the Communists' more respectful treatment of the peasantry as they marched through the countryside (in comparison to that of the KMT soldiers); the CCP's more successful appeal to the Chinese sense of nationalism; and Chiang Kai-shek's unwillingness to undertake reforms that would benefit the

RED GUARDS: ROOTING OUT THOSE "ON THE CAPITALIST ROAD"

During the Cultural Revolution, Mao Zedong called upon the country's young people to "make revolution." Called "Mao's Red Guards," their ages varied, but for the most part they were teenagers.

Within each class and school, various youths would band together in a Red Guard group that would take on a revolutionary-sounding name and would then carry out the objective of challenging people in authority. But the people in authority—especially school-teachers, school principals, bureaucrats, and local leaders of the Communist Party—initially ignored the demands of the Red Guards that they reform their "reactionary thoughts" or eliminate their "feudal" habits.

The Red Guards initially had no real weapons and could only threaten. Since they were considered just misdirected children by those under attack, their initial assaults had little effect. But soon the frustrated Red Guards took to physically beating and publicly humiliating those who stubbornly refused to obey them. Since Mao had not clearly defined precisely what should be their objectives or methods, the Red Guards were free to believe that the ends justified extreme and often violent means. Moreover, many Red Guards took the opportunity to take revenge against authorities, such as teachers who had given them bad grades. Others (at right) would harangue crowds on the benefits of Maoism and the evils of foreign influence.

The Red Guards went on rampages throughout the country, breaking into people's houses and stealing or destroying their property, harassing people in their homes in the middle of the night, stopping girls with long hair and cutting it off on the spot, destroying the files of ministries and industrial enterprises, and clogging up the transportation system by their travels throughout the country to "make revolution." Different Red Guard factions began to fight with one another, each claiming to be the most revolutionary.

Mao eventually called on the army to support the Red Guards in their effort to challenge "those in authority taking the capitalist road." This created even more confusion, as many of the Red Guard groups actually supported the people they were supposed to be attacking. But their revolutionary-sounding names and their pretenses at being "Red" (Communist) confused the army. Moreover, the army was divided within itself and did not particularly wish to overthrow the Chinese Communist Party authorities, the main supporters of the military in their respective areas of jurisdiction.

Since the schools had been closed, the youth of China were not receiving any formal education during this period. Finally, in 1969, Mao called a halt to the excesses of the Red Guards. They were disbanded and sent home. Some were sent to work in factories or out to the countryside to labor in the fields with the peasants. But

New York World-Telegram and Sun Newspaper Photograph Collection/ Library of Congress LC-USZ62-134168

"Anti-revoluntionary" leaders in dunce caps for public shame by Red Guards in Beijing, January 26, 1967.

the chaos set in motion during the Cultural Revolution did not come to a halt until the arrest of the Gang of Four, some 10 years after the Cultural Revolution had begun.

During the "10 bad years," when schools were either closed or operating with a minimal program, children received virtually no formal education beyond an elementary school level. As a result, China's development lagged behind its neighbors such as Japan and South Korea.

peasantry, advance economic development, and control corruption. Still, even had the KMT made greater efforts to reform, any wartime government confronted with the demoralization of the population ravaged by war, inflation, economic destruction, and the humiliation of a foreign occupation would have found it difficult to maintain the loyal support of its people. Even the middle class eventually deserted the KMT. Many of those industrial and commercial capitalists who had supported the Nationalists now joined with the CCP to rebuild China. Others, however, stayed behind only because they were unable to flee to Hong Kong or Taiwan.

One thing is clear: The Chinese Communists did not gain victory because of

support from the Soviet Union; for the Soviets, who were anxious to be on the winning side in China, chose to give aid to the KMT until it was evident that the Communists would win. Furthermore, the Communists' victory rested not on superior weapons but, rather, on a superior strategy, support from the Chinese people, and (as Mao Zedong believed) a superior political "consciousness." It was because of the Communist victory over a technologically superior army that Mao thereafter insisted on the superiority of "man over weapons" and the importance of the support of the people for an army's victory. The relationship of the soldiers to the people is, Mao said, like the relationship of fish to water— without the water, the fish will die.

THE PEOPLE'S REPUBLIC OF CHINA

The Red Army's final victory came rapidly—far faster than anticipated. Suddenly China's large cities fell to the Communists, who now found themselves in charge of a nation of more than 600 million people. They had to make critical decisions about how to unify and rebuild the country. They were obligated, of course, to fulfill their promise to redistribute land to the poor and landless peasantry in return for the peasants' support of the Communists during the Civil War. The CCP leaders were, however, largely recruited from among the peasantry; and like revolutionary fighters everywhere, knew how to make a revolution but had little experience with governance. So, rejected

一定要把揭批"四人帮"的伟大斗争进行到底

International Institute of Social History/Stefan R. Landsberger Collection (http://www.iisg.nl/~landsberger)
A Cultural Revolution—style poster. Below the poster, the inscription reads, "We must definitely carry forward the great struggle in thoroughly exposing and criticizing the Gang of Four."

THE GANG OF FOUR

The current leadership of the Chinese Communist Party views the Cultural Revolution of 1966–1976 as having been a period of total chaos that brought the People's Republic of China to the brink of political and economic ruin. While Mao Zedong is criticized for having begun the Cultural Revolution with his ideas about the danger of China turning "capitalist," the major blame for the turmoil of those years is placed on a group of extreme radicals labeled the "Gang of Four."

The Gang of Four consisted of Jiang Qing, Mao's wife, who began playing a key role in China's cultural affairs during the early 1960s; Zhang Chunqiao, a veteran party leader in Shanghai; Yao Wenyuan, a literary critic and ideologue; and Wang Hongwen, a factory worker catapulted into national prominence by his leadership of rebel workers during the Cultural Revolution.

By the late 1960s, these four individuals were among the most powerful leaders in China. Drawn together by common political interests and a shared belief that the Communist Party should be relentless in ridding China of suspected "capitalist roaders," they worked together to keep the Cultural Revolution on a radical course. One of their targets had been Deng Xiaoping, who emerged as China's paramount leader in 1978, after the members of the Gang of Four had been arrested.

Although they had close political and personal ties to Mao and derived many of their ideas from him, Mao became quite disenchanted with them in the last few years of his life. He was particularly displeased with the unscrupulous way in which they behaved as a faction within the top levels of the party. Indeed, it was Mao who coined the name Gang of Four, as part of a written warning to the

radicals to cease their conspiracies and obey established party procedures.

The Gang of Four hoped to take over supreme power in China following Mao's death, on September 9, 1976. However, their plans were upset less than a month later, when other party and army leaders had them arrested—an event that is now said to mark the formal end of the "10 bad years" or "Cultural Revolution." Removing the party's most influential radicals from power set the stage for the dramatic reforms that have become the hallmark of the post-Mao era in China. In November 1980, the Gang of Four were put on trial in Beijing. They were charged with having committed serious crimes against the Chinese people and accused of having had a hand in "persecuting to death" tens of thousands of officials and intellectuals whom they perceived as their political enemies. All four were convicted and sentenced to long terms in prison.

by the Western democratic/capitalist countries because of their embrace of communism, and desperate for aid and advice, the Communists turned to the Soviet Union for direction and support. They did this in spite of the Soviet leader Joseph Stalin's fickle support of the Chinese Communists throughout the 1930s and '40s.

The Soviet Model

In the early years of CCP rule, China's leaders "leaned to one side" and followed the Soviet model of development in education, the legal system, the economic system, and elsewhere. The Soviet economic model favored capital-intensive industrialization, but all the Soviet "aid"

had to be repaid. Furthermore, following the Soviet model required a reliance on Soviet experts and well-educated Chinese, whom the Communists were not sure they could trust. Without Soviet support in the beginning, however, it is questionable whether the CCP would have been as successful as it was in developing China in the 1950s.

The Maoist Model

China soon grew exasperated with the limitations of Soviet aid and the inapplicability of the Soviet model to Chinese circumstances. China's preeminent leader, Mao Zedong, proposed a Chinese model of development more appropriate to Chinese circumstances. What came to be known as the "Maoist model" took account of China's low level of development, poverty, and large population. Mao hoped to substitute China's enormous manpower for expensive capital equipment by organizing people into ever larger working units.

In 1958, in what became known as the "Great Leap Forward," Mao Zedong launched his model of development. It was a bold scheme to rapidly accelerate the pace of industrialization so that China could catch up with the industrialized states of the West. In the countryside, land was merged into large communes, untested and controversial planting techniques were introduced, and peasant women were engaged fully in the fields in order to increase agricultural production. The communes became the basis for industrializing the countryside through a program of peasants building their own "backyard furnaces" to smelt steel. The Maoist model assumed that those people possessing a proper revolutionary, or "red" (communist), consciousness—that is, a commitment to achieving communism—would be able to produce more than those who were "expert" but lacked revolutionary consciousness. In the cities, efforts to increase industrial production through longer work days, and overtaxing industrial equipment, likewise led to a marked decline in production and industrial wastage.

The Maoist model of extreme "egalitarianism"—captured in the Chinese expression "all eat out of the same pot"—and "continuous revolution," was a rejection of the Soviet model of development, which Mao came to see as an effort to hold the Chinese back from more rapid industrialization. In particular, the Soviets' refusal to give the Chinese the most advanced industrial-plant equipment and machinery, or to share nuclear technology with them, made Mao suspicious of their intentions.

Sino–Soviet Relations Sour

For their part, the Soviets believed that the Maoist model was doomed to failure. The Soviet leader Nikita Khrushchev denounced the Great Leap Forward as "irrational"; but he was equally distressed at what seemed a risky scheme by Mao Zedong to bring the Soviets and Americans into direct conflict over the Nationalist-controlled Offshore Islands in the Taiwan Strait. The combination of what the Soviets viewed as Mao's irrational economic policy and his risk-taking confrontation with the United States prompted the Soviets to abruptly withdraw their experts from China in 1959. They packed up their bags, along with spare parts for Soviet-supplied machinery and blueprints for unfinished factories, and returned home.

The Soviets' withdrawal, combined with the disastrous decline in production resulting from the policies of the Great Leap Forward and several years of bad weather, set China's economic development back many years. Population figures now available indicate that millions died in the years from 1959 to 1962, mostly from starvation and diseases caused by malnutrition. The catastrophic consequences of the Great Leap Forward resulted in the leadership paying no more than lip service to Mao Zedong's ideas. The Chinese people were not told that Mao Zedong bore blame for their problems, but the Maoist model was abandoned for the time being. More pragmatic leaders took over the direction of the economy, but without further support from the Soviets. Not until 1962 did the Chinese start to recover their productivity gains of the 1950s.

By 1963, the Sino–Soviet split had become public, as the two Communist powers found themselves in profound disagreement over a wide range of issues: whether socialist countries could use capitalist methods, such as free markets, to advance economic development; appropriate policies toward the United States; whether China or the Soviet Union could claim to follow Marxism-Leninism more faithfully, entitling it to lead the Communist world. By the mid-1960s, the Sino-Soviet relationship had deteriorated to the point that the Chinese were worried that the Soviets might launch a military attack on them.

The Cultural Revolution

In 1966, Mao launched what he termed the "Great Proletarian Cultural Revolution." Whether Mao Zedong hoped to provoke an internal party struggle and regain control over policy, or (as he alleged) to re-educate China's exploitative, corrupt, and oppressive officials in order to restore a revolutionary spirit to the Chinese people and to prevent China from abandoning socialism, is unclear. He called on China's youth to "challenge authority," particularly "those revisionists in authority who are taking the capitalist road." If China continued along its "revisionist" course, he said, the achievements of the Chinese revolution would be undone. China's youth were therefore urged to "make revolution."

Such vague objectives invited abuse, including personal feuds and retribution for alleged past wrongs. Determining just who was "Red" and committed to the Communist revolution, and who was "reactionary" itself generated chaos, as people tried to protect themselves by attacking others—including friends and relatives. During that period, people's cruelty was immeasurable. People were psychologically, and sometimes physically, tortured until they "admitted" to their "rightist" or "reactionary" behavior. Murders, suicides, ruined careers, and broken families were the debris left behind by this effort to "reeducate" those who had strayed from the revolutionary path. It is estimated that approximately 10 percent of the population—that is, *80 million people*—became targets of the Cultural Revolution, and that tens of thousands lost their lives during these years of political violence.

The Cultural Revolution attacked Chinese traditions and cultural practices as being feudal and outmoded. It also destroyed the authority of the Chinese Communist Party, through prolonged public attacks on many of its most respected leaders. Policies changed frequently in those "10 bad years" from 1966 to 1976, as first one faction and then another gained the upper hand. Few leaders escaped unscathed. Ultimately, the Chinese Communist Party and Marxist-Leninist ideology were themselves the victims of the Cultural Revolution. By the time the smoke cleared, the legitimacy of the CCP had been destroyed, and the people could no longer accept the idea that the party leaders were infallible. Both traditional Chinese morality and Marxist-Leninist values had been thoroughly undermined.

Reforms and Liberalization

With the death of Mao Zedong and the subsequent arrest of the politically radical "Gang of Four" (which included Mao's wife) in 1976, the Cultural Revolution came to an end. Deng Xiaoping, a veteran leader of the CCP who had been purged twice during the "10 bad years," was "rehabilitated" in 1977.

By 1979, China once again set off down the road of construction and put an end to the radical Maoist policies of "continuous revolution" and the idea that it was more important to be "red" than "expert." Saying that he did not care whether the cat was black or white, as long as it caught mice, Deng Xiaoping pursued more pragmatic, flexible policies in order to modernize China. In other words, Deng did not care if he used capitalist methods, as long as they helped modernize China. He deserves credit for opening up China to the outside world and to reforms that led to the liberalization of both the economic and the political spheres. When he died in 1997, Deng left behind a country that, despite some setbacks and reversals, had already traveled a significant distance down the road to liberalization and modernization.

In spite of Deng Xiaoping's pragmatic policies, and Mao Zedong's clear responsibility for precipitating policies that were devastating to the Chinese people, Mao has never been defrocked in China; for to do so would raise serious questions about the legitimacy of the CCP. China's leaders have admitted that, beginning with the Anti-Rightest Campaign of 1957 and the Great Leap Forward of 1958, Mao made "serious mistakes"; but the CCP insists that these errors must be seen within the context of his many accomplishments and his commitment, even if sometimes misdirected, to Marxism-Leninism. In contrast to the Gang of Four and others who were condemned as "counter-revolutionaries," Mao has been called a "revolutionary" who made "mistakes." As recently as the 17th National Congress of the CCP in 2007, Mao Thought (the Chinese adaptation of Marxism-Leninism to Chinese conditions) remained enshrined in the party's constitution as providing the foundation for continued CCP rule.

The Challenge of Reform

The erosion of traditional Chinese values, then of Marxist-Leninist values and faith in the Chinese Communist Party's leadership, and finally of Mao Thought, left China without any strong belief system. Such Western values as materialism, capitalism, individualism, and freedom swarmed into this vacuum to undermine both Communist ideology and the traditional Chinese values that had provided the glue of society. Deng Xiaoping's prognosis had proven correct: The "screen door" through which Western science and technology (and foreign investments) could flow into China was unable to keep out the annoying "insects" of Western values. The screen door had holes that were too large to prevent this invasion.

China's leadership in the reform period has not been united. The less pragmatic, more ideologically oriented "conservative" or "hard-line" leadership (who in the new context of reforms could be viewed as ideologues of a Maoist vintage) challenged the introduction of liberalizing economic reforms precisely because they threatened to undo China's earlier socialist achievements and erode Chinese culture. To combat the negative side effects of introducing free-market values and institutions, China's

leadership launched a number of "mass campaigns": the campaign in the 1980s against "spiritual pollution"—the undermining of Chinese values;[2] a repressive campaign following the brutal crackdown against those challenging the leadership in Tiananmen Square in 1989; on-going campaigns against corruption; and campaigns to "strike hard" against crime and to "get civilized."[3]

Since 1979, in spite of setbacks, China's leadership has been able to keep the country on the path of liberalization. As a result, the economy has had an average annual growth rate of 9.5% for the last 30 years. It is now ranked as the fourth largest economy in the world. China has dramatically reformed the legal and political system as well, even though much work remains to be done. The third generation of the PRC leadership was headed by Jiang Zemin, who led China throughout the 1990s and into the twenty-first century. In turn, Jiang stepped down from his position as party leader in 2001, as president in 2002, and as the head of the Military Affairs Commission in 2004. China's leaders now operate within what is a younger and increasingly well-institutionalized and better-educated system of collective leadership. The problems that the leadership of President Hu Jintao and Premier Wen Jiabao faces as a consequence of China's rapid modernization and liberalization are formidable: massive and growing unemployment; increasing crime, corruption, and social dislocation; a lack of social cohesion; and challenges to the CCP's monopoly on power put into play by its policies of liberalization, pluralization, and modernization. The forces of rapid growth and social and economic modernization have taken on a momentum of their own. China's increasing involvement in the international community has also put into motion seemingly uncontrollable forces, some of which are destablizing, and others that are contributing to demands for political reform. As will be noted below in the discussion of these issues, the real concern for China is not whether China will engage in further reform and democratization, but whether it can maintain stability in the context of this potentially destabilizing international and domestic environment.

The Student and Mass Movement of 1989

Symbolism is very important in Chinese culture; the death of a key leader is a particularly significant moment. In the case of Hu Yaobang, the former head of the CCP, his sudden death in April 1989 became symbolic of the death of liberalizing forces in China. The deceased leader's career and its meaning were touted

as symbols of liberalization, even though his life was hardly a monument to liberal thought. More conservative leaders in the CCP had removed him from his position as the CCP's general-secretary in part because he had offended their cultural sensibilities. Apart from everything else, Hu's suggestion that the Chinese turn in their chopsticks for knives and forks, and not eat food out of a common dish because it spread disease, were culturally offensive to them.

Hu's death provided students with a catalyst to place his values and policies in juxta-position with those of the then increasingly conservative leadership.[4] The students' reassessment of Hu Yaobang's career, in a way that rejected the party's evaluation, was in itself a challenge to the authority of the CCP's right to rule China. The students' hunger strike in Tiananmen Square—essentially in front of party headquarters—during the visit of the Soviet Union President, Mikhail Gorbachev, to China was, even in the eyes of ordinary Chinese people, an insult to Chinese leadership. Many Chinese later stated that the students went too far, as by humiliating the leadership, they humiliated *all* Chinese.

Part of the difficulty in reaching an agreement between the students and China's leaders was that the students' demands changed over time. At first they merely wanted a reassessment of Hu Yaobang's career. But quickly the students added new demands: dialogue between the government and the students (with the students to be treated as equals with top CCP leaders), retraction of an offensive *People's Daily* editorial, an end to official corruption, exposure of the financial and business dealings of the central leadership, a free press, the removal of the top CCP leadership, and still other actions that challenged continued CCP rule.

The students' hunger strike, which lasted for one week in May, was the final straw that brought down the wrath of the central leadership. Martial law was imposed in Beijing. When the citizens of Beijing resisted its enforcement and blocked the armies' efforts to reach Tiananmen Square to clear out the hunger strikers, both students and CCP leaders dug in; but both were deeply divided bodies. Indeed, divisions within the student-led movement caused it to lose its direction; and divisions within the central CCP leadership incapacitated it. For two weeks, the central leadership wrangled over who was right and the best course of action. On June 4, the "hard-liners" won out, and they chose to use military power rather than a negotiated solution with the students.

Did the students make significant or well-thought-out statements about "democracy" or realistic demands on China's leaders? The short and preliminary answer is no; but then, is this really the appropriate question to ask? One could argue that what the students *said* was less important than what they *did*: They mobilized the population of China's capital and other major cities to support a profound challenge to the legitimacy of the CCP's leadership. Even if workers believed that "You can't eat democracy," and even if they participated in the demonstrations for their *own* reasons (such as gripes about inflation and pensions), they did support the students' demand that the CCP carry out further political reforms. This was because the students successfully promoted the idea that if China had had a democratic system rather than authoritarian rule, the leadership would have been more responsive to the workers' bread-and-butter issues.

Repression Within China Following the Crackdown

By August 1989, the CCP leadership had established quotas of "bad elements" for work units and identified 20 categories of people to be targeted for punishment. But people were more reluctant than in the past to follow orders to expose their friends, colleagues, and family members, not only because such verdicts had often been reversed at a later time, but also because many people questioned the CCP's version of what happened in Beijing on June 4. Although the citizenry worried about informers, there seemed to be complicity from top to bottom, whether inside or outside the ranks of the CCP, in refusing to go along with efforts to ferret out demonstrators and sympathizers with the prodemocracy, antiparty movement. Party leaders below the central level appeared to believe that the central government's leadership was doomed; for this reason, they dared not carry out its orders. Inevitably, there would be a reversal of verdicts, and they did not want to be caught in it.

As party leaders in work units droned on in mandatory political study sessions about Deng Xiaoping's important writings, workers wondered how long it would be before the June 4 military crackdown would be condemned as a "counterrevolutionary crime against the people." Individuals in work units had to fill out lengthy questionnaires. A standard one had 24 questions aimed at "identifying the enemy." Among them were such questions as, "What did you think when Hu Yaobang died?" "When Zhao Ziyang went to Tiananmen Square, what did you think? Where were you?" At one university, each faculty member's questionnaire had to be verified by two people (other than one's own family) or the individual involved would not be allowed to teach.[5]

As part of the repression that followed the military crackdown in June 1989, the government carried out arrests of hundreds of those who participated in the demonstrations. During the world's absorption with the Persian Gulf War in 1991, the government suddenly announced the trials and verdicts on some of China's best known leaders of the 1989 demonstrations. Of those who were summarily executed, available information indicates that almost all were workers trying to form labor unions. All the other known 1989 student and dissident leaders were eventually released, although some were deported to the West as a condition of their release. The government has also occasionally re-arrested 1989 protesters for other activities. In 1998, for example, some former protesters made bold attempts to establish a new party to challenge Chinese Communist Party rule. Although their efforts to register this new party were at first tolerated, several were later arrested, tried, and sentenced to prison. Finally, as discussed below, the government has attempted to ferret out and arrest activist leaders of the Falun Gong.

In spite of these important exceptions, many repressive controls were relaxed, and China's mass media have steadily expanded the parameters of allowable topics and opinions. Today, although there are occasional arrests of individuals who are blatantly challenging CCP rule, and although the establishment of a competing party is not tolerated, the leadership is more focused on harnessing the talents of China's best and brightest for the country's modernization than it is on controlling dissent. No longer a revolutionary party, the CCP is intent on effectively governing and developing China.

THE PEOPLE OF CHINA

Population Control

In 2008, China's population was estimated to be over 1.3 billion. In the 1950s, Mao had encouraged population growth, as he considered a large population to be a major source of strength: Cheap human labor could take the place of expensive technology and equipment. No sustained attempts to limit Chinese population occurred until the mid-1970s. Even then, because there were no penalties for those Chinese who ignored them, population control programs were only marginally successful.

In 1979, the government launched a serious birth-control campaign, rewarding couples giving birth to only one child with work bonuses and priority in housing. The only child was later to receive preferential treatment in university admissions and job assignments (a policy eventually abandoned). Couples who had more than one child, on the other hand, were to be penalized by a 10 percent decrease in their annual wages, and their children would not be eligible for free education and health care benefits.

The one-child policy in China's major cities was rigorously enforced, to the point where it was almost impossible for a woman to get away with a second pregnancy. Who was allowed to have a child, as well as when she could give birth, was rigidly controlled by the woman's work unit. Furthermore, with so many state-owned enterprises paying close to half of their entire annual wages as "bonuses," authorities came up with additional sanctions to ensure compliance. Workers were usually organized in groups of 10 to 30 individuals. If any woman in the group gave birth to more than one child, *the entire group* would lose its annual bonus. With such overwhelming penalties for the group as a whole, pressures for a couple not to give birth to a second child were enormous.

To ensure that any unauthorized pregnancy did not occur, women who had already given birth were required to stand in front of x-ray machines (fluoroscopes) to verify that their IUDs (intrauterine birthcontrol devices) were still in place. Abortions could and would be performed throughout the period of a woman's unsanctioned pregnancy. (The moral issues that surround abortions for some Christians are not concerns for the Chinese.)

The effectiveness of China's family planning policy in the cities has been due not merely to the surveillance by state-owned work units, neighborhood committees, and the "granny police" who watch over the families in their residential areas. Changed social attitudes also play a critical role, and urban Chinese now accept the absolute necessity of population control in their overcrowded cities.

The one-child policy in China's cities has led to a generation of remarkably spoiled children. Known as "little emperors," these only children are the center of attention of six anxious adults (the parents and two sets of grandparents), who carefully scrutinize their every movement. It has led to the overuse of medical services by these parents and grandparents, who rush their only child/grandchild to the doctor at the first signs of a sniffle or sore throat. It has also led to overfed, even obese, children. Being overweight used to be considered a hedge against bad times, and the Chinese were initially pleased that their children were becoming heavier. A common greeting showing admiration had long been, "You have become fat!" But as contemporary urban Chinese adopt many of the values associated in the developed world with becoming wealthier, they are changing their perspectives on weight. Jane Fonda–style exercise programs are now a regular part of Chinese television, and weight-loss salons and fat farms are coming into vogue for China's well-fed middle class. Still, most people view the major purpose of exercise as staying healthy and keeping China a strong nation, not looking attractive.

The strictly enforced and administered family planning program has been undermined by a number of trends. First, in the cities, there are large migrant populations who are really under no one's control: the villages from which they fled have no responsibility for them; and the cities to which they migrate rarely issue them a "household registration" certificate, so they really belong to no official's jurisdiction. Yet, rural migrant families usually prefer to have only one child, as in their tenuous economic circumstances, taking care of more than one would make survival in a new city far more difficult. Second, well-to-do entrepreneurs who live in private housing can avoid population-control measures because they are not part of any public housing or work unit. They are willing to pay all the relevant fines and bribes necessary to have as many children as they want. Nevertheless, even they are unlikely to have more than two children. Indeed, some members of China's growing middle class are deciding not to have children, for the same reasons as in other more developed societies: they want to pursue careers and spend time and money in ways that leave little room for children. There are more and more such "DINK" (double income no kids) families now. Third, in recent years, there has been a more relaxed enforcement of the one-child policy because of the demographic crisis on the horizon: too few young people to support the large number of elderly people in future years.

One step the government has taken to address this inverted population pyramid is to allow those married couples who both come from one-child families to have two children. The government has also tried to grapple with one of the unintended side-effects of the one-child policy: the aborting of female fetuses. Given the cultural preference for males, a certain percentage of female fetuses are aborted. (This has resulted in a lopsided male-female ratio of at least 105:100, although in some areas it is said to be as high as 125:100. These are, however, much debated figures. The

problem of a lopsided sex ratio is true in many Asian countries, including India and South Korea.) The sex of fetuses is usually known because of the widespread use in China of ultrasound machines. To use these machines to reveal the sex of the child is illegal, but for a very small bribe, doctors will usually do so. In addition, although female infanticide is illegal, it sometimes happens, especially in rural areas. So the government has promulgated several new laws and has investigated several thousand cases of alleged abuse of sex-identification of fetuses.

In the meantime, China's orphanages have absorbed some of the unwanted girl babies, now much sought after in the West. In 2007, however, China instituted new regulations that make it harder for foreigners to adopt Chinese babies (almost all of whom are girls—boys are usually only put up for adoption if there is a physical or mental defect). Arguably, one of the reasons for this change in policy is because of the other demographic crisis resulting from the one-child policy—tens of millions of men coming of marriage age without women to marry. Apart from societal unhappiness, the lack of brides has led to a sharp increase in the kidnapping of young women, as well as the practice of selling girls as brides in rural marketplaces when they reach marriageable age (usually to men who live in remote villages that have little to offer a new bride).

In the vast rural areas of China, where some three-quarters of the population still live, efforts to enforce the one-child policy have met with less success than in the cities, because the benefits and punishments are not as relevant for peasants. After the communes were disbanded in the early 1980s and families were given their own land to till, peasants wanted sons, to do the heavy farm labor. As a result, the government's policy in the countryside became more flexible. In some villages, if a woman gives birth to a girl and decides to have another child in hopes of having a boy, she may pay the government a substantial fee (usually an amount more than the entire annual income of the family) in order to be allowed to do so. Yet, in an ironic reflection of this still very male-dominant society, today's farming, which is far more physically demanding and less lucrative than factory jobs, is increasingly left to the women, while the men go off to towns and cities to make their fortunes.

Some analysts suggest that at least several million peasants have taken steps to ensure that their female offspring are not counted toward their one-child (and now, in some places, two-child) limit: One strategy is for a pregnant woman simply to move

to another village to have her child. Since the local village leaders are not responsible for women's reproduction when they are not from their own village, women are not harassed into getting an abortion in other villages. If the child is a boy, the mother can simply return to her native village, pay a fine, and register him; if a girl, the mother can return and not register the child. Thus a whole generation of young girls is growing up in the countryside without ever having been registered with the government. Since, except for schooling, peasants have few claims to state-supplied benefits anyway, they may consider this official nonexistence of their daughters a small price to pay for having as many children as necessary until giving birth to a boy. And if this practice is as common as some believe, it may mean that China will not face quite such a large demographic crisis in the ratio between males and females as has been projected.

Males continue to be more valued in Chinese culture because only sons are permitted to carry on traditional Chinese family rituals and ancestor worship. This is unbearably painful for families without sons, who feel that their entire ancestral history, often recorded over several hundred years on village-temple tablets, is coming to an end. As a result, a few villages have changed the very foundations of ancestral worship: They now permit daughters to continue the family lineage down the female line. The government itself is encouraging this practice, and it is also changing certain other family-related policies. For example, it used to be the son who was responsible under the law for taking care of their parents. This meant that parents whose only child was a girl could not expect to be supported in their old age. Now, both sons and daughters are legally responsible. Furthermore, it is hoped that a new system of social security and pensions for retired people will gradually lead the state and employers to absorb the responsibility for caring for the elderly.

China's strict population-control policies have been effective: Since 1977, the population has grown at an *average* annual rate of 1.1 percent, one of the lowest in the developing world. (As of 2008, the annual population growth rate was 0.629 percent—considerably below the fertility replacement rate of 2.1.) Yet, even this low rate works out to an average annual population *increase* for several years to come. (This is because previous generations had large numbers of offspring.) The dilemma is this: on the one hand, the growing population is a drain on China's limited resources and poses a threat to its environment and economic development.

Chinese billboard promoting one-child family.

Alastair Drysdale (DAL/mhhe010359)

As China continues to provide a substantial percentage of its citizens with a higher standard of living, the continuing pollution of China's air, water, and land, and the depletion of nonrenewable resources and energy are leading to ecological crises that are increasingly difficult to redress. On the other hand, there are concerns that the population replacement rate is too low to provide enough workers to support the growing elderly population. Yet, arguably the productivity of new generations of workers will be far higher; for as farmers abandon the land and move into cities, their productivity (that is, their return on labor) increases; and so does the productivity of workers who move into less labor-intensive jobs, or move from manufacturing into the service sector. As a result, it could well turn out that it will take far fewer younger workers to support China's larger retired community than it did in the past. And, as is the case in developed countries now facing problems of a burgeoning retired population, those beyond the retirement age who are still able may simply keep working.

Women

It is hardly surprising that overlaying (but never eradicating) China's traditional culture with a communist ideology in which men and women are supposed to be equal has generated a bundle of contradictions. Under Chinese Communist Party rule, women have long had more rights and opportunities than women in almost any other developing country, and in certain respects, more than women in some developed countries. For example, Chinese women were expected to work, not stay at home. And, in state-owned enterprises, they received from three to twelve months of paid maternity leave and child care in the workplace, decades before this became common practice in the Western countries. Although Chinese women rarely broke through the "glass ceiling" to the highest levels of the workplace or the ruling elite, and were often given "women's work," their pay scale was similar to that of men. Furthermore, an ideological morality that insisted on respect for women as equals (with both men and women being addressed as "comrades") combined with a de-emphasis on the importance of sexuality, resulted in at least a superficial respect for women that was rare before the Communist period.

The economic reforms that began in 1978, however, precipitated changes in the manner in which women are treated, and in how women act. While many women entrepreneurs and workers benefit as much as the men from economic reforms, there have also been certain throwbacks to earlier times that have undercut women's equality. Women are now treated much more as sex objects than they used to be; and while some women revel in their new freedom to beautify themselves, some companies will hire only women who are perceived as physically attractive, and many enterprises are now using women as "window dressing." For example, women dressed in *qipao*—the traditional, slim-fitting Chinese dress slit high on the thigh—stand outside restaurants and other establishments to entice customers. At business meetings, many women have become mere tea-pourers. In newspapers, employment ads for Chinese enterprises often state in so many words that only young, good-looking women need apply.

The emphasis on profits and efficiency since the reforms has also made state-run enterprises reluctant to hire women because of the costs in maternity benefits and because mothers are still more likely than fathers to be in charge of sick children and the household. Under the socialist system, where the purpose of an enterprise was not necessarily to make profits but to fulfill such socialist objectives as the equality of women and full employment, women fared better. Economic reforms, which emphasize profitability, have provided enterprise managers with the excuse they need not to hire women. Whatever the real reason, they can always claim that their refusal to hire more women or to promote them is justified: Women are more costly, or less competent, or less reliable.

National Minorities

Ninety-two percent of the population is Han Chinese. Although only 8 percent is classified as "national minorities," they occupy more than 60 percent of China's geographical expanse. These minorities inhabit almost all of the border areas, including Tibet, Inner Mongolia, and Xinjiang. The stability and allegiance of the border areas are important for China's national security. Furthermore, China's borders with the many neighboring countries are poorly defined, and members of the same minority usually live on both sides of the borders.

To address this issue, China's central government pursued policies designed to get the minorities on the Chinese side of the borders to identify with the Han Chinese majority. Rather than admitting to this objective of undermining distinctive national identities, the CCP leaders phrased the policies in terms of getting rid of the minorities' "feudal" customs, such as religious practices, which are contrary to the "scientific" values of socialism. Teaching children their native language was often prohibited. At times these policies have been brutal and have caused extreme bitterness among the minorities, particularly the Tibetans and the Uighurs (who practice Islam) in the northwest border province of Xinjiang. The extreme policies of the "10 bad years" that encouraged the elimination of the "four olds" led to the wanton destruction of minority cultural artifacts, temples, mosques, texts, and statuary.

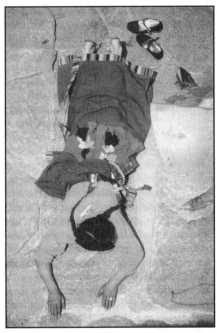

© Glowimages, Inc./Punchstock RF

Buddhist worshipper in Tibet.

© Glowimages, Inc./Punchstock RF

Jokhang Temple, a Buddhist temple in Lhasa, Tibet.

In the 1980s, the Deng Xiaoping leadership conceded that Beijing's harsh assimilation policies had been ill-conceived, and it tried to gain the loyalty of the national minorities through more culturally sensitive policies. Minority children are now taught their own language in schools, alongside the "national" language (Mandarin). By the late 1980s, however, the loosening of controls had led to further challenges to Beijing's control, so the central government tightened up security in Xinjiang and reimposed marital law in Tibet in an effort to quell protests and riots against Beijing's discriminatory policies. Martial law was lifted in Tibet in 1990, but security has remained tight ever since. The terrorist attacks on the United States on September 11, 2001, led to even greater surveillance and controls on those minority groups that practice Islam and are believed to have ties with terrorist organizations in the Middle East.

Tibet

The Dalai Lama is the most important spiritual leader of the Tibetans, but he lives in exile in India, where he fled after a Chinese crackdown on Tibetans in 1959. He has stepped up his efforts to reach some form of accommodation with China. The Dalai Lama insists that he is not pressing for independence, only for greater autonomy; and that as long as he is in charge, Tibetans will use only non-violent methods to this end. The Dalai Lama believes that more Tibetan control over their own affairs

is necessary to protect their culture from extinction. Nevertheless, the people who surround the Dalai Lama are far more militant and see autonomy as only the first step toward independence from China.

In the past, the Chinese government made a concerted effort to assimilate Tibetans by eradicating Tibetan cultural practices and institutions that differentiated them from the majority Han culture. These policies were largely abandoned during the 1980s. At this point, the major threat to Tibetan culture comes from globalization, and from Chinese entrepreneurs who, thanks to economic liberalization policies, have taken over many of the commercial and entrepreneurial activities of Tibet. Ironically, the Tibetan feelings about the Chinese mirror the feelings of the Chinese toward the West: The Tibetans want Chinese technology and commercial goods, but not the values that come with the people providing those goods and technology. And among Tibetans, as among the Chinese, the young are more likely to want to become part of the modern world, to be modern and hip, and to leave behind traditional culture and values. Young Tibetans in Lhasa have been swept up in efforts to make money, a pleasure somewhat reduced by the fact that the increasingly large number of Chinese entrepreneurs in Lhasa usually make higher profits than they do. If Tibetan culture is to survive, Tibetans need to take on a modern identity, one that allows them to be both Tibetan and modern at the same time. Otherwise, the sheer dynamism of Han Chinese culture and globalization may well overwhelm Tibetan culture.[6]

Not all Tibetans accept the Dalai Lama's preferred path of nonviolence. In 1996, Beijing revealed that there were isolated bombing incidents and violent clashes between anti-Chinese Tibetans (reportedly armed) and Chinese authorities. The government, in response, sealed off most monasteries in Lhasa, the capital of Tibet. Beginning in the late 1990s, however, China decided to restore many of Tibet's monasteries—in part to placate Tibetans, in part to attract tourists. China has also made it far easier for foreigners to travel to Tibet. By 2006 it had completed a new highway across the length of the vast Qinghai Province plateau to connect Tibet with the rest of China; and another engineering feat—a railroad through the Tibetan mountains to the capital, Lhasa.

As a result of a policy to alleviate poverty in Tibet, the autonomous region now receives more financial aid from the central Chinese government than any other province or autonomous region in China. Tibetans are better fed, clothed, and housed than in the past; but Tibet still remains China's poorest administrative region. Generous state subsidies have not generated development. This is largely because of disastrous, centrally conceived policies, a bloated administrative structure, a large Chinese military presence to house and feed, disdain for Tibetan culture, and incompetent Han cadres who have little understanding of local issues and rarely speak Tibetan.[7] Tibet's landlocked, remote location and its lack of arable land certainly exacerbate problems in development.

Nevertheless, in recent years, Tibetan farmers have discovered that they can produce a valuable caterpillar fungus, *Cordyceps sinensis* (also called "winter worm, summer grass"). The fungus consumes caterpillars, then produces a columnar growth that shoots through the soil. It can be harvested and dried. It is much sought after by the Chinese as an herbal remedy for enhanced health, longevity, and male potency. Overnight, some of Tibet's poorest farmers have gained considerable wealth from cultivation of the caterpillar. Tibet's tourist industry is also suddenly booming, thanks to an expanded airport, new hotels, fewer restrictions by the Chinese government, and the determination of both Chinese and Western travel agencies to provide opportunities for tourists to visit "Shangrila."

None of this is meant to suggest that Tibet is going to leave poverty behind any time soon, even though the Chinese government is fully engaged in an anti-poverty program in Tibet. Regardless of what actions the Chinese government takes to develop Tibet, moreover, it is viewed with suspicion: New roads or railroads? The better for the Chinese to exploit Tibetan resources and even to invade. Encouraging tourism in Tibet or sending Tibetans to higher-quality Chinese schools outside of Tibet? The better to destroy Tibetan culture. Allowing Chinese entrepreneurs to do business in Tibet or desperately poor youth from neighboring provinces to go to Tibet for work? The better to take away jobs from Tibetans. Projects to develop Tibet's infrastructure for development? The better to destroy its environment. In short, Tibetans tend to regard all of Beijing's policies, and Han cadres in Tibet, with suspicion.

Tibet's anger toward China's central government was exacerbated by Beijing's decision in 1995 not to accept the Tibetan Buddhists' choice (chosen according to traditional Tibetan Buddhist ritual) of a young boy as the reincarnation of the second-most important spiritual leader of the Tibetans, the Panchen Lama, who died in 1989. Instead, Beijing substituted its own six-year old candidate. The Tibetans' choice, meanwhile, is living in seclusion somewhere in Beijing, under the watchful eye of the Chinese. China's concern is that any new spiritual leader could become a focus for a new push for Tibetan independence—an eventuality it wishes to avoid.

Inner Mongolia

Inner Mongolia (an autonomous region under Beijing's control) lies on the southern side of Mongolia, which is an independent state. Beijing's concern that the Mongolians in China would want to unite with Mongolia led to a policy that diluted the Mongol population with what has grown to be an overwhelming majority of Han Chinese. According to the 2000 national census, the national minority (largely Mongol) population was only 4.93 million—a mere 20.76% of the total population of 23.76 million. Inner Mongolia's capital, Huhhot, is essentially a Han city, and assimilation of Mongols into Han culture in the capital is almost complete. Mongolians are dispersed throughout the vast countryside as shepherds, herdsmen, and farmers and retain many of their ethnic traditions and practices.

Events in (Outer) Mongolia have led China's central leadership to keep a watchful eye on Inner Mongolia. In 1989, Mongolia's government—theoretically independent but in fact under Soviet tutelage until—decided to permit multiparty rule at the expense of the Communist Party's complete control; and in democratic elections held in 1996, the Mongolian Communist Party was ousted from power.

Beijing has grown increasingly concerned that these democratic inklings might spread to their neighboring cousins in Inner Mongolia, with a resulting challenge to one-party CCP rule. China's leadership worries that the Mongols in Inner Mongolia may try to secede from China and join with the independent state of Mongolia because of their shared culture. So far, however, those Inner Mongolians who have traveled to Mongolia have been surprised by the relative lack of development there and have shown little interest in drumming up a secessionist movement. Nevertheless, privatization of the economy, combined with an insensitivity to Mongolian culture have led to periodic demonstrations against the Han Chinese-dominated government.

Muslim Minorities

In the far northwest, the predominantly Muslim population—particularly the Uyghur minority—of Xinjiang Autonomous Region continues to challenge the authority of China's central leadership. The loosening of policies aimed at assimilating the minority populations into the Han (Chinese) culture has given a rebirth to Islamic culture and practices, including prayer five times a day, architecture in the Islamic style, traditional Islamic medicine, and teaching Islam in the schools. With the dissolution of the Soviet Union in 1991 into 15 independent states, the ties between the Islamic states on China's borders (Kazakhstan, Kyrgyzstan, and Tajikistan, as well as Afghanistan and Pakistan) have accelerated rapidly.

Beijing is concerned that China's Islamic minorities may find that they have more in common with these neighboring Islamic nations than with the Chinese Han majority and may attempt to secede from China. Signs of a growing, worldwide Islamic movement have exacerbated Beijing's anxieties about controlling China's Islamic minorities. The 9/11/01 attacks by Islamic terrorists, followed by the U.S.–led "war on terrorism" throughout the world, have led China to intensify its efforts to root out Islamic radicals. Although some analysts argue that the war on terrorism has given Beijing an ideal pretext for cracking down on what is a legitimate desire for national independence by Uyghur Muslims in Xinjiang, others accept Beijing's view that those using violence (including bombs) are "terrorists," not "freedom fighters."

Uyghurs who have engaged in terrorism are not motivated by religious fanaticism, but rather, by a desire to achieve a concrete, pragmatic goal: Xinjiang's secession from China. Still, in the last decade, they have received funding from the Islamic world, including, it is believed, from terrorist groups located therein. The Uyghurs do not, however, accept the tenets of Islamic fundamentalists, nor that they view their struggle against Chinese rule as a struggle of good against evil. (Indeed, it has often been noted that Islam is much more moderate, tolerant, and progressive as it spreads eastward.) Evidence that the Uyghurs are engaged in an out-and-out political struggle for independence from Chinese rule would be that Uyghur violence in Xinjiang has not been in form of terrorist attacks on the local Han population but, rather, on the state structure of the governing Han.

China's nearly 9 million Hui—Han Chinese who practice Islam—are also classified as a "national minority," but over many centuries, they have become so integrated into mainstream Chinese culture that at this point in history their only remaining distinct characteristic is their practice of Islam. They speak standard Chinese and live together with other Han. Although a large number of Hui live in one autonomous region, Ningxia, they are also spread out throughout China. In general, in spite of shared Islamic beliefs, they do not identify with Uyghur nationalism, which is seen as particular to Uyghur ethnicity, and not to a broader Islamic identity.

Religion

Confucianism

Confucianism is the "religion" most closely associated with China. It is not, however, a religion in Western terms, as there is no place for gods, faith, or many other beliefs associated with formal religions. But like most religions, it does have a system of ethics for human relationships; and it adds to this what most religions do not have, namely, principles for good governance that include the hierarchical ordering of relationships, with obedience and subordination of those in lower ranks to those in higher ranks.

The Chinese Communists rejected Confucianism until the 1980s, but not because they saw it as an "opiate of the masses." (That was Karl Marx's description of religion, which he viewed as a way of trapping people in a web of superstitions, robbing them of their money, and causing them to passively endure their miserable lives on Earth.) Instead, they denounced Confucianism for providing the ethical rationale for a system of patriarchy that allowed officials to insist on obedience from subordinates. During the years in which "leftists" such as the Gang of Four set the agenda, moreover, the CCP rejected Confucianism for its emphasis on education as a criterion for joining the ruling elite. Instead, the CCP favored ideological commitment—"redness"—as the primary criterion for ruling. The reforms since 1979, however, have emphasized the need for an educated elite, and Confucian values of hard work and the importance of the family are frequently referred to. The revival of Confucian values has, in fact, provided an important foundation for China's renewed emphasis on national identity and Chinese culture as a substitute for the now nearly defunct values of Marxism-Leninism-Mao Thought.

Buddhism

Buddhism has remained important among some of the largest of the national minorities, notably the Tibetans and Mongols. The CCP's efforts to eradicate formal Buddhism have been interpreted by the minorities as national oppression by the Han Chinese. As a result, the revival of Buddhism since the 1980s has been associated with efforts by Tibetans and Mongolians to assert their national identities and to gain greater autonomy in formulating their own policies. Under the influence of the more moderate policies of the Deng Xiaoping reformist leadership, the CCP reconsidered its efforts to eliminate religion. The 1982 State Constitution permits religious freedom, whereas previously only atheism was allowed. The state has actually encouraged the restoration of Buddhist temples, in part because of Beijing's awareness of the continuing tensions caused by its efforts to deny minorities their respective religious practices, and in part because of a desire to attract both tourists and money to the minority areas.

But Buddhism is far more widespread than in just Tibet and Inner Mongolia. Indeed, popular Buddhism, which is full of stories and Buddhist mythology, is pervasive throughout the rural population—and even among some urban populations. Popular Buddhist beliefs are even worked into many of the sects, cults, and folk religions in China. Today, Buddhist temples are frequented by increasingly large numbers of Chinese, who go there to propitiate their ancestors and to pray for good health and more wealth.

Folk Religions

For most Chinese, folk religions are far more important than any organized religion.[8] The CCP's best efforts to eradicate folk religions and to impart in their place an educated "scientific" viewpoint have failed. Animism—the belief that nonliving things have spirits that should be respected through worship—continues to be practiced by China's vast peasantry. Ancestor worship—based on the belief that the living can communicate with the dead and that the dead spirits to whom sacrifices are ritually made have the ability to bring a better (or worse) life to the living—once again absorbs much of the income of China's peasants. The costs of offerings, burning paper money, and using shamans and priests to perform rituals that will heal the sick, appease the ancestors, and exorcise ghosts (who are often poorly treated ancestors returned to haunt their descendants) at times of birth, marriage, and death, can be financially burdensome. But the willingness of peasants to spend money on traditional religious folk practices is contributing to the reconstruction of practices prohibited in earlier decades of Communist rule.

Taoism, Qigong, and Falun Gong

Taoism, which requires its disciples to renounce the secular world, has had few adherents in China since the early twentieth century. But during the repression that followed the crackdown on Tiananmen Square's prodemocracy movement in 1989, many Chinese who felt unable to speak freely turned to mysticism and Taoism. *Qigong,* the ancient Taoist art of deep breathing, had by 1990 become a national pastime. Some 30 Taoist priests in China took on the role of national soothsayers, portending the future of everything from the weather to China's political leadership. What these priests said—or were believed to have said—quickly spread through a vast rumor network in the cities. Meanwhile, on Chinese Communist Party–controlled television, qigong experts swallowed needles and thread, only to have the needles subsequently come out of their noses perfectly

threaded. It is widely believed that, with a sufficient concentration of *qi* (vital energy or breath), a practitioner may literally knock a person to the ground.[9] The revival of Taoist mysticism and meditation, folk religion, and formal religions suggests a need to find meaning from religion to fill the moral and ideological vacuum created by the near-collapse of Communist values.

Falun Gong ("Wheel of Law"), which the government has declared a "sect"—and hence not entitled to claim a constitutional right to practice religion freely—has been charged with involvement in a range of illegal activities. Falun Gong is a complex mixture of Buddhism, Taoism, and qigong practices—the last relying on many ideas from traditional Chinese medicine. According to its adherents, the focus is on healing and good health, but it also has a millennial component, predicting the end of the world and a bad ending for those who are not practitioners. According to the government, the sect's practices can endanger people's health and have in fact caused the deaths of hundreds. It also accuses the sect of being a front for antigovernment political activities.

In 1999, thousands of Falun Gong adherents, some from distant provinces surrounded CCP headquarters, on the edge of Tiananmen Square in Beijing. Hundreds were arrested, but most were soon released and sent back to their home provinces. Others were sent to labor camps or jailed, and some died while incarcerated.[10] In many state-owned work units, officials continue to meet regularly to discuss the dangers of Falun Gong, to encourage followers to end their participation in Falun Gong, and to root out its leaders.

Religious practice often provides the foundation for illegal or "black" societies. Falun Gong and a number of other sects have been accused of using their organizations as fronts for drugs, smuggling, prostitution, and other illegal activities. Religious sects and black societies are widely believed to provide the basis of power for candidates for office. In the countryside, religion can become a tool of the family clans, who sometimes use it to pressure villagers to vote for their candidates.

Christianity

Christianity, which was introduced in the nineteenth and early twentieth centuries by European missionaries, has several million known adherents; and its churches, which were often used as warehouses or public offices after the Communist victory in 1949, have been reopened for religious practice. Bibles in several editions are available for purchase in many large-city bookstores. A steady stream of Christian

DENG XIAOPING = TENG HSIAO-P'ING. WHAT IS PINYIN?

Chinese is the oldest of the world's active languages and is now spoken and written by more people than any other modern language. Chinese is written in the form of characters, which have evolved over several thousand years from picture symbols (like ancient Egyptian hieroglyphics) written on oracle bones to the more abstract forms now in use. Although spoken Chinese varies greatly from dialect to dialect (for example, Mandarin, Cantonese, Shanghai-ese), the characters used to represent the language remain the same throughout China. Dialects are really just different ways of pronouncing the same characters.

There are more than 50,000 different Chinese characters. A well-educated person may be able to recognize as many as 25,000 characters, but basic literacy requires familiarity with only a few thousand.

Since Chinese is written in the form of characters rather than by a phonetic alphabet, Chinese words must be transliterated so that foreigners can pronounce them. This means that the sound of the character must be put into an alphabetic approximation.

Since English uses the Roman alphabet, Chinese characters are Romanized. (We do the same thing with other languages that are based on non-Roman alphabets, such as Russian, Greek, Hebrew, and Arabic.) Over the years, a number of methods have been developed to Romanize the Chinese language. Each method presents what the linguists who developed it believe to be the best way of approximating the sound of Chinese characters. *Pinyin* (literally, "spell sounds"), the system developed in the People's Republic of China, has gradually become the most commonly accepted system of Romanizing Chinese.

⊙	⊖	⊟	日	rì sun
☽	☽	☽	月	yuè moon
彳	勹	儿	人	rén person
朩	朩	朩	木	mù tree

Chinese characters are the symbols used to write Chinese. Modern Chinese characters fall into two categories: one with a phonetic component, the other without it. Most of those without a phonetic component developed from pictographs. From ancient writing on archaeological relics we can see their evolution, as in the examples shown (from left to right) above.

However, other systems are still used in areas such as Taiwan. This can cause some confusion, since the differences between Romanization systems can be quite significant. For example, in pinyin, the name of China's former leader is spelled Deng Xiaoping. But the Wade-Giles system, which was until recently the Romanization method most widely used by Westerners, transliterates his name as Teng Hsiao-p'ing. Same person, same characters, but a difference in how to spell his name in Roman letters.

---

proselytizers flow to China in search of new converts. Today's churches are attended as much by the curious as by the devout. As with eating Western food in places such as McDonald's and Kentucky Fried Chicken, attending Christian churches is a way that some Chinese feel they can participate in Western culture. Some Chinese want to become Christians because they see that in the West, Christians are rich and powerful. They believe that Christianity helps explain the wealth and power of Western capitalists, and hope that converting to Christianity will do the same for them.

The government generally permits mainstream Christian churches to practice in China, but it continues to exercise one major control over Roman Catholics: Their loyalty must be declared to the state, not to the pope. The Vatican is prohibited from involvement with China's priesthood, and Beijing does not recognize the validity of the Vatican's appointment of bishops and cardinals for China. Underground "house churches," primarily for smaller Christian sects, offshoots of mainstream Protestant religions, and papal Catholics, are forbidden. Nevertheless, they seem to flourish as officials busy themselves with addressing far more pressing social isues.

Since the mid-1990s, the government has tried to clamp down on non-mainstream Christian churches as well as religious sects,

arresting and even jailing some of their leaders. They have justified their actions on the grounds that, as in the West, some of the churches are involved in practices that endanger their adherents; some are actually involved in seditious activities against the state; and some are set up as fronts for illegal activities, including gambling, prostitution, and drugs.

Marxism-Leninism-Mao Zedong Thought

In general, Marxists are atheists. They believe that religions hinder the development of "rational" behavior and values that are so important to modernization. Yet societies seem to need some sort of spiritual, moral, and ethical guidance. For Communist party—led states, Marxism was believed to be adequate to fulfill this role. In China, however, Marxism-Leninism was reshaped by Mao Zedong Thought to accommodate for Chinese culture and conditions. Paramount among these conditions was that China was a predominantly peasant society, not a society in which there was a capitalist class exploiting large numbers of urban workers. The re-packaged ideology became known as Marxism-Leninism-Mao Zedong Thought. The Chinese leadership believed that it provided the ethical values necessary to guide China toward communism; and it was considered an integrated, rational thought system.

Nevertheless, this core of China's Communist political ideology exhibited many of the trappings of religions. It included scriptures (the works of Marx, Lenin, and Mao, as well as party doctrine); a spiritual head (Mao); and ritual observances (particularly during the Cultural Revolution, when Chinese were forced to participate in the political equivalent of Bible study each day). Largely thanks to the shaping of this ideology by Maoism, it included moral axioms that embodied traditional Chinese—and, some would say, Confucian—values that resemble teachings in other religions. Thus the moral of Mao's story of "The Foolish Old Man Who Wanted to Remove a Mountain" is essentially identical to the Christian principle "If you have faith you can walk on water," based on a story in the New Testament. Like this teaching, the essence of Mao Zedong Thought was concerned with the importance of a correct moral (political) consciousness.

In the 1980s, the more pragmatic leadership focused on liberalizing reforms and encouraged the people to "seek truth from facts" rather than from Marxism Leninism-Mao Zedong Thought. As a result, the role of ideology declined, in spite of efforts by more conservative elements in the political leadership to keep it as a guiding moral and political force. Participants in the required weekly "political study" sessions in most

COMMUNES: PEASANTS WORK OVERTIME DURING THE GREAT LEAP FORWARD

In the socialist scheme of things, communes are considered ideal forms of organization for agriculture. They are supposed to increase productivity and equality, reduce inefficiencies of small-scale individual farming, and bring modern benefits to the countryside more rapidly through rural industrialization.

These objectives are believed to be attained largely through the economies of scale of communes; that is, it is presumed that things done on a large scale are more efficient and cost-effective. Thus, using tractors, harvesters, trucks, and other agricultural machinery makes sense when large tracts of land can be planted with the same crops and plowed at one time. Similarly, a communal unit of 30,000 to 70,000 people can support small-scale industries, since, in such a large work unit, not everyone has to work in the fields.

Because of its size, a commune can support small-scale industries, as well as other types of organizations that smaller work units could not. A commune, for example, can support a hospital, a high school, an agricultural-research organization, and, if the commune is wealthy enough, even a "sports palace" and a cultural center for movies and entertainment.

During the Great Leap Forward, launched in 1958, peasants were—much against their will—forced into these larger agricultural and administrative units. They were particularly distressed that their small remaining private plots were, like the rest of their land, collectivized. Communal kitchens were to prepare food for everyone. Peasants were told that they had to eat in the communal mess halls rather than in the privacy of their own homes. And,

they were ordered to build "backyard furnaces" to smelt steel and bring the benefits of industry to the countryside—part of Mao Zedong's idea of "closing the gap" between agriculture and industry, and between countryside and city.

When the combination of bad policies and bad weather led to a severe famine, widespread peasant resistance forced the government to retreat from the Great Leap Forward policy and abandon the communes. But a modified commune system remained intact in much of China until the late 1970s, when the government ordered communes to be dissolved. A commune's collective property was then distributed to the peasants within it, and a system of "contract responsibility" was launched. Individual households are again, as before 1953, engaged in small-scale agricultural production on private plots of land.

---

urban work units abandoned any pretense of interest in politics. Instead, they focused on such issues as "how to do our work better" (that is, how to become more efficient and make a profit) that were in line with the more pragmatic approach to the workplace. Nevertheless, campaigns like the "get civilized" and anticorruption ones retain a strong moralistic tone.

Ideology has not been entirely abandoned. In the context of modernizing the economy and raising the standard of living, the current leadership is still committed to building "socialism with Chinese characteristics." Marxist-Leninist ideology is still being reformulated in China; but it is increasingly evident that few true believers in communism remain. Rarely does a Chinese leader even mention Marxism-Leninism in a speech. Leaders instead focus on modernization and becoming more efficient; they are more likely to discuss interest rates and trade balances than ideology. Fully aware that they need something to replace their own nearly defunct guiding ideological principles, however, and fearing that pure materialism and consumerism are inadequate substitutes, China's leaders seem to be relying on patriotism, nationalism, and national identity as the key components of a new ideology. Its primary purpose is very simple: economic modernization and support of the leadership of the Chinese Communist Party.

Undergirding China's nationalism is a fierce pride in China's history, civilization, and people. Insult, snub, slight, or

challenge China, and the result is certain to be a country united behind its leadership, against the offender. To oppose the CCP or its objective of modernization is viewed as "unpatriotic." China's nationalism, on the other hand, is fired by anti-foreign sentiments. These sentiments derive from the belief that foreign countries are—either militarily, economically, or through insidious cultural invasion—attempting to hurt China or to intervene in China's sovereign affairs by telling China's rulers how to govern properly. This is most notably the case whenever the Western countries condemn China for its human-rights record. U.S. support for Taiwan, and the U.S. bombing of the Chinese Embassy in Belgrade, Yugoslavia, during the Kosovo War in May 1999, fueled Chinese nationalism and injected even more tension into Sino–American relations. China's decision to join with the United States in its war on terrorism since 9/11 has, however, resulted in a toned-down nationalism and a less strident approach to international relationships. China's growing entanglement in a web of international economic and political relationships has also contributed to a softening of its nationalistic stance.

Language

By the time of the Shang Dynasty, which ruled in the second millennium B.C., the Chinese had a written language based on "characters." Over 4,000 years, these characters, or "ideographs," have evolved from

being pictorial representations of objects or ideas into their present-day form. Each character usually contains a phonetic element and one (or more) of the 212 symbols called "radicals" that help categorize and organize them.[11] Before the New Culture Movement of the 1920s, only a tiny elite of highly educated men could read these ideographs, which were organized in the difficult grammar of the classical style of writing, a style that in no way reflected the spoken language. All this changed with language reform in the 1920s: The classical style was abandoned, and the written language became almost identical in its structure to the spoken language.

Increasing Literacy

When the Chinese Communists came to power in 1949, they decided to facilitate the process of becoming literate by allowing only a few thousand of the more than 50,000 Chinese characters in existence to be used in printing newspapers, official documents, and educational materials. However, since a word is usually composed of a combination of two characters, these few thousand characters form the basis of a fairly rich vocabulary: Any single character may be used in numerous combinations in order to form many different words. The Chinese Communists have gone even further in facilitating literacy by simplifying thousands of characters, often reducing a character from more than 20 strokes to 10 or even fewer.

In 1979, China adopted a new system, *pinyin,* for spelling Chinese words and names. This system, which uses the Latin alphabet of 26 letters, was created largely for foreign consumption and was not widely used within China. The fact that so many characters have the same Romanization (and pronunciation), plus cultural resistance, have thus far resulted in ideographs remaining the basis for Chinese writing. There are, as an example, at least 70 different Chinese ideographs that are pronounced *zhu,* but each means something different. Usually the context is adequate to indicate which word is being used. But when it may not be clear which of many homonyms is being used, Chinese often use their fingers to draw the character in the air.

Something of a national crisis has emerged in recent years over the deleterious effect of computer use on the ability of Chinese to write Chinese characters from memory. Computers are set up to write Chinese characters by choosing from multiple Chinese words whose sound is rendered into a Latin alphabet. As a result, computer users no longer need to remember how to write the many strokes in Chinese characters—they simply scroll down to the correct Chinese character under the sound of, say, "Zhen." Then they press the "enter" key. The problem is that, without regular practice writing out characters, it is easy to forget how to write them—even for Chinese people. It is a problem akin to the loss of mathematical skills due to the use of calculators and computers.

Spoken Chinese

The Chinese have shared the same written language over the last 2,000 years, regardless of which dialect of Chinese they spoke. (The same written characters were simply pronounced in different ways, depending on the dialect.) Building a sense of national unity was difficult, however, when people needed interpreters to speak with someone living even a few miles away. After the Communist victory in 1949, the government decided that all Chinese would speak the same dialect in order to facilitate national unity. A majority of the delegates to the National People's Congress voted to adopt the northern dialect, Mandarin, as the national language, and required all schools to teach in Mandarin (usually referred to as "standard Chinese").

In the countryside, however, it has been difficult to find teachers capable of speaking and teaching Mandarin; and at home, whether in the countryside or the cities, the people have continued to speak their local dialects. The liberalization policies that began in 1979 have had as their by-product a discernible trend back to speaking local dialects, even in the workplace and on the streets. Whereas a decade ago a traveler could count on the national language being spoken in China's major cities, this is no longer the case. As a unified language is an important factor in maintaining national cohesion, the re-emergence of local dialects at the expense of standard Chinese threatens China's fragile unity.

One force that is slowing this disintegration is television, for it is broadcast almost entirely in standard Chinese. As there is a growing variety of interesting programming available, it may be that most Chinese will make an effort to maintain or even acquire the ability to understand standard Chinese. Many television programs have Chinese characters (representing the words being spoken) running along the bottom of the screen. This makes it less necessary for viewers to understand spoken standard Chinese; but it makes it more necessary for those who do not speak standard Chinese to be literate in order to enjoy television programs.

Education

The People's Republic of China has been remarkably successful in educating its people. Before 1949, less than 20 percent of the population could read and write. Today, nine years of schooling are compulsory. In the larger cities, 12 years of schooling is becoming the norm, with children attending either a vocational middle school or a college-preparatory school. Computer use is increasingly common in urban schools.

It is difficult to enforce the requirement of nine years of school in the impoverished countryside. Still, close to 90 percent of those children living in rural areas attend at least primary school. Village schools, however, often lack rudimentary equipment such as chairs and desks. Rural education also suffers from a lack of qualified teachers, as any person educated enough to teach can probably get a better-paying job in the industrial or commercial sector. But the situation is in flux, because as rural families are having fewer children than before, more can now afford the cost of educating their children. In 2006, the government abolished school fees, but there remain significant costs for poor villagers to educate their children. Still, as the goals of rural families have changed from preparing their children for farming to preparing them for factory work and office jobs in the towns and cities, education is seen as all the more important. So, at the same time that the collective basis for funding schools has deteriorated, in some villages many more farmers are able and willing to pay the necessary costs for schooling their children.

At the other end of the spectrum, many more students are now pursuing a college-oriented curriculum than will ever go on to college. From 1998 to 2004, China doubled the number of students it admitted to universities, from 2.1 to 4.2 million students.[12] Nevertheless, only about 5 percent of the senior middle school graduates will pass the university entrance examinations and be admitted. As a result, many who had prepared for a college curriculum are inappropriately educated for the workplace. The government is attempting to augment vocational training for high school students, but it is also increasing the number of slots available in colleges and universities. Private high schools and colleges are becoming increasingly popular as parents try to optimize the chances for their only child to climb the academic ladder in order to gain social and economic success. Enrollments in on-line education courses, especially in business, have also soared in numbers as China's economy becomes increasingly specialized and demands greater skills and expertise for jobs.

Political Education

Until the reforms that began in 1979, the content of Chinese education was suffused with political values and objectives. A considerable amount of school time—as much as 100 percent during political campaigns—was devoted to political education. Often this amounted to nothing more than learning by rote the favorite axioms and policies of the leading faction in power. When that faction lost power, the students' political thought had to be reoriented in the direction of the new policies and values. History, philosophy, literature, and even foreign languages and science were laced with a political vocabulary.

The prevailing political line has affected the balance in the curriculum between political study and the learning of skills and scientific knowledge. Beginning in the 1960s, the political content of education increased dramatically until, during the Cultural Revolution, schools were shut down. When they reopened in the early 1970s, politics dominated the curriculum. When Deng Xiaoping and the "modernizers" consolidated their power in the late 1970s, this tendency was reversed. During the 1980s, in fact, schools jettisoned the study of political theory because both administrators and teachers wanted their students to do well on college-entrance examinations, which by then focused on academic subjects. As a result, students refused to clog their schedules with the

(D. Falcone/PhotoLink/DAL19099)

Communes were disbanded by the early 1980s. In some areas, however, farmers have continued to work their land as a single unit in order to benefit from the economies of scale of large tracts of land.

study of political theory and the CCP's history. The study of Marxism and party history was revived in the wake of the events of Tiananmen Square in 1989, with the entering classes for many universities required to spend the first year in political study and indoctrination, sometimes under military supervision; but this practice was abandoned after two years. Today, political study has again been confined to a narrow part of the curriculum, in the interest of giving students an education that will help advance China's modernization.

Study Abroad

Since 1979, when China began to promote an "open door" policy, more than 100,000 PRC students have been sent for a university education to the United States, and tens of thousands more have gone to Europe and Japan. China has sent so many students abroad in part because the quality of education had seriously deteriorated during the Cultural Revolution, and in part because China's limited number of universities can accommodate only a tiny percentage of all high school graduates. Although an increasingly large number of Chinese universities are able to offer graduate training, talented Chinese students still travel abroad to receive advanced degrees.

Chinese students who have returned home have not always met a happy fate. Many of those educated abroad who were in China at the time of the Communists' victory in 1949, or who returned to China thereafter, were not permitted to hold leadership positions in their fields. Ultimately they were the targets of class-struggle campaigns and purges in the 1950s, '60s, and '70s, precisely because of their Western education. For the most part, those students who returned to China in the 1980s found that they could not be promoted because of the continuation of a system of seniority.

Since 1992, however, when Deng Xiaoping announced a major shift in economic and commercial policy to support just about anything that would help China become rich and powerful, the government has offered students significant incentives to return to China, including excellent jobs, promotions, good salaries, and even the chance to start new companies. Chinese students educated abroad are also recruited for their expertise and understanding of the outside world by the rapidly multiplying number of joint ventures in China, and by universities that are establishing their own graduate programs. Today, fully one third of students educated abroad return to live in China.

The Chinese government also now sees those Chinese who do stay abroad as forming critical links for China to the rest of the world. They have become the bridges over which contracts, loans, and trade flow to China, and are viewed as a positive asset. Finally, like immigrants elsewhere, Chinese who settle abroad tend to send remittances back to their families in China. These remittances amount to hundreds of millions of U.S. dollars in foreign currency each year and are valuable not just to the family recipients but also to the government's bank reserves.

Chinese studying abroad learn much about liberal democratic societies. Those who have returned to China bring with them the values at the heart of liberal-democratic societies. While this does not necessarily mean that they will demand the democratization of the Chinese political system, they do bring pluralistic liberal-democratic ideas to their own institutions. Some have been instrumental in setting up institutions such as "think tanks," have encouraged debate within their own fields, and have been insistent that China remain open to the outside world through the Internet, travel, conferences, and communications.

THE ECONOMIC SYSTEM

A Command Economy

Until 1979, the Chinese had a centrally controlled command economy. That is, the central leadership determined the economic policies to be followed and allocated all of the country's resources—labor, capital, land, and raw materials. It also determined how much each enterprise, and even each individual, would be allocated for production and consumption. Once the Chinese Communist Party leadership determined the country's political goals and the correct ideology, the State Planning Commission and the State Economic Commission would then decide how to implement these objectives through specific policies for agriculture and industry and the allocation of resources. This is in striking contrast to a capitalist laissez-faire economy, in which government control over both consumers and producers is minimal and market forces of supply and demand play the primary role in determining the production and distribution of goods.

The CCP leadership adopted the model of a centralized planned economy from the Soviet Union. Such a system was not only in accord with the Leninist model of centralized state governance; it also made sense for a government desperate to unify China after more than 100 years of internal division, instability, and economic collapse. Historically, China suffered from the ability of large regions to evade the grasp of central control over such matters as currency and taxes. The inability of the Nationalist government to gain control over the country's economy in the 1930s and early 1940s undercut its power and contributed to its failure to win control over China. Thus, the Chinese Communist Party's decision to centralize economic decision making after 1949 helped the state to function as an integrated whole.

Over time, however, China's highly centralized economy became inefficient and too inflexible to address the complexity of the country's needs. Although China possesses a large and diverse economy, with a broad range of resources, topography, and climate, its economic planners made policy as if it were a uniform, homogeneous whole. Merely increasing production was itself considered a contribution to development, regardless of whether a market for the products existed or whether the products actually helped advance modernization.

State planning agencies, without the benefit of market research or signals from the marketplace, determined whether or not a product should be manufactured, and in what quantity. For example, the central government might set a goal for a factory to manufacture 5 million springs per year—without knowing if there was even a market for them. The factory management did not care, as the state was responsible for marketing the products and paid the factory's bills. If the state had no buyer for the springs, they would pile up in warehouses; but rarely would production be cut back, much less a factory be closed, as this would create the problem of employing the workers cut from the factory's payroll. Economic inefficiencies of this sort were often justified because socialist political objectives such as full employment were being met. Even today the state worries about shutting down a state-owned factory that is losing money, because it creates unemployment. In turn, unemployment leads to popular anger and provides a volatile, unstable environment, ripe for public political protest. Quality control was similarly not as important an issue as it should have been for state-run industries in a centrally planned economy. Until market reforms began in 1979, the state itself allocated all finished products to other industries that needed them. If a state-controlled factory made defective parts, the industry using them had no recourse against the supplier, because each factory had a contract with the state, not with other factories. It was the state that would pay for additional parts to be made, so the enterprises did not bear the costs.

As a result, China's economic development under the centralized political leadership of the CCP occurred by fits and starts. Much waste resulted from planning that did not take into account market factors of supply and demand. Centrally set production quotas took the place of efficiency and profitability in the allocation of resources. Although China's command economy was able to meet the country's most important industrial needs, problems like these took their toll over time. Enterprises had little incentive to raise productivity, quality, or efficiency when doing so did not affect their budgets, wages, or funds for expansion.

Agricultural Programs

By the late 1950s, central planning was causing significant damage to the agricultural sector. Regardless of geography or climate, China's economic planners repeatedly ordered the peasants to restructure their economic production units according to one centralized plan. China's peasants, who had supported the CCP in its rise to power before 1949 in order to acquire their own land, had enthusiastically embraced the CCP's fulfillment of its pledge of "land to the tillers" after the Communists took over in 1949. But in 1953, the leadership, motivated by a belief that small-scale agricultural production could not meet the production goals of socialist development, ordered all but 15 percent of the arable land to be pooled into "lower-level agricultural producer cooperatives" of between 300 and 700 workers. The remaining 15 percent of land was to be set aside as private plots for the peasants, and they could market the produce from these plots in private markets throughout the countryside. Then, in 1956, the peasants throughout the country were ordered into "higher-level agricultural producer cooperatives" of 10 times that size, and the size of the private plots allotted to them was reduced to 5 percent of the cooperatives' total land.

Many peasants felt cheated by these wholesale collectivization policies. When in 1958 the central leadership ordered them to move into communes 10 times larger still than the cooperatives they had just joined, they were irate. Mao Zedong's Great Leap Forward policy of 1958 forced all peasants in China to become members of communes: enormous economic and administrative units consisting of between 30,000 and 70,000 people. Peasants were required to relinquish their private plots, and turn over their private utensils, as well as their household chickens, pigs, and ducks, to the commune. Resisting this mandate, many peasants killed and ate their livestock. Since private enterprise was no longer permitted, home industries ground to a halt.

CCP chairman Mao's vision for catching up with the West was to industrialize the vast countryside. Peasants were therefore ordered to build "backyard furnaces" to smelt steel. Lacking iron ore, much less any knowledge of how to make steel, and under the guidance of party cadres who themselves were ignorant of steelmaking, the peasants tore out metal radiators, pipes, and fences. Together with pots and pans, they were dumped into their furnaces. Almost none of the final smelted product was usable. Finally, the central economic leadership ordered all peasants to eat in large, communal mess halls. This was reportedly the last straw for a people who valued family above all else. Being deprived of time alone with their families for meals, the peasants refused to cooperate further in agricultural collectivization.

When the catastrophic results of the Great Leap Forward policy poured in, the CCP retreated—but it was too late. Three subsequent years of bad weather, combined with the devastation wreaked by these policies and the Soviet withdrawal of all assistance, brought economic catastrophe. Demographic data indicate that in the "three bad years" from 1959 to 1962, more than 20 million Chinese died from starvation and malnutrition-related diseases.

Courtesy of Ron Church (rchurch01)

Chinese street shops in the 1980s.

By 1962, central planners had condoned peasants returning to production units that were smaller than communes. Furthermore, peasants were again allowed to farm a small percentage of the total land as private plots, to raise domestic animals for their own use, and to engage in household industries. Free markets, at which the peasantry could trade goods from private production, were reopened. The commune structure was retained throughout the countryside, however; and until the CCP leadership introduced the contract responsibility system in 1979, it provided the infrastructure of rural secondary school education, hospitals, and agricultural research.

Other centrally determined policies, seemingly oblivious to reality, compounded the P.R.C.'s difficulties in agriculture. Maoist policies carried out during both the Great Leap Forward and renewed during the Cultural Revolution included attempts to plant three crops per year in areas that for climatic reasons can only support two (as the Chinese put it, "Three times three is not as good as two times five"); and "close planting," which often more than doubled the amount of seed planted, with the result that all of it grew to less than full size or simply wilted for lack of adequate sunshine and nutrients.

A final example of centrally determined agricultural policy bringing catastrophe was the decision during the Cultural Revolution that "the whole country should grow grain." The purpose was to establish China's self-sufficiency in grain. Considering China's immense size and diverse climates, soil types, and topography, a policy ordering everyone to grow the same thing was doomed to failure. Peasants were ordered to plow under fields of cotton and cut down rubber plantations and fruit orchards, planting grain in their place. China's central planning was largely done by the CCP, not by economic or agricultural experts, and they ignored overwhelming evidence that grain would not grow well, if at all, in some areas. These policies ignored the fact that China would have to import everything that it had replaced with grain, at far greater costs than it would have paid for importing just grain. Peasant protests were futile in the face of local-level Communist Party leaders who hoped to advance their careers by implementing central policy. The policy of self-sufficiency in grain was abandoned only with the arrest of the Gang of Four in 1976.

Economic Reforms: Decentralization and Liberalization

In 1979, Deng Xiaoping undertook reform and liberalization of the economy, a critical component of China's modernization program. The government tried to maintain centralized state control of the direction of policy and the distribution and pricing of strategic and energy resources, while decentralizing decision making down to the level of the township and village. Decentralization was meant to facilitate more rational decision making, based on local conditions, needs, and efficiency. Although the state has retained the right to set overall economic priorities, township and village enterprises (TVEs), as well as larger state-owned enterprises, have been encouraged to respond to local market forces of supply and demand. Centrally determined quotas and pricing for most products have been phased out, and enterprises now contract with one another rather than with the state. Thus the government's role as the go-between in commercial transactions—and as the central planner for everything in the economy—is gradually disappearing.

Since the introduction of market capitalism in the 1980s, the economy has become increasingly privatized. Some 70 percent of China's gross national product (GNP) is now produced by these nonstate enterprises. They compete with state-run enterprises to supply goods and services, and if they are not profitable, they go bankrupt.

On the other hand, some state-run enterprises that operate at a loss continue to be subsidized by the government rather than shut down. One reason is that the enterprises are in a sector over which the state wants to keep control, such as energy, raw materials, and steel production. Another reason is fear of the destabilizing impact of a high level of unemployment if the state closes down large state-run enterprises. Subsidies and state-owned bank loans (which will not be repaid) to unprofitable enterprises consume a significant portion of the state's budget. China's membership in the World Trade Organization (WTO) since 2001 has, however, forced China's large state-owned enterprises to become efficient, or else perish in the face of foreign competition. In the meantime, the government continues to close down the most unprofitable state-run enterprises, and it counts on the entrepreneurial sector and foreign investors to fuel economic growth and absorb the unemployed.

In addition, under a carefully managed scheme, the government has started to sell off some state-run industries to TVEs, the private sector, and foreign investors. Whoever buys them must in most cases guarantee some sort of livelihood, even if not full employment, to the former employees of the state-run enterprises. The new owners, however, have far more freedom to make a profit than did the enterprises when they were state-owned. The state is also slowly introducing state-run pension and unemployment funds to care for those workers who lose their jobs when state-owned enterprises are shut down.

Today, the agricultural sector is almost fully market-driven. The "10,000 yuan" household (about U.S. $1,200), once a measure of extraordinary wealth in China, has become a realizable goal for most peasants. Free markets are booming in China, and peasants may now produce whatever they can get the best price for in the market, once they have filled their grain quotas to the state. Wealthy rural towns are springing up throughout the agriculturally rich and densely populated east coast, as well as along China's major transportation routes.

Problems Created by Economic Reforms
Disputes Over Property

One downside of privatization and marketization is a distinct increase in disputes among villagers. There are disputes over who gets to use the formerly collectively owned goods, such as tractors, harvesters, processing equipment, and boats for transporting goods at harvest time. And with formerly collective fields turned into a patchwork of small private plots, villagers often protest when others cross their land with farm equipment. Theoretically, the land that is "leased" to the peasants is collectively owned by the village, but in practice the land is treated as the private property of the peasants. Those who choose to leave their land may contract it out to others, so some peasants have amassed large tracts of land suitable for large-scale farm machinery. To encourage development, the government has permitted land to be leased for as long as 30 years and for leased rights to be inherited. Furthermore, peasants have built houses on what they consider their own land, itself a problem because it is usually arable land. Nevertheless, the village councils also have some ability to reallocate land so that soldiers and others who return to settle in the villages can receive adequate land to farm.

With the growth of free enterprise in the rural towns since 1979, some 60 million to 100 million peasants have left the land to work for higher pay in small-scale rural industry or in cities. It is not just that the wages are higher, but also that the peasants are burdened by the arbitrary imposition of local taxes and fees. Combined with the low profits on agricultural products and the unpredictability of weather, farmers seek better wages in local enterprises or migrate to the cities. Others leave because their land has been confiscated by the local government for development. Rarely compensated adequately, if at all, for their land, they are forced to leave the villages for towns and cities. Parents often migrate together, but are unable to bear the costs of taking their children with them, so they are left with their relatives or friends—or to

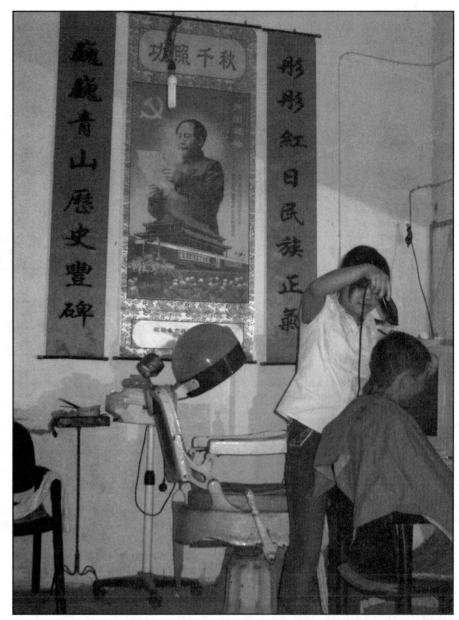

(Courtesy of Suzanne Ogden/sogden033)

Small private businesses in towns and cities are part of what is driving the growth of individual wealth in China. This hair-cutting salon is in a town in Anhui Province. A poster on the wall indicates the continuing reverence for Mao Zedong in many parts of China.

fend for themselves, alone. To address the problems being created by the confiscation of agricultural land, as well as to stop the boom in building "development zones" for no specific need or purpose, the government cancelled some 4,800 of the 6,866 development zones that had sprung up throughout China. The Ministry of Land and Resources has discovered that, of the total zones, 70 percent had illegally acquired land, or had confiscated the land and then left it unused. The measure shut down about 65 percent of the total land area planned for development zones, and returned some of the land to agricultural use.[13]

Instability and Crime

For some, especially those able to find employment in the booming construction industry in many small towns and cities, migration has brought a far better standard of living. But tens of millions of unemployed migrants clog city streets, parks, and railroad stations. They have been joined by equally large numbers of workers from bankrupt state-owned enterprises. Together, they have contributed to a vast increase in criminality and social instability. According to Chinese government reports, there were more than

25

CHINA'S SPECIAL ECONOMIC ZONES

In 1979, China opened four "Special Economic Zones" (SEZs) within the territory of the People's Republic of China as part of its program to reform the socialist economy and to encourage foreign investment. The SEZs were allowed a great deal of leeway in experimenting with new economic policies. For example, Western management methods, including the right to fire unsatisfactory workers (something unknown under China's centrally planned economy), were introduced into SEZ factories. Laws and regulations on foreign investment were greatly eased in the SEZs in order to attract foreign capital. Export-oriented industries were established with the goal of earning large amounts of foreign exchange in order to help pay for importing technology for modernization. To many people, the SEZs looked like pockets of capitalism inside the socialist economy of the P.R.C.; indeed, they are often referred to as "mini-Hong Kongs." In 1984, 14 coastal cities were allowed to open up development zones to help attract foreign investment.

© IMS Communications, Ltd/Capstone Design/FlatEarth Images RF
A Shenzhen street at night.

The largest of the Special Economic Zones is Shenzhen, which is located just across the border from the Hong Kong New Territories. Over several decades, Shenzhen was transformed from a sleepy little rural town to a large, modern urban center and one of China's major industrial cities. The city boasts broad avenues and skyscrapers, and a standard of living that is among the highest in the country.

But with growth and prosperity have come numerous problems. The pace of construction has outstripped the ability of the city to provide adequate services to the growing population. Speculation and corruption have been rampant, and crime is a more serious problem in Shenzhen than in most other parts of China. Strict controls on immigration help stem the flood of people who are attracted to Shenzhen in the hopes of making their fortune.

Nevertheless, the success of Shenzhen and other Special Economic Zones led the leadership to expand the concept of SEZs throughout the country, most notably Shanghai's new Pudong district. The special privileges, such as lower taxes, that foreign businesses and joint ventures could originally enjoy only in these zones were expanded first along the coast and then to the interior, so that it too could benefit from foreign investment. By 2004, there were 6,866 "development zones," formed largely by confiscating agricultural land from the peasantry.

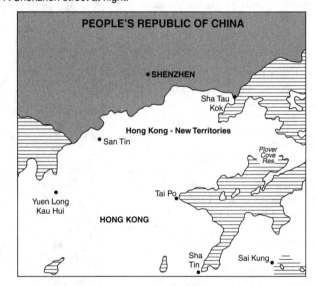

Shenzhen is the largest of China's SEZs. It is located close to the Hong Kong New Territories.

74,000 "mass incidents" (protests and riots) in 2004, a 30 percent increase over the 58,000 reported in 2003, and more than six times the number it reported 10 years earlier.[14] In 2005 over 87,000 such demonstrations occurred.

Problems Arising From a Mixed Economy

Still other problems arose from the post–1979 reform policies that led to a mixed socialist and capitalist economy. For example, with decentralization, industrial enterprises tried to keep their profits but "socialize" their losses. That is, profitable enterprises (whether state-owned, collective TVEs, or private) try to hide their profits to avoid paying taxes to the state. State-owned enterprises that are losing money ask the

state for subsidies to keep them in business. For this reason, the amount of profits turned over to the state was not commensurate with the dramatic increase in the value of industrial output since 1979. In the last decade, however, this situation has been ameliorated as China has become a primarily market-driven economy. Almost all prices are now market-determined, except for energy, water, and natural resources. Although it is common in almost all market economies for the state to regulate the prices of energy and utilities, the fact that certain other commodities and products in short supply are still regulated by the state continues to create problems in China.[15]

Products such as rolled steel, glass, cement, or timber are either hoarded as a safeguard against future shortages, or

resold at unauthorized higher prices. By doing so, these enterprises make illegal profits for themselves and deprive other enterprises of the materials they need for production. In short, the remnants of a mixed economy, combined with the lack of a strong regulatory state to administer the economy, provide many opportunities for corruption and abuse of the system.

Further, while private and collective enterprises rely on market signals to determine whether they will expand production facilities, the state continues to centrally allocate resources based on a national plan. A clothing factory that expands its production, for instance, requires more energy (coal, oil) and water, and more cotton. The state, already faced with inadequate energy resources to keep most industries operating

Courtesy of Suzanne Ogden (sogden030)

Water buffalo cultivating rice in China.

at full capacity, continues to allocate the same amount to the now-expanded factory. Profitable enterprises want a greater share of centrally allocated scarce resources, but find they cannot acquire them without the help of "middlemen" and a significant amount of under-the-table dealing. Corruption has, therefore, become rampant at the nexus where the capitalist and socialist economies meet.

Widespread corruption in the economic sector has led the Chinese government to wage a series of campaigns against economic crimes such as embezzlement and graft. An increasing number of economic criminals are going to prison, and serious offenders are sometimes executed. Until energy and transportation bottlenecks and the scarcity of key resources are dealt with, however, it will be extremely difficult to halt the bribery, smuggling, embezzlement, and extortion now pervasive in China. The combination of relaxed centralized control, the mandate for the Chinese people to "get rich," and a mixed economy have exacerbated what was already a problem under the socialist system. In a system suffering from serious scarcities but controlled by bureaucrats, it is political power, not the market, that determines who gets what. This includes not only goods, but also opportunities, licenses, permits, and approvals.

Although the Chinese may now purchase in the market many essential products previously distributed through bureaucratically controlled channels, there are still many goods available only through the "back door"—that is, through people they know and with whom they exchange favors or money. Scarcity, combined with bureaucratic control, has led to "collective corruption": Individuals engage in corrupt practices, even cheat the state, in order to benefit the enterprise for which they work. Since enterprises not owned by the state will not be bailed out if they suffer losses, the motivation for corrupt activities is stronger than under the previous system.

Liberalization of the economy is providing a massive number and variety of goods for the marketplace. The Chinese people may buy almost any basic consumer goods in stores or the open markets. But the nexus between continued state control and the free economy still fuels a rampant corruption that threatens the development of China's economy.

The mixed economy, then, provides the environment in which corruption has increased; but it is further exacerbated by the sheer amount of money in China today. Before 1979, corruption tended to involve exchanges of favors, many of which amounted to giving access, a privilege, or a necessary document to someone in exchange for another favor. Today, corruption is about getting large amounts of money through various deals. Further, unlike in most developing countries, corruption is not just at the top. It is widespread, all the way to the bottom of the economic ladder.

Some argue that the fact that so many people at all rungs of the economic ladder can share in the cashing out of corrupt activities allows it to be tolerated.[17]

Still, there is a huge amount of wealth concentrated in the elite, if for no other reason than that they have the "connections" and access to gain wealth. Figures indicate that 90 percent of China's billionaires are, in fact, children of the senior party-state elite.[18] The ability of corrupt individuals to abscond to a foreign country has made capital flight an increasingly worrisome issue. China's Ministry of Commerce reported that thousands of corrupt officials (many of whom are said to be the children and relatives of political leaders) have illegally transferred China's wealth to companies registered in offshore tax shelters and financial havens.[19]

Unequal Benefits

Not all Chinese have benefited equally from the 30 years of economic reforms. Those who inhabit cities in the interior, and peasants living far from cities and transportation lines or tilling less arable land, have reaped far fewer rewards. And although the vast majority of Chinese have seen some improvement in their standard of living, short-term gains in income are threatened in the long term by the deterioration of the infrastructure for education and medical care in large parts of China's hinterland. This deterioration is due to the elimination of the commune as the underlying institution for funding these services. Wealthier peasants send their children into the larger towns and cities for schooling.

In healthcare, the Communist government has overseen dramatic improvements in the provision of social services for the masses. Largely because of its emphasis on preventive medicine and sanitation, life expectancy has increased from 45 years in 1949 to 73 years (overall) today. The government has successfully eradicated many childhood diseases and has made great strides against other diseases, such as malaria and tuberculosis. The privatization of medicine in recent years has, however, meant that many no longer have guaranteed access to medical treatment. The press has highlighted many cases in which, if they cannot pay, they will not be treated. Wealthier families, on the other hand, can travel to the more comprehensive health clinics and hospitals farther away, although in some areas, they have actually built local schools and private hospitals. In recent years, under the leadership of Hu Jintao and Wen Jiabao, the state has stepped back in to address these issues of unequal access, in part because they are giving rise to social instability. Among their many policies has been the elimination of school fees for children who attend rural schools.

Nevertheless, the visible polarization of wealth, which had been virtually eradicated in the first 30 years of Communist rule, continues to deepen in the context of capitalism and a poorly regulated free market. The creation of a crassly ostentatious wealthy class and a simply ostentatious middle class, in the context of high unemployment, poverty, and a mobile population, is breeding the very class conflict that the Chinese Communists fought a revolution to eliminate. When reforms began 30 years ago, street crime was almost unheard of in China's cities. Now it is a growing problem, one that the government fears may erode the legitimacy of CCP rule if left uncontrolled.

Mortgaging the Future

One of the most damaging aspects of the capitalist "get-rich" atmosphere prevailing in China is the willingness to sacrifice the future for short-term profits. The environment continues to be deeply degraded by uncontrolled pollution; the rampant growth of new towns, cities, and highways; the building of houses on arable land; the overuse of nonrenewable water resources; and the destruction of forests. Some state institutions, including schools, have turned the open spaces (such as playgrounds) within their walls into parking lots in China's crowded cities to provide spaces for the rapidly growing number of privately owned cars.

To sustain its rapid economic growth, China has had to add new power-generating capacity, 90 percent of which is from new coal-fired plants, at the *annual* rate (as of 2006) of "the entire capacity of the UK and Thailand combined, or about twice the generating assets of California."[20] China's primary source of energy is coal, followed by oil, both of which emit substantial greenhouse gases (such as carbon dioxide) to the environment. In 2008, China became the world's largest producer of greenhouse gases. But regardless of how much it contributes to global warming, China is already suffering from its effects. The government is concerned about the impact of global warming on China's future economic growth and food security, as well as its role in generating severe weather patterns, desertification, and flooding. Environmental deterioration is, in turn, causing social instability. Indeed, each year there is an increasing number of major protests—often violent—from communities affected by environmental degradation. Since 1997, pollution disputes submitted to legal or administrative resolution have increased at an annual rate of about 25 percent. By 2002, the actual number of disputes reported as submitted for solution had reached 500,000.[21]

Health problems arising from polluted air and contaminated water are affecting both rural and urban populations. Cities that used to have clear blue skies before economic reforms began 30 years ago now infrequently see the sun. Coal-burning plants, which produce significant amounts of air particulates, supply two-thirds of China's energy needs. With close to 70 percent of China's rivers and lakes severely polluted, even boiled water is not fit to drink. In Beijing, 90 percent of the underground water supply on which it relies is contaminated. To add to its woes, a 60-billion-dollar pipeline is having to be built to transfer water from the south to the north, especially for Beijing.

So, even though China's government takes the same stance as most other developing countries—namely, that the *developed* countries should pay for their efforts to reduce greenhouse gases (and sulfur dioxide, which causes acid rain), China realizes it has to take its own actions before it is too late. Moreover, with Beijing hosting the 2008 Olympic Games, the government wants to be sure that air quality is improved quickly. The problem is that the State Environment Protection Agency (SEPA) is one of China's weakest ministries. It must compete against other powerful ministries that want to promote economic development, regardless of the environmental costs. The government also promotes car ownership and consumption of durable goods such as air conditioners and washing machines, all of which consume considerable energy and thereby exacerbate the pollution. In the meantime, officials receive promotion based on how much they have advanced economic growth in their localities. This puts them at cross purposes with SEPA's goals of regulating pollution, and causes them to blatantly ignore state environmental regulations.

Added to the demand for energy created by economic growth is the hugely inefficient use of energy, with some products requiring as much as 10 to 20 times more energy to produce than in more efficient economies, such as Japan, the U.S., and Germany. So, in 2006, environmental policy, instead of capping greenhouse gas emissions, chose to reduce the amount of energy used in the production of a product. The central government is now demanding that major state enterprises as well as provincial governors sign contracts in which they pledge "to reduce the amount of energy consumed relative to economic output by 20 percent over five years." If China succeeds in doing so, even though economic output will continue to grow, the amount of energy used will grow at a much slower rate.[22]

THE CHINESE LEGAL SYSTEM
Ethical Basis of Law

In imperial China, the Confucian system provided the basis for the traditional social and political order. Confucianism posited that good governance should be based on maintaining correct personal relationships among people, and between people and their rulers. Ethics were based on these relationships. A legal system did exist, but the Chinese resorted to it in civil cases only in desperation, for the inability to resolve one's problems oneself or through a mediator usually resulted in considerable "loss of face"—a loss of dignity or standing in the eyes of others. (In criminal cases, the state normally became involved in determining guilt and punishment.)

This perspective on law carried over into the period of Communist rule. Until legal reforms began in 1979, most Chinese preferred to call in CCP officials, local neighborhood or factory mediation committees, family members, or friends to settle disputes. Lawyers were rarely used, and only when mediation failed did the Chinese resort to the courts. By contrast, the West lacks both this strong support for

Neighborhood mediation in China.

the institution of mediation and the concept of "face." So Westerners have difficulty understanding why China has had so few lawyers, and why the Chinese have relied less on the law than on personal relationships when problems arise.

Like Confucianism, Marxism-Leninism is an ideology that embodies a set of ethical standards for behavior. After 1949, it easily built on China's cultural predisposition toward ruling by ethics instead of law. Although Marxism-Leninism did not completely replace the Confucian ethical system, it did establish new standards of behavior based on socialist morality. These ethical standards were embodied in the works of Marx, Lenin, and Mao, and in the Chinese Communist Party's policies; but in practice, they were frequently undercut by preferential treatment for officials.

Legal Reforms

Before legal reforms began in 1979, the Chinese cultural context and the socialist system were the primary factors shaping the Chinese legal system. Since 1979, reforms have brought about a remarkable transformation in Chinese attitudes toward the law, with the result that China's laws and legal procedures—if not practices and implementation—look increasingly like those in the West. This is particularly true for laws that relate to the economy, including contract, investment, property, and commercial laws. The legal system has evolved to accommodate its more market-oriented economy and privatization. Chinese citizens have discovered that the legal system can protect their rights, especially in economic transactions. In 2004, 4.4 million civil cases were filed, double the number 10 years earlier. This is a strong indication that the Chinese now are more aware of their legal rights, and believe they can use the law to protect their rights and to hold others (including officials) accountable for their actions.[23] Still, in many civil cases (such as disputes with neighbors and family members), the Chinese remain inclined to rely on mediation and traditional cultural values in the settling of disputes.

Law and Politics

From 1949 until the legal reforms that began in 1979, Chinese universities trained few lawyers. Legal training consisted of learning law and politics as an integrated whole; for according to Marxism, law is meant to reflect the values of the "ruling class" and to serve as an instrument of "class struggle." The Chinese Communist regime viewed law as a branch of the social sciences, not as a professional field of study. For this reason, China's citizens tended to view law as a mere propaganda tool, not as a means for protecting their rights. They had never really experienced a law-based society. Not only were China's laws and legal education highly politicized, but politics also pervaded the judicial system.

With few lawyers available, few legally trained judges or prosecutors in the courts, and even fewer laws to refer to for standards of behavior, inevitably China's legal system has been subject to abuse. China has been ruled by people, not by law; by politics, not by legal standards; and by party policy, not by a constitution. Interference in the judicial process by party and local state officials has been all too common.

After 1979, the government moved quickly to write new laws. Fewer than 300 lawyers, most of them trained before 1949 in Western legal institutions, undertook the immense task of writing a civil code, a criminal code, contract law, economic law, law governing foreign investment in China, tax law, and environmental and forestry laws. One strong motivation for the Chinese Communist leadership to formalize the legal system was its growing realization, after years of a disappointingly low level of foreign investment, that the international business community was reluctant to invest further in China without substantial legal guarantees.

Even China's own potential entrepreneurs wanted legal protection against the *state* before they would assume the risks of developing new businesses. Enterprises, for example, wanted a legal guarantee that if the state should fail to supply resources contracted for, it could be sued for losses issuing from its nonfulfillment of contractual obligations. Since the leadership wanted to encourage investment, it needed to supplement economic reforms with legal reforms. Codification of the legal system fostered a stronger basis for modernization and helped limit the party-state's abuse of the people's rights.

In addition, new qualifications have been established for all judicial personnel. Demobilized military officers who became judges and prosecutors during the Cultural Revolution have been removed from the judiciary. Judges, prosecutors, and lawyers must now have formal legal training and pass a national judicial examination. It is hoped that judicial personnel endowed with higher qualifications and larger salaries, as well as judicial systems that are financially autonomous from local governments will diminish judicial corruption and enhance the autonomy of judicial decisions.[24]

Criminal Law

Procedures followed in Chinese criminal courts have differed significantly from those in the United States. Although the concept of "innocent until proven guilty" was introduced in China in 1996, it is still presumed that people brought to trial in criminal cases are guilty. This presumption is confirmed by the judicial process itself. That is, after a suspect is arrested by the police, the procuratorate (*procuracy,* the investigative branch of the judiciary system) will spend considerable time and effort examining the evidence gathered by the police and establishing whether the suspect is indeed guilty. This is important

to understanding why 99 percent of all the accused brought to trial in China are judged guilty. Indeed, had the facts not substantiated their guilt, the procuracy would have dismissed their cases before going to trial.

In short, then, those adjudged to be innocent would never be brought to trial in the first place. For this reason, court trials function mainly to present the evidence upon which the guilty verdict is based—not to weigh the evidence to see if it indicates guilt—and to remind the public that criminals are punished. A trial is a "morality play" of sorts: the villain is punished, justice is done, the people's interests are protected. In addition, the trial process continues to emphasize the importance of confessing one's crimes, for those who confess and appear repentant in court will usually be dealt more lenient sentences. Criminals are encouraged to turn themselves in, on the promise that their punishment will be less severe than if they are caught. Those accused of crimes are encouraged to confess rather than deny their guilt or appeal to the next level, all in hopes of gaining a more lenient sentence from the judge.

This type of system, which tends to focus on confession, not on fact finding, is weighted against the innocent. The result is that police are more inclined to use brutal tactics in order to exact a confession; but of course, police in Western liberal-democratic countries also have been known to use brutality, and even torture, to get a confession.

Another serious problem with the Chinese system was that the procuracy, which investigated the case, also prosecuted the case. Once the procuracy established "the facts," they were not open to question by the lawyer or the representative of the accused. (In China, a person may be represented by a family member, friend, or colleague, largely because there are not enough lawyers to fulfill the guarantee of a person's "right to a defense.") The lawyer for the accused was not allowed to introduce new evidence, make arguments to dismiss the case based on technicalities or improper procedures (such as wire tapping), call witnesses for the defendant, or make insanity pleas for the client. Instead, the lawyer's role in a criminal case was simply to represent the person in court and to bargain with the court for a reduced sentence for the repentant client.

The 1996 legal reforms were aimed at improving the rights of the accused: They may now call their own witnesses and introduce their own evidence, they cannot be held for more than 30 days without being formally charged with a crime, and they are supposed to have access to a lawyer within several days of being formally

arrested. But many suspects are still not accorded these rights.

The accused have the right to a defense, but it has always been presumed that a lawyer will not defend someone who is guilty. Most of China's lawyers are still employed and paid by the state. As such, a lawyer's obligation is first and foremost to protect the state's interests, not the individual's interests at the expense of the state. Lawyers who acted otherwise risked being condemned as "counter-revolutionaries" or treasonous. Small wonder that after 1949, the study of law did not attract China's most talented students.

Today, however, the law profession is seen as potentially lucrative and increasingly divorced from politics. Lawyers can now enter private practice or work for foreigners in a joint venture. The All-China Lawyers Association, established in 1995 by the Ministry of Justice to regulate the legal profession, also functions as an interest group to protect the rights of lawyers against the state. Thus, when in recent years lawyers have found themselves in trouble with the law because they have defended the political rights of their clients against the state, the association tries to protect them.

Lawyers in Civil and Commercial Law

In the areas of civil and commercial law, the role of the lawyer has become increasingly important since the opening of China's closed door to the outside world. Because foreign trade and investment have become crucial to China's development, the government has made an all-out effort to train many more lawyers. In today's China, upholding the law is no longer simply a matter of correctly understanding the party "line" and then following it in legal disputes. China's limited experience in dealing with economic, liability, corporate, and contractual disputes in the courts, as well as the insistence by foreign investors that Chinese courts be prepared to address such issues, have forced the leadership to train lawyers in the intricacies of Western law and to draft countless new laws and regulations. To protect themselves against what is difficult to understand in the abstract, the Chinese used to refuse to publish their newly written laws. Claiming a shortage of paper or the need to protect "state secrets," they withheld publication of many laws until their actual impact on China's state interests could be determined. This practice frustrated potential investors, who dared not risk capital investment in China until they knew exactly what the relevant laws were. Today, however, the complexity of both foreign-investment issues and the

CENTRAL GOVERNMENT ORGANIZATION OF THE PEOPLE'S REPUBLIC OF CHINA

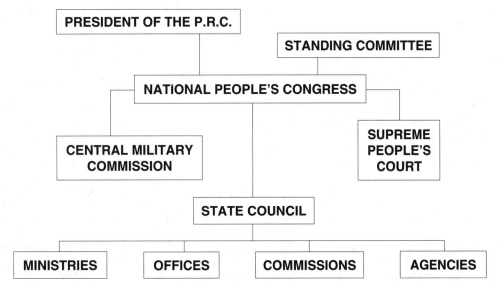

This central government organization chart represents the structure of the government of the People's Republic of China as it appears on paper. However since all of the actions and overall doctrine of the central government must be reviewed and approved by the Chinese Communist Party, political power ultimately lies with the party. To ensure this control, virtually all top state positions are held by party members.

THE CHINESE COMMUNIST PARTY (CCP)

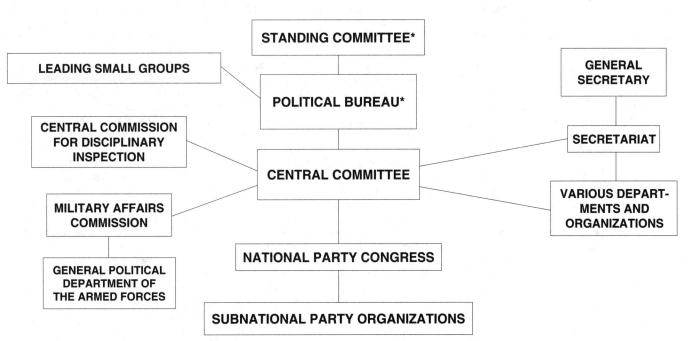

*The Political Bureau and its Standing Committee and the "Leading Small Groups" are the most powerful organizations within the Chinese Communist Party and are therefore the real centers of power in the P.R.C.

entrepreneurial activities of China's own citizens have led the Chinese government to publish most of its laws as quickly as possible.

THE POLITICAL SYSTEM

The Party and the State

In China, the Chinese Communist Party is the fountainhead of power and policy. But not all Chinese people are party members. Although the CCP has some 70 million members, this number represents only 5 percent of the population. Joining the CCP is a competitive, selective, rigorous process. Some have wanted to join out of a commitment to Communist ideals, others in hopes of climbing the ladder of success, still others to gain access to limited goods and opportunities. Ordinary Chinese are generally suspicious of the motives of those who do join the party. Many well-educated Chinese have grown cynical about the CCP and refused to join. Still, those who travel to China today are likely to find that many of the most talented people they meet are party members. Party hacks who are ideologically adept but incompetent at their work are gradually being squeezed out of a party desperate to maintain its leading position in a rapidly changing China.

Today's Party wants the best and brightest of the land as members, and it wants it to represent "the people" more broadly. In 2001, Jiang Zemin, then general-secretary of the CCP, laid the groundwork for this with his "theory of the three represents": The Party was from that point on to represent not just the workers and peasants, but *all* the people's interests, including both intellectuals and capitalists. This addition to party theory indicates that the Chinese Communist Party recognizes the important role that intellectuals and business people have played—and will play—in modernizing China; but it also acknowledges the reality that many individuals already within the Party have become capitalists. By enshrining this theory in the party constitution at the 16th Party Congress in 2002, the party was in effect attempting to shore up its legitimacy as China's ruling party. At the same time, it was in effect announcing that it had relinquished its role as a revolutionary party in favor of its new position as the *governing* party of China.

The CCP is still China's ultimate institutional authority. Although in theory the state is distinct from the party, in practice the two overlapped almost completely from the late 1950s to the early 1990s. Efforts to keep the party from meddling in the day-to-day work of the government and management of economic enterprises have

had some effect; but in recent years, more conservative leaders within the CCP have exerted considerable pressure to keep the Party in charge.

The state apparatus consists of the State Council, headed by the premier. Under the State Council are the ministries and agencies and "people's congresses" responsible for the formulation of policy. The CCP has, however, exercised firm control over these state bodies through interlocking organizations. CCP branches exist within all government organizations; and at every administrative level from the central government in Beijing down to the villages, almost everyone in a leadership position is also a party member.

Corruption in the Political System

China's political system is subject to enormous abuses of power. The lines of authority within both the CCP and the state system are poorly defined, as are the rules for selection to top leadership positions. In the past, this allowed individuals like Mao Zedong and the Gang of Four to usurp power and rule arbitrarily. By the late 1980s, China's bureaucracy appeared to have become more corrupt than at any time since the People's Republic of China came into being in 1949. Anger at the massive scale of official corruption was, in fact, the major factor unifying ordinary citizens and workers with students during the antigovernment protests in the spring of 1989.

Although campaigns to control official corruption continue, the problem appears to be growing even worse. Campaigns do little more than scratch the surface. This is in part because with so many opportunities to make money in China, especially for party and state officials whose positions give them the inside track for making profitable deals, the potential payoff for corruption can be huge—and the risks of getting caught appear small. This is particularly true in the case of selling off of state-owned assets. In most cases, state-owned enterprises that have been closed down, or privatized, have been turned over to the relatives of China's leaders for managing. The same is true in real estate: land, which used to be completely state-owned, is now controlled by partly privatized land companies, run by the relatives of leaders, who take huge profits for themselves when they make deals with investors and real estate developers. One problem is that Chinese institutions lack the transparency, acquired through financial checks within the system and open access to accounting books, that could help rein in corruption. The situation is exacerbated by a society that by its complicity encourages official corruption.

Individuals may write letters to the editors of the country's daily newspapers or to television stations to expose corruption. Many Chinese, especially those living in the countryside, feel that the only way in which local corruption will be addressed is if the media send reporters to investigate and publicly expose criminality. The China Central Television station has aired a popular daily program in prime time that records the successes of China's public security system in cracking down on official corruption and crime. The press also devotes substantial space to sensational cases of official corruption, in part because it helps sell newspapers. The media only has the resources, however, to address comparatively few of the numerous cases begging for investigation. Furthermore, those reporters who have threatened to expose scandals, abuses of authority, and inappropriate local policies are often harassed, or even had violence used against them by those who might suffer from such a report. And in 2007, the government was reported to have shut down the investigative branches of the papers with more aggressive reporters. There is evidence, on the other hand, that some reporters have actually used the threat of reporting a scandal to extort money from local officials in order to cover it up.

So far, most efforts to control official corruption have had little effect. Officials continue to use their power to achieve personal gain, trading official favors for others' services (such as better housing, jobs for their children, admission to the right schools, and access to goods in short supply), or for wining and dining. Getting things done in a system that requires layers of bureaucratic approval still depends heavily upon a complex set of personal connections and relationships, all reinforced through under-the-table gift giving. This stems in part from the still heavily centralized aspect of Chinese governance, and in part from the overstaffing of a bureaucracy that is plagued by red tape. Countless offices must sign off on requests for anything from installing a telephone to processing a request for a license or additional electrical outlets. This gives enormous power to individual officials who handle those requests, allowing them to ask for favors in return, or to stone-wall if the payoff is inadequate.

In today's more market-oriented China, officials have lost some of their leverage over the distribution of goods. Now, instead of waiting for a work unit official to decide whose turn it is to purchase a bicycle or who will have the right to live in a two-bedroom apartment, anyone with adequate funds may buy virtually anything

Embassy of the People's Republic of China

Chinese Communist Party 17th national congress October 2007.

they want. In a society where prostitution is banned brothels can be run in the open, virtually without interference from the police, who are bribed to look the other way. In short, officials may have lost control over the distribution of many consumer goods, but they have kept their ability to facilitate or obstruct access to many services, documents, licenses, and so on.

Controlling the abuse of official privilege is difficult in part because of the large discretionary budgets that officials have, and in part because the Chinese have made an art form out of going around regulations. For example, the government issued a regulation stipulating that governmental officials doing business could order only four dishes and one soup at a meal. But as most Chinese like to eat well, especially at the government's expense, the restaurants accommodated them by simply giving them much larger plates on which they put many different dishes, and then wrote it up as if it were just one dish.

The definition of corrupt behavior has also become more complex as the country moves from a socialist economy to a market economy. In the initial stages of introducing a market economy, selling imported goods in China for high profits was considered corrupt, as was paying middlemen to arrange business transactions. In the 1980s, some businesspeople were arrested, and even executed, for such activities. Now, it is assumed that those importing goods from abroad will make as large a profit as possible; and instead of looking at middlemen as the embodiment of corruption, government regulations allow them to be paid a transaction "fee." Yet, middlemen continue many activities considered corrupt, such as demanding a fee for introducing potential investors to appropriate officials—in part because the middlemen must in turn pay the officials for agreeing to meet with the potential investors—even though it is their job to do so.

Reform of party-state institutions and procedures has been an important avenue through which the government has attempted to curb corruption; but its broader goal in reforming the party state has been to improve the quality of China's leadership. Otherwise, China's leaders worry, the Chinese Communist Party may lose its legitimacy. Reforms have encouraged, even demanded, that the Chinese state bureaucracy reward merit more than mere seniority, and expertise more than political activism. And in 1996, the government's practice of allowing officials to stay in one ministry during their entire career was replaced by new regulations requiring officials from divisional chiefs up to ministers and provincial governors to be rotated every five years. Restrictions on tenure in office have brought a much younger generation of leaders into power; and they have placed a time limit on any one individual's access to power. The emphasis on a collective leadership since reforms began in 1979 has, moreover, made it virtually impossible for a leader to develop a personality cult, such as that which reached fanatical proportions around CCP chairman Mao Zedong during the Cultural Revolution. These reforms have dramatically reshaped the leadership structure and process. But other reforms, such as an anti-nepotism regulation that prohibits any high official from working in the same office as a spouse or direct blood relative, have seemingly had little effect on the overall pattern of officials using their power and access to put family members in positions where they can acquire significant wealth.

CONTEXT FOR DEMOCRACY

Cultural and Historical Authoritarianism

The Chinese political system reflects a history, political culture, and values entirely different from those in the West. For millennia, Chinese thought has run along different lines, with far less emphasis on such ideals as individual rights, privacy, and limits on state power. The Chinese political tradition is weighed down with a preference for authoritarian values, such as obedience and subordination of individuals to their superiors in a rigidly hierarchical system, and a belief in the importance of moral indoctrination. China's rulers have throughout history shown greater concerns for establishing their authority and maintaining unity in the vast territory and population they control than in protecting individual rights. Apart from some of China's intellectuals, the overwhelming majority of the Chinese people have appeared to be more afraid of chaos than an authoritarian ruler. Even today, the Chinese people seem more concerned that their leaders have *enough* power to control China than

that the rights of citizens vis-à-vis their leaders be protected.

This is not to suggest that Confucianism and China's other traditions did not contain some mention of such rights. They did; but the *dominant* strand of Chinese political culture was authoritarian. It was critical in shaping the development of today's political system. As a result, when the Communists came to power in 1949, they were trying to operate within the context of an inherited patriarchal culture, in which the hierarchical values of superior–inferior and subordination, loyalty, and obedience prevailed over those of equality; and in which there was a historical predisposition toward official secrecy; a fear of officials and official power; and a traditional repugnance for courts, lawyers, and formal laws that protected individual rights. Thus, when Western democratic values and institutions were introduced, China's political culture and institutions were ill prepared to embrace them.

China's limited experience with democracy in the twentieth century was bitter. Virtually the entire period from the fall of China's imperial monarchy in 1911 to the Communist victory in 1949 was marred by warlordism, chaos, war, and a government masking brutality, greed, and incompetence under the label of "democracy." Although it is hardly fair to blame this period of societal collapse and externally imposed war on China's efforts to practice "democracy" under the "tutelage of the Kuomintang," the Chinese people's experience of democracy was nevertheless negative.

Moreover, the Chinese Communists condemned Western liberal democracy for being too weak a political system to prevent the Great Depression and two world wars in the twentieth century. In any event, foreign values were always suspect in China, as foreigners had repeatedly declared war on China in order to advance their own national interests. China was inclined to view the propagation of liberal democratic values as just one more effort by Western countries to enhance their own national power.

Experience with the Western powers and China's own efforts to implement democracy before 1949, together with China's traditional political culture, help explain the people's reluctance to embrace Western liberal democratic ideals. During the period of the Republic of China (1912–1949), China's "democratic" political and legal institutions proved inadequate to guarantee the nation's welfare, or to protect individual rights. Even under Communist rule, the one period described as "democratic mass rule" (the Cultural Revolution, from 1966 to 1976) was in fact a period of mass

(Courtesy of Suzanne Ogden/sogden076)

This is a meeting room for the Chinese Communist Party branch in Huang village, Anhui Province. Below the banner for the "Mobilization meeting for Huang village's progressive educational activities," is the oath for those who join the party.

tyranny. For the Chinese, the experience of relinquishing power to "the masses" turned into the most horrific period of unleashed terrorism and cruelty they had experienced since the Communist takeover in 1949. Most analysts would argue that this was in no respect a "democracy," but rather the result of the Chinese people being manipulated by an ever-shifting nouveau elite, who were in a desperate competition with other pretenders to power. To those Chinese who experienced the Cultural Revolution firsthand, this was what could happen if China became democratic.

Socialist Democracy

When the CCP came to power in 1949, it inherited a country torn by civil war, internal rebellion, and foreign invasions for more than 100 years. The population was overwhelmingly illiterate and desperately poor, the economy in shambles. The most urgent need was for order and unity. China made great strides in securing its borders and ending internal fighting and chaos. Despite some serious setbacks and mistakes under the leadership of Mao Zedong, moreover, China also succeeded in establishing effective institutions of government and enhancing the material well-being of its people. But in the name of order and stability, China's leaders also severely limited the development of "democracy" in its Western liberal-democratic sense.

The Chinese people are accustomed to "eating bitterness," not to standing up to authority. The traditional Confucian emphases on the group rather than the individual and on respect for authority continue to this day, although modernization, internationalization, and disenchantment with the CCP leadership have diminished their powerful cultural hold. Rapid modernization has likewise undermined Marxist Leninist-Maoist values, the glue that, along with traditional values, had helped hold China together. None of this, however, necessarily bodes well for the propagation of democratic values; for the destabilizing social effects of a loss of values, and the concomitant rise of aggressive nationalism and materialism, hardly provide a receptive environment for liberal democratic values.

Nevertheless, since 1949, and especially since the reform period began in 1979, there has been a gradual accretion of individual rights for Chinese people. These include greater freedom of speech; access to far more information and a diversity of perspectives; the right to vote in local elections; and development of the rights to privacy, to choose one's own work (as opposed to being assigned by the government), to move and work in different locations, to own private property, and many more. Moreover, the impersonal market forces of supply and demand, combined with an abundant variety of consumer goods, have undercut the power of officials to control the distribution

of resources and opportunities in the society. The result is that the Chinese are no longer beholden to officials to supply them in exchange for favors, gift giving, banqueting, and outright bribery. This equality of access in the marketplace contributes to a greater sense of control by the people over their daily lives.

Unfortunately, even as such rights grow, other very important rights previously enjoyed by the Chinese people—such as a job, health care, housing, and education—are being eroded. Such "welfare rights" have provided the context in which other rights have gained meaning. At the same time that it has led to greater political and societal rights, then, economic liberalization has contributed to the polarization of wealth and destabilization of Chinese society.

Patterns of political participation are also changing. Participation in the political process at the local level has already led to greater responsiveness by local officials to the common people's needs. Village officials are more inclined than in the past to seek out advice for improving the economic conditions in their localities, and incompetent village officials are usually unable to gain reelection. In spite of local elections and other efforts to advance village democracy, however, villagers in many parts of China do not believe that elections have made much of a difference. Even in those areas where there has been extraordinary economic development, villagers do not necessarily see the connection of elections and democratization with prosperity.[25]

China has experienced only limited open popular demand for democracy. When the student-led demonstrations in Beijing began in 1989, the demands for democratic reforms were confined largely to the small realm of the intellectual elite—that is, students and well-educated individuals, as well as some members of the political and economic ruling elite. The workers and farmers of China remained more concerned about bread-and-butter issues—inflation, economic growth, unemployment, and their own personal enrichment—not democratic ideals.

By the mid-1990s, many Chinese had discovered that they could get what they wanted through channels other than mass demonstrations, because of the development of numerous alternative groups, institutions, and processes. Many of these groups are not political in origin, but the process by which they are pressing for policy changes in the government is highly political. When reforms began in 1979, there was only a handful of such groups. By the end of 2006, there were 346,000 interest groups and associations, commonly

Villagers standing in line to vote, September 2001, near Shanghai.

called NGOs (non-governmental organizations) in the West, but labeled as "civilian organizations" in China.[26]

While all such organizations are headed by a member of the CCP (usually a retired person), they reflect and promote the interests of their membership. Indeed, it is in the self-interest of the appointed party head of the organization to advance its power and respond to the requests of the membership to represent their interests at higher levels. As an example, the party-state instituted an association to which small entrepreneurs in each city and town must belong. The association's purpose is to assert some level of control over a totally unsupervised arena of small business and commerce activity, but it also promotes the interests of its members; for entrepreneurs engaged in legitimate businesses do not want to have to compete against unregistered businesses that flog shoddy, illegal, and even dangerous products. Further, by helping crack down on those whose products violate copyright and trademark regulations, the association helps promote legitimate businesses.

In many areas, such as environmental protection, education, healthcare, and poverty reduction, interest groups, associations, foundations, and charities work together with the government to advance their causes. The fact that each group must be registered with the government and led by a party-state official need not, in most cases, be viewed as a negative factor. Indeed, the existence of a party-state official at the top ensures access to power that an organization would not otherwise have. Sometimes, the government has

demanded that all "civilian associations," foundations, and charities re-register, in part because countless businesses have tried to avoid taxes by claiming to be "civilian organizations," charities, or foundations. The government likewise prohibits democracy-promoting organizations from registering. Organizations that are funded by foreigners are always watched carefully, and when they appear to cross the line and become involved in sponsoring political movements, the government shuts them down.

It is perhaps ironic that the Chinese Communist Party's penchant for organizing people has resulted in teaching them organizational skills that they now use to pressure the government to change policy.[27] They work through these organizations to protect and advance their members' interests within the framework of existing law and regulations.

Even those Chinese not working through officially organized associations ban together to petition local officials using the organizational techniques they learned from the CCP. For example, urban neighborhoods join forces to stop local noise pollution emanating from stereos blasting on the street where thousands of Chinese engage in ballroom dancing, or from the cymbals, tambourines, gongs, and drums of old ladies doing "fan dancing" on the city streets.[28] In turn, the dancers petition the local officials to maintain their "right" to express themselves through dancing in the streets, some of the few public spaces available to them in a crowded urban environment.

The tendency to organize around issues and interests in China today is more than a reflection of the decline of the role of Communist ideology in shaping policy. It also reflects the government's focus on problem solving and pragmatic concerns in policy-making. Many constituencies take advantage of this approach to issues and policy. Although China has never been homogeneous and uncomplicated, it is certainly a far more complex economy, society, and polity today than it was before 1980. Today's China has far more diverse needs and interests than was the case previously, and specialized associations and interest groups serve the need of articulating these interests.

Compared to Western liberal democratic systems, Chinese citizens are politically passive. But is this a sign of satisfaction with the CCP regime? Is Chinese submissiveness a sign of "collusion" with their oppressors? One could argue that, like Eastern Europeans, the Chinese have participated in their own political oppression simply by complying with the demands of the system. As the Czech Republic's then-president Vaclav Havel stated, "All of us have become accustomed to the totalitarian system, accepted it as an unalterable fact and therefore kept it running. . . . None of us is merely a victim of it, because all of us helped to create it together.[29]

Can we say that the Chinese, any more than the Czechs, collaborated with their authoritarian rulers if they did not flee into exile under Communist rule, or did not refuse to work? Is anyone who docs not actively revolt against an oppressive system necessarily in collusion with it? In the case of China, one cannot assume that the major reason why people are not challenging the Communist system is out of fear of punitive consequences—although those who want to directly challenge CCP rule through the formation of new political parties or trade unions, or through the explicit public criticism of China's top political leaders do indeed risk punishment. The more logical explanation is that the Chinese have developed a completely different style from that of citizens in Western liberal democratic countries for getting what they want. This style is largely based on cultivating personal relationships rather than more formal and open institutionalized forms of political participation. More "democratic" behavioral skills can, of course, be acquired through practice; and as the Chinese political system gradually adopts more liberal democratic practices, the political culture is likely to evolve—indeed, it *is* evolving—in a more democratic direction.

Students, Intellectuals, and Business People as Potential Forces for Democratization

Democratization in China has been hampered by the people's inability to envision an alternative to CCP rule. What form would it take? How would it get organized? And if the CCP were overthrown, who would lead a new system? These questions are still far from being answered. So far, no dissident leadership capable of offering an alternative to CCP leadership, and laying claim to popular support, has formed. Even the mass demonstrations in 1989 were not led by either a worker, a peasant, or even an intellectual with whom the common people could identify:

> [C]ompared with the intellectuals of Poland and Czechoslovakia, for example, Chinese intellectuals have little contact with workers and peasants and are not sensitive to their country's worsening social crisis; they were caught unawares by the democratic upsurge of 1989, and proved unable to provide the people with either the theoretical or practical guidance they needed.[30]

In fact, during the Tiananmen protests in 1989, students were actually annoyed by the workers' participation in the demonstrations. They wanted to press their own political demands—not the workers' more concrete, work-related issues. Some Chinese believe that the students' real interest in setting forth their own demands was because they wanted to enhance their own prestige and power vis-à-vis the regime: The students' major demands were for a "dialogue" with the government as "equals," and for free speech. These issues were of primary interest to them, but of little interest to the workers of China. Many Chinese believe that had the leaders of the 1989 demonstrations suddenly been catapulted to power, their behavior would have differed little from the ruling CCP elite. The student movement itself admitted to being authoritarian, of kowtowing to its own leaders, and of expecting others to obey rather than to discuss decisions. As one Beijing University student wrote during the 1989 Tiananmen Square protests:

> The autonomous student unions have gradually cut themselves off from many students and become a machine kept constantly on the run in issuing orders. No set of organizational rules widely accepted by the students has emerged, and the democratic mechanism is even more vague.[31]

In any event, few of those who participated in the demonstrations in 1989 are interested in politics or political leadership today. Most have thrown themselves into business and making money.

Apart from students and intellectuals, some of the major proponents of democratic reform today hail from China's newly emerging business circles; but these groups have not united to achieve reform, as they neither like nor trust each other. Intellectuals view venture capitalists "as uncultured, and business people as driven only by crass material interests." The latter in turn regard intellectuals and students as "well-meaning but out of touch with reality and always all too willing and eager to serve the state" when it suits their needs.[32] Moreover, although the business community is interested in pushing such rights as the protection of private property and the strengthening of the legal system in the commercial and economic spheres, it tends to be more supportive of the regime's "law and order" values than of democratic values; for an unstable social and political environment would not be conducive to economic growth.

Those who wanted reforms (or even the overthrow of Communist Party rule) but left China and remain abroad have lost their political influence. Apart from everything else, it is difficult for those living abroad to make themselves heard in China, even if their articles are published or appear on the Web. Although they may keep in touch with the dissident movement in China, their influence is largely limited to their ability to supply it with funds. Doing so, however, often gets the recipients in China in trouble. Today's college students in China are among the strongest supporters of the Chinese government.

The Impact of Global Interdependency on Democratization

Since the late 1970s, the cultural context for democracy in China has shifted. The expansion of the international capitalist economy and increasing cultural and political globalization have led to a social and economic transformation of China. For the first time in Chinese history, a significant challenge to the "we–they" dichotomy—of China against the rest of the world—is occurring. This in turn has led many Chinese to question the heretofore assumed superiority of Chinese civilization.

Such an idea does not come easily for a people long-accustomed to hearing about China's greatness. Hence the fuss caused by *River Elegy*, a TV documentary series first shown on Chinese national television in 1988. In this series, the film producers

Digital Vision/Getty Images RF
Woman with personal organizer.

argued that the Chinese people must embrace the idea of global interdependency—technological, economic, and cultural. To insist at that time in history on the superiority of Chinese civilization, with the isolation of China from the world of ideas that this implied, would only contribute to China's continued stagnation. The series suggested that the Chinese must see themselves as equal, not superior to, others; and as interdependent with, not as victims of, others. Such concepts of equality, and the opening up of China to ideas from the rest of the world, have led to a remarkable transformation of the Chinese political, cultural, and economic landscape.

In 2007, a 12-part TV documentary series, *Rise of the Great Powers,* aired by CCTV (China Central Television) examined how great powers have risen in history, and whether and why rising powers became involved in war. The fact that a television documentary, nearly ten years after the *River Elegy* series, was focused on a different set of issues and questions for China's role in the world in itself reflects how much China's self-perceptions and role in the world have changed.

The Press and Mass Media

At the time that the student-led demonstrations for democracy began in Beijing's Tiananmen Square in the spring of 1989, China's press had grown substantially and become increasingly liberalized. By the end of 2007, China had about 550 million cell phones. China's Internet users reached 253 million in early 2008. Both numbers are still growing. With some 2,000 newspapers,

STOCK MARKETS, GAMBLING, AND LOTTERIES

China has had two stock markets since the late 1980s. One was created in the Special Economic Zone (SEZ) of Shenzhen; the other in Shanghai. With only seven industries originally registered on them, strict rules about how much daily profit or loss (1.2 percent for the Shanghai exchange until July 1992) a stock could undergo, and deep public suspicion that these original issues of stocks were worthless, these markets got off to a slow start. But when these same stocks were worth five times their original value just a year later, the public took notice. Rumors—as important in China as actual news—took over and exaggerated the likelihood of success in picking a winning stock. The idea of investors actually losing money, much less a stock-market crash, did not seem to be an idea whose time had come.

Because China is still largely a cash economy, a stock-market transaction can be complicated. Instead of just telephoning a stockbroker and giving an order, with a simple bank transfer or check to follow shortly, many Chinese must still appear in person, stand in line, and pay cash on the spot. Taiwan has added its own angle to the stock-mania by selling to the Mainlanders small radios that are tuned in to only one frequency—stock market news. Local branches of the stock market and brokerages are popular places for retired people to spend the day watching their stocks on the boards. In Shanghai, they can also tune into "Stock Market Today," a popular local television program. Issuing, buying, and selling stocks has at times been a near-national obsession. Not only do ordinary companies selling commercial goods, such as computers and clothing, issue stocks. So do taxicab companies and even universities. Thus far, few such stocks are actually listed on the national stock exchanges; but employees of these work units are eager to purchase the stocks. In most cases, the original issues are sold at far higher prices than their face value, as employees (and even nonemployees) eagerly buy up fellow employees' rights to purchase stocks, at grossly inflated prices. Presumably, the right of employees to own stock in their own work unit will make them eager to have it do well, and thus increase efficiency and profits.

Even as China's economy continued to roar along with double-digit growth in the twenty-first century, the ardor for wheeling and dealing in the stock market cooled considerably. Companies were making money, but stock prices were in the doldrums, with a 2003 poll indicating that 90 percent of investors had lost money.[34] Then, in 2006, investors fueled a 130 percent surge. The bull market was largely due to a massive inflow of speculative funds from both foreign investment, and domestic investment from Chinese investors hoping to profit more from the stock market than from leaving their money in banks, where they rarely earn more than 2 percent per annum.

The underlying problems in China's stock markets, however, remain a concern. First, they are not regulated by outside auditors, which means that investors cannot trust the information in company reports. Scandals involving stocks all too often erupt in the Chinese media. Second, the state itself usually owns the majority of voting shares—often as much as two-thirds of the shares of China's leading companies. (These shares were until recently also "untradable" shares, meaning the companies were not really private at all, and

© Photodisc/Getty Images RF

Shanghai Pudong financial district.

should not have been listed on a public stock exchange.) This results in the state's preferred policies, which are often based on bureaucratic and political concerns, rather than private investors and the market determining company strategies and profitability for, say, the technology, telecommunications, or heavy industrial sector. Because a state enterprise or state agency is usually the majority stockholder, moreover, it can by its own purchases and sales determine the price of a stock. The small investor is simply a pawn, and really has little chance to make a profit.

Companies that are owned and run by state agencies and ministries, such as the Ministry of Defense, have used state funds to invest in both domestic and international stocks and real estate. They have sometimes lost millions of yuan in the process. As a result, the government now prohibits state-run units from investing state money in stocks and real estate. Nevertheless, some still do so indirectly, thereby evading the laws.

Learning from Western practices and catering to a national penchant for gambling (illegal, but indulged in nevertheless, in mahjong and cards), the Chinese have also begun a number of lotteries. Thus far, most of these have been for the purpose of raising money for specific charities or causes, such as for victims of floods and for the disabled. Recently, because the items offered, such as brand-new cars, have been so desirable, the lotteries have generated billions of yuan in revenue. The government has found these government-controlled lotteries to be an excellent way of addressing the Chinese penchant for gambling while simultaneously generating revenues to compensate for those it seems unable to collect through taxes.

Finally, companies follow such Western marketing gimmicks for increasing sales as putting Chinese characters on the inside of packages or bottle caps to indicate whether the purchasers have won a prize. With a little Chinese ingenuity, the world could witness never-before-imaged realms of betting and competitive business practices that appeal to people's desire to get something for nothing.

9,000 magazines, and 600 publishing houses, the Chinese are able to express a wider variety of viewpoints and ideas than at any time since the CCP came to power in 1949. The production of millions of television sets, radios, short-wave radios, cassette recorders, and VCRs also facilitated the growth of the mass media in China. They were accompanied

by a wide array of foreign audio and video materials. The programs of the British Broadcasting Corporation (BBC) and the Voice of America (VOA), the diversification of domestic television and radio programs (a choice made by the Chinese government and facilitated by satellite communication), and the importation and translation of foreign

books and magazines—all contributed to a more pluralistic press in China. In fact, by 1989, the stream of publications had so overwhelmed the CCP Propaganda Department that it was simply no longer able to monitor their contents.

During the demonstrations in Tiananmen Square, the international press in Beijing, unlike the Chinese press, was freely filming the events and filing reports on the demonstrations. The Chinese press then took a leap into complete press freedom. With camera operators and microphones in hand, Chinese reporters covered the student hunger strike that began on May 13 in its entirety; but with the imposition of martial law in Beijing on May 20, press freedom came to a crashing halt.

In the immediate aftermath of the brutal crackdown on Tiananmen Square demonstrators in June 1989, the CCP imposed a ban on a variety of books, journals, and magazines. The government ordered the "cleansing" of media organizations, with "bad elements" to be removed and not permitted to leave Beijing for reporting. All press and magazine articles written during the prodemocracy movement, as well as all television and radio programs shown during this period, were analyzed to see if they conformed to the party line. If they did not, those individuals responsible for editing were dismissed. And, as had been the practice in the past, press and magazine articles once again had to be on topics specified by the editors, who were under the control of the Propaganda Department of the CCP. In short, press freedom in China suffered a significant setback because of the pro-democracy demonstrations in the spring of 1989.

In the new climate of experimentation launched by Deng Xiaoping in 1992, however, the diversity of television and radio programs soared. China's major cities now have multiple channels carrying a broad range of programs from Hong Kong, Taiwan, South Korea, Japan, and the West. These programs, whether soap operas about the daily life of Chinese people living in Hong Kong and Taiwan, or art programs introducing the world of Western religious art through a visual art history tour of the Vatican, or in news about protests and problems faced by other nations in the world expose the Chinese to values, events, ideas, and standards of living previously unknown to them. They are even learning about the American legal process through China's broadcasting of American television dramas that focus on police and the judicial system. Chinese are fascinated that American police, as soon as they arrest suspects, inform them that they have "the right to remain silent" and "the right to a lawyer." Such programs may do more to promote reform of the Criminal Procedure Code than anything human rights groups do.

Today, television ownership is widespread. In addition to dozens of regular channels, China has numerous cable stations. And virtually all families have radios. Round-the-clock, all-news radio stations broadcast the latest political,

economic, and cultural news and conduct live interviews; and radio talk shows take phone calls from anonymous listeners about everything from sex to political and economic corruption. There are even blatant critiques of police brutality,[33] and analyses of failed government policies on everything from trade policy to health care and unemployment. There is also far better coverage of social and economic news in all the media than previously, and serious investigative reporting on corruption and crime. A popular half-hour program during evening prime time looks at cases of corruption and crime that are being investigated, or have been solved. Figures indicate the exponential growth of the media. The number of books published annually in China rose from about 5,000 in 1970 to about 104,000 in 1995. The number of newspapers grew from 42 in 1970 to over 2,000 by the year 2005, with a circulation of over 100 million. (In China, almost all work units post a number of newspapers in glass cases outside, so the readership is far higher than the circulation numbers.) Most of the newspapers also have their own websites. Similarly, the number of magazines grew from a handful in 1970 to more than 9,000 by 2005—an official number that excludes the large number of nonregistered magazines and illegal publications. Xinhua (New China) News Agency has more than 100 branches throughout the world that report on news for the Chinese people. There are hundreds of radio stations, and the number of television stations grew to 3,000 by 2005. Close to 90 percent of the population has access to television. CCTV-9, the "CNN" of China, is a slick, English-language program that is watched in many parts of the world, and actually has broader viewership in Asia than does CNN. By 2005, there were 750 cable-television stations and an estimated 125 million households with cable television access, with millions of new subscribers being added each year. The government's National Cable Company is forming a countrywide network to expand services geographically and to include new Internet and telecommunications connections.[35]

This effort to expand Internet availability indicates the government's dilemma: It wants China to modernize rapidly, and to have the scientific, economic, commercial, and educational resources on the Internet available to as many as possible. It has demanded that all government offices be updated to use the Internet in order to improve communication, efficiency, and transparency. At the same time, it wants to control which websites can be accessed, and what type of material may be made available to China's citizens on those sites.

In spite of the government's best efforts, the Internet is virtually uncontrollable. Angry and inflammatory commentary on events in China, and even criticism of China's leadership, appear with increasing regularity. Some sites are closed down because they violate the unstated boundaries of acceptable commentary; but it is difficult in a computer-saavy world to block access to all sites that the government might find irritating, if not downright seditious. China's Internet users know what is going on in the world; and they can spend their time chatting to dissidents abroad and at home on e-mail if they so choose. But most prefer to use the Internet for business, news, sports, games, music, socializing, and, of course, pornography. The Chinese, in fact, seem to spend most of their time on the Internet for entertainment and playing games, in contrast to Americans' preference for using it primarily for information. China's largest Internet company, Ten-cent, dominates 80 percent of China's market, far more than Google dominates in the U.S. market. This is due largely to the complete package of entertainment it offers (with a preference for playing games, forming communities, and adopting virtual personas—avatars), as well as its mobile instant-messaging service. In China, 70 percent of the Internet's users are under the age of 30; whereas in the U.S., some 70 percent are *over* the age of 30.[36] With print and electronic media so prolific and diverse, much of it escapes any monitoring whatsoever, especially newspapers, magazines, and books. Even the weekend editions of the remaining state-run newspapers print just about any story that will sell. Often about a seamier side of Chinese life, they undercut the puritanical aspect of communist rule and expanding the range of topics available for discussion in the public domain. Were the state able to control the media, it would, at the very least, crack down on pornographic literature on the streets.

The sheer quantity of output on television, radio, books, and the press allows the Chinese people to make choices among the types of news, programs, and perspectives they find most appealing. Their choices are not necessarily for the most informative or the highest quality, but for the most entertaining. Because the media (with few exceptions) are market-driven, consumers' preferences, not government regulations or ideological values, shape programming and publishing decisions.

This market orientation results from economic reforms. By the 1990s, the government had cut subsidies to the media, thereby requiring that even the state-controlled media had to make money or be shut down. This in turn meant that the news stories it presented had to be more newsworthy in order to sell advertising and subscriptions. Even in the countryside, the end of government subsidies to the media has spurred publication. Thinking there is money to be made, township and village enterprises, as well as private entrepreneurs, have set up thousands of printing facilities during the last 10 to 15 years.[37] In short, "Even though China's media can hardly be called free, the emergence of divergent voices means the center's ability to control people's minds has vanished."[41]

The party tends, however, to concentrate its limited resources on the largest and influential journals, magazines, newspapers, and publishing houses. It seems to have written off the rest as the inevitable downside of a commercialized media market—and the part that it no longer supports, nor controls, financially. Funded by advertising and consumer demand, the media must now "march to the market." Nevertheless, Beijing is trying to tighten its control over the media system by instituting a penalty point system. In 2007, the Chinese Communist Party's propaganda department announced the new system of points-based penalties, whereby each media outlet will be allocated 12 points. If it uses up its 12 points, it may be closed. Point deductions are based on the seriousness of the media outlet's action. This will supplement the existing system in which the CCP's propaganda department and the government's media regulator have jointly decided when to issue warnings, remove offending executives or reports, or otherwise punish a media organization. The new approach is portrayed as an effort to increase "social harmony," and seemed to be increasing in 2007 intensity before the 17th National Party Congress and the Beijing 2008 Olympics.[38] As for China's film industry, because it produces relatively few films each year, it is more heavily censored than print media. Furthermore, all films are shot in a small number of studios, making control easier. Finally, a film is likely to have a much larger audience than most books, and so the censors are concerned that it be carefully reviewed before being screened.[39] Zhang Yimou, China's renowned film director and producer, and recipient of numerous international film awards, has had the screening in China of one after another of his films banned. A publication of the Party School of the Chinese Communist Party condemned his 2006 blockbuster, *Curse of the Golden Flower,* as "ugly" and "blood-thirsty," transgressing the moral limits of Chinese art. And yet, the film has not been banned in China, and has wracked up tens of millions of dollars in profits.[40]

Human Rights and Democracy: The Chinese View

Surveys indicate that most urban Chinese citizens believe the government has adopted policies that have greatly improved their daily lives. Many have seen the government's law-and-order campaigns—which sometimes involve crackdowns on perceived dissidents (such as Falun Gong activists)—as necessary to China's continued economic prosperity and political stability. They have tended to be far more interested in the prospect of a higher standard of living than in the rights of dissidents.

Even China's intellectuals no longer seem interested in protest politics. They do not "love the party," but they accept the status quo. Some just want a promotion and to make money. Others have become advisers to the government's think tanks and advisory committees. Many have gone into business. As one university professor put it, it is easy to be idealistic in one's heart; but to be idealistic in action is a sign of a true idealist, and there haven't been many of those in China since 1989. Today in China, it is difficult to find any student or member of the intellectual elite who demonstrated in Tiananmen Square in 1989 doing anything remotely political.

Still, those who are discontent with party rule have far more outlets today for their grievances: the mass media, and journals, as well as think tanks, policy advisory committees, and professional associations that actually influence policy. Street protests are no longer considered the best way for the educated and professional classes to change policy, although ordinary workers and peasants resort to them with increasing frequency.

Many members of China's elites are committed to reform, but the number of idealists committed to democracy—or communism—is limited. Few Chinese, including government officials, want to discuss communist ideology, and even fewer agree on what democracy means. They prefer to talk about business and development, and do so in terms familiar to capitalists throughout the world, but also in terms of the overall objective of strengthening China as a nation. In this respect, they are appealing to the strong nationalism that has virtually replaced communism as the normative glue holding the country together.

Apart from their changed perspectives on what really matters, many Chinese feel that they do not know enough to challenge government policy on human rights issues. Why should they risk their careers to fight for the rights of jailed dissidents about whom they know almost nothing, they ask.

They know of the abuse of human rights in Western liberal democracies, such as the killing of student protesters at Kent State by the National Guard during the Vietnam War, the many deaths attributed to the British forces in Northern Ireland, the torture of American-held prisoners in Iraq and in Guantanamo Bay. When the U.S. State Department issues its annual human rights report, which inevitably makes harsh criticism of China, Beijing replies with an equally damning condemnation of human rights abuses by the United States. In 2007, it noted the "increased willingness by Washington to spy on its own citizens by monitoring telephone calls, computer connections, and travels."[42]

The Chinese people have heard of the unseemly behavior of several student leaders of the Tiananmen Square demonstrations, both during the movement in 1989 and after it. They wonder aloud if in the treatment of criminal suspects and those suspected of treason or efforts to harm the country—especially suspected terrorists—Western democratic states exhibit more virtuous behavior than does China. Some Chinese intellectuals argue that the recent difficulties in the United States and other Western democracies indicate that their citizens frequently elect the wrong leaders, people who not only make bad policies but who are also increasingly involved in corrupt money politics—the very issue of most concern to the Chinese. This, they suggest, indicates that democracy is no more able than socialism to produce good leaders. Furthermore, many support the view that the Chinese people are inadequately prepared for democracy because of a low level of education. The blatant political maneuverings and other problems surrounding the 2000 U.S. presidential election hardly offered reassurance as to the virtues of American democracy; nor did the American 2003 invasion and subsequent occupation of Iraq. The minimal response by the U.S. government to those challenging the administration, and the unwillingness of Congress to debate the war years after the invasion give the Chinese the impression that "the people" were not necessarily listened to, and that a democracy does not necessarily have an effective system of "checks and balances."

Within China, it is frequently the people, rather than the government, who demand the harshest penalties for common criminals, if not political dissidents. And it is China's own privileged urbanites who often demand that the government ignore the civil rights of other citizens. For example, urban residents in Beijing have repeatedly demanded that the government remove migrant squatters and their shantytowns,

A crowded classroom in a school for children of migrants in Beijing. As of 2007, all migrant children were supposed to be put into the city's state-funded schools, but it is not clear this will happen immediately.

asserting that they are breeding grounds for criminality in the city. And they resist the government allowing migrants to attend the city's public schools or receive health-care. Many ordinary people now seem to accept the government's overall assessment of the events of the spring of 1989, which is that the demonstrations in Tiananmen Square posed a threat to the stability and order of China and justified the military's crackdown. To many Chinese people, no less than to their government, stability and order are critical to the continued economic development of China. Advancement toward democracy and protection of human rights take a back seat.

INTERNATIONAL RELATIONS

From the 1830s onward, foreign imperialists nibbled away at China's territorial sovereignty, subjecting China to one national humiliation after another. As early as the 1920s, both the Nationalists and the Communists were committed to unifying and strengthening China in order to rid it of foreigners and resist further foreign incursions. When the Communists achieved victory over the Nationalists in 1949, they vowed that they would never again allow foreigners to tell China what to do. The "century of humiliation" beginning from the "Opium War" in 1839 is essential to understanding China's foreign policy in the period of Chinese Communist rule.

From Isolation to Openness

By the early 1950s, the Communists had forced all but a handful of foreigners to leave China. The target of the United States' Cold War policy of "isolation and containment," China under Chairman Mao Zedong charted an independent, and eventually an isolationist, foreign policy. Even China's relations with socialist bloc countries were suspended after the Cultural Revolution began in 1966. China took tentative steps toward re-establishing relations with the outside world with U.S. president Richard Nixon's visit to China in 1972, but it did not really pursue an "open door" policy until more pragmatic "reformers" gained control in 1978. By the 1980s, China was hosting several million tourists annually, inviting foreign investors and foreign experts to help with China's modernization, and allowing Chinese to study and travel abroad. Nevertheless, inside the country, contacts between Chinese and foreigners were still affected by the suspicion on the part of ordinary Chinese that ideological and cultural contamination comes from abroad and that association with foreigners might bring trouble.

These attitudes have moderated considerably, to the point where some Chinese are willing to socialize with foreigners, invite them to their homes, and even marry them. However, this greater openness to things foreign sits uncomfortably together with a new nationalism that has emerged since the West so heavily criticized, and punished, China for the military crackdown on Tiananmen Square demonstrators in June 1989.

© blue jean images/Getty Images RF

Students on grounds of Summer Palace in Beijing.

A strong xenophobia (dislike and fear of foreigners) and an awareness of the history of China's victimization by Western and Japanese imperialism mean that the Chinese are likely to rail at any effort by other countries to tell them what to do. The Chinese continue to exhibit this sensitivity on a wide variety of issues, from human rights to China's policies toward Tibet and Taiwan; from intellectual property rights to prison labor and environmental degradation.

Ordinary Chinese people tended to concur with the government's anger over the U.S. threat of economic sanctions to challenge China's human rights policies (something that is no longer possible since China joined the World Trade Organization [WTO] in 2001). They were enraged by the American bombing of the Chinese Embassy in Belgrade during the war in Yugoslavia, which the U.S. government insisted was by error, not intent; the crash of a U.S. spy plane with a Chinese jet in 2001, which the Chinese believed to be in their own airspace; efforts to prevent China from entering the World Trade Organization or becoming a site for the Olympics; American accusations of Chinese spying and stealing of American nuclear-weapons secrets, charges that appeared to the Chinese to be motivated by hostility toward China, especially when they were ultimately dismissed for lack of evidence; American accusations of illegal campaign funding by the Chinese; the on- going human-rights barrage; the strengthening of U.S. military ties with Japan and Taiwan; and continued American interference in China's efforts to regain control of Taiwan.

Only a narrow line separates a benign nationalism essential to China's unity, however, and a popular nationalism with militant overtones threatens to career out of control.[43] These aspects of nationalism worry China's government, whose primary concerns remain economic growth and stability. The government does not want to be forced into war by a militant nationalism. Nevertheless, China's xenophobia continues to show up in its efforts to keep foreigners isolated in certain living compounds; to limit social contacts between foreigners and Chinese; to control the import of foreign literature, films, and periodicals; and in general to limit the invasion of foreign political and cultural values in China. Since 1996, in an effort to protect China's culture, the government has ordered television stations to broadcast only Chinese-made programs during prime time. In 2007, the government limited television stations to showing "ethically inspiring TV series" during prime time. Programs broadcast during prime time must likewise "keep script and video records for future censorship against vulgarity."[44] The government has also attempted to enhance national pride through economic success; and by participation in international events, including the Olympic and Asian Games, music competitions, and film festivals.

Yet, in some respects, the resistance to the spread of foreign values in China is proving to be a losing battle, with growing numbers of foreigners in China; television swamped with foreign programs; Kentucky Fried Chicken, McDonald's, Starbucks, and Pizza Hut ubiquitous; "Avon calling"

at several million homes;[45] bodybuilding, disco, cell phones, and Internet becoming part of the culture. Further, with millions of Chinese tourists and officials tromping through the world, vast numbers of foreign investors in China, China's hosting of trade fairs, international meetings, and the 2008 Olympics, as well as a heavy reliance on foreign experts to help China reform its economic, legal, financial, and banking systems, and set up a commodities and futures market, China is awash with values that contend with traditional Chinese ones. China is now a full participant in the international economic and financial system: it is the third-largest global trading country, and gives foreign aid to developing countries, especially in Africa. It is an important participant in the war on terrorism, and a key player in Interpol and other efforts to control international crime syndicates, smuggling of weapons and drugs, and international trafficking in children and women. China today is seen by most countries as a partner rather than an adversary, a part of the solution, not the problem (such as in negotiations with the North Koreans over their nuclear weapons program). Its powerful economy and investments abroad have earned it respect (leavened with fear) worldwide. Today, China is a key international actor. It cannot be dismissed as a poor country without the wherewithal to enter the modern world.

China is a much more open country than at any time since 1949. This is in spite of the efforts by the party's more conservative wing to limit the impact of foreign ideas about democracy and individual rights on the political system, as well as the impact from "polluting" values embedded in foreign culture. Over time, however, conservatives have lost the battle to limit foreign influence, due more to the inexorable forces of globalization, communication, and the Internet than to any struggle behind closed doors with political adversaries. At the same time, although China's flourishing business community and growing middle class have little interest in disrupting the emphasis on stability by calling for greater political democracy, they nevertheless encourage, and benefit from, China's greater openness. Foreign investment in China (annual total foreign direct investment in the last few years has averaged around US$60 billion) far outstrips foreign investment in any other developing country. This is due not just to China's potential market size but also to the favorable investment climate created by the party-state. Fully one-third of China's manufacturing output is produced by foreign companies in China (both in the form of joint ventures with the Chinese, and wholly- owned foreign companies), indicating just how important foreign investment is to China's economy. (This is an important fact to remember when critics denounce China's trade surplus; that is, a considerable percentage of those exports are actually produced by companies wholly or partly owned by parent companies located in countries to which China exports its products.) China's openness, especially since joining the WTO in 2001, has forced its own enterprises to compete not just against imports, but also against foreign firms that have invested in China. China's service sector has been opened up to foreign competition. By 2007, foreign banks, insurance companies, securities firms, and telecommunications could compete on an increasingly equal basis.[46]

When it comes to the economy, then, the government has seemed less worried about the invasion of foreign values than anxious to attract foreign investment. China sees a strong economy as the key to both domestic stability and international respect. The government's view now seems to be: If it takes nightclubs, discos, exciting stories in the media, stock markets, rock concerts, the Internet, and consumerism to make the Chinese people content and the economy flourish under CCP rule, then so be it.

THE SINO–SOVIET RELATIONSHIP

While forcing most other foreigners to leave China in the 1950s, the Chinese Communist regime invited experts from the Soviet Union to China to give much-needed advice, technical assistance, and aid. This convinced the United States (already certain that Moscow controlled communism wherever it appeared) that the Chinese were puppets of the Soviets. Indeed, until the Great Leap Forward in 1958, the Chinese regime accepted Soviet tenets of domestic and foreign policy along with Soviet aid. But China's leaders soon grew concerned about the limits of Soviet aid and the relevance of Soviet policies to China's conditions—especially the costly industrialization favored by the Soviet Union. Ultimately, the Chinese questioned their Soviet "big brother" and turned to the Maoist model of development, which aimed to replace expensive Soviet technology with human labor. Soviet leader Nikita Khrushchev warned the Chinese of the dangers to China's economy in undertaking the Great Leap Forward; but Mao Zedong interpreted this as evidence that the Soviet "big brother" wanted to hold back China's development.

The Soviets' refusal to use their military power in support of China's foreign-policy objectives further strained the Sino–Soviet relationship. First in the case of China's confrontation with the United States and the forces of the "Republic of China" over the Offshore Islands in the Taiwan Strait in 1958, and then in the Sino-Indian border war of 1962, the Soviet Union backed down from its promise to support China. The Soviets also refused to share nuclear technology with the Chinese. The final blow to the by-then fragile relationship came with the Soviet Union's signing of the 1963 Nuclear Test Ban Treaty. The Chinese denounced this as a Soviet plot to exclude China from the "nuclear club" that included only Britain, France, the United States, and the Soviet Union. Subsequently, Beijing publicly broke party relations with Moscow. In 1964 China denotated its first nuclear bomb.

The Sino–Soviet relationship, already in shambles, took on an added dimension of fear during the Vietnam War, when the Chinese grew concerned that the Soviets (and Americans) might use the war as an excuse to attack China. China's distrust of Soviet intentions was heightened in 1968, when the Soviets invaded Czechoslovakia in the name of the "greater interests of the socialist community"—which, they contended, "overrode the interests of any single country within that community." Soviet skirmishes with Chinese soldiers on China's northern borders soon followed. Ultimately, it was the Chinese leadership's concern about the Soviet threat to China's national security that, in 1971, caused it to reassess its relationship with the United States and led to the establishment of diplomatic relations with China in 1979. Indeed, the real interest of China and the United States in each other was as a "balancer" against the Soviet Union. Thus, in the midst of the Cold War, which began in 1947 and did not end until the late 1980s, China had moved out of the Soviet-led camp; yet China did not begin benefiting from friendship with Western countries in the power balance with the Soviet Union until it gained the seat in the United Nations in 1971.

The Sino–Soviet relationship moved toward reconciliation only near the end of the Cold War. In 1987, the Soviets began making peaceful overtures: They reduced troops on China's borders and withdrew support for Vietnam's puppet government in neighboring Cambodia. Beijing responded positively to the new *glasnost* ("open door") policy of the Soviet Communist Party's General Secretary, Mikhail Gorbachev. Border disputes were settled and ideological conflict between the two Communist giants abated; for with the Chinese themselves shelving Marxist dogma in their economic policies, they could hardly continue to denounce the Soviet Union's "revisionist" policies and make self-righteous claims to ideological orthodoxy. With both the Soviet Union and China abandoning their earlier battle over who should lead the Communist camp, they shifted away from conflict over ideological and security issues to cooperation on trade and economic issues. Today, China and Russia have significant trade, and their relationship is based on national interests, not ideology.

From "People's War" to Cyber War

With the collapse of Communist party rule, first in the Central/Eastern European states in 1989, and subsequently in the Soviet Union, the dynamics of China's foreign policy changed dramatically. Apart from fear that their own reforms might lead to the collapse of CCP rule in China, the breakup of the Soviet Union into 15 independent states removed China's ability to play off the two superpowers against each other: The formidable Soviet Union simply no longer existed. Yet its fragmented remains had to be treated seriously, for the state of Russia still has nuclear weapons and shares a common border of several thousand miles with China, and the former Soviet republic of Kazakhstan shares a border of nearly 1,000 miles.

The question of what type of war the Chinese military might have to fight has affected its military modernization. For many years, China's military leaders were in conflict over whether China would have to fight a high-tech war or a "people's war," in which China's huge army would draw in the enemy on the ground and destroy it. In 1979, the military modernizers won out, jettisoning the idea that a large army, motivated by ideological fervor but armed with hopelessly outdated equipment, could win a war against a highly modernized military such as that of the Soviet Union. The People's Liberation Army (PLA) began by shedding a few million soldiers and putting its funds into better armaments. A significant catalyst to further modernizing the military came with the Persian Gulf War of 1991, during which the CNN news network broadcasts vividly conveyed the power of high-technology weaponry to China's leaders.

In the nationwide rush to become prosperous, the PLA plunged into the sea of business. China's military believed that it was allocated an inadequate budget for modernization, so it struck out on its own along the capitalist road to raise money. By the late 1990s, the PLA had become one of the most powerful actors in the Chinese economy. It had purchased considerable property in the Special Economic Zones near Hong Kong; acquired ownership of major tourist hotels and industrial enterprises; and invested in everything from golf courses, brothels, and publishing houses to CD factories and the computer industry, as a means for funding military modernization. In 1998, however, President Jiang Zemin demanded that the military relinquish its economic enterprises and return to its primary task of building a modern military and protecting China. The promised payoff was that China's government would allocate more funding to the PLA, making it unnecessary for it to rely on its own economic activities.

In recent years, China's military has purchased weaponry and military technology from Russia as Moscow scales back its own military in what sometimes resembles a going-out-of-business sale; but in doing so, China's military may have simply bought into a higher level of obsolescence, since Russia's weaponry lags years behind the technology of the West. China possesses nuclear weapons and long-distance bombing capability, but its ability to fight a war beyond its own borders is quite limited. Asian countries, torn between wondering whether China or Japan will be a future threat to their territory, do not seem concerned by China's military modernization, except when China periodically makes threatening statements about Taiwan or the Spratly Islands in the South China Sea. Even here, however, Beijing usually relies on economic and diplomatic instruments. In the case of Taiwan, it is essentially tying Taiwan's economy to the mainland by welcoming economic investment and trade; the hope is ultimately to bring Taiwan under the control of Beijing without a war. In the case of the Spratlys, under whose territorial waters there is believed to be significant oil deposits, Beijing has reached tentative agreement with the five governments involved in competing claims to the Spratlys to avoid the possibility of armed clashes.

Nevertheless, in spite of China's remarkable economic and diplomatic gains since the reform period began in 1979, the leadership continues to modernize China's military capabilities. Beijing is ever alert to threats to its national security, but there are no indications that it is preparing for aggression against any country. China's military modernization is primarily aimed at defensive capabilities and maintaining its deterrent capability against an American nuclear attack. It has also increased the number of missiles it aims at Taiwan in response to repeated suggestions by Taiwan's former President, Chen Shui-bian, that Taiwan would declare independence. With the arrival of the George W. Bush administration in Washington in early 2001,

the American leadership began to seriously consider the possibility of deploying a limited "national missile defense" (NMD) in the United States, and even to deploy a "theater missile defense" (TMD) around Japan—and possibly Taiwan. Were a missile-defense system successfully deployed, it would limit the ability of China to prevent Japan or the United States from attacking it—or to prevent Taiwan from declaring independence. By providing a protective shield, TMD would allow Taiwan to declare independence with impunity. TMD is, then, perceived by Beijing as an aggressive move by the United States, and helps explain China's efforts to substantially increase the number of missiles it aims at Taiwan in order to overcome any defensive system (including "theater missile defense") that might be installed.

The PLA's doctrine has transformed from "the People's War" to "limited local war under information conditions," according to China's 2004 Defense White Paper.

China's leadership is, in any event, primarily concerned with economic development. China is working to become an integral part of the international economic, commercial, and monetary systems. It has rapidly expanded trade with the international community, even more so since joining the World Trade Organization in 2001. Today, China focuses its efforts primarily on infrastructure development and investment, not just in China but throughout the world. With the exponential growth in per capita income for more than 200 million Chinese, China is pressed to acquire natural resources to satisfy rocketing increases in consumer demand. It is investing heavily in resources for the future in Latin America, Southeast Asia, Africa, and the Middle East. It is ironic that China, considered "the sick man of Asia" in the early 20th century, should now in the 21st century be buying up companies not just in the developing world, but also in Europe and the United States; and that it has, along with Japan, become the "banker" for the United States, buying American debt and keeping the U.S. dollar from declining still further in value, especially when the United States is suffering from a severe financial crisis now. For these reasons, China holds substantial bargaining power vis-à-vis the United States and many other countries in the world.

THE SINO–AMERICAN RELATIONSHIP

China's relationship with the United States has historically been an emotionally turbulent one.[47] During World War II, the United States gave significant help to the Chinese,

who at that time were fighting under the leadership of the Nationalist Party, headed by General Chiang Kai-shek. When the Americans entered the war in Asia, the Chinese Communists were fighting together with the Nationalists in a "united front" against the Japanese, so American aid was not seen as directed against communism.

After the defeat of Japan at the end of World War II, the Japanese military, which had occupied much of the north and east of China, was demobilized and sent back to Japan. Subsequently, civil war broke out between the Communists and Nationalists. The United States attempted to reconcile the two sides, but to no avail. As the Communists moved toward victory in 1949, the KMT leadership fled to Taiwan. Thereafter, the two rival governments each claimed to be the true rulers of China. The United States, already in the throes of the Cold War because of the "iron curtain" falling over Eastern Europe, viewed communism in China as a major threat to its neighbors.

Korea, Taiwan, and Vietnam

The outbreak of the Korean War in 1950 helped the United States to rationalize its decision to support the Nationalists, who had already lost power on the mainland and fled to Taiwan. The Korean War began when the Communists in northern Korea attacked the non-Communist south. When United Nations troops (mostly Americans) led by American general Douglas MacArthur successfully pushed Communist troops back almost to the Chinese border and showed no signs of stopping their advance, the Chinese—who had frantically been sending the Americans messages about their concern for China's own security, to no avail—entered the war. The Chinese forced the UN troops to retreat to what is today still the demarcation line between North and South Korea. Thereafter, China became a target of America's Cold War isolation and containment policies.

With the People's Republic of China condemned as an international "aggressor" for its action in Korea, the United States felt free to recognize the Nationalist government in Taiwan as the legitimate government to represent all of China. The United States supported the Nationalists' claim that the people on the Chinese mainland actually wanted the KMT to return to the mainland and defeat the Chinese Communists. As the years passed, however, it became clear that the Chinese Communists controlled the mainland and that the people were not about to rebel against Communist rule.

Sino–American relations steadily worsened as the United States continued to build up a formidable military bastion with an

© AP Photo/Ed Wray

Chinese acrobats perform to warm up the crowd at the Olympic weightlifting competition at the Beijing 2008 Olympics in Beijing, China Monday, Aug.11, 2008.

estimated 100,000 KMT soldiers in the tiny islands of Quemoy and Matsu in the Taiwan Strait, just off China's coast. Tensions were exacerbated by the steady escalation of U.S. military involvement in Vietnam from 1965 to the early 1970s. China, fearful that the United States was really using the war in Vietnam as the first step toward attacking China, concentrated on civil-defense measures: Chinese citizens used shovels and even spoons to dig air-raid shelters in major cities such as Shanghai and Beijing, with tunnels connecting them to the suburbs. Some industrial enterprises were moved out of China's major cities in order to make them less vulnerable in the event of a massive attack on concentrated urban areas. The Chinese received a steady barrage of what we would call propaganda about the United States "imperialist" as China's number-one enemy; but it is important to realize that the Chinese leadership actually *believed* what it told the people, especially in the context of the United States' steady escalation of the war in Vietnam toward the Chinese border, and the repeated "mistaken" overflights of southern China by American planes bombing North Vietnam. Apart from everything else, it is unlikely that China's leaders would have made such an immense expenditure of manpower and resources on civil-defense measures had they not truly believed that the United States was preparing to attack China.

Diplomatic Relations

By the late 1960s, China was completely isolated from the world community,

including the Communist bloc. It saw itself as surrounded on all sides by enemies—the Soviets to the north and west, the United States to the south in Vietnam as well as in South Korea and Japan, and the Nationalists to the east in Taiwan. Internally, China was in such turmoil from the Cultural Revolution that it appeared to be on the verge of complete collapse.

In this context, Soviet military incursions on China's northern borders, combined with an assessment of which country could offer China the most profitable economic relationship, led China to consider the United States as the lesser of two evil giants and to respond positively to American overtures. In 1972, President Richard Nixon visited China. When the U.S. and China signed the Shanghai Communique at the end of his visit, the groundwork was laid for reversing more than two decades of hostile relations.

Thus began a new era of Sino–American friendship, but it fell short of full diplomatic relations. This long delay in bringing the two states into full diplomatic relations reflected not only each country's domestic political problems but also mutual disillusionment with the nature of the relationship. Although both sides had entered the relationship with the understanding of its strategic importance as a bulwark against the Soviet threat, the Americans had assumed that the 1972 opening of partial diplomatic relations would lead to a huge new economic market for American products; the Chinese assumed that the new ties would quickly lead the United States to end its diplomatic relations with Taiwan. Both were disappointed.

Nevertheless, pressure from both sides eventually led to full diplomatic relations between the United States and the People's Republic of China on January 1, 1979.

The Taiwan Issue in U.S.–China Relations

Because the People's Republic of China and the Republic of China both claimed to be the legitimate government of the Chinese people, the establishment of diplomatic relations with the former necessarily entailed breaking them with the latter. Nevertheless, the United States continued to maintain extensive, informal economic and cultural ties with Taiwan. It also continued the sale of military equipment to Taiwan. Although these military sales are still a serious issue, American ties with Taiwan have diminished, while China's own ties with Taiwan have grown steadily closer since 1988. Taiwan's entrepreneurs have become one of the largest groups of investors in China's economy. More than one million people from Taiwan, about 5% of Taiwan's population, live on the mainland, with 500,000 living in Shanghai alone. Taiwan used to have one of the cheapest labor forces in the world; but because its workers now demand wages too high to remain competitive, Taiwan's entrepreneurs have dismantled many of its older industries and reassembled them on the mainland. With China's cheap labor, these same industries are now profitable, and both China's economy and Taiwan's entrepreneurs benefit. Taiwan's businesspeople are also investing in new industries and new sectors, and they are competing with other outside investors for the best and brightest Chinese minds, so the relationship has already moved beyond simply exploiting the mainland for cheap labor and raw materials.

Ties with the mainland have also been enhanced since the late 1980s by the millions of tourists from Taiwan, most of them with relatives on the mainland. They bring both presents and good will. Family members who had not seen one another since 1949 have reestablished contact, and "the enemy" now seems less threatening.

China hopes that its economic reforms and growth, which have substantially raised the standard of living, will make reunification more attractive to Taiwan. This very positive context has, however, been disturbed over the years by events such as the military crackdown on the demonstrators in Tiananmen Square in 1989, and efforts by Taiwan's leaders to move towards independence. In 1996, China responded to such efforts by "testing" its missiles in the waters around Taiwan. High-level talks to discuss eventual reunification were broken off and now occur on a sporadic basis. The 2000 election of the Democratic Progressive Party candidate, Chen Shui-bian as president (and his re-election in 2004), led to still more crises with Beijing. President Chen, who campaigned on the platform of an independent Taiwan, refused to acknowledge Beijing's "one China" principle, and he insisted that Taiwan negotiate with the P.R.C. as "an equal." This further strained the relationship and led to raising the bellicosity decibel level in Beijing. Nevertheless, both sides recognize it is in their interests for the foreseeable future to maintain the status quo—a peaceful and profitable relationship in which Taiwan continues to act as an independent state, but does not declare its independence. In 2008, the pro-independence Chen was replaced by KMT's Ma Ying-jeou, who favors a more conciliatory policy toward mainland China.

So far, the battle between Taipei and Beijing remains at the verbal level. At the same time, massive investments by Taiwan in the mainland and the 2000 opening of Taiwan's Offshore Islands of Quemoy and Matsu for trade with the P.R.C. are bringing the two sides still closer together. Their two economies are becoming steadily more intertwined, and both sides benefit from their commercial ties. This does not mean that they will soon be fully reunified in law. Furthermore, there remains the black cloud of Beijing possibly using military force against Taiwan if it declares itself an independent state. Beijing refuses to make any pledge never to use military force to reunify Taiwan with the mainland, on the grounds that what it does with Taiwan is China's internal affair. In Beijing's view, no other country has a right to tell China what to do about Taiwan.

Human Rights in U.S.–China Relations

Since U.S. president Jimmy Carter established diplomatic relations with China in 1979, each successive American president has campaigned on a platform that decried the abuse of human rights in China and vowed, if elected, to take strong action, including economic measures, to punish China. The Chinese people have been confused and distraught at this prospect. They do not see the point in punishing hundreds of millions of Chinese for human rights abuses committed not by the people, but by their leadership. Nor do they necessarily believe that their own government has been more abusive of human rights than other states that seem to escape scrutiny. In any event, within a few months (if not sooner) of being sworn in, each successive president has abandoned his campaign platform and taken a more moderate approach to China.

Why was this? Once inauguration day was over, it was quickly explained to the new president that the United States dare not risk jeopardizing its relations with an

increasingly powerful state containing one-quarter of the world's population through punitive measures. Boycotts would probably give Japan and other countries a better trading position while undercutting the opportunity for Americans to do business with China. By 2000, President Bill Clinton had managed to get Congress to vote for "permanent normal trading relations" (PNTR). No longer would normal trade

relations with China be subjected each spring to a congressional review of its human-rights record. This in turn cleared the way for China to join the World Trade Organization with an American endorsement in 2001. Under WTO rules, one country may not use trade as a weapon to punish another for political reasons.

Clinton's China policy was also shaped by a new strategy of "agreeing to disagree"

Timeline: PAST

1842
The Treaty of Nanking cedes Hong Kong to Great Britain

1860
China cedes the Kowloon Peninsula to Great Britain

1894–1895
The Sino–Japanese War

1895–1945
Taiwan is under Japanese colonial control

1898
China leases Northern Kowloon and the New Territories (Hong Kong) to Great Britain for 99 years

1900–1901
The Boxer Rebellion

1911
Revolution and the overthrow of the Qing Dynasty

1912–1949
The Republic of China

1921
The Chinese Communist Party (CCP) is established

1931
Japanese occupation of Manchuria (the northeast province of China)

1934–1935
The Long March

1937–1945
The Japanese invasion and occupation of much of China

1942–1945
The Japanese occupation of Hong Kong

1945–1949
Civil war between the KMT and CCP

The KMT establishes the Nationalist government on Taiwan. Keeps name of Republic of China

The People's Republic of China is established

1950
The United States recognizes the Nationalist government in Taiwan as the legitimate government of all China

1958
The "Great Leap Forward"; the Taiwan Strait crisis (Offshore Islands)

1963
The Sino–Soviet split becomes public

1966–1976
The "Cultural Revolution"

1971
The United Nations votes to seat the P.R.C. in place of the R.O.C.

1972
U.S. president Richard Nixon visits the P.R.C.; the Shanghai Communique

1976
Mao Zedong dies; removal of the Gang of Four

1977
Deng Xiaoping returns to power

1979
The United States recognizes the P.R.C. and withdraws recognition of the R.O.C.

1980s–1990s
Resumption of arms sales to Taiwan

The Shanghai Communique II: the United States agrees to phase out arms sales to Taiwan

China and Great Britain sign an agreement on Hong Kong's future Sino–Soviet relations begin to thaw

China sells Silkworm missiles to Iran and Saudi Arabia

Student demonstrations in Tiananmen Square; military crackdown; political repression follows

Deng encourages "experimentation" and the economy booms

The United States bombs the Chinese Embassy in Belgrade; says "an accident" Deng Xiaoping dies; Jiang Zemin assumes power

PRESENT

2000s
China bans the Falun Gong sect.

Terrorist attacks of 9/11 lead to stronger ties between China and the United States, but China opposes the war on Iraq

SARS (Severe Acute Respiratory Syndrome) outbreak

Hu Jintao and Wen Jiabao take over the reins of the party and government from outgoing Jiang Zemin in a peaceful transition of power

2006
China becomes the fourth largest economy, the third largest global trader.

2008
Olympics in Beijing

China's first space walk

on certain issues such as human rights, while efforts continued to be made to bring the two sides closer together. This strategy came out of a belief that China and the United States had so many common interests that neither side could afford to endanger the relationship on the basis of a single issue. The American policy of "engagement" with China, which began with the Clinton administration, was based on the belief that isolating China had proven counterproductive. The administration argued that human rights issues could be more fruitfully addressed in a relationship that was more positive in its broader aspects. "Engagement" allowed the two countries to work together toward shared objectives, including the security of Asia.

Although President George W. Bush initially appeared intent on ending engagement, and treating China as a "strategic adversary," the Bush administration soon abandoned this policy—an act made complete by the September 11, 2001 terrorist attacks on the United States. After those events, President Bush told the world, "You are either with us or against us." China, not wishing to needlessly bring trouble on itself, immediately sided with the United States in the war on terrorism. This had important implications for the role that human rights could play in the U.S.–China relationship; for with the focus on terrorism, human rights took a back seat, even in the United States itself. With critics across the political spectrum raising countless questions about the American government's treatment of suspected terrorists, the United States was hardly in a position to be pressing for improved human rights in China. Just as important, the United States did not want to raise gratuitous questions concerning China's alleged derogation of human rights when it needed China on its side, not just in the war on terrorism, but on almost every issue of international significance.

In spite of the White House's tendency to be pro-China and avoid the issue of human rights, the U.S. Congress has been a different matter. It was Congress that pressed the human rights agenda, especially under President Clinton. Indeed, during his second term in office, Congress used Clinton's favorable treatment of China as one more reason for trying to force him out of office. Coupled with 9/11, the curtailing of American liberties, and numerous accusations of the American abuse of the rights of those under detention in Guantanamo and Iraq, the Chinese human rights issue virtually disappeared from the congressional agenda. In the 2008 U.S. presidential election, China's human rights did not become a campaign issue. U.S.–China relations today are more likely to suffer from trade and monetary issues than from human rights concerns.

THE FUTURE

Since 1979, China has moved from being a relatively closed and isolated country to one that is fully engaged in the world. China's agenda for the future is daunting. It must avoid war; maintain internal political stability in the context of international pressures to democratize; continue to carry out major economic, legal, and political reforms without destabilizing society and endangering CCP control; and sustain economic growth while limiting environmental destruction.

Since the death of Deng Xiaoping in 1997, China has carried out smooth leadership transitions. The central party-state leadership has never deviated from the road of reform.

Strong economic growth has been crucial to the continuing legitimacy of the CCP leadership in the eyes of the Chinese people. The party may, however, some day change its name to one more reflective of its actual policies—not communism but capitalism, combined with socialist social policies. To some degree, it has adopted policies similar to those of European leftist parties, which tend to label themselves as "democratic socialist" or "socialist democratic" parties. Whatever name it adopts, the Chinese Communist Party is unlikely to allow the creation of a multiparty system any time soon that could challenge its leadership.

Governing the world's largest population is a formidable task, one made even more challenging by globalization. The integration of China into the international community has heightened the receptivity of China's leaders to pressures from the international system on a host of specific issues: human rights, environmental protection, intellectual property rights, prison labor, arms control, and legal codes. China's leadership insists on moving at its own pace and in a way that takes into account China's culture, history, and institutions; but China is now subject to globalizing forces, as well as internal social and economic forces, that have a momentum of their own.

In the meantime, China, like so many other developing countries, must worry about the polarization of wealth, high levels of unemployment, uncontrolled economic growth, environmental degradation, and the strident resistance by whole regions within China against following economic and monetary policies formulated at the center. It is also facing a major HIV/AIDS epidemic, a potential collapse of the banking and financial systems, the need to finance a social safety net and retirement pensions, a demographic crisis, and a looming threat to its state-owned enterprises as a result of China's entry into the WTO. To wit, the international community is pressing

China to revalue the Chinese currency, the *yuan,* so that Chinese goods will be priced higher, thus making them less competitive internationally. Common criminality, corruption, and social instability provide additional fuel that could one day explode politically and bring down Chinese Communist Party rule.

At this time there is no alternative leadership waiting in the wings to take up the burden of leading China and ensuring its stability. An unstable China would not be in anyone's interest, neither that of the Chinese people, nor any other country. An insecure and unstable China would be a more dangerous China, and it would be one in which the Chinese people would suffer immeasurably.

NOTES

1. Pam Woodall, "The Real Great Leap Forward, *The Economist,* October 2, 2004, p. 6.

2. A concern about "spiritual pollution" is not unique to China. It refers to the contamination or destruction of one's own spiritual and cultural values by other values. Europeans are as concerned about it as the Chinese and have, in an effort to combat spiritual pollution, limited the number of television programs made abroad (i.e., in the United States) that can be broadcast in European countries.

3. The essence of the "get civilized" campaign was an effort to revive a value that had seemingly been lost: respect for others and common human decency. Thus, drivers were told to drive in a "civilized" way—that is, courteously. Ordinary citizens were told to act in a "civilized" way by not spitting or throwing garbage on the ground. Students were told to be "civilized" by not stealing books or cheating, keeping their rooms and bathrooms clean, and not talking loudly.

4. The turmoil that ensued after his death had also ensued after the death of the former beloved premier, Zhou Enlai. Similar turmoil followed the death of another recently arrived hero of the students. Indeed, the central leadership was almost paralyzed when, in January 2005, Zhao Ziyang, the Secretary General of the CCP at the time of the Tiananmen demonstrations in 1989, died. Zhao, who was dismissed from his position because in the end he supported the students' demands for political reform, had been accused of trying to "split" the party. He spent the next 15 years, until his death, under house arrest in Beijing.

5. "Campaign to Crush Dissent Intensifies," *South China Morning Post* (August 9, 1989).

6. Susan K. McCarthy, "The State, Minorities, and Dilemmas of Development in Contemporary China," *The Fletcher Forum of World Affairs,* Vol. 26:2 (Summer/Fall 2002).

7. June Teufel Dreyer, "Economic Development in Tibet under the People's Republic

of China," *Journal of Contemporary China,* Vol. 12, no. 36 (August 2003), pp. 411–430.

8. For excellent detail on Chinese religious practices, see Robert Weller, *Taiping Rebels, Taiwanese Ghosts, and Tiananmen* (Seattle: University of Washington Press, 1994); and Alan Hunter and Kimk-wong Chan, *Protestantism in Contemporary China* (Cambridge: Cambridge University Press, 1993). The latter notes that Chinese judge gods "on performance rather than theological criteria" (p. 144). That is, if the contributors to the temple in which certain gods were honored were doing well financially and their families were healthy, then those gods were judged favorably. Furthermore, Chinese pray as individuals rather than as congregations. Thus, before the Chinese government closed most temples, they were full of individuals praying randomly, children playing inside, and general noise and confusion. Western missionaries have found this style too casual for their own more structured religions (p. 145).

9. Professor Rudolf G. Wagner (Heidelberg University). Information based on his stay in China in 1990.

10. Richard Madesen, "Understanding Falun Gong," *Current History* (September 2000), Vol. 99, No. 638, pp. 243–247.

11. For a better understanding of how Chinese characters are put togther, see John DeFrancis, *Visible Speech: The Diverse Oneness of Writing Systems* (Honolulu: University of Hawaii Press, 1989); and Bob Hodge and Kam Louie, *The Politics of Chinese Language and Culture: The Art of Reading Dragons* (New York: Routledge, 1998.)

12. "Number of University Students Recruited Doubles in Six Years," *People's Daily Online* (December 7, 2004).

13. Cao Desheng, "China Cancels 4,800 Development Zones," *China Daily,* August 24, 2004.

14. Howard W. French "Alarm and Disarray on Rise in China," *The New York Times,* August 24, 2005.

15. Nicholas R. Lardy, "China's Economy: Problems and Prospects," *Foreign Policy Research Institute,* Vol. 12, no. 4 (Feb. 2007), online at www.fpri.org

16. Desheng Cao, "China cancels 4,800 Development Zones," *China Daily,* August 24, 2004.

17. Yan Sun, "Corruption, Growth, and Reform," *Current History,* September 2005, pp. 257–263.

18. According to research done by the Research Office of the State Council, the Chinese Academy of Social Sciences, and the Party School's Research Office, the main source of the billionaires' wealth was, among other things, "Legal or illegal commissions from introducing foreign investments . . .; Importing facilities and equipment with . . . prices . . . usually 60 percent to 300 percent higher than market prices; . . . Developing and selling land with bank loans and zero costs; . . .

Smuggling, tax evasion. . . . Obtaining and pocketing loans from banks without collateral." For this and other sources of wealth for Chinese billionaires, see Mo Ming, "90 Percent of China's Billionaires Are Children of Senior Officials," http://financenews.com/ausdaily/

19. Jonathan Watts, "Corrupt Officials Have Cost China 330 Million Pounds in 20 Years," *The Guardian* (August 20, 2004).

20. Richard McGregor, "China's Power Capacity Soars," *Financial Times,* February 6, 2007.

21. Yuanyuan Shen (Tsinghua University Law School), seminar, Harvard University Center for the Environment, China Project, October 20, 2005.

22. *Shai Oster,* "China Tilts Green: Climate Concerns Sway Beijing," *The Wall Street Journal,* February 13, 2007.

23. Philip P. Pan, "In China, Turning the Law into the People's Protector," *The Washington Post Foreign Service* (Dec. 28, 2004), p. A1.)

24. Suzanne Ogden, *Inklings of Democracy in China* (Cambridge: Harvard University Asia Center and Harvard University Press, 2002), pp. 234–236.

25. Based on the author's trip to interview village leaders in 2000 and the author's visit with President Carter to monitor elections in a Chinese village in 2001. See Ogden, pp. 183–220.

26. "Chinese NGOs increase to 346,000 last year," posted February 4, 2007, at www.chinaelections.org

27. For an excellent analysis of how the "patterns of protest" in China have replicated the "patterns of daily life," see Jeffrey N. Wasserstrom and Liu Xinyong, "Student Associations and Mass Movements," in Deborah S. Davis, Richard Kraus, Barry Naughton, Elizabeth J. Perry, eds., *Urban Spaces in Contemporary China: The Potential for Autonomy and Community in Post-Mao China* (Cambridge: Cambridge University Press and Woodrow Wilson Center Press, 1995), pp. 362–366, 383–386. The authors make the point that students learned how to organize, lead, and follow in school. This prepared them for organizing so masterfully in Tiananmen Square. The same was true for the workers who participated in the 1989 protests "not as individuals or members of 'autonomous' unions but as members of *danwei* delegations, which were usually organized with either the direct support or the passive approval of work-group leaders, and which were generally led onto the streets by people carrying flags emblazoned with the name of the unit." p. 383.

28. In 1996–1997, the citizens of Beijing who were unable to sleep through the racket finally forced the government to pass a noise ordinance that lowered the decibel level allowed on streets by public performers, such as the fan and ballroom dancers.

29. Vaclav Havel, as quoted by Timothy Garton Ash, "Eastern Europe: The Year of Truth," *New York Review of Books* (February 15, 1990), p. 18, referenced in Giuseppe De

Palma, "After Leninism: Why Democracy Can Work in Eastern Europe," *Journal of Democracy,* Vol. 2, No. 1 (Winter 1991), p. 25, note 3.

30. Liu Binyan, "China and the Lessons of Eastern Europe," *Journal of Democracy,* Vol. 2, No. 2 (Spring 1991), p. 8.

31. Beijing University student, "My Innermost Thoughts—To the Students of Beijing Universities" (May 1989), Document 68, in Suzanne Ogden, et al., eds., *China's Search for Democracy,* pp. 172–173.

32. Vivienne Shue, in a speech to a USIA conference of diplomats and scholars, as quoted and summarized in "Democracy Rating Low in Mainland," *The Free China Journal* (January 24, 1992), p. 7.

33. Joyce Barnathan, et al., "China: Is Prosperity Creating a Freer Society?" *Business Week* (June 6, 1994), p. 98.

34. Jim Yardley, "Chinese United by Common Goal: A Hot Stock Tip," *The New York Times* (January 30, 2007), pp A1, A10.

35. These figures are a composite, taken from the Chinese government website on "Mass Media," http://www.china.org.cn/english/features/Brief/193358.htm (Feb. 10, 2007); and "Lexis-Nexis Country Report, 1999: China," http://www.lexis-nexis.com.

36. David Barboza, "Internet Boom in China is Built on Virtual Fun," *The New York Times* (Feb. 5, 2007), pp. A1, A4.

37. Wang, in Davis, pp. 170–171.

38. Cary Huang, "Beijing Tightens Media Grip with Penalty Points System," *South China Morning Post,* Feb. 9, 2007.

39. Wang Meng (former minister of culture and a leading novelist in China), speech at Cambridge University (May 23, 1996). An example of a movie banned in China is the famous producer Chen Kaige's *Temptress Moon.* This movie, which won the Golden Palm award at the Cannes Film Festival in 1993, is, however, allowed to be distributed abroad. The government has adopted a similar policy of censorship at home but distribution abroad for a number of films, including *Farewell My Concubine,* by China's most famous film directors.

40. "Party Magazine Attacks Morality of Chinese Films," (article published on Feb. 9 2007, posted Feb. 10, 2007), www.chinaelections.org). Zhang Yimou's film *House of Flying Tigers,* and Chen Kaige's film *The Promise,* were also condemned by the party periodical, *The Study Times.*

41. Barnathan, et al., pp. 98–99.

42. For the Chinese response in 2007, see Edward Cody, "China: Bush Has No Right to Criticize on Human Rights," *Washington Post,* March 8, 2007.

43. For more on Chinese nationalism, see Suzanne Ogden, "Chinese Nationalism: The Precedence of Community and Identity Over Individual Rights," *Asian Perspective,* vol. 25, no. 4 (2001), pp. 157–185.

44. China to Show Only "Ethically Inspiring TV Series in Prime Time from Next Month" Published and posted Jan. 22, 2007 on www.chinaelections.org

45. In 1998, Avon was, at least temporarily, banned from China, as were other companies that used similar sales and marketing techniques. Too many Chinese found themselves bankrupted when they could not sell the products that they had purchased for resale.

46. Lardy, "China's Economy . . . ," (February 2007), ibid.

47. For excellent analyses of the Sino–American relationship from the nineteenth century, see Warren Cohen, *America's Response to China: A History of Sino–American Relations,* 3rd ed. (New York: Columbia University Press, 1990); Richard Madesen, *China and the American Dream: A Moral Inquiry* (Berkeley, CA: University of California Press, 1995); Michael Schaller, *The United States and China in the Twentieth Century,* 2nd ed. (New York: Oxford University Press, 1990); David Shambaugh, ed., *American Studies of Contemporary China* (Armonk, NY: M.E. Sharpe, 1993); and David Shambaugh, *Beautiful Imperialist: China Perceives America, 1972–1990* (Princeton, NJ: Princeton University Press, 1991).

Hong Kong Map

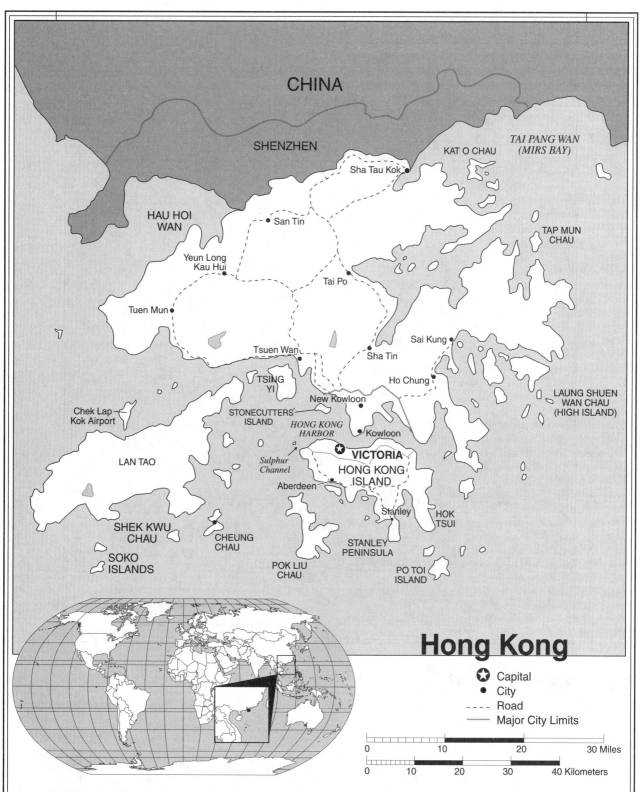

Hong Kong

- ⭐ Capital
- ● City
- --- Road
- — Major City Limits

Hong Kong is comprised of the island of Hong Kong (1842), the Kowloon Peninsula and Stonecutters' Island (1860), the New Territories (1898) that extend from Kowloon to the Chinese land border; and 230 adjacent islets. Land is constantly being reclaimed from the sea, so the total land area of Hong Kong is continually increasing by small amounts. All of Hong Kong reverted to Chinese sovereignty on July 1, 1997. It was renamed the Hong Kong Special Administrative Region.

Hong Kong (Hong Kong Special Administrative Region)

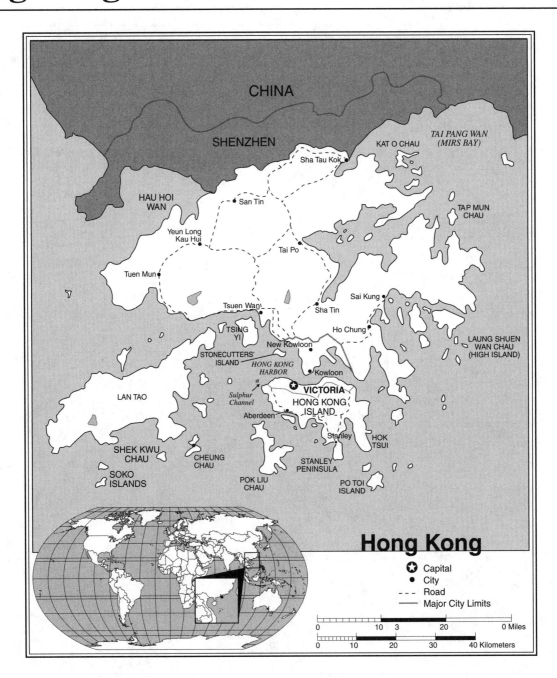

Hong Kong Statistics

GEOGRAPHY

Area in Square Miles (Kilometers):
421 (1,092) (about six times the size of Washington, D.C.)
Geographical Features: hilly to mountainous, with steep slopes; lowlands in the north; more than 200 islands
Climate: tropical

Environmental Concerns: air and water pollution

PEOPLE
Population

Total: 7,018,636 (July 2008 est.)
Annual Growth Rate: 0.532% (2008 est.)
Ethnic Makeup: 95% Chinese (mostly Cantonese); 5% others

Religions: local religions (Buddism and Taoism) 90%; Christian 10%
Major Languages: Chinese (Cantonese) 89.2% (official); other Chinese dialects 6.4%; English 3.2% (official).

Health

Life Expectancy at Birth: 81.77 years (*male:* 79.07 years; *female:* 84.69 years) (2008)

Infant Mortality Rate: 2.93 deaths/1,000 live births
Total Fertility Rate: 1 child born/woman (2008 est.)
Physicians Available: 1.3/1,000 people
HIV/AIDS—Adult Prevalence Rate: 0.1% (2003 est.)

EDUCATION

Adult Literacy Rate: 93.5%
Education expenditures: 3.9% of GDP (2006)

COMMUNICATION

Telephones—main lines in use: 3.875 million (2007)
Telephones—mobile cellular: 10.55 million (2007)
Internet Users: 3.961 million (2007)
Television Broadcast Stations: 55 (2 TV networks, each broadcasting on 2 channels) (2007)

TRANSPORTATION

Airports: 2 (2007)
Heliports: 5 (2007)
Paved Roadways: 2,009 km (2007)

GOVERNMENT

Type: Special Administrative Region (SAR) of China
Head of State: President of China Hu Jintao (since March 2003)
Head of Government: Chief Executive Donald Tsang (since June 2005)
National Holiday: National Day (Anniversary of the Founding of the People's Republic of China), October 1. July 1 is celebrated as Hong Kong SAR Establishment Day
Constitution: The Basic Law, approved in March 1990 by China's National People's Congress, is Hong Kong's "mini-constitution"
Legal system: based on English common law
Political Parties: Association for Democracy and People's Livelihood or ADPL; Citizens Party; Civic Party; Democratic Alliance for the Betterment and Progress of Hong Kong or DAB; Democratic Party; Frontier Party; League of Social Democrats; Liberal Party
Suffrage: direct election—18 years of age for a number of non-executive positions; universal for permanent residents living in the territory of Hong Kong for the past seven years; indirect election—limited to about 220,000 members of functional constituencies and an 800-member election committee drawn from broad regional groupings, central government bodies, and municipal organizations

MILITARY

Military Expenditures (% of GDP): None. Defense is the responsibility of China.
Current Disputes: none

ECONOMY

Currency: Hong Kong dollar (HKD)
Exchange Rate: U.S.$1 = 7.75 HKD (December 2008)

Per Capita Income (Purchasing Power Parity): $42,000 (2007 est.)
GDP (official exchange rate): $206.7 billion (2007 est.)
GDP - Real Growth Rate: 6.4% (2007 est.)
Unemployment Rate: 4% (2007 est.)
Agriculture: fresh vegetables; poultry; pork; fish
Industries: textiles; clothing; tourism; banking; shipping; electronics; plastics; toys; watches; clocks
Exports: $345.9 billion f.o.b., including re-exports (2007 est.)
Exports Partners: China 48.7%; U.S. 13.7%; Japan 4.5% (2007)
Exports Commodities: electrical machinery and appliances; textiles; apparel; footwear; watches and clocks; toys; plastics; precious stones; printed material
Imports: $365.6 billion (2007 est.)
Imports Partners: China 46.3%; Japan 10%; Taiwan 7.1%; Singapore 6.8%; U.S. 4.9%; South Korea 4.2% (2007)
Imports Commodities: raw materials and semi-manufactures; consumer goods; capital goods; foodstuffs; fuel (most is re-exported)

SUGGESTED WEB SITES

http://www.cia.gov/library/publications/the-world-factbook/geos/hk.html
http://www.gov.hk/en/about/sitemap.htm
http://www.WorldBank.org
http://www.state.gov
http://www.civic-exchange.org

Hong Kong Report

Hong Kong, the "fragrant harbor" situated on the southeastern edge of China, was under British rule, characterized as the "pearl of the Orient," from 1842 until 1997. The British colonial administration supported a market economy in the context of a highly structured and tightly controlled political system. This allowed Hong Kong's dynamic and vibrant people to shape the colony into one of the world's great success stories. The history of Hong Kong's formation and development, its achievements, and its handling of the difficult issues emanating from a "one country, two systems" formula since it was returned to Chinese rule in 1997 provide one of the most fascinating stories of cultural, economic, and political transition in the world. Hong Kong's "borrowed time" has ended; but its efforts to shape itself into the "Manhattan of China" are in full swing.

HISTORY

In the 1830s, the British sale of opium to China was creating a nation of drug addicts. Alarmed by this development, the Chinese imperial government banned opium; but private British "country traders," sailing armed clipper ships, continued to sell opium to the Chinese by smuggling it (with the help of Chinese pirates) up China's coast and rivers. In an effort to enforce the ban, the Chinese imperial commissioner, Lin Zexu, detained the British in Canton (Guangzhou) and forced them to surrender their opium. Commissioner Lin took the more than 21,000 chests of opium and destroyed them in public.[1]

The British, desperate to establish outposts for trade with an unwilling China, used this siege of British warehouses as an excuse to declare war on the Chinese. Later called the Opium War (1839–1842), the conflict ended with China's defeat and the Treaty of Nanjing.

Great Britain did not wage war against the Chinese in order to sell an addictive drug that was banned by the Chinese government. Rather, the Chinese government's attack on the British opium traders, whose status as British citizens suddenly proved convenient to the British government, provided the necessary excuse for Great Britain getting what it really wanted: free trade with a government that had restricted trade with the British to one port, Canton. It also allowed London to assert Great Britain's diplomatic equality with China, which considered itself the "Central Kingdom" and superior to all other countries. The Chinese imperial government's demand that all "barbarians," including the British, kowtow to the Chinese emperor, incensed the British and gave them further cause to set the record straight.

The China trade had been draining the British treasury of its gold and silver species; for the British purchased large quantities of Chinese porcelain, silk, tea, and spices, while the Chinese refused to purchase the products of Great Britain's nineteenth-century Industrial Revolution. Smug in their belief that their cultural and moral superiority was sufficient to withstand any military challenge from a "barbarian" country, the Chinese saw no need to develop a modern military or to industrialize. An amusing example of the thought process involved in "Sinocentrism"—the belief that China was the center of the world and superior to all other countries—was Imperial Commissioner Lin's letter to Queen Victoria. Here he noted "Britain's dependence on Chinese rhubarb, without which the English would die of constipation."[2] China's narrow world view blinded it to the growing power of the West and resulted in China's losing the opportunity to benefit from the Industrial Revolution at an early stage. The Opium War turned out to be only the first step in a century of humiliation for China—the step that led to a British foothold on the edge of China.

For their part, the British public did not generally see the sale of opium as a moral issue, or that large-scale addiction was a possible outcome for China. Opium was available for self-medication in Britain, was taken orally (not smoked as it was in China), was administered as a tranquilizer for infants by the working class, and was not considered toxic by the British medical community at that time.[3] Great Britain's colonial government in Hong Kong remained dependent on revenues from the sale of opium until Hong Kong was occupied by Japan during World War II.[4]

The Treaty of Nanjing gave the British the right to trade with the Chinese from five Chinese ports; and Hong Kong, a tiny island off the southern coast of China, was ceded to them "in perpetuity." In short, according to the practices of the colonizing powers of the nineteenth century, Hong Kong became a British colony forever. The Western imperialists were still in the acquisition phase of their history. They were not contemplating that one day the whole process of colonization might be reversed. As a result, Great Britain did not foresee that it might one day have to relinquish the colony of Hong Kong, either to independence or to Chinese rule.

Hong Kong Island's total population of Chinese villagers and people living on boats then numbered under 6,000. From 1842 onward, however, Hong Kong became the primary magnet for Chinese immigrants fleeing the poverty, chaos, and cruelty of China in favor of the relatively peaceful environment of Hong Kong under British rule. Then, in 1860, again as a result of a British victory in battle, the Chinese ceded to the British "in perpetuity" Stonecutters' Island and a small (3 1/2 square miles) but significant piece of land facing the island of Hong Kong: Kowloon Peninsula. Just a few minutes by ferry (and, since the 1970s, by tunnel) from Hong Kong Island, it became an important part of the residential, commercial, and business sectors of Hong Kong. The New Territories, the third and largest part (89 percent of the total area) of what is now known as "Hong Kong," were not granted "in perpetuity" but were merely leased to the British for 99 years under the second Anglo–Chinese Convention of Peking in 1898. The New Territories, which extended from Kowloon to the Chinese land border, comprised the major agricultural area supporting Hong Kong.

The distinction between those areas that became a British colony (Hong Kong Island and Kowloon) and the area "leased" for 99 years (the New Territories) is crucial to understanding why, by the early 1980s, the British felt compelled to negotiate with the Chinese about the future of "Hong Kong"; for although colonies are theoretically colonies "in perpetuity," the New Territories were merely leased, and would automatically revert to Chinese sovereignty in 1997. Without this large agricultural area, the rest of Hong Kong could not survive; the leased territories had, moreover, become tightly integrated into the life and business of Hong Kong Island and Kowloon.

Thus, with the exception of the period of Japanese occupation (1942–1945) during World War II, Hong Kong was administered as a British Crown colony from the nineteenth century onward. After the defeat of Japan in 1945, however, Britain almost did not regain control over Hong Kong because of the United States, which insisted that it did not fight World War II in order to return colonies to its allies. But Britain's leaders, both during and after World War II, were determined to hold on to Hong Kong because of its symbolic, economic, and strategic importance to the British Empire. India, Singapore, Malaya, Burma—all could be relinquished, but not Hong Kong.[5] Moreover, although during World War II, a U.S. presidential order had stated that at the end of the war, Japanese troops in Hong Kong were to surrender to Chiang Kai-shek, the leader of the Republic of China, it did

not happen. Chiang, more worried about accepting surrender of Japanese troops in the rest of China before the Chinese Communist could, did not rush to Hong Kong. Meanwhile, a British fleet moved rapidly to Hong Kong to pre-empt Chiang occupying Hong Kong, even though Chiang averred he would not have stayed. The British doubted this, and argued that Hong Kong was still British sovereign territory and would itself accept the surrender of the Japanese.[6]

At the end of the civil war that raged in China from 1945 to 1949, the Communists' Red Army stopped its advance just short of Hong Kong. Beijing never offered an official explanation. Perhaps it did not want to get into a war with Britian in order to claim Hong Kong, or perhaps the Chinese Communists calculated that Hong Kong would be of more value to them if left in British hands. Indeed, at no time after their victory in 1949 did the Chinese Communists attempt to force Great Britain out of Hong Kong, even when Sino-British relations were greatly strained, as during China's "Cultural Revolution."[7]

This did not mean that Beijing accepted the legitimacy of British rule. It did not. After coming to power on the mainland in 1949, the Chinese Communist Party held that Hong Kong was a part of China stolen by British imperialists, and that it

THE SECOND ANGLO/CHINESE CONVENTION CEDES THE KOWLOON PENINSULA TO THE BRITISH

The second Anglo/Chinese Convention, signed in 1860, was the result of a string of incidents and hostilities among the Chinese, the British, and the French. Although the French were involved in the outbreak of war, they were not included in the treaty that resulted from conflict.

The catalyst for the war was that, during a truce, the Chinese seized the chief British negotiator and executed 20 of his men. In reprisal, the English destroyed nearly 200 buildings of the emperor's summer palace and forced the new treaty on the Chinese. This called for increased payments ("indemnities") by the Chinese to the English for war-inflicted damages as well as the cession of Kowloon Peninsula to the British.

was merely "occupied" by Great Britain. Hence the notion of Hong Kong as "a borrowed place living on borrowed time." The People's Republic of China insisted that Hong Kong not be treated like other colonies; for the process of decolonization has in practice meant sovereignty and freedom for a former colony's people.[8] China was not about to allow Hong Kong to become independent. After the People's Republic of China gained the China seat in the United Nations in 1971, it protested the listing of Hong Kong and Macau (a Portuguese colony) as colonies by the UN General Assembly's Special Committee on Colonialism. In a letter to the Committee, Beijing insisted they were merely

> part of Chinese territory occupied
> by the British and Portuguese
> authorities. The settlement of
> the questions of Hong Kong and
> Macao is entirely within China's
> sovereign right and does not at all
> fall under the ordinary category of
> colonial territories. Consequently
> they should not be included in the
> list of colonial territories covered by
> the declaration on the granting of
> independence to colonial countries
> and peoples. . . . The United
> Nations has no right to discuss
> these questions.[9]

China made it clear that, unlike other colonies, Hong Kong's colonial subjects did not have the option of declaring independence, for overthrowing British colonial rule would have led directly to the re-imposition of China's control. And although there is for the Hong Kong Chinese a cultural identity as Chinese, after 1949 few wanted to fall under the rule of China's Communist Party government. Furthermore, Beijing and London as a rule did not interfere in Hong Kong's affairs, leaving these in the capable hands of the colonial government in Hong Kong. Although the colonial government formally reported to the British Parliament, in practice it was left to handle its own affairs. Still, the colonial government did not in turn cede any significant political power to its colonial subjects.[10]

No doubt the Chinese Communists were ideologically uncomfortable after winning control of China in 1949 in proclaiming China's sovereign rights and spouting Communist principles while at the same time tolerating the continued existence of a capitalist and British-controlled Hong Kong on its very borders. China could have acquired control within 24 hours simply by shutting off Hong Kong's water supply from the mainland. But China profited from the British presence there and, except for occasional flareups, did little to challenge it.

By 1980, the Hong Kong and foreign business communities had grown increasingly concerned about the expiration of the British lease on the New Territories in 1997. The problem was that all land in the New Territories (which by then had moved from pure agriculture to becoming a major area for manufacturing plants, housing, and commercial buildings) was *leased* to businesses or individuals, and the British colonial government could not grant any land lease that expired after the lease on the New Territories expired. Thus, all land leases—regardless of which year they were granted—would expire three days in advance of the expiration of the main lease on the New Territories on July 1, 1997. As 1997 grew steadily closer, then, the British colonial government had to grant shorter and shorter leases. Investors found buying leases increasingly unattractive. The British colonial government felt compelled to do something to calm investors.[11]

For this reason, it was the British, not the Chinese, who took the initiative to press for an agreement on the future status of the colony and the rights of its people. Everyone recognized the inability of the island of Hong Kong and Kowloon to survive on their own, because of their dependence upon the leased New Territories for food, and because of the integrated nature of the economies of the colonial and leased parts of Hong Kong. Everyone (everyone, that is, except for British prime minister Margaret Thatcher) also knew that Hong Kong was militarily indefensible by the British and that the Chinese were unlikely to permit the continuation of British administrative rule over Hong Kong after it was returned to Chinese sovereignty.[12] So, a series of formal Sino–British negotiations over the future of Hong Kong began in 1982. By 1984, the two sides had reached an agreement to restore all three parts of Hong Kong to China on July 1, 1997.

The Negotiations Over the Status of Hong Kong

Negotiations between the People's Republic of China and Great Britain over the future status of Hong Kong got off to a rocky start in 1982. Prime Minister Thatcher set a contentious tone for the talks when she claimed, after meeting with Chinese leaders in Beijing, that the three nineteenth century treaties that gave Great Britain control of Hong Kong were valid according to international law; and that China, like other nations, had an obligation to honor its treaty commitments. Thatcher's remarks infuriated China's leaders, who denounced the treaties that resulted from imperialist aggression as "unequal," and lacking legitimacy in the contemporary world.

Both sides realized that Chinese sovereignty over Hong Kong would be reestablished in 1997 when the New Territories lease expired, but they disagreed profoundly on what such sovereignty would mean in practice. The British claimed that they had a "moral commitment" to the people of Hong Kong to maintain the stability and prosperity of the colony. Both the British and the Hong Kong population hoped that Chinese sovereignty over Hong Kong might be more symbolic than substantive and that some arrangement could be worked out that would allow for continuing British participation in the administration of the area. The Chinese vehemently rejected what they termed "alien rule in Chinese territory" after 1997, as well as the argument that the economic value of a Hong Kong *not* under its administrative power might be greater.[13] Great Britain agreed to end its administration of Hong Kong in 1997, and together with China worked out a detailed and binding arrangement for how Hong Kong would be governed under Chinese sovereignty.

The people of Hong Kong itself did not formally participate in these negotiations over the colony's fate. Although the British and Chinese consulted various interested parties in the colony, they chose to ignore many of their viewpoints. China was particularly adamant that the people of Hong Kong were Chinese and that the government in Beijing represented *all Chinese* in talks with the British.

In September 1984, Great Britain and the People's Republic of China initialed the Joint Declaration on the Question of Hong Kong. It stated that, as of July 1, 1997, Hong Kong would become a "Special Administrative Region" (SAR) under the control of the central government of the People's Republic of China. The Chinese came up with the idea of "one country, two systems," whereby, apart from defense and foreign policy, the Hong Kong SAR would enjoy a high degree of autonomy. Hong Kong would maintain its current social, political, economic, and legal systems alongside China's systems; would remain an international financial center; and would retain its ability to establish independent economic (but not diplomatic) relations with other countries.

The Sino–British Joint Liaison Group was created to oversee the transition to Chinese rule. Any changes in Hong Kong's laws made during the transition period, if they were expected to continue after 1997, had to receive final approval from the Joint Liaison Group. If there were disagreement within the Liaison Group between the British and

Chinese, they were obligated to talk until they reached agreement. This procedure gave China veto power over any proposed changes in Hong Kong's governance and laws proposed from 1984 to 1997.[14] When London's newly appointed governor, Christopher Patten, arrived in 1992 and attempted to change some of the laws that would govern Hong Kong after 1997, China had reason to use that veto power.

The Basic Law

The Basic Law is the crucial document that translates the *spirit* of the Sino–British Joint Declaration into a legal code. Often referred to as a "mini-constitution" for Hong Kong after it became a SAR on July 1, 1997, the Basic Law essentially defines where Hong Kong's autonomy ends and Beijing's governance over Hong Kong begins. The British had no role in formulating the Basic Law, as the Chinese considered it an internal, sovereign matter. In 1985, China established the Basic Law Drafting Committee, under the direction of the National People's Congress (NPC). The Committee had 59 members—36 from the mainland, 23 from Hong Kong. Of the latter, almost all were "prominent figures belonging to high and high-middle strata," with Hong Kong's economic elite at its core. In addition, China established a "Consultative Committee" in Hong Kong of 180 members. Its purpose was to function as a nonofficial representative organ of the people of Hong Kong from all walks of life, an organ that would channel their viewpoints to the Basic Law Drafting Committee. By so including Hong Kong's elite and a Hong Kong–wide civic representative organ in consultations about the Basic Law, China hoped to provide political legitimacy to the Basic Law.[15] Once the Basic Law was approved in April 1990 by China's NPC, the final draft was promulgated.

The Basic Law gave Hong Kong a high degree of autonomy after 1997, except in matters of foreign policy and defense, which fell under Beijing's direct control. The government was to be made up of local civil servants and a chief executive chosen by an "Election Committee" appointed by the Standing Committee of the National People's Congress.[16] The chief executive was given the right to appoint key officials of the Special Administrative Region (subject to Beijing's approval). Provisions were made to allow some British and other foreign nationals to serve in the administration of the SAR, if the Hong Kong government so desired. An elected Legislature was made responsible for formulating the laws.[17] The maintenance of law and order remained the responsibility of local authorities, but

China took over from the British the right to station military forces in Hong Kong. The local judicial and legal system were to remain basically unchanged, but China's NPC reserved the right to approve all new laws written between 1990 and 1997.[18]

Thus, the Joint Declaration and Basic Law brought Hong Kong under China's rule, with the National People's Congress in Beijing accorded the right of the final interpretation of the meaning of the Basic Law in case of dispute; but the Basic Law allows Hong Kong considerable independence over its economy, finances, budgeting, and revenue until the year 2047. China is thus committed to preserving Hong Kong's "capitalist system and lifestyle" for 50 years and has promised not to impose the Communist political, legal, social, or economic system on Hong Kong. It also agreed to allow Hong Kong to remain a free port, with its own internationally convertible currency (the Hong Kong dollar), over which China would not exercise authority. The Basic Law states that all Hong Kong residents shall have freedom of speech, press, publication, association, assembly, procession, and demonstration, as well as the right to form and join trade unions, and to strike. Freedom of religion, marriage, choice of occupation, and the right to social welfare are also protected by law.[19]

Beijing agreed to continue to allow the free flow of capital into and out of Hong Kong. It also agreed to allow Hong Kong to enter into economic and cultural agreements with other nations and to participate in relevant international organizations as a separate member. Thus, Hong Kong was not held back from membership in the World Trade Organization (WTO) by China's earlier inability to meet WTO membership qualifications. Similarly, Hong Kong is a separate member of the World Bank, the Asian Development Bank, and the Asian-Pacific Economic Conference (APEC). Hong Kong is also allowed to continue issuing its own travel documents to Hong Kong's residents and to visitors.

When China promulgated the Basic Law in 1990, Hong Kong residents by the thousands took to the streets in protest, burning their copies of it. Some of Hong Kong's people saw Britain as having repeatedly capitulated to China's opposition to plans for political reform in Hong Kong before 1997, and as having traded off Hong Kong's interests in favor of Britain's own interests in further trade and investment in China. Hong Kong's business community, however, supported the Basic Law, believing that it would provide for a healthy political and economic environment for doing business. Other Hong Kong residents believed that it was Hong Kong's commercial value,

not the Basic Law, that would protect it from a heavy-handed approach by the Chinese government.

The Joint Declaration of China and Great Britain (1984), and the Basic Law (1990) are critical to understanding China's anger in 1992 when Governor Patten proceeded to push for democratic reforms in Hong Kong without Beijing's agreement—particularly since Patten's predecessor, Governor David Wilson, always did consult Beijing and never pushed too hard. After numerous threats to tear up the Basic Law, Beijing simply stated in 1994 that, after the handover of Hong Kong to Chinese sovereignty in 1997, it would nullify any last-minute efforts by the colonial government to promote a political liberalization that went beyond the provisions in the Basic Law. And that is precisely what China did on July 1, 1997. As is noted later in this report, the changes that Patten advocated were largely last-ditch efforts to confer on Hong Kong's subjects democratic rights that they had never had in more than 150 years of British colonial rule. These rights related largely to how the Legislature was elected, the expansion of the electorate, and the elimination of such British colonial regulations as one requiring those who wanted to demonstrate publicly to first acquire a police permit.

The Chinese people were visibly euphoric about the return of Hong Kong "to the embrace of the Motherland." The large clock in Beijing's Tiananmen Square counted the years, months, days, hours, minutes, and even seconds until the return of Hong Kong, helping to focus the Chinese people on the topic. Education in the schools, special exhibits, the movie *The Opium War* (produced by China), and even T-shirts displaying pride in the return of Hong Kong to China's control reinforced a sense that a historical injustice was at last being corrected. On July 1, 1997, celebrations were held all over China, and the pleasure was genuinely and deeply felt by the Chinese people. In Hong Kong, amidst a drenching rain, celebrations were also held. At midnight on June 30, 1997, 4,000 guests watched as the Union Jack was lowered, and China's flag, together with the new Hong Kong Special Administrative Region flag, were raised. President Jiang Zemin, and Charles, the Prince of Wales, and Tony Blair, Prime Minister of Great Britain, represented their respective countries at the ceremony.[20]

THE SOCIETY AND ITS PEOPLE
Immigrant Population

In 1842, Hong Kong had a mere 6,000 inhabitants. Today, it has over 7 million people. What makes this population distinctive is its predominantly immigrant composition. Waves of immigrants have flooded Hong Kong ever since 1842. Even today, barely half of Hong Kong's people were actually born there. This has been a critical factor in the political development of Hong Kong; for instead of a foreign government imposing its rule on submissive natives, the situation has been just the reverse. Chinese people voluntarily emigrated to Hong Kong, even risking their lives to do so, to subject themselves to alien British colonial rule.

In recent history, the largest influxes of immigrants came as a result of the 1945–1949 Civil War in China, when 750,000 fled to Hong Kong; as a result of the "three bad years" (1959–1962) following the economic disaster of China's Great Leap Forward policy; and from 1966 to 1976, when more than 500,000 Chinese went to Hong Kong to escape the societal turmoil generated by the Cultural Revolution. After the Vietnam War ended in 1975, Hong Kong also received thousands of refugees from Vietnam as that country undertook a policy of expelling many of its ethnic Chinese citizens. Many Chinese from Vietnam risked their lives on small boats at sea to attain refugee status in Hong Kong.

Although China's improving economic and political conditions after 1979 greatly stemmed the flow of immigrants from the mainland, the absorption of refugees into Hong Kong's economy and society remained one of the colony's biggest problems. Injection of another distinct refugee group (the Chinese from Vietnam) generated tension and conflict among the Hong Kong population.

Because of a severe housing shortage and strains on the provision of social services, the British colonial government first announced that it would confine all new refugees in camps and prohibit them from outside employment. It then adopted a policy of sending back almost all refugees who were caught before they reached Hong Kong Island and were unable to prove they had relatives in Hong Kong to care for them. Finally, the British reached an agreement with Vietnam's government to repatriate some of those Chinese immigrants from Vietnam who were believed to be economic rather than political refugees. The first few attempts at this reportedly "voluntary" repatriation raised such an international furor that the British were unable to systematize this policy. By the mid-1990s, however, better economic and political conditions in Vietnam made it easier for the British colonial government to once again repatriate Vietnamese refugees.

Before the July 1, 1997, handover, moreover, Beijing insisted that the British clear the camps of refugees. It was not a problem that China wanted to deal with. As it turned out, the British failed to clear the camps, leaving the job to the Chinese after the handover. The last one was closed in the summer of 2000. Today, China still maintains strict border controls, in an effort to protect Hong Kong from being flooded by Chinese from the mainland who are hoping to take advantage of the wealthy metropolis, or just wanting to look around and shop in Hong Kong.[21]

The fact that China's economy has grown rapidly for the last 30 years, especially in the area surrounding Hong Kong, has diminished the poverty that led so many Mainlanders to try illegally emigrating to Hong Kong. Nevertheless, overpopulation is still an important social issue because it stretches Hong Kong's limited resources and has contributed to the high levels of unemployment in recent years. Rulings that have greatly limited the right of Mainlanders with at least one Hong Kong parent (so-called "right-of-abode" seekers) to migrate to Hong Kong have eased concerns somewhat.

Today, the largest number of immigrants to Hong Kong are still Mainlanders; but they are more likely than in the past

United Nations Photo UN74043

Squatter community for refugees in Hong Kong.

to come from distant provinces. Although Hong Kong is made up almost entirely of immigrants and their descendants, the older immigrants look down upon their non-Cantonese-speaking country cousins as "uncivilized." They are socially discriminated against and find it difficult to get the better-paying jobs in the economy. This is in striking contrast to past attitudes: From the 1960s to the 1980s, Hong Kong residents generally expressed deep sympathy with Mainlanders, building rooftop schools for them, and throwing food onto the trucks when the British colonial government transported Mainlanders back to China against their will.[22]

Language and Education

Ninety-five percent of Hong Kong's people are Chinese. The other 5 percent are primarily European, Vietnamese, Filipino, and Indonesian. Although a profusion of Chinese dialects are spoken, the two official languages, English and the Cantonese dialect of Chinese, predominate. Since the Chinese written language is in ideographs, and the same ideographs are usually used regardless of how they are pronounced in various dialects, all literate Hong Kong Chinese are able to read Chinese newspapers—and 95 percent of them do read at least one of the 16 daily newspapers available in Hong Kong.[23] Even before the handover, moreover, the people were intensively studying spoken Mandarin, the official language of China.

Since the handover in 1997, a source of bubbling discontent has been the decision of the Executive Council to require all children to be taught in Chinese. The government's rationale was that the students would learn more if they were taught in their own language. This decision caused an enormous furor. Many Hong Kong Chinese, especially from the middle classes, felt that if Hong Kong were going to remain a major international financial and trading center, its citizens must speak English. Many suspected that the real reason for insisting on Chinese was to respond to Beijing's wishes to bind the Hong Kong people to a deeper Chinese identity. In response to strong public pressures, the Hong Kong government finally relented and allowed 100 schools to continue to use English for instruction. Many of the other schools are, Hong Kong parents complain, suffering from a decline in the quality of education generally, and language skills in particular. Those who can afford it now try to get their children into the growing number of private schools.

Chinese cultural values of diligence, willingness to sacrifice for the future,

A woman, from the Hakka minority in Hong Kong.

commitment to family, and respect for education have contributed to the success of Hong Kong's inhabitants. (The colonial government guaranteed nine years of compulsory and free education for children through age 15, helping to support these cultural values.) As a result, the children of immigrants have received one of the most important tools for material success. Combined with Hong Kong's rapid post–World War II economic growth and

government-funded social-welfare programs, education improved the lives of almost all Hong Kong residents, and allowed remarkable economic and social mobility. A poor, unskilled peasant who fled across China's border to Hong Kong to an urban life of grinding poverty—but opportunity—could usually be rewarded by a government-subsidized apartment, and by grandchildren who graduated from high school and moved on to white-collar jobs.

A fishing family on houseboat in Aberdeen Harbor, Hong Kong.

Since the 1997 handover, the Hong Kong SAR has continued to support compulsory and free education. But in this rapidly changing society, juvenile delinquency is on the rise, because parents are working long hours and spend little time with their children, and an increasing number of those who finish the basic nine years of school now leave the educational system. Criminal gangs *(triads)* recruit them to promote criminal activities.[24]

For those who wish to continue their education beyond high school, access to higher education is limited, so ambitious students work hard to be admitted to one of the best upper-middle schools, and then to one of the even fewer places available in Hong Kong's universities. Hong Kong's own universities are becoming some of the best in the world, and admission is highly competitive. An alternative chosen by many of Hong Kong's brightest students is to go abroad for a college education. This has been important in linking Hong Kong to the West.

Living Conditions

Hong Kong has a large and growing middle class. By 1995, in fact, Hong Kong's per capita income had surpassed that of its colonial ruler, Great Britain.[25] Its people are generally well-dressed; and restaurants, buses, and even subways are full of people yelling into their cell-phones. Enormous malls full of fashionable stores can be found throughout Hong Kong. McDonald's is so much a part of the cityscape that most residents do not realize it has American origins. After school, the many McDonald's are full of teenagers meeting with their friends, doing homework, and sharing a "snack" of the traditional McDonald's meal—hamburgers, fries, and Coca-Cola (served hot or cold). The character Ronald McDonald, affectionately referred to by his Cantonese name, Mak Dong Lou Suk Suk (Uncle McDonald), is recognized throughout Hong Kong.[26]

Nevertheless, Hong Kong's people suffer from extremes of wealth and poverty. The contrast in housing that dots the landscape of the colony dramatically illustrates this. The rich live in luxurious air-conditioned apartments and houses on some of the world's most expensive real estate. They may enjoy a social life that mixes such Chinese pleasures as mahjong, banqueting, and participation in traditional Chinese and religious rituals and festivals with British practices of horseracing, rugby, social clubs, yacht clubs, and athletic clubs for swimming and croquet.[27] (These practices have faded greatly with the exit of the British.) The Chinese have removed the name "Royal" from all of Hong Kong's old social clubs, including the Royal Jockey Club, which today is neither royal nor British. Times have changed: Hong Kong is no longer a colony, and exclusivity is a thing of the past. The mix of Hong Kong people and foreigners in business clubs reflects the fact that Hong Kong's business elite is now both British and Chinese. Of course, memberships in some clubs are still all-British, like cricket clubs, because the Chinese are not interested.[28]

The wealthy are taken care of by cooks, maids, gardeners, and chauffeurs, most of whom are Filipino. The Hong Kong people—and the government—greatly prefer hiring Filipinos to hiring mainlander Chinese, as the former are better trained, speak English, and are less likely to try to apply for permanent residency in Hong Kong. (The preference for hiring Filipinos adds to the sense the Chinese Mainlanders have of being discriminated against.) Virtually all members of the Filipino workforce (estimated to be about 200,000) have Sundays off, and they more or less take over the parks, and even the streets in Hong Kong Central, where they camp out for the day with their compatriots. The government dares not intervene to get them off the streets, lest it be accused of racism or violating their civil liberties. The Filipinos often complain about exploitation and abuse by Hong Kong employers.

There is a heavier concentration of Mercedes, Jaguars, Rolls Royces, and other luxury cars—not to mention cellular phones, car faxes, and fine French brandy—in Hong Kong than anywhere else in the world.[29] Some Hong Kong businessmen spend lavishly on travel, entertainment, and mistresses. Their mistresses, however, now tend to live in Shenzhen, the "Special Economic Zone" (SEZ) just 40 minutes by train from Hong Kong Central. Purchasing an apartment for them and paying for their upkeep are cheaper there, as are the karaoke bars, golf courses, bars, and massage parlors. Hong Kong is now for the wealthier and more sedate businessmen, while Shenzhen is more attractive to Hong Kong's young professionals.

The wealthiest business people have at least one bodyguard for each member of their families. Conspicuous consumption and what in the West might be considered a vulgar display of wealth are an ingrained part of the society. Some Hong Kong businesspeople, who have seemingly run out of other ways to spend their money, spend several hundred thousand dollars just to buy a lucky number for their car license plate. One Hong Kong businessman built a magnificent home in Beijing that replicates the style of the Qing Dynasty and features numerous brass dragons on the ceilings, decorated with three pounds of gold leaf.[30]

In stark contrast to the lifestyles of the wealthy business class, the vast majority of Hong Kong's people live in crowded high-rise apartment buildings, with several poor families sometimes occupying one apartment of a few small rooms, and having inadequate sanitation facilities.[31] Beginning in the mid-1950s, the British colonial government built extensive low-rent public housing, which today accommodates about half of the population. These government-subsidized housing projects easily become run down and are often plagued by crime. But without them, a not-insignificant percentage of the new immigrant population would have continued to live in squalor in squatter villages with no running water, sanitation, or electricity.

When he took office in 1997, Hong Kong's first chief executive, Tung Chee-hwa, made a significant commitment to provide more government-funded housing and social-welfare programs—some 85,000 new apartments were to be built each year. But in 2000, Tung suddenly announced that he had scrapped that policy

two years earlier because of falling real-estate prices (owing to the Asian economic crisis)—without telling anyone. The result is a housing scarcity, and the rents for the apartments in the few new residential buildings are far beyond the means of the average Hong Kong resident.

The Economy

A large part of the allure of Hong Kong has been its combination of a dynamic economy with enlightened social welfare policies. The latter were possible not just because of the British colonial government's commitment to them but also because the flourishing Hong Kong economy provided the resources for them. Hong Kong had a larger percentage of the gross domestic product (GDP) available for social welfare than most governments, for two reasons. First, it had a low defense budget to support its approximately 12,000 British troops (including some of the famous Gurkha Rifles) stationed in the colony for external defense (only 0.4 percent of the GDP, or 4.2 percent of the total budget available). Second, the government was able to take in substantial revenues (18.3 percent of GDP) through the sale of land leases.[32]

Now, of course, China is in charge of Hong Kong's defense. Land leases came to an end in 1997 with the return of Hong Kong's leased territories to China, but the sale of land is still the primary source of government revenue. Continuing the system established by the British colonial government, the Hong Kong government makes money by selling land one piece at a time to its handful of real-estate developers, who then build on the land.[33] This is how Hong Kong can continue to finance governmental expenditures without any income tax, sales taxes, or capital gains tax; and with a low profit tax (16.5 percent) for corporations, and a flat 15 percent tax on salaries that kicks in at such a high level that a large percentage of those working in Hong Kong pay nothing at all.

The result is that Hong Kong is a great place to do business, but the cost of private housing is beyond the means of most of Hong Kong's middle class; and, having made its money by selling land to the land developers, the government must then turn around and use a substantial portion of that money to subsidize public housing so that rent is affordable. Half of Hong Kong's populace receives housing free or at minimal (subsidized) rent, but the middle class cannot afford to buy housing. Many have moved to more affordable housing in the Shenzhen Special Economic Zone across the border in China. This may explain in part why the Hong Kong population has

fallen by at least 300,000 people in the last few years.

Hong Kong's real estate system has affected the people's viewpoint on housing. Unlike in the West, people do not view the purchase of an apartment as a place where they might want to reside for an indefinite period. Rather, they see it more like buying a stock, and they might buy and sell it within one year in order to make a profit. Before the Asian financial crisis that hit Hong Kong in 1997, this was a fairly sure bet; but housing prices have been much lower, and many people have lost their savings by speculating in housing.

Beijing's greatest concern before the handover in 1997 was that the colonial administration had dramatically increased welfare spending—65 percent in a mere five years.[34] From Beijing's perspective, the British appeared determined to empty Hong Kong's coffers, leaving little for Beijing to use elsewhere in China. The Chinese believed that the British were setting a pattern to justify Hong Kong's continuing expenditures in the next 50 years of protected autonomy. As it turned out, however, the British did not try to deplete Hong Kong assets, and China's companies were deeply involved even in the vastly expensive new airport that the British insisted on building before their departure. (It opened in July 1998, one year after the handover.)

No sooner had China taken back Hong Kong than, suddenly, the Asian economic financial crisis broke out, first in Thailand, and then throughout Asia. It wreaked havoc on Hong Kong's economy and challenged its financial and economic system. Beijing, instead of interfering with the decisions made by Hong Kong to address the crisis, took a hands-off approach, except to offer to support the Hong Kong dollar against currency speculators by using China's own substantial foreign-currency reserves of U.S. $150 billion to sustain the Hong Kong dollar's peg to the U.S. dollar. Furthermore, China did not take the easy route of devaluing the Chinese yuan, which would have sent Asian markets, and Hong Kong's in particular, into a further downward spiral.

The Asian financial and economic crisis (1997–2002) brought a severe downturn in living conditions in Hong Kong. Growing increasingly anxious about the situation, the Hong Kong population pressured their government to intervene and do more to ease the pain. They demanded that the government take a more activist role in providing social welfare, controlling environmental degradation, and regulating the economy. In response to such pressure, the government required taxis to stop using diesel fuel and enacted some of the toughest emissions standards in the world.[35] The government also committed more to social welfare than it had under British rule. In addition, it intervened in the financial markets, purchasing large amounts of Hong Kong dollars to foil attempts by speculators to make a profit from selling Hong Kong dollars. It also intervened in the Hong Kong stock market, using up some 25 percent of its foreign-currency reserves to purchase large numbers of shares in Hong Kong companies in a risky but ultimately successful effort to prevent a further slide of the stock market.

Hong Kong's woes were aggravated, however, by the world economic turndown that began in 2000, made worse by the September 11, 2001 terrorist attacks on the United States, and by the outbreak of the SARS (severe acute respiratory syndrome) epidemic in early 2003 in the next-door Chinese province of Guangdong. It quickly spread to Hong Kong, showing the vulnerability of Hong Kong's geographical position on the edge of China. The life-threatening illness (with close to a 5 percent mortality rate) and the initial reluctance of China to furnish information about the spread of the epidemic in China led to disaster for Hong Kong's tourist industry and economy in 2003. Meanwhile, pollution from the coal-fired plants in the flourishing economy next door in southern China led to rapidly deteriorating air quality in Hong Kong. A survey taken each year from 1992 to 2007 indicates that by the end of 2003, the satisfaction of the Hong Kong people with the government reached its nadir, with only 51 percent of those surveyed "satisfied" with their life in Hong Kong.[36]

Before the 1997 return of Hong Kong to China, many analysts predicted that Beijing would undercut Hong Kong's prosperity through various political decisions limiting political freedom, tampering with the legal system, and imposing economic regulations that would endanger growth. Instead, Beijing left Hong Kong in the hands of its hand-picked Chief Executive, Tung Chee-hwa. Tung, however, proved unable to save Hong Kong's economy from the Asian financial crisis and rapidly lost popularity. To wit, although the economy recovered, its growth rate has remained only half that of the China mainland. The local press severely criticized Tung for having too literally interpreted Beijing's promise to the rest of the world in 1997 that Hong Kong would not change. Indeed, Hong Kong has changed so little in the years since the handover that it seems to be losing its dominant position in Asia as a major financial and commercial center to Shanghai and Singapore. Just as worrisome, Taiwan has emerged as the Asian leader in computer

Copyright IMS Communication Ltd/Capstone Design/FlatEarth Images RF (DAL022C14)
Bamboo scaffolding in Hong Kong.

technology, while Hong Kong has fallen further behind in the technology sweepstakes. Tung resigned in March 2005 due to "health reasons," just 3 years into his second term. Donald Tsang, a lifelong civil servant, became the new Chief Executive.

The erosion of Hong Kong's leadership in Asia is blamed not on Beijing, but on the government's lack of vision and its catering to the real-estate "tycoons"—the mere half dozen individuals who hold the vast majority of Hong Kong's wealth in their hands.[37] More than anything else, Hong Kong's loss of its international character and relative decline as an Asian city are blamed on its "official obsession with mainland relations."[38] Yet, regardless of how others view Hong Kong, its citizens seem generally pleased with their government's relationship with the mainland, especially in the last few years.[39]

The collapse of Hong Kong's real estate prices in the wake of the Asian economic crisis did, however, result in their turning to technology as a new source of wealth for Hong Kong, and themselves. The Internet is empowering small entrepreneurs. But Hong Kong's economy is plagued with other problems emanating from monopolistic and duopolistic control of many sectors in the economy.[40] A more cynical view is that Hong Kong businesspeople are sycophants to both the Hong Kong and Beijing governments: their customary operating procedure is to make money not through creativity but through their connections—a practice common on the mainland as well.

Hong Kong's real estate and stock markets have bounced back from the Asian financial crisis, but remain volatile. For the time being, Hong Kong's greatest protection against substantial turmoil and a prolonged recession is the stability and growth of China's economy, which continues to bubble along at an average of 9 percent per year. Hong Kong businesspeople have heavily invested in China. Were its growth to falter, so would Hong Kong's.

Hong Kong as a World Trade and Financial Center

From the moment Hong Kong became a colony, the British designated it as a free port. The result is that Hong Kong has never applied tariffs or other major trade restrictions on imports. Such appealing trade conditions, combined with Hong Kong's free-market economy, deepwater harbor, and location at the hub of all commercial activities in Asia, have made it an attractive place for doing business. Indeed, from the 1840s until the crippling Japanese occupation during World War II, Hong Kong served as a major center of China's trade with both Asia and the Western world.

The outbreak of the Korean War in 1950 and the subsequent United Nations embargo on exports of strategic goods to China, as well as a U.S.–led general embargo on the import of Chinese goods, forced Hong Kong to reorient its economy. To combat its diminished role as the middleman in trade with the mainland of China, Hong Kong turned to manufacturing. At first, it manufactured mainly textiles. Later, it diversified into other areas of light consumer goods and developed into a financial and tourist center.

Today, Hong Kong continues to serve as a major trade and financial hub, with thousands of companies located there for the purpose of doing business with China. Even Mainland China companies try to have headquarters in Hong Kong, for reasons related to foreign exchange, taxes, and stock listing issues. Hong Kong also remains a middleman in trade with China, with more than one-third of China's total trade still flowing in and out of China through Hong Kong. A full 80 percent of Hong Kong's container port traffic, in fact, goes to and from Southern China. So Hong Kong's economy is still closely tied to China's economy.

In addition, Hong Kong has actually shifted its own manufacturing base into China. Back in 1980, when almost half of Hong Kong's workforce labored in factories and small workshops, Hong Kong was on the verge of pricing itself out of world markets because of its increasingly well-paid labor and high-priced real estate. Just then, China, with its large and cheap labor supply, inexpensive land, and abundant resources, initiated major internal economic reforms that opened up the country for foreign investment. As a result, Hong Kong transferred its manufacturing base over the border to China, largely to the contiguous province of Guangdong. By the late 1990s, more than 75 percent of the Hong Kong workforce was in the service sector, with only 13 percent remaining in manufacturing. In short, the vast majority of Hong Kong workers in the manufacturing sector have been replaced by some 5 million Chinese laborers who now work in the tens of thousands of factories either owned or contracted out to Hong Kong businesses on the mainland.[41]

Hong Kong's many assets, including its hard-working, dynamic people, have made it into the world's tenth-largest trading economy. But it is facing much competition. In 2005, Singapore surpassed it to become the world's busiest container port, with Shanghai's and Shenzhen's ports hot on its heels. This does not mean that Hong Kong is not profiting from this shift, however, as it is Hong Kong investors who are helping the Mainland's ports grow. Similarly, as of 2007, Hong Kong had dropped from third to seventh as a place for foreign exchange trade. Still, it remains one of the world's largest banking centers, and has grown to become Asia's third-largest stock market, thanks to increased listings of companies from the China Mainland. Considering its tiny size and population, these are extraordinary achievements.

Hong Kong has, then, many competitors from other "dragons" in Asia; but given the rapid growth of the Asian economies over the last 30 years, there is no reason why other major financial and trade centers in Asia would necessarily harm Hong Kong's economy. Shanghai's or Shenzhen's growth need not come at Hong Kong's expense. In fact, the booming SEZ of Shenzhen is really an extension of Hong Kong's growth and power, as is most of Southern China. Perhaps Singapore presents the greatest challenge to Hong Kong's position as a financial center. And changes in the trade environment, such as South Korea establishing full diplomatic relations with China in 1992, have allowed it to deal directly with China, thereby bypassing Hong Kong as an entrepôt for trade and business with China. But Hong Kong's entrepreneurs and businesses remain efficient, flexible, and able to incorporate such changes into their business strategies successfully.

The Special Economic Zones (SEZs)

As part of its economic reform program and "open door" policy that began in 1979, China created Special Economic Zones in areas bordering or close to Hong Kong in order to attract foreign investment. SEZs, until recent years under far more liberal regulations than the rest of China, blossomed in the 1980s and 1990s. Various branches of China's government themselves invested heavily in the SEZs in hopes of making a profit. In the 1990s, even China's military developed an industrial area catering to foreign investors and joint ventures in one of China's SEZs, Shenzhen, as part of its effort to compensate for insufficient government funding for the military. It called its policy "one army, two systems"—that is, an army involved with both military and economic development.[42] Brushing aside its earlier preference for a puritanical society, China's military was as likely to invest in nightclubs, Western-style hotels, brothels, and health spas in the SEZs as it was in the manufacturing sector. In 1998, however, Beijing ordered the military to divest itself of its economic enterprises, so it no longer runs nonmilitary enterprises in Shenzhen.

The bulk of foreign investment in the SEZs comes from Hong Kong Chinese, either with their own money or acting as middlemen for investors from Taiwan, the United States, and others. Most direct foreign investment in China, in fact, comes *through* Hong Kong, either by setting up companies in Hong Kong, or using Hong Kong companies as intermediaries. In turn, China is the single largest investor in Hong Kong, and its state-owned enterprises and

joint ventures also set up companies in Hong Kong. Thus, this integrated area of South China, encompassing Hong Kong, the SEZs, and the provinces of Guangdong, Fujian, and Hainan Island, has become a powerful new regional economy on a par with other Asian "little dragons."

Indeed, even before China took over Hong Kong in 1997, South China had already become an integral part of Hong Kong's empire, with profound political as well as economic implications. Many Hong Kong people who regularly cross into Shenzhen SEZ (and even own property there) pressure the Shenzhen government to be responsive to their interests. Hong Kong's media coverage of Shenzhen affairs also puts pressure on the SEZ's administrators to be more responsive to public concerns, such as the exploitation of Mainlanders working under contract in Hong Kong–owned firms.[43]

At the same time, Hong Kong's growing ties with the SEZs and cross-border trade generally is causing serious problems, including the restructuring of the workforce as jobs in the manufacturing sector move across the Hong Kong border for cheaper labor. The result is a downward pressure on wages in Hong Kong, although many economists believe this will make Hong Kong more competitive. In any event, the Hong Kong business community is moving to integrate the economy even more fully with the mainland to take advantage of China's future growth.

Sensitivity of the Economy to External Political Events

Hong Kong's economic strength rests on its own people's confidence in their future—a confidence that has fluctuated wildly over the years. When Beijing undertook economic-retrenchment policies, partially closed the "open door" to international trade and investment, engaged in political repression, or rattled its sabers over Taiwan, Hong Kong's stock market would gyrate, its property values declined, and foreign investment would go elsewhere. Not knowing what the transition to Chinese sovereignty would bring, Hong Kong's professional classes emigrated at the rate of about 60,000 people per year between 1990 and 1997. This drain of both talent and money out of the colony was as serious a concern for China as it was for Hong Kong.

London's refusal to allow Hong Kong citizens to emigrate to the United Kingdom contributed to a sense of panic among the middle and upper classes in Hong Kong—those most worried about their economic and political future under Communist rule.

Other countries were, however, more than willing to accept these well-educated, wealthy immigrants, who came ready to make large deposits in their new host country's banks. Once emigrants gained a second passport (a guarantee of residency abroad in case conditions warrant flight), however, they tended to return to Hong Kong, where opportunities abound for entrepreneurs and those in the professions, such as doctors, architects, and engineers.

Beijing's verbal intimidation of Hong Kong dissidents who criticized China in the period following the Tiananmen crackdown in 1989, and again when Governor Christopher Patten began whipping up Hong Kong fervor for greater democratic reforms from 1992 to 1997, also aroused anxiety in the colony. Hong Kong's anxiety that Great Britain would trade the colony's democratic future for good relations with China was later counterbalanced by concern that Patten's efforts to inject Hong Kong with a heavy dose of democratization before its return to China's control would lead to China dealing harshly with Hong Kong's political freedoms after 1997. In the end, Patten's blunt refusal to abide by the terms agreed to in the Basic Law, namely, that China would have to agree to any changes made before 1997, merely led to a reversal of Patten's changes after the handover, and no more.

China's sovereignty over Hong Kong has not had a negative effect on its economy. Occasionally China's statements concerning Hong Kong's economy, judicial system, or politics have sent shock waves throughout the colony, causing the Hang Sang stock market to take a nose dive out of fears that China would ignore the principles in the Basic Law guaranteeing Hong Kong's 50 years of autonomy. Similarly, the 2003 SARS epidemic had a catastrophic impact on Hong Kong's economy. Such volatility demonstrates just how sensitive Hong Kong is to Beijing's policies and actions. Nevertheless, in the years since the handover, millions of Hong Kong citizens have relinquished their British passports for Hong Kong Special Administrative Region passports. Apart from pressures from China for them to do so, it indicates a belief that their future lies with Hong Kong and China, not Great Britain.

China is sensitive to the possibility of its policies or statements destabilizing Hong Kong. Indeed, in the ten years since the handover, Beijing has exercised unusual restraint so as to avoid being seen to interfere in Hong Kong's affairs. For example, Beijing no longer permits Chinese ministry officials to visit or oversee their counterparts in Hong Kong without clearance, lest it be interpreted as interference.

Furthermore, it is the Hong Kong government, not the Ministry of Foreign Affairs office in Hong Kong, that deals with all of the foreign consulates in Hong Kong. And, unlike the British Commonwealth Office, which always sent copies of government documents to the Hong Kong government, China's Ministry of Foreign Affairs does not, again to avoid being accused of interference.[44]

Because Beijing has tread lightly in Hong Kong, most businesses already located there have remained. In fact, many foreign corporations rushed to establish themselves in Hong Kong before the handover in order to avoid the unpredictable, lengthy, and expensive bureaucratic hassle of trying to gain a foothold in the China mainland lying beyond Hong Kong. Even Taiwan's enterprises in Hong Kong have stood firm; for without direct trade and transport links between China and Taiwan, Hong Kong is still the major entrepôt for trade between the two places. Many Chinese mainland corporations also establish footholds in Hong Kong to ease the problem of foreign hard-currency transfer and to avoid a host of other difficulties that plague mainland businesses.

Nevertheless, the overall profile of the foreign business community has changed substantially since 1997. Many British went home, leaving their companies in the hands of capable Hong Kong Chinese managers, a reflection of the end of the colonial era in the business community as well as in the political system; but the percentage of Americans and Europeans doing business in Hong Kong has increased significantly.

Crime

Although Hong Kong is still characterized by a high level of social stability, a high crime rate continues to plague society. For more than a decade, ordinary criminality has been steadily augmented by crime under the control of competing Chinese triads. This is in part because the housing and community and mutual-aid groups of the 1970s and 1980s, which used to help the police track down criminals, disappeared. Their disappearance also contributed to increasing juvenile delinquency.[45] Opium, largely controlled by the triads, continues to be used widely by the Chinese. As a commentator once put it:

> Opium trails still lead to Hong Kong . . . and all our narcotic squads and all the Queen's men only serve to make the drug more costly and the profits more worthwhile. It comes in aeroplanes and fishing junks, in hollow pipes

and bamboo poles and false decks and refrigerators and pickle jars and tooth paste tubes, in shoes and ships and sealing wax. And even cabbages.[46]

Today, Hong Kong remains one of the largest entrepôts for drugs, and the number of drug addicts is skyrocketing. This is in no small part because social and economic liberalization on the mainland has allowed its people to move about freely. Hong Kong triads work in collaboration with triads across the border. Young people cross the border to Shenzhen to buy drugs (originating in Myanmar (Burma), which they then smuggle back across Hong Kong's border. In turn, those recruited in Shenzhen provide a base in the mainland for Hong Kong triads to deal in drugs, prostitutes, and guns, and to set up underground banks and transport illegal immigrants across the border.[47]

Cooperation between Hong Kong and Chinese mainland drug investigators is complicated by Hong Kong's legal system, which still differs from the legal system of the rest of China. The critical difference is that Hong Kong does not have capital punishment. And China, committed to not changing Hong Kong's legal system for 50 years, has not pressured Hong Kong to change its law on the death penalty. Dozens of crimes such as drug dealing, punishable by execution in the rest of China, will result at most in a life sentence in Hong Kong.

Before the handover, when Hong Kong investigators asked the Chinese to turn over drug dealers to the Hong Kong authorities, the Chinese expended significant resources to find the criminals and turn them over. But when the Chinese asked the Hong Kong drug authorities to do the same, they went so far as to arrest the suspects, but refused to turn them over to China's public security office because of the fairly strong chance that a person convicted on charges of selling drugs in China would be executed. At first China wanted to copy the Singapore model of executing drug dealers, but it soon realized that would mean the execution of thousands. Now only the biggest drug dealers are executed. (The problems emanating from cross-border crime are discussed further in this report, under the topic "The Legal System and the Judiciary.")

Hong Kong's organized crime has long been powerful in the areas of real estate; extortion from massage parlors, bars, restaurants, and clubs; illegal gambling; smuggling; the sale of handguns (illegal for ordinary people to purchase); prostitution; and drugs. And, as is common in other Asian countries, gangs are often hired by corporations to deal with debtors and others who cause them difficulties. Triads have also expanded into kidnapping for ransom, and taken on some unexpected roles. As an example, when the British governor in Hong Kong, Christopher Patten, upset Beijing with his proposals for further democratization of Hong Kong before 1997, the Chinese Communist regime allegedly recruited triad members to begin harassing those within the Hong Kong government who were supporting Patten's proposals. (And, when Patten's dog disappeared one day in 1992 during the crisis stage of Sino–British relations, one rumor had it that the Chinese Communists had kidnapped the dog and were going to ransom it in exchange for halting political reform in Hong Kong. The other rumor was that Patten's pet had been flown into China to be served up for breakfast to Deng Xiaoping. Of course, neither rumor was true.)

POLITICS AND POLITICAL STRUCTURE

Politics and the political structure have changed greatly since the days of Hong Kong's colonial government, when the British monarch, acting on the advice of the prime minister, would appoint a governor, who presided over the Hong Kong government's colonial administration. Colonial rule in Hong Kong may be characterized as benevolent, consultative, and paternalistic, but it was nonetheless still colonial. Although local people were heavily involved in running the colony and the colonial government interfered very little in the business activities and daily lives of Hong Kong Chinese, the British still controlled the major levers of power and filled the top ranks in the government.

The colony's remarkable political stability until the handover in 1997 was, then, hardly due to any efforts by the British to transplant a form of Western-style democracy to Hong Kong. But, the colonial Hong Kong government did seek feedback from the people through the hundreds of consultative committees that it created within the civil service. Similarly, although the British ultimately controlled both the Legislative Council (LegCo) and Executive Council (ExCo), these governmental bodies allowed Hong Kong's socioeconomic elites to participate in the administration of the colony, even if they were unable to participate in the *formulation* of policy. Some 300 additional advisory groups as well as numerous partly elected bodies—such as the municipal councils (for Hong Kong Island and Kowloon), the rural committees (for the New Territories), and district boards—also had considerable autonomy

in managing their own affairs. This institutionalized consultation among Chinese administrators and the colonial government resulted in the colony being governed by an elite informed by and sensitive to the needs of the Hong Kong people. As was common to British colonial administration elsewhere, the lower levels of government were filled with the local people. Rarely was political dissent expressed outside the government.[48]

The relatively high approval rating of British colonial rule helps explain why only a small portion of the mere 6 percent of registered voters actually voted. With the government assuring both political stability and strong economic growth, the people of Hong Kong spent most of their time and energy on economic pursuits, not politics. In any event, given the limited scope of democracy in Hong Kong, local people had little incentive to become politically involved. For this reason, as the handover came nearer, Hong Kong residents grew increasingly concerned that there were few competent and trustworthy leaders among the Hong Kong Chinese to take over.[49] They also worried that a government controlled by leaders and bureaucrats who held foreign passports or rights of residence abroad would not be committed to their welfare. Although Beijing withdrew its demand before the handover that all governmental civil servants swear an oath of allegiance to the government of China and turn in their British passports, many did so anyway (including the first chief executive, Tung Chee-hwa).

The colonial government remained stable, then, because it was perceived to be trustworthy, competent, consultative, and capable of addressing the needs of Hong Kong's people. Most Hong Kong citizens also believed that a strong political authority was indispensable to prosperity and stability, and they worried that the formation of multiple political parties could disrupt that strong authority. Thus, what is seen in the West as a critical aspect of democracy was viewed by the people in Hong Kong as potentially destabilizing.

Nevertheless, by the late 1980s, many Hong Kong Chinese began to demand that democratic political reforms be institutionalized before the Chinese Communists took over in 1997. The ability of the departing colonial government to deal with these increased pressures to democratize Hong Kong was, however, seriously constricted by the 1982 Joint Declaration and the Basic Law of 1990, which required Beijing's approval before the British could make any changes in the laws and policies governing Hong Kong. The people of Hong Kong awoke to the fact that their interests and

those of the colonial government were no longer compatible. Britain's policy toward Hong Kong had become a mere appendage of British policy toward China, and the status quo was frozen. The Hong Kong colonial government had, essentially, lost its independence to Beijing and London.[50]

What was "handed over" on July 1, 1997, was sovereign control of Hong Kong. Hong Kong became a Special Administrative Region of China, with Beijing guaranteeing autonomy for 50 years in the political, legal, economic, and social realms. But Hong Kong would be governed by its new "constitution," the Basic Law, written by China's leaders. This document provided for certain changes to be made *after* the handover. Notably, Article 23 required the Hong Kong Legislative Council to outlaw treason, succession, subversion, and sedition, as well as other activities that could endanger China's national security. That is, Hong Kong was expected to outlaw, and punish, those individuals and organizations operating in Hong Kong who in the view of Beijing might pose a threat to China's security; but for five years, nothing was done to define how Article 23 could be implemented (see below).

Similarly, for five years after the 1997 handover, there was no real change in the government—except, of course, that Hong Kong's chief executive reported to Beijing, not London. The structure of the post-1997 government, outlined in great detail in the Basic Law, was to be, like Hong Kong's colonial government: structured on a separation of powers among the executive, legislative, and judicial branches of government, serving to check the arbitrary use of power by any single individual or institution of the government. This separation of powers, however, never did exist within the framework of a representative democracy. Thus, the government today remains similar in many respects to what it was under colonial rule, with power continuing to be centralized in the executive branch. LegCo cannot even initiate substantive legislation without the approval of the chief executive, or hold the chief executive accountable for his actions. In effect, Hong Kong under the Basic Law has retained the colonial model put in place by the British in the nineteenth century.

China has made some changes in Hong Kong's government to bring it into greater correspondence with its own government structure, even if in some cases this is merely a matter of changing names. In 2002, under a new "ministerial" system, Beijing changed the Basic Law to allow the chief executive to appoint all 14 policy secretaries in the cabinet of 20. (The others are leading politicians, including two heads of progovernment parties, and close personal advisers.) Previously, cabinet secretaries were senior civil servants who were, at least in theory, politically neutral. Now that they are appointed, they serve at the chief executive's discretion, which means that their political views weigh heavily in their selection. This has raised further questions concerning the accountability of the government to the Legislature.[51]

The Executive Council is run by Hong Kong's chief executive. Fortunately, continuity was maintained in the first years after the handover, when most of the cabinet heads under British colonial rule agreed to serve under the first chief executive. Sole decision-making authority remains vested in the chief executive, although ultimately Beijing must approve of any of ExCo's policies. So far, Beijing has chosen not to exercise this approval in a way that hampers the chief executive's policy-making authority.

Since 1982, the Hong Kong Transition Project has taken the pulse of Hong Kong each year through an extensive survey of public opinion on a variety of issues related to the impact of the transition of Chinese sovereignty. The level of satisfaction has been consistently much higher in the post-handover period than in the 15 years leading up to it.[52] Furthermore, the percentage of those satisfied with the performance of the PRC government in dealing with Hong Kong affairs remained unusually high. In fact, Hong Kong public opinion in Nov. 2003 continued to give a far higher approval rating to Beijing's leadership than to Hong Kong's chief executive: Those "satisfied" or "very satisfied" with Beijing's dealing with Hong Kong affairs were 72 percent of those polled; whereas for Chief Executive Tung, the approval rating in the same 2003 poll was a humiliating 21 percent. Moreover, satisfaction with the overall performance of the Hong Kong government fell from 66 percent approval in June 1997 (still under British rule), to 20 percent by Nov. 2003.[53]

Problems with becoming the first chief executive of Hong Kong were understandable: As a colony, Hong Kong had bred strong civil servants, but no real political leaders who had had opportunities to make political decisions. So Beijing had to pick someone whom they felt was safe, but who inevitably lacked real leadership experience. Tung Chee-hwa was a businessman, an elitist who opposed the welfare state and supported "Asian values" of a strong central leadership and obedient citizenry.[54] Tung Chee-hwa's popularity one year after he took office (49 percent were satisfied or very satisfied with his performance in July 1998) was quickly eroded by his inability to

Courtesy of Bruce Argetsinger (Bargetsinger01)

Small businesses on a busy Hong Kong street.

effectively address a number of problems, including fallout from the Asian financial and economic crisis that began within a few months of his entering office. Tung was blamed not only for plummeting land prices and the government's incompetence, but also for his reluctance to intervene in order to relieve the people's suffering that resulted from the crisis. The infrequency of his appearances in front of LegCo, and his refusal to consult with LegCo representatives, caused significant conflict and anger. Although it was the executive branch's role to deal with the financial crisis in Hong Kong, LegCo still believed that it should have been consulted.[55]

Although Beijing reappointed Tung for a second term in 2002, Beijing was not pleased with his performance. This was

largely because of the growing number of demonstrations and protests directed at his government, and the dissatisfaction of the people of Hong Kong with his performance. By late 2003, some 58 percent of Hong Kong people polled said they would support China's President Hu Jintao and Premier Wen Jiabao if they were to dismiss Tung for his performance.[56]

Suddenly, in March 2005, Tung resigned, apparently under pressure from Beijing. Because two years remained in his term as Chief Executive, it led to a major constitutional crisis; for the Basic Law lacked procedures for dealing with a mid-term replacement. Beijing managed to engineer the choice of Donald Tsang, a member of the Executive Council, to fill out the term, which ends in 2007. Beijing has already ruled out any possibility that it will allow universal suffrage and full democracy for the elections of the next chief executive at that time (or of the Legislative Council in 2008—only 30 of its 60 legislators are directly elected at present). Although China has pledged significant autonomy for Hong Kong, Beijing argued that nothing in the Basic Law obligates it to allow Hong Kong to fully democratize on its own timetable. The real reason for China's reluctance to let Hong Kong move ahead is, no doubt, because it will put Hong Kong far in front of the pace of democratization in some of China's major cities, such as Beijing and Shanghai.[57]

Efforts to get the economy back on track were, as noted above, stymied greatly by events beyond the chief executive's control—the Asian financial crisis, the global recession that followed the terrorist attacks on the United States on September 11, 2001; and the SARS epidemic that erupted in 2003. Nevertheless, as the public and the press saw it, the fault for failure to revive the economy lay at the feet of the Hong Kong government, and especially the Chief Executive, not external forces (or Beijing). If, they argued, the Chief Executive had appointed advisers based on competence instead of politics, he would have received better advice.

Hong Kong residents generally believe, then, that Hong Kong's problems arise not from Beijing's control but, rather, from the incompetence of their own government. So the critical question for the Chief Executive is no longer how autonomous he is of Beijing's control. Instead, it is whether he can maintain his legitimacy as the head of Hong Kong's government. In this respect, Donald Tsang has thus far done quite well. In a March 2006 survey concerning his performance since taking office, fully 76 percent were "satisfied" with Tsang as Chief Executive.[58] But most Hong Kong people would prefer direct elections for all LegCo members and district council members, as well as for the chief executive. Presently, the latter is appointed by the Beijing-controlled Election Committee.

Article 23 of the Basic Law

As noted earlier, Article 23 outlaws treason, secession, subversion, and sedition. It also prohibits the theft of "state secrets," political activities of foreign political organizations in Hong Kong, and the establishment of ties with foreign political organizations by political organizations in Hong Kong. It had been left up to the Hong Kong government to give teeth to Article 23 so that it could be implemented, but it had not done so.

© IMS Communications, Ltd/Capstone Design/FlatEarth Images RF.
Flags of Hong Kong and China flying side by side

The purpose of Article 23 is to protect the national security of China as a whole by defining the types of activities in Hong Kong that would be punishable by law. It was one thing to define terms such as "subversion" as it applied to the rest of mainland China; it was another thing to define these terms for residents of Hong Kong. This had to be done without jeopardizing the fundamental rights given to Hong Kong people in the Basic Law, some of which have not been given to the rest of the Chinese.

The terrorist attacks of 9/11 spurred the Hong Kong government's Security Bureau to submit a bill to amend Article 23. In early 2003, after a year-long period of public consultation, Chief Executive Tung submitted a draft bill to LegCo. This predictably caused a public uproar, as it brought back fears that Beijing might have pressured the government to limit the guaranteed rights of people in Hong Kong. The public was particularly worried about a constriction of freedom of the media to report news; and the rights to demonstrate and protest, to associate with foreign organizations or with organizations banned on the mainland, to access Internet sites, and to organize pressure groups and political groups. There was also concern that the new definitions of "treason," "subversion," and "sedition" might mean that journalists who managed to get hold of unpublished government documents, or refusal to reveal their anonymous sources, could be charged with "theft of state secrets."[59]

The concerns about the potential limits on individual freedom by Article 23 has spilled over into a concern for the rule of law in Hong Kong, which is the basis for protecting all other freedoms. The possibility that the Hong Kong government might resort to secret trials on cases relating to proscription of certain local organizations, and that "mere association between a local organization and a proscribed one on the Mainland" might be grounds for arrest, also caused anxiety. On July 1, 2003, 500,000 people demonstrated in Hong Kong against the draft bill. Finally, after further demonstrations, and Beijing's realization that the suggested amendments were destabilizing Hong Kong and causing hostility toward Beijing, the bill to amend Article 23 was withdrawn without any date for reconsideration. The impact of this is dramatically illustrated by polls that asked about the performance of China's government in dealing with Hong Kong affairs: In June 2003, before the July 1st demonstrations, there was a 57 percent satisfaction rate with Beijing; 6 months later, after the withdrawal of the legislation, the satisfaction rate shot up to 72 percent.[60] The fact that Beijing in this case catered to the will of the Hong Kong people seems to have won enormous good will for China.

Political Parties and Elections

On July 1, 1997, China immediately repealed Governor Patten's expansion of the franchise for the 1995 elections, which had lowered the voting age to 18 and extended the vote to all of Hong Kong's adult population (adding 2.5 million people to the voting rolls)—without consulting Beijing. As the Joint Declaration

Apartment complexes in Hong Kong.

required that China had to agree to even a small increase in democracy in the Hong Kong colony, Beijing was within its rights when it repealed the changes and replaced the Legislature elected under those rules. A 400-member "Provisional Legislature," already selected by China's Preparatory Committee, replaced it on July 1, 1997.

Why did Beijing cancel the results of the 1995 elections? China's leaders viewed the last-ditch colonial government's efforts to install a representative government in Hong Kong as part of a conspiracy to use democracy to undercut China's rule in Hong Kong after 1997. They believed that the last-minute political reforms could, in fact, jeopardize Hong Kong's prosperity and stability by permitting special interests and political protest to flourish; and that Hong Kong's social problems—narcotics, violence, gangs, prostitution, an underground economy—required that Hong Kong be controlled, not given democracy. China therefore adopted a status quo approach to Hong Kong. After all, Hong Kong's political system under British colonial control had been imposed from the outside. This system worked well and kept Hong Kong stable and prosperous. Beijing merely wanted to replace a colonial ruler with a Chinese one.[61]

Nor did Beijing want a situation in which those citizens living in Hong Kong enjoyed substantially more rights than the rest of China's population. This could easily lead to pressure on Beijing to extend those rights to all Chinese. If Beijing is going to give greater political rights to its people, it would rather do so on its own timetable. Nevertheless, Beijing has kept its promises not to interfere in Hong Kong's political system after the handover.

In the 1995 elections, Hong Kong's Democratic Party, whose political platform called for major changes to the Basic Law in order to give Hong Kong people more democratic rights, won two-thirds of the vote. Although Beijing canceled the results of that election upon gaining control over Hong Kong in July 1997, Beijing immediately rescheduled the elections for May 1998; and when those elections led to the reelection of the same number of Democratic Party members as before, Beijing made no effort to remove them from the legislature.[62]

In the fall 2004 LegCo elections, the Democratic Party and their allies won 25 of the 60 seats, meaning that the pro-government/pro-Beijing parties still control the legislature after several rounds of elections. In that election, however, only

30 of the seats were chosen by direct election from the citizenry. The other 30 were chosen by what are called "functional constituencies," which tend to be more conservative, pro-business, and pro-Beijing. So, even though the democratic camp won the majority of the electoral vote, they still were not able to gain a majority of the seats.

The pan-democrats managed to win 24 of the 60 seats in the 2008 LegCo election. Many analysts attribute the electoral results to the preference of the electorate for better local governance over deadlines for democratization. The democracy camp lacks a meaningful platform of political, social, and economic policies that would improve conditions in Hong Kong and be attractive to the electorate. Analysts also point to the disarray within the democracy camp, which seems unable to agree on anything other than that more democracy would be a good thing, and that they should stand in opposition to government policies.

Beijing has warned the pro-democracy group not to move forward with any plan to hold a referendum on direct elections before the original timetable called for them. Combined with this warning, however, have been significant efforts by China to enhance economic integration between

Hong Kong and the mainland provinces bordering it. China has also made it easier for Chinese tourists to go to Hong Kong—a potential boon to the flagging tourist industry in Hong Kong.[63] This may help explain why the pro-Beijing forces maintained control of LegCo.

Under British colonial rule, ordinary citizens were rarely involved in politics. Today, there is much greater involvement, but a lingering suspicion of and lack of enthusiasm for politics and political parties in Hong Kong. The lack of a coherent platform and strong leadership in the democracy camp, as well as its failure to bring about change in government policies, contributes to a feeling of political inefficacy—a sense that there is little ordinary citizens can do to shape policy. This view is also influenced by a belief that there is a not altogether healthy alliance between big business and government.

On the other hand, the government has the support of some remarkably strong pro-Beijing parties, especially the Democratic Alliance for the Betterment of Hong Kong (DAB). (It may not be appropriate to call the DAB pro-Beijing, but it does make more efforts to work with China for common goals and opposes it far less frequently than many in the democracy camp do.) The DAB has joined up with other "patriotic" (that is, pro-China/pro-government) parties in a loose coalition. The coalition works *with* the government to make policies focused on environmental, social, and economic issues. Many are suspicious of the DAB ties to the government, and concerned about the funding of the DAB by the Chinese government; but it and Hong Kong's "patriotic" organizations are highly effective at mobilizing people at the local level and responding to their concerns on issues important to their daily lives.

It is difficult for the Democratic Party to make inroads on the seats assigned to functional constituencies, which usually go to pro-government business people. This unfair, indeed undemocratic, system, whereby a mere 180,000 individuals could vote for the 30 functional constituency seats, while 3.5 million voted for the other 30 seats, is a residual system set up by the British colonial government.

The complicated electoral system virtually guarantees business groups dominance in the Legislature. This is one factor accounting for both Beijing and the Hong Kong government's tolerating the Democratic Party and its political protests, even when the protesters publicly denounce Beijing's leaders. That is, with rare exceptions (such as the protests led by the democracy camp against the bill to amend Article 23), their protests are without consequences.

Besides, LegCo is a rather powerless political body. It is poorly funded, so legislators cannot afford the kind of research support that is essential to making effective policy proposals. And while in session, LegCo meets only once a week, at which time legislators give speeches written for them by their staffs.[64] This is hardly the stuff of impassioned legislative debate and policy making.

Beijing has tolerated the gadfly role of the Democratic Party, no doubt hoping that this hands-off policy will help bring Taiwan into negotiations for unification with the mainland sooner. The Hong Kong government has also kept channels open to Democratic Party leaders. The Democratic Party has, in turn, adopted a more moderate stance toward both Beijing and the government than it might otherwise have done—a position facilitated by the departure of several of the party's more radical leaders—and the public's concerns that it not stir up problems that could destabilize Hong Kong.[65]

The Democratic Party's minority position within the Legislature condemns it to the position of a critic and complainer.[66] In the post-transition period, the Hong Kong people believe that the party's demands for greater democracy have not been appropriate to the problems at hand. These problems include the "bird flu," which threatened public health and forced the government to kill the entire stock of chickens in Hong Kong; the red tide, which killed hundreds of thousands of fish; a disastrous opening of the new airport in 1998; the right-of-abode seekers in Hong Kong; the drop in real-estate values, increased unemployment, bankruptcies of retail stores, and a dramatic decline in tourism. These were not the sorts of problems for which the Democratic Party's call for changes in the Basic Law, a timetable for democratization, and opposition to Beijing have been relevant. Indeed, the vast majority of the public has wanted government intervention to address these problems. Thus, the many street demonstrations that occur tend not to be directed to broad demands for democracy but, rather, to pressing public policy issues. They reflect the frustration of the population in the legislature's ineffectiveness in shaping government policy.

The Legal System and the Judiciary

Under colonial rule, Hong Kong's judiciary was independent. After 10 years under the "one country, two systems" envisioned in the Basic Law, it has remained so. Judges are appointed and serve for life. English common law, partly adapted to accommodate Chinese custom, has been at the heart of the legal system. Much of the confidence in Hong Kong as a good place to live and do business has been based on the reputation of its independent judiciary for integrity and competence, the stability of the legal and constitutional system, and Hong Kong's adherence to the rule of law.

China has allowed Hong Kong's legal system to rely on such legal concepts as habeas corpus, legal precedent, and the tradition of common law, which do not exist in China. Beijing has not subjected Hong Kong's legal system to the Communist Party Politburo's guidelines for the rest of China. But on political matters such as legislation, human rights, civil liberties, and freedom of the press, the Basic Law offers inadequate protection. For example, the Basic Law provides for the Standing Committee of the National People's Congress (NPC) in Beijing, not the Hong Kong courts, to interpret the Basic Law and to determine whether future laws passed by the Hong Kong Legislature conflict with the Basic Law.

Furthermore, although Beijing had promised Hong Kong that the chief executive will be accountable to the Legislature, the Basic Law gives the chief executive the power to dissolve the Hong Kong Legislature and veto bills. The relationship of Hong Kong's Basic Law to China's own Constitution remains in limbo. The fundamental incompatibility between the British tradition (in which the state's actions must not be in conflict with the laws) and China's practice of using law as a tool of the state, as well as China's conferring and withdrawing rights at will, is at the heart of the concern about Chinese rule over Hong Kong.[67]

The first case to be tried by the Hong Kong courts after July 1, 1997, was that of an American streaker who ran nude in crowded downtown Hong Kong and was easily apprehended. In this rather amusing case, the court fined and released the defendant. Serious questions soon arose, however, about the handling of cross-border crime. As noted earlier, the source of the problem is that Hong Kong does not have capital punishment, and China does. In the past, when Hong Kong has arrested a P.R.C. citizen wanted for a criminal activity that is punishable in China by execution, it has refused to turn the person over to China's judicial authorities.

The position of the Hong Kong courts is that a Hong Kong citizen cannot be tried in China for *any* crimes committed in Hong Kong, even if caught in China, because of its judicial independence under the "one country, two systems" structure. But, according to Article 7 of China's Criminal Code, China has the right to prosecute a Chinese national who commits a crime *anywhere* in the world, providing the crime was either planned in, or had consequences in, China.[68] The assertion of such a broad jurisdiction over Chinese nationals inevitably puts it in conflict with Hong Kong's judicial system. Because so many criminals straddle the border between the Hong Kong SAR and mainland China, and because they have different criminal codes, there are many levels of conflict and ambiguity to resolve. In the ten years since the handover, the increasingly porous borders between Hong Kong and the rest of China, the greater mobility of the Chinese people, and the open market economy have seemed like an open invitation to Hong Kong's triads not only to expand their crime rings within China, but also to take refuge there. At the same time, citizens of China who commit capital crimes in mainland China sometimes try to enter Hong Kong, where capital punishment is prohibited.

Polls over the years have indicated that residents (including those who really do not know anything about the Basic Law's provisions) are satisfied with the Basic Law and the rule of law in Hong Kong.[69] In addition, most residents think that Beijing has adhered to the Basic Law, but they have not been pleased that the Hong Kong government has several times dragged Beijing into Hong Kong affairs. One of the most notable examples was the Hong Kong government's request to China's National People's Congress in 1999 to rule on the "right of abode" for Mainlanders with at least one Hong Kong parent. (At the time of the NPC's ruling, 1.4 million Mainlanders were claiming eligibility.) The Hong Kong judiciary's decision was overturned, a result that came as a great relief to Hong Kong residents who were more afraid of overcrowding than they were of Beijing's interference. Nevertheless, as of 2008, the right to abode is still an uncomfortable issue; for although there is sympathy for these settlers' plight (many have lived and worked in Hong Kong for most of their lives), the settlers are usually the fruit of relationships between mainland Chinese women and married Hong Kong men who frequently go to the mainland for business, a point that does not sit well with many citizens, especially Hong Kong women.

Public Security

Under the "one country, two systems" model, Hong Kong continues to be responsible for its own public security. The British colonial military force of about 12,000 has been replaced by a smaller Chinese People's Liberation Army (PLA) force of about 9,000. The military installations used by the British forces were turned over to the PLA. In efforts to reassure the Hong Kong populace that the primary purpose of the military remains the protection of the border from smuggling and illegal entry, and for general purposes of national security, soldiers are mostly stationed across the Hong Kong border in Shenzhen. Some are also stationed, however, in heavily populated areas, to serve as a deterrent to social unrest and mass demonstrations against the Chinese government. No doubt the high cost of keeping soldiers in metropolitan Hong Kong was also a factor in the PLA decision to move most of its troops to the outskirts.

Apart from diminishing the interactions between the PLA soldiers and the Hong Kong people, China has done much to ensure that the troops do not become a source of tension. To the contrary, China wants them to serve as a force in developing a positive view of Chinese sovereignty over Hong Kong. As part of their "charm offensive," the soldiers must be tall (at least 5 feet 10 inches); have "regular features" (that is, be attractive); be well read (with all officers having college training, and all ordinary soldiers having a high school education); know the Basic Law; and be able to speak both the local dialect of Cantonese and simple English.[70] In short, the PLA, which has no such requirements for its regular soldiers and officers, has trained an elite corps of soldiers for Hong Kong. No doubt the hope is that a well-educated military will be less likely to provoke problems with Hong Kong residents. In fact, PLA troops are even permitted to date and marry local Hong Kong women!

Press, Civil Rights, and Religious Freedom

China's forceful crackdown on protesters in Beijing's Tiananmen Square in 1989 and subsequent repression traumatized the Hong Kong population. China warned the Hong Kong authorities that foreign agents might use such organizations as the Hong Kong Alliance in Support of the Patriotic Democratic Movement in China (a coalition of some 200 groups) to advance their intelligence activities on the mainland, and even accused that group of "playing a subversive role in supporting the pro-democracy movement."[71] China also announced that it would not permit politically motivated mass rallies or demonstrations against the central government of China after the handover. As it turns out, Beijing has done little to stop the rallies and protests by such diverse groups as doctors, students, property owners, social workers, and civil servants, Mainlanders demanding the right to abode in Hong Kong, or event protests against the bill to amend Article 23. Such protests occur regularly in Hong Kong. Indeed, even Jiang Zemin, during one of his final trips to Hong Kong as president of China, had to face the potential humiliation by the thousands of Falun Gong demonstrators protesting Beijing's crackdown on the religious group in China. (Rather than prohibiting the group members from protesting, Hong Kong authorities took Jiang along a route where they were not so visible.) Beijing has, however, used subtle and not-so-subtle intimidation to discourage Hong Kong from supporting prodemocracy activities, suggesting that such acts would be "treasonous." In addition, those individuals who assisted the Tiananmen demonstrators in Beijing in 1989, and those leaders of the annual demonstrations in Hong Kong to protest China's use of force to crack down on Tiananmen demonstrators, are blacklisted in China. Were they to try to go to the mainland, they could be arrested for sedition. Only when the chief executive himself has intervened on their behalf have they been allowed to cross the Hong Kong border.

One freedom that Hong Kong subjects under British rule had was freedom of the press. Hong Kong had a dynamic press that represented all sides of the political spectrum. Indeed, it even tolerated the Chinese Communist Party's sponsorship of both its own pro-Communist, pro-Beijing newspaper, and its own news bureau (the New China News Agency) in Hong Kong, which, until the handover, also functioned as China's unofficial foreign office in Hong Kong.

Concerns remain that China may one day crack down on Hong Kong's press, but they pale in comparison with other concerns. Indeed, when asked in a 2006 survey about 14 different issues, those evoking the lowest levels of concern were freedom of the press (8 percent), freedom of assembly (7 percent), and freedom of speech (7 percent). (By contrast, 48 percent were "very worried" about air and water pollution.)[72] This is not surprising, as China so far has done little to challenge Hong Kong's press freedom. The exceptions are primarily concerning matters that China considers "internal affairs." The Hong Kong press has received warnings not to speak favorably about Taiwan independence; but in general, members of the Hong Kong press have mastered the art of knowing where to draw the line so as not to offend Beijing. Self-censorship is nothing new for Hong Kong's (or China's) press; and even under the British, it was necessary. How Beijing will respond to a Hong Kong press that openly challenges the Chinese Communist Party remains to be seen; but in China itself, political analyses are no longer confined to parroting the Communist Party's line, and investigative reportage is encouraged. Further, the Hong Kong press does not hesitate to engage in searing criticisms of the chief executive, even though he is appointed by Beijing. In short, a major rollback of press freedom in Hong Kong seems unlikely.

As for religious freedom, Beijing has stated that as long as a religious practice does not contravene the Basic Law, it will be permitted. Given the fact that China's tolerance of religious freedom on the mainland has expanded dramatically since it began liberalizing reforms in 1979, this does not seem to be a likely area of tension. Even in the case of Falun Gong, a sect that is banned on the mainland but has strong support in Hong Kong, thus far Beijing does not seem inclined to pressure the Hong Kong government to restrict its activities.

THE FUTURE

The future is, of course, unpredictable; but so far, there is a "business as usual" look about Hong Kong. Hong Kong still appears much as it did before its return to China's sovereign control. And although some analysts believe that power is imperceptibly being transferred to Beijing, Deng Xiaoping's promise that "dancing and horseracing would continue unabated" has been kept. "U.S. aircraft carriers still drop anchor and disgorge their crews into the Wanchai district's red-light bars. Anti-China demonstrators continue their almost weekly parades through the Central district. . . . Meanwhile, the People's Liberation Army has made a virtue of being invisible."[73] It seems that fears of Hong Kong becoming just another Chinese city were misplaced.

China's leaders have promised that for 50 years after 1997, the relationship between China and the Hong Kong Special Administrative Region will be "one country, two systems." Moreover, China's leaders clearly want their cities to look more like Hong Kong, not the other way around. In fact, with China's commercial banks starting to act much the same as banks in any capitalist economy, the phasing out of China's state-run economy in favor of a market economy, a budding stock market, billions of dollars in foreign investment, and entry into the World Trade Organization, China's economy is looking more like Hong Kong's and less like a centrally planned socialist economy. China's leaders have repeatedly stated the importance of foreign investment, greater openness, and experimentation; and they are doing

everything possible to integrate the country into the global economy. The imposition of a socialist economy on Hong Kong is, at this point, unthinkable.

China's political arena is also changing so profoundly that the two systems, which just 20 years ago seemed so far apart, are now much closer. China has undergone some political liberalization, (increasing electoral rights at the local level, permitting freedom in individual lifestyles, mobility, and job selection, and according greater freedom to the mass media). The rapid growth of private property and business interests is also bringing significant social change to China, including the proliferation of interest groups and associations to promote their members' interests.

Southern China's extraordinary economic boom has made Hong Kong optimistic about the future. Many of its residents see a new "dragon" emerging, one that combines Hong Kong's technology and skills with China's labor and resources. Others, however, do not see Hong Kong happily working as one unit with China. Instead, they see Hong Kong as a rival competing with Shanghai and with the many new ports that China is building; and even with Shenzhen, which borders Hong Kong and also now has a deepwater container port. Shenzhen is developing a high-quality pool of labor that costs just one-tenth that of Hong Kong, so many corporations are moving their operations—and their wealth—across the border to China. Moreover, the P.R.C. no longer needs Hong Kong as an entrepôt to export its products. Not only can it now do so through its own ports, but it is also building plants in other countries, such as India, where it will manufacture and export goods that otherwise would have gone through Hong Kong. In addition, China's membership in the WTO as of 2001, as well as its increasingly direct contacts and trade with Taiwan, could easily lead to a partial eclipse of Hong Kong.

Some Hong Kong analysts believe that the greatest threat to Hong Kong's success is not political repression and centralized control from Beijing; rather, it would take the more insidious form of China's bureaucracy and corruption simply smothering Hong Kong's economic vitality. One concern is that mainland companies operating in Hong Kong may be allowed to stand above the law or to use their Hong Kong ties to exert inappropriate influence on behalf of pro-China business interests and corrupt the Hong Kong economy.[74] So far, Hong Kong has escaped this fate, and is still considered one of the least corrupt business environments in the world. Another concern is that China may bring the features of the Singapore political model to

Hong Kong, whereby it would be ruled by pro-China business tycoons who are insensitive to the political, social, and economic concerns of other groups, and where democratic parties would find it impossible to gain a majority in a legislative system stacked against them. Political rights and freedom would also be restricted by moving toward a Singapore political model.[75] Yet another worry is that the dangers lie *within* Hong Kong, notably the minimalist efforts of the Hong Kong government to reshape it in a way that allows it to remain competitive.

Timeline: PAST

A.D. 1839–1842
The first Opium War between China and Great Britain. Ends with Treaty of Nanjing, which cedes Hong Kong to Britain

1860
The Chinese cede Kowloon and Stonecutter Island to Britain. They became part of Hong Kong

1898
England gains a 99-year lease on the New Territories, which also became part of Hong Kong

1911
A revolution ends the Manchu Dynasty; the Republic of China is established

1941
The Japanese attack Pearl Harbor and take Hong Kong; Hong Kong falls under Japanese control

1949
The Communist victory in China produces massive immigration into Hong Kong

1980s
Great Britain and China agree to the return of Hong Kong to China

1990s
China resumes control of Hong Kong on July 1, 1997

PRESENT

1997–2002
Hong Kong's efforts to recover from the Asian economic and financial crisis are hindered by a worldwide economic downturn

2003
Outbreak of SARS. After massive demonstrations, government withdraws bill to amend the Basic Law, Article 23, on sedition from further consideration

2005
Chief Executive Tung Chee-hwa abruptly resigns. Donald Tsang becomes the new Chief Executive.

2007
Donald Tsang is re-elected

2008
LegCo election

Beijing has an important stake in its take-over of Hong Kong not being perceived as disruptive to its political or economic system, and that Hong Kong's residents and the international business community believe in its future prosperity. Policies and events that threatened that confidence in the 1980s led to the loss of many of Hong Kong's most talented people, technological know-how, and investment. China does not want to risk losing still more.[76] Beijing also wants to maintain Hong Kong as a major free port and the regional center of trade, financing, shipping, and information—although it is also doing everything possible to turn Shanghai into a competitive center.[77]

William Overholt has labeled the major underlying sources of tension between Hong Kong and Beijing as the "Three Confusions:" Beijing's "confusion of Hong Kong, where there is virtually no separatist sentiment, with Taiwan;" confusion due to a failure to distinguish between the types of lawful demonstrations that have traditionally taken place in Hong Kong on a regular basis "with disruptive demonstrations in the mainland;" and confusion because of Beijing's failure to distinguish between some of the older leaders of the democracy movement "with the moderate loyal sentiments of the overwhelming majority of the democratic movement."[78] To the degree that China can eliminate such confusion, it will be able to avoid many problems with Hong Kong.

Finally, regardless of official denials by the government in Taiwan, Beijing's successful management of "one country, two systems" in Hong Kong will profoundly affect how Taiwan feels about its own peaceful integration with the mainland. If Beijing wants to regain control of Taiwan by peaceful means, it is critical that it handle Hong Kong well.

NOTES

1. R. G. Tiedemann, "Chasing the Dragon," *China Now,* No. 132 (February 1990), p. 21.

2. Jan S. Prybyla, "The Hong Kong Agreement and Its Impact on the World Economy," in Jurgen Domes and Yu-ming Shaw, eds., *Hong Kong: A Chinese and International Concern* (Boulder, CO: Westview Special Studies on East Asia, 1988), p. 177.

3. Tiedemann, p. 22.

4. Steven Tsang, *A Modern History of Hong Kong* (New York: I.B.Tauris, 2004), p. 271.

5. Siu-kai Lau, "The Hong Kong Policy of the People's Republic of China, 1949–1997," *Journal of Contemporary China* (March 2000), Vol. 9, No. 23, p. 81.

6. Tsang, pp. 133–135.

7. Robin McLaren, former British ambassador to China, seminar at Cambridge University, Centre for International Relations (February 28, 1996).

8. Ambrose Y. C. King, "The Hong Kong Talks and Hong Kong Politics," in Domes and Shaw, p. 49.

9. Hungdah Chiu, Y. C. Jao, and Yual-li Wu, *The Future of Hong Kong: Toward 1997 and Beyond* (New York: Quorum Books, 1987), pp. 5–6.

10. Siu-kai Lau, "Hong Kong's 'Ungovernability' in the Twilight of Colonial Rule," in Zhiling, Lin and Thomas W. Robinson, *The Chinese and Their Future: Beijing, Taipei, and Hong Kong* (Washington, D.C.: The American Enterprise Institute Press, 1994), pp. 288–290.

11. McClaren.

12. McLaren noted that it was not easy to convince Prime Minister Thatcher in her "post-Falklands mood" (referring to Great Britain's successful defense of the Falkland Islands, 9,000 miles away, from being returned to Argentine rule), that Hong Kong could not stay under British administrative rule even after 1997.

13. T. L. Tsim, "Introduction," in T. L. Tsim and Bernard H. K. Luk, *The Other Hong Kong Report* (Hong Kong: The Chinese University Press, 1989), p. xxv.

14. Norman J. Miners, "Constitution and Administration," in Tsim and Luk, p. 2.

15. King, pp. 54–55.

16. Annex I, Nos. 1 and 4 of *The Basic Law of the Hong Kong Special Administrative Region of the People's Republic of China* (hereafter cited as *The Basic Law*). Printed in *Beijing Review,* Vol. 33, No. 18 (April 30–May 6, 1990), supplement. This document was adopted by the 7th National People's Congress on April 4, 1990.

17. For specifics, see Annex II of *The Basic Law* (1990).

18. Article 14, *The Basic Law* (1990).

19. Articles 27, 32, 33, and 36, *The Basic Law* (1990).

20. Tsang, p. 271.

21. Chinese cities on the mainland are overrun by transients. On a daily basis, Shanghai alone has well over a million visitors, largely a transient population of country people. Hong Kong does not feel that it can handle such an increase in its transient population.

22. James Tang and Shiu-hing (Sonny) Lo, University of Hong Kong, interview in Hong Kong (June 2000).

23. Michael E. DeGolyer, director, *1982–2007 Hong Kong Transition Project: Accountability & Article 23* (Hong Kong: Hong Kong Baptist University, December 2002), pp. 43–44. These newspapers include several that are pro-Beijing.

24. Tang and Lo.

25. In 1995, Hong Kong's per capita GDP was U.S.$23,500. Wang Gungwu and Wong Siu-lun, eds., *Hong Kong in the Asian-Pacific Region: Rising to the New Challenge* (Hong Kong: University of Hong Kong, 1997), p. 2.

26. James L. Watson, "McDonald's in Hong Kong: Consumerism, Dietary Change, and the Rise of a Children's Culture," in James L. Watson, ed., *Golden Arches East: McDonald's in East Asia* (Palo Alto, CA: Stanford University Press, 1997), pp. 77–109.

27. Tsim, in Tsim and Luk, p. xx.

28. Howard Gorges (South China Holdings Corporation), interview in Hong Kong (June 2000).

29. Wang and Wong, p. 3.

30. Keith B. Richburg, "Uptight Hong Kong Countdown," *The Washington Post* (July 2, 1996), pp. A1, A12.

31. An average apartment measures 20 feet by 23 feet, or 460 square feet.

32. Tsim, in Tsim and Luk, p. xxi.

33. The purchaser of the property pays tax, develops the property, and then pays a 2 percent tax on every real-estate transaction (renting or selling) that occurs thereafter.

34. Keith B. Richburg, "Chinese Muscle-Flexing Puts Hong Kong Under Pessimistic Pall," *The Washington Post* (December 26, 1996), p. A31.

35. For information on Hong Kong's problems with pollution, including from car emissions, see http://www.epd.gov.hk/epd/english/environmentinhk/air/air_maincontent.html

36. The Hong Kong Transition Project, *Parties, Policies, and Political Reform in Hong Kong* (Hong Kong: Hong Kong Baptist University, 2006), p. 15.

37. The six largest real-estate companies are among the top 20 companies in the Hang Seng Index of stocks. Others are banks and technology companies. The largest is Cheong Kong Holdings, under Li Kashing's control. Companies linked to him and his son accounted for 26 percent of the total market capitalization of the Hang Seng Index! *Asiaweek* (May 26, 2000), pp. 33–36.

38. Philip Bowring, "Meanwhile: China Changes, Not Hong Kong," *International Herald Tribune* (Feb. 12, 2007).

39. In surveys done since 1995, the percentage "satisfied" with the relationship with the mainland" has fluctuated widely. The lowest level of satisfaction (21 percent) was recorded in 1995, the highest (71 percent) in November 2005. The most recent survey, November 2006, recorded satisfaction at 62 percent. See The Hong Kong Transition Project, *Parties, Policies, and Political Reform in Hong Kong* (Hong Kong: Hong Kong Baptist University (2006), p. 51.

40. Al Reyes, journalist (*Asiaweek),* interview in Hong Kong (June 16, 2000).

41. "Is Hong Kong Ripe for a Bit of Central Planning?" *The Economist* (April 12, 1997).

42. Tammy Tam, "Shenzhen Industrial Estate Developed to Boost Military Funds," *The Hong-Kong Standard* (September 5, 1989), p. 1.

43. Shiu-hing Lo, "Hong Kong's Political Influence on South China," *Problems of Post-Communism,* Vol. 46, No. 4 (July/August 1999), pp. 33–41.

44. Tang and Lo; Christine Loh, LegCo legislator and founder of the Citizens' Party, interview in Hong Kong (June 2000). Loh did not run for reelection in September 2000. She is a businessperson-turned-politician. She has been a self-described "armchair critic" of the British and Hong Kong SAR governments, and is generally supportive of the business community.

45. Tang and Lo.

46. John Gordon Davies, "Introduction," *Hong Kong Through the Looking Glass* (Hong Kong: Kelly & Walsh, 1969).

47. Tang and Lo.

48. King, in Domes and Shaw, pp. 45–46.

49. Prybyla, in Domes and Shaw, pp. 196–197; and Lau, in Lin and Robinson, p. 302.

50. Lau, in Lin and Robinson, pp. 293–294, 304–305.

51. Willy Wo-Lap Lam, "New Faces to Star in Hong Kong's New Cabinet," CNN Web site (June 24, 2002).

52. In June 1997, just before the July 1 hand-over, only 45 percent were "satisfied," and 41 percent were "dissatisfied." DeGolyer, *Hong Kong Transition Project,* 1982–2007, Table 145, p. 103; http://www.hkbu.edu.hk/ hktp.

53. Hong Kong Transition Project, *Listening to the Wisdom of the Masses:Hong Kong People's Attitudes toward Constitutional Reforms* (Hong Kong: Civic Exchange and Hong Kong Transition Project, 2004), Tables 38, 135, 9, pp. 32, 68, 14.

54. Loh, interview.

55. "Silent Treatment: Hong Kong's Chief and Its Legislature Aren't Talking," *Far Eastern Economic Review* (September 17, 1998), p. 50. Hong Kong Transition Project, *Listening to the Wisdom,* Table 25, pp. 22–23.

56. Hong Kong Transition Project, *Listening to the Wisdom* (2004), Table 135, p. 68.

57. Frank Ching, "Beijing Loath to Cast the Fate of Elections in Hong Kong to the Wind," *The Japan Times,* August 2, 2006.

58. The Hong Kong Transition Project, *Parties, Policies, and Political Reform in Hong Kong,* (2006), p. 54.

59. Data based on surveys done in November 2002. The government submitted the proposed changes to Article 23 two months earlier. In almost all categories of rights, and across all occupations, ages, education, and so on, Hong Kong people showed an increase in concern about rights because of the potential amendments to Article 23. Hong Kong Transition Project, *Listening to the Wisdom,* (2004) pp. 36–39, 49–66.

60. Ibid., Table 38, p. 32.

61. King, in Domes and Shaw, pp. 51, 56, 57.

62. In the 1998 elections, 20 members of LegCo were for the first time elected directly; and of these, 13 seats went to the Democratic Party. Of the remaining 40 seats, which were indirectly elected, seven went to the Democratic Party.

63. Mark Magnier, "Hong Kong Warned to Drop Vote Idea," *LA Times,* Nov. 10, 2004.

64. Loh, interview (June 2000).

65. Alvin Y. So, "Hong Kong's Problematic Democratic Transition: Power Dependency or Business Hegemony? *The Journal of Asian Studies,* Vol. 59, No. 2 (May 2000), pp. 375–376.

66. According to the Hong Kong Transition Project 2000 polls, only 30 percent of the people believe that political parties wield significant influence on the government, whereas 74 percent think that Beijing officials do. Michael E. DeGolyer, director, *The Hong Kong Transition Project: 1982–2007* (Hong Kong: Hong Kong Baptist University, 2000), p. 25.

67. James L. Tyson, "Promises, Promises. . . ." *The Christian Science Monitor* (April 20, 1989), p. 2.

68. "Another Place, Another Crime: Mainland Trial of Alleged Gangster Puts 'One Country, Two Systems' to Test," *Far Eastern Economic Review* (November 5, 1998), pp. 26–27.

69. DeGolyer, The Hong Kong Transition (2000) 2000, pp. 3–8. Of students, 54 percent are satisfied, 28 percent neutral.

70. Kevin Murphy, "Troops for Hong Kong: China Puts Best Face on It," *The International Herald Tribune* (January 30, 1996), p. 4.

71. Miu-wah Ma, "China Warns Against Political Ties Abroad," *The Hong Kong Standard* (September 1, 1989), p. 4; and Viola Lee, "China 'Trying to Discourage HK People,' " *South China Morning Post* (August 21, 1989). The article, which originally appeared in an *RMRB* article in July, was elaborated upon in the August edition of *Outlook Weekly,* a mouthpiece of the CCP.

72. The Hong Kong Transition Project, *Parties, Policies, and Political Reform in Hong Kong* (2006), p. 19.

73. "Hong Kong: Now the Hard Part," *Far Eastern Economic Review* (June 11, 1998), p. 13.

74. Michael C. Davis, "Constitutionalism and Hong Kong's Future," *Journal of Contemporary China* (July 1999), Vol. 8, No. 21, pp. 271.

75. *Ibid.,* pp. 269, 273.

76. For extensive surveys on which types of people might want to leave Hong Kong, and for what reasons, see The Hong Kong Transition Project, *Parties, Policies, and Political Reform in Hong Kong* (Hong Kong: Hong Kong Baptist University, 2006.

77. Kai-Yin Lo, "A Big Awakening for Chinese Rivals: Hong Kong and Shanghai Look Afar," *International Herald Tribune,* January 20, 2005.

78. William Overholt, Testimony, "The Hong Kong Legislative Election of Sept 12, 2004: Assessment and Implications" (Testimony presented to the Congressional-Executive Commission on China on Sept. 23, 2004), (Santa Monica: RAND Corporation, 2004), p. 7.

Taiwan Map

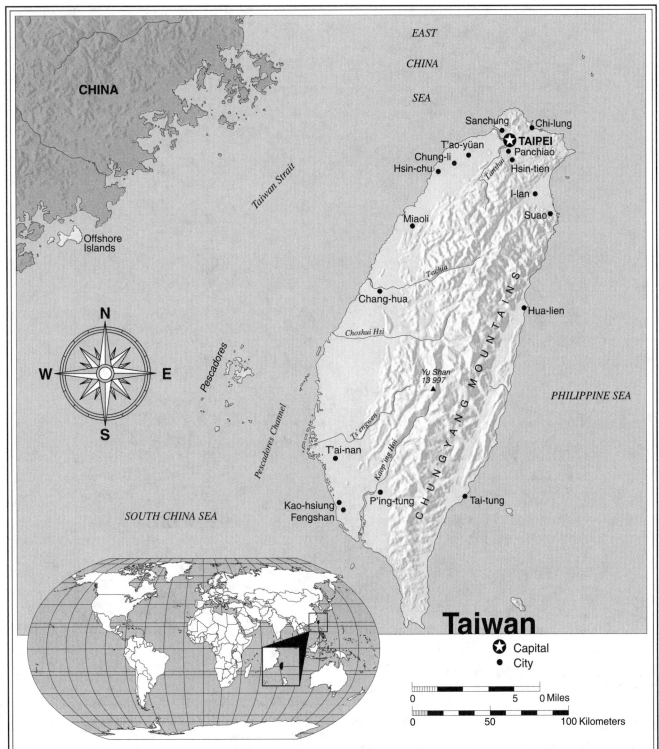

Taiwan was the center of the government of the Republic of China (Nationalist China) after 1949. According to international law, Taiwan is a part of China. Taiwan consists of the main island, 15 islands in the Offshore Islands group, and 64 islands in the Pescadores Archipelago. While the Pescadores are close to Taiwan, the Offshore Islands are only a few miles off the coast of mainland China.

Taiwan

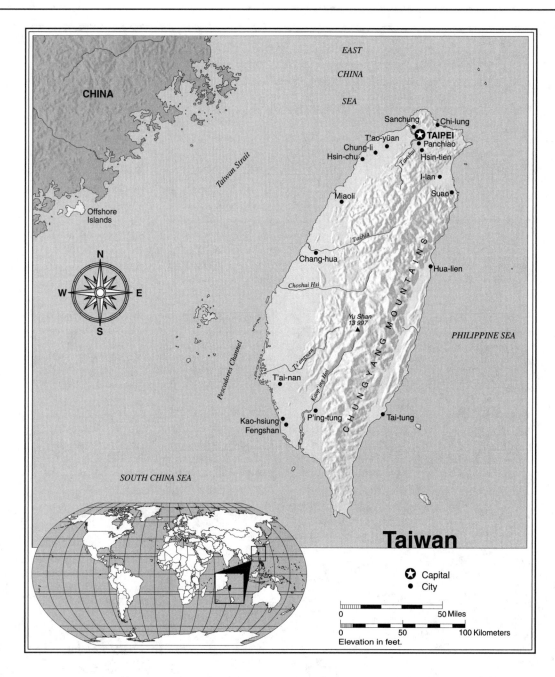

Taiwan Statistics

GEOGRAPHY

Area in Square Miles (Kilometers):
13,892 (35,980) (slightly smaller than Maryland and Delaware combined)
Capital (Population): Taipei (2,622,933) (September 2008)
Environmental Concerns: water and air pollution; contamination of drinking water; radioactive waste; trade in endangered species

Geographical Features: mostly rugged mountains in east; flat to gently rolling plains in west
Climate: tropical; marine

PEOPLE

Population

Total: 22,920,946 (July 2008 est.)
Population Growth Rate: 0.238% (2008 est.)

Sex Ratio: 1.0175 male(s)/female (2008 est.)
Life Expectancy: Total Population: 77.76 years (*male:* 74.89 years; *female:* 80.89 years) (2008 est.)
Total Fertility Rate: 1.13 children born/woman (2008 est.)
Religions: mixture of Buddhist and Taoist 93%; Christian 4.5%; other 2.5%
Languages: Mandarin Chinese (official), Taiwanese, Hakka dialects

Education

Adult Literacy Rate: 96.1%

ECONOMY

Currency: New Taiwan dollar (TWD)
Exchange Rate: U.S.$1 = 33.4 TWD
(December 2008)
GDP (Purchasing Power Parity):
$695.4 billion (2007 est.)
GDP (Official Exchange Rate):
$383.3 billion (2007 est.)
GDP Real Growth Rate: 5.7% (2007 est.)
*GDP Per Capita (Purchasing Power
Parity):* $30,100 (2007 est.)
GDP Composition by Sector: agriculture:
1.4%; industry: 27.5%; services:
71.1% (2007 est.)
Unemployment Rate: 3.9% (2007 est.)
Inflation Rate (Consumer Prices): 1.8%
(2007 est.)
Exports: $246.5 billion f.o.b. (2007 est.)
Exports Commodities: electronic and
electrical products; metals; textiles;
plastics; chemicals; auto parts (2002)
Exports Partners: China 32.4%; U.S.
12.9%; Hong Kong 8.5%; Japan 6.4%;
Singapore 5% (2007)
Imports: $215.1 billion f.o.b. (2007 est.)
Imports Commodities: electronic and
electrical products; machinery;
petroleum; precision instruments;
organic chemicals; metals (2002)
Imports Partners: Japan 22.1%; U.S.
13%; China 10.9%; South Korea 7.3%;
Saudi Arabia 4.8%; Singapore 4.5%
(2007)

COMMUNICATION

Telephones—Main Lines: 14.497 million
(2006)
Telephones—Mobile Cellular:
24.302 million (2007)
Television Broadcast Stations: 76 (46
digital and 30 analog) (2007)
Internet Users: 14.76 million (2007)

TRANSPORTATION

Airports: 41 (2007)
Railways: 1,588 km (2007)
Roadways: 40,262 km; 38,171 km paved
(includes 976 km of expressways)
(2007)
Ports: Chilung (Keelung), Kaohsiung,
Taichung

GOVERNMENT

Government Type: multiparty democracy
Major Parties: Kuomintang (Chinese
Nationalist Party); Democratic
Progressive Party; People First
Party; Taiwan Solidarity Union;
New Party
National Day: October 10 (Anniversary
of the Chinese Revolution in 1911)
Head of State: Ma Ying-jeou (since May
2008)
Head of Government: Premier (President
of the Executive Yuan) Lio Chao-
shiuan (since May 2008)
Suffrage: universal at 20 years of age

MILITARY

Military Branches: Army, Navy
(includes Marine Corps), Air Force,
Coast Guard Administration, Armed
Forces Reserve Command, Combined
Service Forces Command, Armed
Forces Police Command
Military Expenditures: 2.2% of GDP
(2006)

SUGGESTED WEB SITES

http://www.cia.gov/library/publications/
the-world-factbook/geos/tw.html
http://www.gio.gov.tw
http://www.etaiwannews.com/Taiwan
http://www.mac.gov
.tw/english/index1-e.htm

Taiwan Report

Taiwan, today a powerful economic player in Asia, was once an obscure island off the coast of China, just 90 miles away. Taiwan has also been known as Formosa, Free China, the Republic of China, Nationalist China and Republic of China on Taiwan. It was originally inhabited by aborigines from Southeast Asia. By the seventh century A.D., Chinese settlers had begun to arrive. The island was subsequently "discovered" by the Portuguese in 1590, and Dutch as well as Spanish settlers followed. Today, the aborigines' descendants, who have been pushed into the remote mountain areas by the Chinese settlers, number under 400,000, a small fraction of the 23 million people now living in Taiwan. Most of the population is descended from people who emigrated from the Chinese mainland's southern provinces before 1885, when Taiwan officially became a province of China. Although their ancestors originally came from China, they are known as *Taiwanese,* as distinct from the Chinese who fled the mainland from 1947 to 1949. The latter are called *Mainlanders* and represent less than 20 percent of the island's population. After 1949, the Mainlanders dominated Taiwan's political elite; but the "Taiwanization" of the political realm that began after Chiang Kai-shek's death in 1975 and the political liberalization since 1988 have allowed the native Taiwanese to take up their rightful place within the elite.

The Manchus, "barbarians" who came from the north, overthrew the Chinese rulers on the mainland in 1644 and established the Qing Dynasty. In 1683, they conquered Taiwan; but because Taiwan was an island 90 miles distant from the mainland and China's seafaring abilities were limited, the Manchus paid little attention to it and exercised minimal sovereignty over the Taiwanese people. With China's defeat in the Sino–Japanese War (1894–1895), the Qing was forced to cede Taiwan to the Japanese. The Taiwanese people refused to accept Japanese rule, however, and proclaimed Taiwan a republic. As a result, the Japanese had to use military force to gain actual control over Taiwan.

For the next 50 years, Taiwan remained under Japan's colonial administration. Japan helped to develop Taiwan's agricultural sector, a modern transportation network, and an economic structure favorable to later industrial development. Furthermore, the Japanese developed an educated workforce, which proved critical to Taiwan's economic growth.

With Japan's defeat at the end of World War II (in 1945), Taiwan reverted to China's sovereignty. In the meantime, the Chinese had overthrown the Manchu Dynasty (1911) and established a republican form of government on the mainland. Beginning in 1912, China was known as the Republic of China (R.O.C.). Thus, when Japan was defeated in 1945, it was Chiang Kai-shek who, as head of the R.O.C. government, accepted the return of the island province of Taiwan to R.O.C. rule. When some of Chiang Kaishek's forces were dispatched to shore up control in Taiwan in 1947, tensions quickly arose between them and the native Taiwanese. The ragtag, undisciplined military forces of the KMT (the Kuomintang, or Nationalist Party) met with hatred and contempt from the local people. They had grown accustomed to the orderliness and professionalism of the Japanese occupation forces and were angered by the incompetence and corruption of KMT officials. Demonstrations against

MCCARTHYISM: ISOLATING AND CONTAINING COMMUNISM

The McCarthy period in the United States was an era of rabid anti-communism. McCarthyism was based in part on the belief that the United States was responsible for losing China to the Communists in 1949 and that the reason for this loss was the infiltration of the U.S. government by Communists. As a result, Senator Joseph McCarthy *(pictured here)* spearheaded a "witchhunt" to ferret out those who allegedly were selling out American interests to the Communists. McCarthyism took advantage of the national mood in the Cold War era that had begun in 1947. At that time, the world was seen as being divided into two opposing camps: Communists and capitalists.

The major strategy of the Cold War, as outlined by President Harry Truman in 1947, was the "containment" of communism. This strategy was based on the belief that if the United States attempted—as it had done with Adolf Hitler's aggression against Czechoslovakia (the first step toward World War II)—to appease communism, it would spread beyond its borders and threaten other free countries.

The purpose of the Cold War strategy was, then, to contain the Communists within their national boundaries and to isolate them by hindering their participation in the international economic system and in international organizations. Hence, in the case of China, there was an American-led boycott against all Chinese goods, and the

Wisconsin Historical Society (WHi8006)

Joseph McCarthy.

United States refused to recognize the People's Republic of China as the legitimate representative of the Chinese people within international organizations.

---

rule by Mainlanders occurred in February 1947. Relations were badly scarred when KMT troops killed thousands of Taiwanese opposed to mainland rule. Among those murdered were many members of the island's political and intellectual elite.

Meanwhile, the KMT's focus remained on the mainland, where, under the leadership of General Chiang Kai-shek, it continued to fight the Chinese Communists in a civil war that had ended their fragile truce during World War II. Civil war raged from 1945 to 1949 and diverted the KMT's attention away from Taiwan. As a result, Taiwan continued, as it had under the Qing Dynasty's rule, to function quite independently of Beijing. In 1949, when it became clear that the Chinese Communists would defeat the KMT, General Chiang and some 2 million members of his loyal military, political, and commercial elite fled to Taiwan, moving with them the R.O.C. government which they claim to be the true government of China. This declaration reflected Chiang's determination to regain control over the mainland, and his conviction that the more than 600 million people living on the mainland would welcome the return of the KMT to power.

During the McCarthy period of the "red scare" in the 1950s (during which Americans believed to be Communists or Communist sympathizers—"reds"—were persecuted by the U.S. government), the United States supported Chiang Kai-shek. In response to the Chinese Communists' entry into the Korean War in 1950, the United States applied its Cold War policies

of support for any Asian government that was anti-Communist, regardless of how dictatorial and ruthless it might be, in order to "isolate and contain" the Chinese Communists. It was within this context that in 1950, the United States committed itself to the military defense of Taiwan and the off-shore islands in the Taiwan Strait, by ordering the U.S. Seventh Fleet to the Strait and by giving large amounts of military and economic aid to Taiwan. General Chiang Kai-shek continued to lead the government of the Republic of China on Taiwan until his death in 1975, at which time his son, Chiang Ching-kuo, succeeded him.

One China, Two Governments

Taiwan's position in the international community and its relationship to the government in Beijing have been determined by perceptions and values as much as by actions. In 1949, when the R.O.C. government fled to Taiwan, the Chinese Communists renamed China the "People's Republic of China" (P.R.C.), and they proclaimed the R.O.C. government illegitimate. Later, Mao Zedong, the P.R.C.'s preeminent leader until his death in 1976, was to say that adopting the new name instead of keeping the name "Republic of China" was the biggest mistake he ever made, for it laid the groundwork for future claims of "two Chinas." Beijing claimed that the P.R.C. was the legitimate government of all of China, including Taiwan. Beijing's attempt to regain de facto control over Taiwan was, however, forestalled first by the

outbreak of the Korean War and thereafter by the presence of the U.S. Seventh Fleet in the Taiwan Strait.

Beijing has always insisted that Taiwan is an "internal" Chinese affair, that international law is therefore irrelevant, and that other countries have no right to interfere. For its part, until 1995, the government of Taiwan agreed that there was only one China and that Taiwan was a province of China. But by 1995–1996, the political parties had begun debating the possibility of Taiwan declaring itself an independent state.

Although the Chinese Communists' control over the mainland was long evident to the world, the United States managed to keep the R.O.C. in the China seat at the United Nations by insisting that the issue of China's representation in the United Nations was an "important question." This meant that a two-thirds affirmative vote of the UN General Assembly, rather than a simple majority, was required. With support from its allies, the United States was able to block the P.R.C. from winning this two-thirds vote until 1971. Once Secretary of State Henry Kissinger announced his secret trip to Beijing in the summer of 1971 and that President Richard Nixon would be going to China in 1972, the writing was on the wall. Allies of the United States knew that U.S. recognition of Beijing as China's legitimate government would eventually occur, so there would no longer be pressure to block the P.R.C. from membership in the United Nations. They quickly jumped ship and voted for Beijing's representation.

CHIANG KAI-SHEK: DETERMINED TO RETAKE THE MAINLAND

Until his dying day, President Chiang Kai-shek, whose memorial hall is *pictured here,* maintained that the military, led by the KMT (Kuomintang, or Nationalist Party), would one day return to the mainland and, with the support of the Chinese people living there, defeat the Communist government. During the years of Chiang's presidency, banner headlines proclaimed daily that the Communist "bandits" would soon be turned out by internal rebellion and that the KMT would return to control on the mainland. In the last years of Chiang Kai-shek's life, when he was generally confined to his residence and incapable of directing the government, his son, Chiang Ching-kuo, always had two editions of the newspaper made that proclaimed such unlikely feats, so that his father would continue to believe these were the primary goals of the KMT government in Taiwan. In fact, a realistic appraisal of the situation had been made long before Chiang's death in 1975, and most of the members of the KMT only pretended to believe that recovery of the mainland was imminent.

Chiang Ching-kuo, although continuing to strengthen Taiwan's defenses, turned his efforts to building Taiwan into an economic showcase in Asia. Taiwan's remarkable growth and a certain degree of political liberalization were the hallmarks of his leadership. A man of the people, he shunned many of the elitist practices of his father and the KMT ruling elite, and he helped to bring about the Taiwanization of both the KMT party and the government. The "Chiang dynasty" in Taiwan came to an end with Chiang Ching-kuo's death in 1988. It was, in fact, Chiang Ching-kuo who made certain of this, by barring his own sons from succeeding him and by grooming his own successor, a native Taiwanese.

Public Domain

Chiang Kai-shek memorial.

As the Taiwanese have gained an increasing amount of power in the last 20 years, they have reasserted their Taiwanese identity. This has led to a fading out of the two Chiangs from Taiwan's history books and public images.

At this critical moment, when the R.O.C.'s right to represent "China" in the United Nations was withdrawn, the R.O.C. could have put forward the claim that Taiwan had the right to be recognized as an independent state, or at least to be granted observer status. Instead, the R.O.C. steadfastly maintained that there was but one China and that Taiwan was merely a province of China. As a result, today Taiwan has no representation in any major international organization under the name of "Republic of China;" and it has representation only as "Chinese Taipei" in organizations in which the P.R.C. is a member—if the P.R.C. allows it any representation at all. With few exceptions, however, Beijing has been adamant about not permitting Taiwan's representation regardless of what it is called.[1]

It is important to understand that at the time Taiwan lost its seat in the United Nations, it was still ruled by the KMT mainlanders, under the name of the Republic of China. The "Taiwanization" of the ruling KMT party-state did not begin until the mid 1970s. As a result, the near 85 percent of the population that was native Taiwanese lacked the right to express their preference for rule by native Taiwanese rather than KMT mainlanders, much less their desire for a declaration of independent statehood. Under martial law, those who had dared to

demand independence were imprisoned, forcing the Taiwan independence movement to locate outside of Taiwan. In short, most of the decisions that have shaped Taiwan's international legal standing through treaties and diplomatic relations were made when the KMT mainlanders held political power. Only after the abandonment of martial law in 1987, and the KMT's decision to allow competing political parties, did the Taiwanese start to assert a different view of Taiwan's future. By then, many would agree, it was too late.

INTERNATIONAL RECOGNITION OF THE P.R.C., AT TAIWAN'S EXPENSE

The seating of the P.R.C. in the United Nations in 1971 thus led to the collapse of Taiwan's independent political standing as the R.O.C. in international affairs. Not wanting to anger China, which has a huge and growing economy and significant military power, the state members of international organizations have given in to Beijing's unrelenting pressure to exclude Taiwan. Furthermore, Beijing insists that in bilateral state-to-state relations, any state wishing to maintain diplomatic relations with it must accept China's "principled stand" on Taiwan—notably, that Taiwan is a province of China and that the People's Republic of China is its sole representative.

Commercial ventures, foreign investment in Taiwan, and Taiwan's investments abroad have suffered little as a result of countries' severing their *diplomatic* relations with Taipei. After being forced to close all but a handful of its embassies as one state after another switched recognition from the R.O.C. to the P.R.C., Taipei simply substituted offices that function as if they are embassies. They handle all commercial, cultural, and official business, including the issuance of visas to those traveling to Taiwan. Similarly, the states that severed relations with Taipei have closed down their embassies there and reopened them as business and cultural offices. The American Institute in Taiwan is a typical example of these efforts to retain ties without formal diplomatic recognition.

Still, Taiwan's government feels the sting of being almost completely shut out of the official world of international affairs. Its increasing frustration and sense of humiliation came to a head in early 1996. Under intense pressure to respond to demands from its people that Taiwan get the international recognition that it deserved for its remarkable accomplishments, Taiwan's president, Lee Teng-hui, engaged in a series of maneuvers to get the international community to confer de facto recognition of its statehood. Not the least of these bold forays was President

Lee's offer of U.S. $1 billion to the United Nations in return for a seat for Taiwan—an offer rejected by the United Nations' secretary-general.

Lee's campaign for election in the spring of 1996 proved to be the final straw for Beijing. Lee had as one of his central themes the demand for greater international recognition of Taiwan as an independent state. Beijing responded with a military buildup of some 200,000 troops in Fujian Province across the Taiwan Strait, and the "testing" of missiles in the waters around Taiwan. Under pressure from the United States not to provoke a war with the mainland, and a refusal on the part of the United States to say exactly what it would do if a war occurred, President Lee toned down his campaign rhetoric. A military conflict was averted. Since 1996, the pattern of Taiwan aggressively discussing independence, followed by China threatening the use of military force and the U.S. warning Taiwan to refrain from rhetoric about independence, has become well-established.

THE OFFSHORE ISLANDS

Crises of serious dimensions erupted between China and the United States in 1954–1955, 1958, 1960, and 1962 over the blockading of supplies to the Taiwan-controlled Offshore Islands in the Taiwan Strait. Thus, the perceived importance of these tiny islands grew out of all proportion to their intrinsic worth. The two major island groups, Quemoy (about two miles from the Chinese mainland) and Matsu (about eight miles from the mainland) are located about 90 miles from Taiwan. As a consequence, Taiwan's control of them made them strategically valuable for pursuing the government's professed goal of retaking the mainland—and valuable for psychologically linking Taiwan to the mainland.

In the first years after their victory on the mainland, the Chinese Communists shelled the Offshore Islands at regular intervals. When there was not a crisis, their shells were filled with pro-Communist propaganda materials, which littered the islands. When the Chinese Communists wanted to test the American commitment to the Nationalists in Taiwan and the Soviet commitment to their own objectives, they shelled the islands heavily and intercepted supplies to the islands. In the end, China always backed down; but in 1958 and 1962, it did so only after going to the brink of war with the United States. By 1979, most states had affirmed Beijing's claim that Taiwan was a province of China through diplomatic recognition of the P.R.C. Beijing's subsequent "peace initiatives" toward Taiwan moved the confrontation over the Offshore Islands to the level of an exchange of gifts by balloons and packages floated across the channel. As a 1986 commentary noted:

> The Nationalists load their balloons and seaborne packages with underwear, children's shoes, soap, toys, blankets, transistor radios and tape recorders, as well as cookies emblazoned with Chiang Ching-kuo's picture and audio tapes of Taiwan's top popular singer, Theresa Teng, a mainland favorite.
>
> The Communists send back beef jerky, tea, herbal medicines, mao-tai and cigarettes, as well as their own varieties of soap and toys.[2]

Because of the dramatic increase in contacts, tourism, trade, and smuggling since the early 1990s, however, such practices have ceased.

The lack of industry and manufacturing on the Offshore Islands led to a steady emigration of their natives to Southeast Asia for better jobs. The civilian population is about 50,000 (mostly farmers) in Quemoy and about 6,000 (mostly fishermen) in Matsu. Until the mid-1990s, the small civilian population in Quemoy was significantly augmented by an estimated 100,000 soldiers. The heavily fortified islands appeared to be somewhat deserted, since the soldiers lived mostly underground: hospitals, kitchens, sleeping quarters—everything was located in tunnels blasted out of granite, including two-lane highways that could accommodate trucks and tanks. Heavily camouflaged anti-artillery aircraft dotted the landscape, and all roads were reinforced to carry tanks.

Taiwan's military administration of Quemoy and Matsu ended in 1992.

Today, Taiwan's armed forces are streamlined, with only some 10,000 troops remaining on the Offshore Islands. Taiwan's Ministry of Defense believes, however, that these troops are better able than the former, larger forces to protect the Offshore Islands, because of improved weapons and technology. Many of the former military installations have become profit-making tourist attractions. Moreover, as of January 2001, the "three mini-links" policy was initiated, with both Quemoy and Matsu allowed to engage in direct trade, transportation, and postal exchange with the mainland. In truth, this change only legalized what had been going on for more than a decade—namely, a roaring trade in smuggled goods between the Offshore Islands and the mainland. Taiwan now seems far more interested in boosting the economy of these islands and increasing links with the mainland than it is concerned with the islands becoming hostages of the mainland. Indeed, Taiwan has moved forward with a plan to secure water for the islands from the mainland, to cope with an increased demand for water it assumes will be generated by growing tourism and business activities.[3] (The first PRC tourists went to Quemoy in Sept. 2004.)

Thus one fiction—that there was no direct trade between Taiwan's Offshore Islands and the mainland—has been abolished. Other fictions wait to be dismantled as Taiwan and the mainland move toward further integration. For example, there is still not supposed to be direct trade between the island of Taiwan and the mainland. All ships are supposed to transship their goods by way of another port, such as Hong Kong or the Ryuku Islands. But now, as soon as ships have left Taiwan, they simply process paperwork with port authorities in the Ryuku Islands by way of fax—that is, without actually ever going there—so they can go directly to the mainland. This eliminates the expensive formalities of transshipments via another port. In short, direct trade has actually been in existence for almost a decade.

CULTURE AND SOCIETY

Taiwan is a bundle of contradictions: "great tradition, small island; conservative state, drastic change; cultural imperialism, committed nationalism; localist sentiment, cosmopolitan sophistication."[4] Over time, Taiwan's culture has been shaped by various cultural elements—Japanese, Chinese, and American culture; localism, nationalism, cosmopolitanism, materialism; and even Chinese mainland culture (in the form of "mainland mania"). At any one time, several of these forces have coexisted and battled for dominance. As Taiwan has become increasingly affected by globalization, the power of the central government to control cultural development has diminished. This has unleashed not just global cultural forces but also local *Taiwanese* culture.[5]

The Taiwanese people were originally immigrants from the Chinese mainland; but their culture, which developed in isolation from that of the mainland, is not the same as the "Chinese" culture of the defeated "Mainlanders" who arrived from 1947 to 1949. Although the Nationalists saw Taiwan largely in terms of security and as a bastion from which to fight against and defeat the Chinese Communist regime on the mainland, "it also cultivated Taiwan as the last outpost of traditional Chinese high culture. Taiwanese folk arts, in particular opera and festivals, did thrive, but as low culture."[6]

The Taiwanese continue to speak their own dialect of Chinese (Taiwanese), distinct from the standard Chinese spoken by the Mainlanders, and almost all Taiwanese engage in local folk-religion practices. However, until the mid-1990s, the Mainlander-controlled central government dictated a cultural policy that emphasized Chinese cultural values in education and the mass media. As a result, the distinctions institutionalized in a political system that discriminated against the Taiwanese were culturally reinforced.

The Taiwanese grew increasingly resistant to efforts by the KMT Mainlanders to "Sinify" them—to force them to speak standard Chinese and to adopt the values of the dominant Chinese Mainlander elite. By the 1990s, state-controlled television offered many programs in the Taiwanese dialect. Today, Taiwanese appear to have won the battle to maintain their cultural identity. Taiwanese legislators are refusing to use Chinese during the Legislature's proceedings, so now Mainlanders in the Legislative Yuan must learn Taiwanese. Indeed, the pendulum appears to have swung the other way, not just in language, but in terms of engineering an appropriate psycho-cultural milieu for an independent Taiwan. For example, former president Chen Shui-bian went through with plans to "de-Sinicise" Taiwan by ridding it of any symbolic connections with the mainland. Thus, he has changed the names of government agencies and state-owned corporations that have "China" in them (for example, China Steel Corporation was renamed Taiwan Steel Corporation). "De-Chiangification," echoing the unofficial but popular "de-Maoification" campaign on the Mainland in the early 1980s, has led to changing the name of the Chiang Kai-shek Airport to Taiwan Taoyuan International Airport, and the gradual disappearance of Chiang memorabilia and removal of icons and statues of Chiang K'ai-shek. Indeed the mayor of Kaoehsiung City personally oversaw the tearing down of a 24 foot high statue at the Chiang K'ai-shek Cultural Center, the second largest in Taiwan and then chopped it into two hundred pieces. Even Sun Yat-sen, the revolutionary who inspired the overthrow of the Manchu Dynasty in 1911, is fading from public memory. Sun Yat-sen established the Republic of China, and Chiang K'ai-shek was his heir to political power on the Mainland, and brought the rule of Chinese mainlanders to Taiwan under the name of Republic of China. In short, the DPP was trying to cut off the Taiwanese from their Chinese heritage. Cynics say the real motivation was that Chen Shui-bian would like to divert the Taiwanese from all the corruption charges he and other members of the DPP were facing. After Ma Ying-jeou became the President in 2008, many of the names have been changed back (for example, Taiwan Post is now China Post again). In any event, such

changes are merely a change in window dressing, given the billions of dollars of investment flowing from Taiwan into the mainland. Investments are doing far more to link Taiwan with the mainland than any mere name change can counter. And, ironically, in the convoluted cultural politics of Taiwan-Mainland relations, the Chinese on the Mainland are busily sprucing up sites for tourists that feature where Chiang K'ai-shek was born, slept, or marched through, and are in the market for the statues of that defeated KMT Generalissimo!

Generally speaking, however, Taiwanese and Mainlander culture need not be viewed as two cultures in conflict, for they share many commonalities. Now that Taiwanese have moved into leadership positions in what used to be exclusively Mainlander institutions, and intermarriage between the two groups has become more common, an amalgamation of Taiwanese and traditional Chinese practices is becoming evident throughout the society. As is discussed later in this report, the real source of conflict is the Taiwanese insistence that their culture and political system not be controlled by Chinese from the mainland, whether they be Nationalists or Communists.

On the other hand, rampant materialism as well as the importation of foreign ideas and goods are eroding both Taiwanese *and* Chinese values. For example, there are more than 3,000 7-Eleven outlets in Taiwan, and customers in central Taipei rarely have to walk more than a few blocks to get to the next one. Starbucks coffee houses, often much larger than those in the United States, are usually so packed it is hard to find a seat. Most major American fast-food franchises, such as Kentucky Fried Chicken and McDonald's, are ubiquitous. They provide "snack" food for Taiwan's teenagers and children—before they settle down for "real" (Chinese) food. The Big Mac culture affects more than waistlines, contributing as it does to a more globalized culture in Taiwan. Although the government has at various times engaged in campaigns to reassert traditional values, the point seems lost in its larger message, which asks all to contribute to making Taiwan an Asian showplace. The government's emphasis on hard work and economic prosperity has seemingly undercut its focus on traditional Chinese values of politeness, the sanctity of the family, and the teaching of culturally based ethics (such as filial piety) throughout the school system. Materialism and an individualism that focuses on personal needs and pleasure seeking are slowly undermining collectively oriented values.[7] In many ways, this seems to parallel what is happening on the China Mainland. In the meantime, unlike their mainland cousins, who have had a 40-

hour, five-day work week since 1996, the Taiwanese did not relinquish an exhausting six day, 48-hour work week until 2001. While playing a part in Taiwan's economic boom of the past decade, the emphasis on materialism has contributed to a variety of problems, not the least of which are the alienation of youth, juvenile crime, the loosening of family ties, and the general decline of community values. The pervasive spread of illicit sexual activities through such phony fronts as dance halls, bars, saunas, "barber shops," and movies on-video/DVD and music-video/DVD establishments, as well as hotels and brothels, grew so scandalous and detrimental to social morals and social order that at one point the government even suggested cutting off their electricity. They nevertheless continue to thrive. Another major activity that goes virtually uncontrolled is gambling. Part of the problem in clamping down on either illicit sexual activities or gambling (both of which are often combined with drinking in clubs) is that organized crime is involved; and that in exchange for bribes, the police look the other way.[8]

THE ENVIRONMENT

The pursuit of individual material benefit without a concomitant concern for the public good has led to uncontrolled growth and a rapid deterioration in the quality of life, even as the people in Taiwan become richer. As Taiwan struggles to catch up with its own success, the infrastructure has faltered. During the hot, humid summers in its largest city, Taipei, air is so dense with pollution that eyes water, hair falls out, and many people suffer from respiratory illnesses. Inadequate recreational facilities leave urban residents with few options but to join the long parade of cars out of the city on weekends, often only to arrive at badly polluted beaches. Taiwan's citizens have begun forming interest groups to address such problems, and public protests about the government's neglect of quality-of-life issues have grown increasingly frequent. Environmental groups, addressing such issues as wildlife conservation, industrial pollution, and waste disposal, have burgeoned; but environmental campaigns and legislation have difficulty keeping pace with the rapid growth of Taiwan's material culture. According to Taiwan's Environmental Protection Agency, for example, from 1990 to 2000, the amount of garbage produced doubled, but without a doubling of capacity to dispose of it. Part of the problem is that in addition to being a very small island, Taiwan is mostly mountainous, so there is virtually nowhere to construct new landfills. Old landfills are filled to capacity and are leaching toxins into the soil. It is not uncommon for garbage simply to be dumped into a river, or left to rot in gullies or wherever it can be dumped unobserved.[9] Some is taken out to sea, and drifts back to the beaches. But new laws that require citizens to sort their garbage into three categories (regular waste, kitchen leftovers, and recyclable materials), and allow the government to fine citizens who do not sort properly, are intended to bring significant declines in the amount of garbage.[10]

Taiwan must continue to battle against the polluting effects of rapidly increasing wealth; for with almost all Taiwanese families owning a refrigerator, air conditioner, and a car or motorcycle (sometimes several), without a commensurate expansion of the island's roads, carbon emissions continue to grow, and air quality continues to deteriorate. Taipei's recent construction of a subway system has helped traffic flow and kept air pollution from worsening even more quickly. However, political roadblocks have confounded efforts to build a high-speed rail system, and efforts to build Taiwan's fourth nuclear-power plant, a critical project for providing clean electrical power, were plagued by political maneuvering. The DPP government, upon arrival in office, first cancelled the construction plan, and then, under pressure from the opposition and in consideration of the billions of dollars already invested in the plant, it overturned the cancellation. But in a sign of the strength of those environmentalists opposed to the building of the plant, the government made several concessions, including a pledge to a goal of a nuclear-free Taiwan in the future. In many respects, the government has shown good faith, and has supported the development of solar energy technology, in which Taiwan has become a leader.[11]

The public concerns about building nuclear-power plants are understandable. Taiwan sits astride an active earthquake zone, and the potential damage to the environment from a nuclear reactor hit by an earthquake is incalculable. Recent major earthquakes have measured as high as 6.7 on the Richter scale and caused significant damage to the island. The antinuclear movement is increasingly active, especially after an accident at one of Taiwan's nuclear-power plants and the discovery that there are more than 5,000 radioactive buildings in Taiwan, including more than 90 in the city of Taipei.[12] The antinuclear movement in Taiwan exemplifies the problem plaguing environmentalists elsewhere: those opposed to building nuclear plants out of fear of a nuclear accident are pitted against those who favor nuclear plants as a source of clean, carbon-free energy as the way to address the problem of carbon

Courtesy of Suzanne Ogden (sogden02)

A busy Buddhist temple in Taipei. Local people make offerings of food and burning incense.

emissions and global warming gases. The debate goes on while, in the meantime, Taiwan's environment continues to be severely damaged and long-term environmental sustainability is brought into question.

Taiwan is not alone in confronting the financial and political dilemmas caused by the need to create a sustainable environment in the context of a pro-growth economic policy, but its situation is perhaps more urgent because of its high population density and individual wealth. With a population of 1,600 persons per square mile, it is one of the most densely populated places in the world. When this is combined with Taiwan having "the highest density of factories and motor vehicles in the world," as well as being one of the highest per capita energy users in East Asia,[13] it is no surprise that the environment has become a serious mainstream issue. Decisions by tens of thousands of Taiwan's manufacturers to relocate abroad, especially to mainland China, is one way Taiwan is able to "export" its pollution.

RELIGION

A remarkable mixture of religions thrives in Taiwan. The people feel comfortable with placing Buddhist, Taoist, and local deities— and even occasionally a Christian saint—together in their family altars and local temples. Restaurants, motorcycle-repair shops, businesses small and large— almost all maintain altars. The major concern in prayers is for the good health and fortune of the family. The focus is on life in this world, not on one's own afterlife.

People pray for prosperity, for luck in the stock market, and even more specifically for the winning lottery number. If the major deity in one temple fails to answer prayers, people will seek out another temple where other deities have brought better luck. Alternatively, they will demote the head deity of a temple and promote others to his or her place. The gods are thought about and organized in much the same way as is the Chinese bureaucracy. In fact, they are often given official clerical titles to indicate their rank within the deified bureaucracy.

Numerous Taiwanese religious festivals honor the more than 100 local city gods and deities. Offerings of food and wine are made to commemorate each one of their birthdays and deaths, and to ensure that the gods answer one's prayers. It is equally important to appease one's deceased relatives. The annual Tomb-Sweeping Festival (*qing ming*) in April is when the whole family cleans up their ancestral grave sites, makes offerings of food, money, and flowers, and burns incense to honor their ancestors.[14]

If they are neglected or offered inadequate amounts of food, money, and respect, they will cause endless problems for their living descendants by coming back to haunt them as ghosts. Even those having trouble with their cars or getting their computer programs to work will drop by the temple to pray to the gods and ancestors— just in case their problems have arisen from giving them inadequate respect. Whole businesses are dedicated to making facsimiles of useful or even luxury items out of paper, such as a car, a house, a computer, an airplane—and these days, paper Viagra as well—which are then brought to a temple and burned, thus sending them to their ancestors for their use.

The seventh month of the lunar calendar is designated "Ghost Month." For the entire month, most do whatever is necessary "to live in harmony with the omnipotent spirits that emerge to roam the world of the living." This includes "preparing doorway altars full of meat, rice, fruit, flowers and beverages as offerings to placate the anxious visitors. Temples [hang] out red lanterns to guide the way for the roving spirits. . . . Ghost money and miniature luxury items made of paper are burned ritualistically for ghosts to utilize along their desperate journey. . . ."[15]

In addition, the people heed a long list of taboos that can have an adverse effect on business during Ghost Month. The real estate industry is particularly hard hit, because people do not dare to move into new houses, out of fear that homeless ghosts might take up permanent residence. Many choose to wait until after Ghost Month to make major purchases, such as cars. Few choose to marry at this time as, according to folk belief, a man might discover that his new bride is actually a ghost! Pregnant women usually choose to undergo Caesarean sections rather than give birth during Ghost Month. And law suits decline because it is believed that ghosts dislike those who bring law suits.[16] (On the mainland of China, the Chinese Communist Party's emphasis on science and the eradication of superstition means that it is far less common there than in Taiwan for people to worry in such a systematic way about propitiating ghosts.)

Finally, there continues to be a preference for seeking medical cures from local temple priests, over either traditional Chinese or modern Western medicine. The concern of local religion is, then, a concern with this life, not with salvation in the afterlife. The attention to deceased ancestors, spirits, and ghosts is quite different from attention to one's own fate in the afterlife.

What is unusual in the case of Taiwanese religious practices is that as the island has become increasingly modern and wealthy, it has not become less religious. Technological modernization has seemingly not brought secularization with it. In fact, aspiring capitalists often build temples in hopes of getting rich. People bring offerings of food; burn incense and bundles of paper money to honor the temple gods; and burn expensive paper reproductions of houses, cars, and whatever other material possessions they think their ancestors might like to have in their ethereal state. They also pay real money to the owner of

their preferred temple to make sure that the gods are well taken care of. Since money goes directly to the temple owner, not to a religious organization, the owner of a temple whose constituents prosper will become wealthy. Given the rapid growth in per capita income in Taiwan since 1980, then, temples to local deities have proliferated, as a builder of a temple was almost guaranteed to get rich if its constituents' wealth grew steadily.

Christianity is part of the melange of religions. About 4 percent of the population is Christian; but it is subject to local adaptations, such as setting off firecrackers inside a church during a wedding ceremony to ward off ghosts, and the display of flashing neon lights around the Virgin Mary. The Presbyterian Church in Taiwan, established in Taiwan by missionaries in 1865, was frequently harassed by the KMT because of its activist stance on social and human rights issues and because it generally supported the Taiwan-independence viewpoint.[17] There are more than 1,200 Presbyterian congregations in Taiwan; but in recent years, there has been a 10 percent drop in members—apparently due to the aging church leaders' inflexibility in responding to modernization and ideas from the outside.[18] The Catholic Church in Taiwan is likewise witnessing a decline in membership; and it is also suffering from the aging of its priests, most of whom had emigrated in the 1940s from the China mainland and are now dying off. There is an ever smaller number of young priests in training to replace them.

As for Confucianism, it is more a philosophy than a religion. Confucianism is about self-cultivation, proper relationships among people, ritual, and proper governance. Although Confucianism accepts ancestor worship as legitimate, it has never been concerned directly with gods, ghosts, or the afterlife. In imperial China, if drought brought famine, or if a woman gave birth to a cow, the problem was the lack of morality on the part of the emperor—not the lack of prayer—and required revolt.

When the Nationalists governed Taiwan, they tried to restore Chinese traditional values and to reinstitute the formal study of Confucianism in the schools. Students were apathetic, however, and would usually borrow Confucian texts only long enough to study for college-entrance exams. Unlike the system of getting ahead in imperial China through knowledge of the Confucian classics, students in present-day Taiwan need to excel in science and math. Yet, although efforts to engage students in the formal study of Confucianism have fallen on deaf ears, Confucian values suffuse the culture. The names of streets, restaurants, corporations,

and stores are inspired by major Confucian virtues; advertisements appeal to Confucian values of loyalty, friendship, and family to sell everything from toothpaste to computers; children's stories focus on Confucian sages in history; and the vocabulary that the government and party officials use to conceptualize issues is the vocabulary of Confucianism—moral government, proper relationships between officials and the people, loyalty, harmony, and obedience.

EDUCATION

The Japanese are credited with establishing a modern school system in Taiwan in the first part of the twentieth century. After 1949, Taiwan's educational system developed steadily. Today, Taiwan offers nine years of free, compulsory education. Almost all school-age children are enrolled in elementary schools, and most go on to junior high schools. More than 70 percent continue on to senior high school. Illiteracy has been reduced to about 6 percent and is still declining. Night schools that cater to those students anxious to test well and make the cut for the best senior high schools and colleges flourish. Such extra efforts attest to the great desire of Taiwan's students to get ahead through education.

Taiwan has one of the best-educated populations in the world, a major factor in its impressive economic development. Its educational system is, however, criticized for its insistence on uniformity through a unified national curriculum, a lecture format that does not allow for student participation, the grueling high school and university entrance examinations, tracking, rote memorization, heavy homework assignments, and humiliating treatment of students by teachers. Its critics say that the system inhibits creativity.[19] There is also a gender bias in education, which results in women majoring in the humanities and social sciences, while men choose science and math majors. Reforms in recent years have tried to modify some of these practices; and Taiwan's burgeoning information-technology and high-tech sectors have added to pressures to train more women in science and technology.

The number of colleges and universities has more than doubled since martial law was lifted. But the 120 colleges and universities now in existence cannot meet the demand for spaces for all qualified students. As a result, many students go abroad for study. From 1950 to 1978, only 12 percent of some 50,000 students who studied abroad returned, a reflection of both the lack of opportunity in Taiwan and the oppressive nature of government in that period. Beginning in the late 1980s, as Taiwan grew more prosperous and the political system more open, this outward flood of human talent, or "brain drain," was stemmed. Nevertheless, the system of higher education has been unable to keep up with the demand for high-tech workers. This has led to a loosening of restrictions on importing high-tech workers from mainland China.[20]

As the economies of mainland China and Taiwan become more intertwined, the options that Taiwanese have in the educational arena are increasing. A growing number of Taiwan's high school graduates choose to go to a university on the mainland. This is in no small part because the vast majority of Taiwan's businesspeople are investing their money in the mainland economy. However, in spite of the fact that many students from Taiwan attend China's leading universities, which produce outstanding graduates whose degrees are readily accepted in the West, Taiwanese students find that their degrees are not properly honored once they return to Taiwan. Indeed, in a poll conducted in Taiwan in 2000, 40.5 percent of respondents believed that academic credentials earned by Taiwan's students in the mainland should have a stricter standard applied than to students graduating in Taiwan; and 6.3 percent believed that they should not be recognized at all.[21] Students have to take a set of exams upon returning from the mainland to validate the legitimacy of their degrees. It would appear, however, that the real reason is political—namely, to challenge the quality of any institutions under the control of the Chinese Communist rulers. The Ma Ying-jeou government is planning to recognize mainland degrees.

HEALTH CARE AND SOCIAL SECURITY

Although Taiwan's citizens have received excellent health care for many years, the health-care system is now facing a crisis. Health care has been a major political issue for candidates running for office. But slower economic growth has produced lower governmental revenues for health care. The elderly, moreover, tend to visit their doctors on a weekly, if not a daily, schedule, not only because their visits are virtually free, but also because that's where all the other elderly people are! Lonely, with time on their hands and an obsession with longevity, the elderly often hang out at hospitals and health clinics. This contributes to the financial crisis of the "medicare" system, for doctors, who are paid by the number of patients they see, are more than happy to see dozens of patients each hour. Indeed, citizens complain that their visits usually last less than a minute!

Still, Taiwan's health care functions admirably. The one issue that continues to bedevil it is that the PRC continues to block its application for even a non-member "observer" status in the World Health Organization (WHO). It does so on the grounds that Taiwan is simply a province of China, not a sovereign state. The 2003 SARS (severe acute respiratory syndrome) epidemic in Hong Kong, China, and Southeast Asian countries also broke out in Taiwan. More recently, bird flu has shown up in Taiwan. But because of the lack of either membership or observer status in WHO, Taiwan's ability to receive or contribute important health data was minimal. This situation potentially jeopardizes not only health care in Taiwan, but health care in the entire world, especially during epidemics.

The Labor Standards Law requires that Taiwanese enterprises provide a pension plan for their employees; but under the old labor standards regulations, 90 percent of employees did not qualify for a pension because they had not worked in the same company for a minimum of 25 years. In 2005, the Labor Pension Retirement Act came into effect, with the result that everyone is now covered. As a result, Taiwan's citizens are not so reliant on their families for support in old age.

WOMEN

The societal position of women in Taiwan reflects an important ingredient of Confucianism. Traditionally, Chinese women "were expected to obey their fathers before marriage, their husbands after, and their sons when widowed. Furthermore, women were expected to cultivate the "Four Virtues": morality, skills in handicrafts, feminine appearance, and appropriate language."[22] In Taiwan, as elsewhere throughout the world, women have received lower wages than men and have rarely made it into the top ranks of government and business—this in spite of the fact that it was women who, from their homes, managed the tens of thousands of small businesses and industries that fueled Taiwan's economic boom.

In the workplace outside the home, women have been treated differently than men. For example, women are not allowed to serve in the armed forces; but until the 1990s, "all female civil servants, regardless of rank, [were] expected to spend half a day each month making pants for soldiers, or to pay a substitute to do this."[23] Women, who make up 40 percent of Taiwan's civil service, find themselves "walking on glue" when they try to move from the lower ranks to the middle and senior ranks of the civil service. By the beginning of 2000,

only 12 percent of the total senior level civil service, and less than a third of intermediate ranks, were made up of women. Those figures had not changed at all by the end of 2004.[24] There have, however, been greater opportunities for women in the last decade. Women are more visible in the media and politics than before. In 2000, for the first time, a woman was elected as vice-president (and was re-elected in 2004); but since 1949, not one of the five branches of government has been headed by a woman.

Because women may now receive the same education as men, and because employment in the civil service is now based on an examination system, women's social, political, and economic mobility has increased.[25] Better education of women has been both the cause and the result of greater advocacy by Taiwan's feminists of equal rights for women. It has also eroded the typical marriage pattern, in which a man is expected to marry a woman with an education inferior to his own.

THE ECONOMY

The rapid growth of Taiwan's economy and foreign trade has enriched Taiwan's population. A newly industrialized economy (NIE), Taiwan long ago shed its "Third World," underdeveloped image. Today, the World Bank classifies it as a "high-income" economy. With a gross domestic product per capita income that rose from U.S.$100 in 1951 to U.S.$16,590 (equivalent in purchasing power parity dollars to $30,100) in 2007, and a highly developed industrial infrastructure and service industry, Taiwan sits within the ranks of some of the most developed economies in the world. As with the leading industrial nations, however, the increasing labor costs for manufacturing and industry have contributed to a steady decline in the size of those sectors as companies relocate to countries with cheaper raw materials and lower wages. Taiwan's economic growth rate from 1953 to 1997 had averaged a phenomenal 8-percent-plus annually; but it has slowed down since the Asian financial crisis that began in 1997. In recent years, a growing percentage of Taiwan's economic growth is due to production on the mainland, where most of Taiwan's manufacturing base has moved.

The government elite initiated most of the reforms critical to the growth of Taiwan's economy, including land redistribution, currency controls, central banking, and the establishment of government corporations. Taiwan's strong growth and high per capita income does not, however, bring with them a lifestyle comparable to that in the most developed Western states. The government has had limited success in addressing many of the problems arising from its breathtakingly fast modernization. In spite of—and in some cases because of—Taiwan's astounding economic growth, the quality of life has deteriorated greatly. Taiwan's cities are crowded and badly polluted, and housing is too expensive for most urbanites to afford more than a small apartment. The overall infrastructure is inadequate to handle traffic, parking, electricity, and other services expected in a more economically advanced society.

Massive air and water pollution; an inadequate urban infrastructure for housing, transportation, electricity, and water; and the rapid acquisition of carbon-emitting consumer goods, especially air conditioners, motorcycles, and automobiles, have made the environment unbearable and transportation a nightmare. Complaints of oily rain, ignitable tap water, stunted crops due to polluted air and land, and increased cancer rates abound. "Garbage wars" over the "not-in-my-back-yard" issue of sanitary landfill placement have led to huge quantities of uncollected garbage.[27] Numerous public-interest groups have emerged to pressure the government to take action. The government has tried to be responsive, but bitterly divisive politics and rampant corruption have complicated finding solutions to these woes, as everyone tries to get ahead in a now relatively open economy.

Taiwan's economic success thus far may also be attributed to a relatively open market economy in which businesspeople have developed international markets for their products and promoted an export-led economy. Taiwan's highly productive workers have tended to lack class consciousness, because they progress so rapidly from being members of the working-class "proletariat" to becoming capitalists and entrepreneurs. Even factory workers often become involved in small businesses.[28]

Now that Taiwan is privatizing those same government corporations that used to have complete control over many strategic materials as well as such sectors as transportation and telecommunications, workers are resisting the loss of their "iron rice bowl" of permanent employment in state enterprises and the civil service. Much like mainland China, the government is concerned that social instability may result if workers, instead of accepting the international trend toward privatization, resists it through street protests.[29] As an increasing number of industrial workers in Taiwan move into white-collar jobs and are replaced by relatively poorly organized immigrant laborers, who are often sent home when the jobs disappear, this problem seems to have been temporarily sidelined.

Sometimes called "Silicon Island," Taiwan has some 1.2 million small and medium-size enterprises, and only a handful of mega-giants. Most of these smaller enterprises are not internationally recognized names, but they provide the heart and even the backbone of technological products worldwide. They make components, or entire products (such as computer hardware), according to specifications set by other, often well-known, large firms, whose names go on the final product. Furthermore, because Taiwan's firms tend to be small and flexible, they can respond quickly to changes in technology. This is particularly true in the computer industry. Thanks to the many students who have gone to the United States to study and then stayed to work in the computer industry's Silicon Valley, there are strong ties with Taiwan's entrepreneurs.[30] Taiwan's development of the information-technology sector has benefited from governmental incentives and from Taiwan's educated labor force. In this sector, low-wage labor is not yet an issue, and Taiwan has become the leading Asian center for information technology (IT) and software.

A stable political environment facilitated Taiwan's rapid growth. So did Taiwan's protected market, which brought protests over Taiwan's unfair trade policies from those suffering from an imbalance in their trade with Taiwan. Since joining the World Trade Organization (WTO) in 2002, Taiwan has shed most of the regulations that have protected its industries from international trade competition and has come into compliance with international intellectual property rights legislation.

For the economy as a whole, there has been a dramatic turnaround since the 1997–2000 Asian financial crisis. By 2004, GDP growth has moved from negative numbers to a positive 3.2 percent. Taiwan came out of its economic downturn largely by increasing commercial links with China, where Taiwanese businesspeople can get better returns on their investment. There are more than 50,000 Taiwanese factories that have created more than 3 million jobs already in mainland China. A 10 percent of China's IT products that are exported are made in Taiwanese factories on the mainland, and Taiwanese firms control a quarter of China's export licenses. Some 10,000 Taiwanese businesspeople travel to the mainland each day. In 2001, Taiwan's government lifted the limits on investment in China by companies and enterprises from U.S.$5 million to U.S.$50 million. The new Ma Ying-jeou government has lifted more investment restrictions. In short, Taiwan's growth is coming from its investments in China.

Indeed, most of Taiwan's businesspeople are more concerned about the survival of their businesses than about national security vis-à-vis the mainland. As a result, they have been sending delegations to China (without authorization from the government) to reassure its leaders that they will not let Taiwan declare independence and will continue to develop economic ties with the mainland. They believe (as does Beijing) that once the two economies are fully integrated, a declaration of independence of Taiwan will be highly unlikely.[31]

By 2007, Taiwanese had invested well over U.S.$150 billion in China. Because of restrictions on trade with the mainland, however, money must first move to Hong Kong or elsewhere, and only then to China. These sorts of maneuvers complicate business investments and irritate Taiwan's business community. Critics contend that former President Chen Shui-bian failed to fulfill his promises to liberalize current restrictions on travel to and from mainland China. As part of his 2004 election campaign, President Chen promised to open direct air passenger and cargo links, to ease restrictions on travel to and from the mainland, and to liberalize regulations prohibiting Taiwanese from raising capital for their China businesses on the Taiwan Stock Exchange.[32] But when Chen left office little progress had been made in these matters. Many in Taiwan's business community are, in fact, distressed that Chen is not doing more to protect and promote business ties with the mainland (which may explain why the business community generally supported the KMT in the 2004 elections). President Ma has been pushing for closer ties across the Taiwan Strait since he took office in May 2008.

Taiwanese enterprises run what amounts to a parallel economy on the mainland that is completely entangled with China's own. In fact, as of 2003, China had become Taiwan's number one trade partner. By 2006, over 22 percent of Taiwan's export trade was with China. Taiwan has a substantial trade surplus with the mainland. Much of China's trade surplus with the United States is, in fact, from Taiwan's enterprises doing business in China. It is estimated that up to one-third of exported consumer goods labeled 'Made in China' are actually made in firms owned by Taiwan's businesspeople in China. "Analysts attribute more than 70 percent of the growth in America's trade deficit with China to the exports of Taiwanese firms."[33] The result is that, as of August 2008, Taiwan held more than $282 billion in its central reserve bank—the third-largest holding of reserve currency and gold in the world.

Finally, although Taipei insists that the government will not establish direct trade links with China until Beijing meets certain conditions, it has passed legislation so that free-trade zones can be established near Taiwan's international airports and harbors. The purpose of these tax-free areas is to encourage foreign businesspeople, including Chinese from the Mainland, to establish companies in Taiwan for the purpose of trade, processing, and manufacturing.[34] Clearly Taipei is trying both to stem the outward flow of Taiwan's investment moneys and to lure more investors to Taiwan by making its business conditions competitive with those of the mainland, Hong Kong, and Asian countries with free trade zones.

Agriculture and Natural Resources

After arriving in Taiwan, the KMT government carried out a sweeping land-reform program: The government bought out the landlords and sold the land to their tenant farmers. The result was equalization of land distribution, an important step in promoting income equalization among the farmers of Taiwan. Today, farmers are so productive that Taiwan is almost self-sufficient in agriculture—an impressive performance for a small island where only 25 percent of the land is arable.

The land-reform program was premised upon one of Sun Yat-sen's famous Three Principles, the "people's livelihood." One of the corollaries of this principle was that any profits from the increase in land value attributable to factors not related to the real value of farmland—such as through urbanization, which makes nearby agricultural land more valuable—would be turned over to the government when the land was sold. As a result, although the price of land has skyrocketed around Taiwan's major cities, and although many farmers are being squeezed by low prices for their produce, they would get virtually none of the increased value for their land if they sold it to developers. Many farmers have thus felt trapped in agriculture. In the meantime, the membership of both China and Taiwan in the World Trade Organization means that cheaper mainland produce flows quite freely into Taiwan. While this has undercut the profits of farmers in such areas as rice, their profits in fruits and other products have benefited by the lifting of trade barriers.

Natural resources, including land, are quite limited in Taiwan. Taiwan's rapid industrialization and urbanization have put a strain on what few resources exist. Taiwan's energy resources, such as coal, gas, and oil, are particularly limited. The result

© Photodisc/Getty Images RF
Taipei 101.

is that the government has had to invest in the building of four nuclear-power plants to provide sufficient energy to fuel Taiwan's rapidly modernizing society and economy. Taiwan has been able to postpone its energy and resource crisis by investing in the development of mainland China's vast natural resources. Taiwan's businesspeople have also moved their industries to other countries where resources, energy, land, and labor are cheaper. They now control a vast network of manufacturing and distribution facilities throughout the world.[35] Taiwan's economy has, in short, continued to grow while at the same time avoiding the problem of resource and energy scarcity through extensive participation in the global economy.

Internationalization of its economy is also part of Taiwan's strategy to thwart the PRC's efforts to cut off its relationships with the rest of the world. With Taiwan's important role in the international economy, it is virtually impossible for its trade, commercial, and financial partners to ignore it. This saves Taiwan from even greater international diplomatic isolation than it already faces in light of its current "non-state" status. In the meantime, its economy is becoming increasingly integrated with that of the Chinese mainland, to the mutual benefit of both economies.

Taiwan as a Model of Economic Development

Taiwan is often cited as a model for other developing economies seeking to lift themselves out of poverty. They could learn some useful lessons from certain aspects of Taiwan's experience, such as the encouragement of private investment and labor productivity, an emphasis on basic health care and welfare needs, and policies to limit gross extremes of inequality. But Taiwan's special advantages during its development have made it hard to emulate. These advantages include its small size, the benefits of improvements to the island's economic infrastructure and educational system made under the Japanese occupation, massive American financial and technical assistance, and a highly favorable international economic environment during Taiwan's early stages of growth.

What has made Taiwan extraordinary among the rapidly developing economies of the world is the government's ability—and commitment—to achieve and maintain a relatively high level of income equality. Although there are homeless people in Taiwan, their numbers are small. Government programs to help the disabled and an economy with moderate unemployment (3.9 percent in 2006) certainly help, as does a tight-knit family system that supports family members in difficult times. The government's commitment to Sun Yat-sen's principle of the "people's livelihood," or what in the West might be called a "welfare state," is still an important consideration in policy formation.

Like China's two stock markets, the regulatory regime of Taiwan's Stock Exchange Corporation (TSEC) is unreliable. Trading in Taiwan's stock market is highly speculative, and foreigners find it difficult to buy shares. The growth of Taiwan's stock market—a market often floating on the thin air of gossip and rumor—has created (and destroyed) substantial wealth almost overnight. Nevertheless, Taiwan's economic wealth remains fairly evenly distributed, contributing to a strongly cohesive social system.

At the same time, Taiwan's rapid economic growth rate, combined with a relatively low birth rate, has led businesses to import foreign laborers to do unskilled jobs that Taiwan's better-paid residents refuse to do. These foreign workers, largely from Thailand, the Philippines, and Indonesia, work at wages too low, with hours too long and conditions too dangerous for Taiwan's own citizens. By the end of 2001, there were more than 304,000 legal foreign workers in Taiwan, and a growing number of illegal foreign workers.

Today, one in five marriages is to someone from outside Taiwan, primarily from mainland China or Southeast Asian countries; and one in seven children is born in these marriages. Thus, the population of

SUN YAT-SEN: THE FATHER OF THE CHINESE REVOLUTION

Sun Yat-sen (1866–1925) was a charismatic Chinese nationalist who, in the declining years of the Manchu Dynasty, played upon Chinese nationalist hostility both to foreign colonial powers and to the Manchu rulers themselves.

Sun (pictured at the right) drew his inspiration from a variety of sources, usually Western, and combined them to provide an appealing program for the Chinese. This program was called the Three People's Principles, which translates the phrase in the Gettysburg Address "of the people, by the people, and for the people" into "nationalism," "democracy," and the "people's livelihood."

This last principle, the "people's livelihood," is the source of dispute between the Chinese Communists and the Chinese Nationalists, both of whom claim Sun Yat-sen as their own. The Chinese Communists believe that the term means socialism, while the Nationalists in Taiwan prefer to interpret it to mean the people's welfare in a broader sense.

Sun Yat-sen is, in any event, considered by all Chinese to be the father of the Chinese Revolution of 1911, which overthrew the enfeebled Manchus. He thereupon declared China to be a republic and named himself president. However, he had to relinquish control immediately to the warlord Yuan Shih-K'ai, who was the only person in China powerful enough to maintain control over all other contending military warlords in China.

When Sun died in 1925, Chiang Kai-shek assumed the mantle of leadership of the Kuomintang, the Chinese Nationalist Party. After the defeat of the KMT in 1949, Sun's widow chose to remain in the People's Republic of China and held high honorary positions until her death in 1982.

Library of Congress Prints and Photographs Division
(LC-USZ62-5972)
Sun Yat-Sen: father of Chinese revolution (1866–1925).

Taiwan, which used to be divided primarily along Mainlander-Taiwanese lines, has a fairly substantial immigrant compotent. Immigrants are still often looked down upon because they are seen as marrying Taiwanese to get ahead economically, and because they tend to come from relatively impoverished backgrounds. Some marry Taiwanese men who are from lower economic and social classes and may even be unemployed, or too sick or old to work. But these immigrant spouses, over 90 percent of whom are women, are essential to a society suffering from the same problems as Mainland China (from which so many of the brides come): a surplus of men of marriageable age, and a rapidly graying population because of a low birthrate.[36]

THE POLITICAL SYSTEM

From 1949 to 1988, the KMT justified the unusual nature of Taiwan's political system with three extraordinary propositions. First, the government of the Republic of China, formerly located on the mainland of China, was merely relocated temporarily on China's island province of Taiwan. Second, the KMT was the legitimate government not just for Taiwan but also for the hundreds of millions of people living on the Chinese mainland under the control of the Chinese Communist Party.[37] Third, the people living under the control of the Communist "bandits" would rush to support the KMT if it invaded the mainland to overthrow the Chinese Communist Party regime. Taiwan's political and legal institutions flowed from these three unrealistic propositions, which reflected hopes, not reality. Underlying all of them was the KMT's acceptance, in common with the Chinese Communist Party, that there was only one China and that Taiwan was a province of that one China. Indeed, until the early 1990s, it was a *crime* in Taiwan to advocate independence.

The Constitution

In 1946, while the KMT was still the ruling party on the mainland, it promulgated a "Constitution for the Republic of China." This Constitution took as its foundation the same political philosophy as the newly founded Republic of China adopted in 1911 when it overthrew China's Manchu rulers on the mainland: Sun Yat-sen's "Three People's Principles" ("nationalism," "democracy," and the "people's livelihood"). Democracy was, however, to be instituted only after an initial period of "party tutelage." During this period, the KMT would exercise virtually dictatorial control while in theory preparing China's population for democratic political participation.

The Constitution provided for the election of a National Assembly (a sort of "electoral college"); a Legislative Yuan ("branch") to pass new laws, decide on budgetary matters, declare war, and conclude treaties; a Judicial Yuan to interpret the Constitution and all other laws and to settle lawsuits; an Executive Yuan to run the economy and manage the country generally; a Control Yuan, the highest supervisory organ, to supervise officials through its powers of censure, impeachment, and auditing; and an Examination Yuan (a sort of personnel office) to conduct civil-service examinations. The Examination Yuan and

Control Yuan were holdovers from Chinese imperial traditions dating back thousands of years.

Because this Constitution went into effect in 1947 while the KMT still held power on the mainland, it was meant to be applicable to all of China, including Taiwan. The KMT government called nationwide elections to select delegates for the National Assembly. Then, in 1948, it held elections for representatives to the Legislative Yuan and indirect elections for members of the Control Yuan. Later in 1948, as the Civil War between Communists and Nationalists on the mainland raged on, the KMT government amended the Constitution to allow for the declaration of martial law and a suspension of regular elections; for by that time, the Communists were taking control of vast geographical areas of China. Soon afterward, the Nationalist government under Chiang Kai-shek fled to Taiwan. With emergency powers in hand, it was able to suspend elections and all other democratic rights afforded by the Constitution.

By October 1949, the Communists had taken control of the Chinese mainland. As a result, the KMT, living in what it thought was only temporary exile in Taiwan, could not hold truly "national" elections for the National Assembly or for the Legislative and Control Yuans as mandated by the 1946 Constitution. But to foster its claim to be the legitimate government of all of China, the KMT retained the 1946 Constitution and governmental structure, as if the KMT alone could indeed represent all of China. With "national" elections suspended, those individuals elected in 1947 from all of China's mainland provinces (534 out of a total 760 elected had fled with General Chiang to Taiwan) continued to hold their seats in the National Assembly, the Legislative Yuan, and the Control Yuan—usually until death—without standing for re-election. Thus began some 40 years of a charade in which the "National" Assembly and Legislative Yuan in Taiwan pretended to represent all of China. In turn, the government of the island of Taiwan pretended to be a mere provincial government under the "national" government run by the KMT. At no time did the KMT government suggest that it would like Taiwan to declare independence as a state.

Although the commitment to retaking the China mainland was quietly abandoned by the KMT government even before Chiang Kai-shek's death, the 1946 Constitution and governmental structure remained in force. This was in spite of the fact that over those many years, numerous members of the three elected bodies died. Special elections were held just to fill their vacant seats. The continuation of this atavistic

system raised serious questions about the government's legitimacy. The Taiwanese, who comprised more than 80 percent of the population but were not allowed to run for election to the Legislative Yuan or National Assembly, accused the KMT Mainlanders of keeping a stranglehold on the political system and pressured them for greater representation. Because the holdovers from the pre-1949 period were of advanced age and often too feeble to attend meetings of the Legislative Yuan (and some of them no longer even lived in Taiwan), it was virtually impossible to muster a quorum. Thus, in 1982, the KMT was forced to "reinterpret" parliamentary rules in order to allow the Legislative Yuan to get on with its work.

Chiang Ching-kuo, Chiang Kai-shek's son and successor, decided to concede reality and began bringing Taiwanese into the KMT. By the time a Taiwanese, Lee Teng-hui, succeeded Chiang Ching-kuo in 1988 as the new Nationalist Party leader and president of the "Republic of China," 70 percent of the party's membership was Taiwanese. Pressures therefore built for party and governmental reforms that would diminish the power of the old KMT Mainlanders. In July 1988, behind the scenes at the 13th Nationalist Party Congress, the leadership requested the "voluntary" resignation of the remaining pre-1949 holdovers. Allegedly as much as U.S. $1 million was offered to certain hangers-on if they would resign, but few accepted. Finally, the Supreme Court forced all those Chinese mainland legislators who had gained their seats in the 1948 elections to resign by the end of 1991.

Under the Constitution, the Legislative, Judicial, Control, and Examination branches hold certain specific powers. Theoretically, this should result in a separation of powers, preventing any one person or institution from the arbitrary abuse of power. In fact, however, none of these branches of government exercised much, if any, power independent of the KMT or the president who was chosen by the KMT until after the first completely democratic legislative elections of December 1992. In short, the KMT and the government were merged, in much the same way as the CCP was merged with the government on the mainland. Indeed, property and state enterprises owned by the government were claimed by the KMT as their own property when they lost control of the presidency in 2000.

Thanks to changes made by President Lee, however, Taiwan now has a far greater separation of powers as well as a two-headed government: The president is primarily responsible for Taiwan's security, and the prime minister (premier) is responsible for the economy, local government, and other broad policy matters.

But problems remain because the president may appoint the prime minister without approval by the Legislature—yet the Legislature has the power to cast a no confidence vote and require new elections if it finds the government's actions unacceptable.

A final consequence of the three propositions upon which political institutions in Taiwan were created was that, after the KMT arrived in 1947, Taiwan maintained two levels of government. One was the so-called national government of the "Republic of China," which ruled Taiwan as just one province of all of China. The other was the actual provincial government of Taiwan, which essentially duplicated the functions of the "national" government, and reported to the "national" government, which for so many years pretended to represent all of China. In this provincial-level government, however, native Taiwanese always had considerable control over the actual functioning of the province of Taiwan in all matters not directly related to the Republic of China's relationship with Beijing. Taiwan's provincial government thus became the training ground for native Taiwanese to ascend the political ladder once the KMT reformed the political system. The Taiwan provincial government was officially "frozen" and essentially abolished in 1998.

Martial Law

The imposition of martial law in Taiwan from 1948 to 1987 is critical to understanding the dynamics of Taiwan's politics. Concerned with the security of Taiwan against subversion, or an invasion by the Chinese Communists, the KMT government had imposed martial law on Taiwan. This allowed the government to suspend civil liberties and limit political activity, such as organizing political parties or mass demonstrations. Thus it was a convenient weapon for the KMT Mainlanders to control potential Taiwanese resistance and to quash any efforts to organize a "Taiwan independence" movement. Police powers were widely abused, press freedoms were sharply restricted, and dissidents were jailed. As a result, the Taiwan Independence Movement was forced to organize abroad, mostly in Japan and the United States. Taiwan was run as a one-party dictatorship supported by the secret police.

Non-KMT candidates were eventually permitted to run for office under the informal banner of *tangwai* (literally, "outside the party"); but they could not advocate independence for Taiwan; and they had to run as individuals, not as members of opposition political parties, which were forbidden until 1989. The combination of international pressures for democratization, the growing confidence of the KMT, a more stable situation on the China mainland, and diminished threats from Beijing led the KMT to lift martial law in July 1987. Thus ended the state of "Emergency" under which almost any governmental use of coercion against Taiwan's citizens had been justified.

Civil Rights

Until the late 1980s, the rights of citizens in Taiwan did not receive much more protection than they did on the Chinese mainland. The R.O.C. Constitution has a "bill of rights," but most of these civil rights never really existed until martial law was lifted in 1987. Civil rights were repeatedly suspended when their invocation by the citizenry challenged KMT power or policies; and opposition political parties were not allowed to organize. Because the "Emergency" regulations provided the rationale for the restriction of civil liberties, the KMT used military courts (which do not accord basic protection of defendants' civil rights) to try what were actually civil cases,[38] arrested political dissidents, and used police repression, such as in the brutal confrontation during the 1980 Kaohsiung Incident.[39]

The 2002 survey by the Taipei-based Chinese Association for Human Rights, as well as the 2004 U.S. Department of State report on Taiwan's human rights indicated that the protection of judicial rights had improved somewhat. There was some improvement in the interrogation of suspects, but protection of suspects in police custody remained inadequate. Some cases of physical abuse of persons in police custody were reported, usually when lawyers were not present for the interrogation, or when the interrogation was not audio- and videotaped, as required by law. In 2003, a law was enacted to limit police powers. Search warrants and police raids of businesses suspected of illegal activities now require stricter proof of "probable cause." Furthermore, if police have failed to follow due process and therefore infringed on a suspect's rights, the suspect can immediately file an administrative appeal. In recent years, no reports of politically motivated disappearances or deaths have been made; and claims of unlawful dentention and arrest are rare.[40] Political rights (civil rights and freedom, equality, democratic consolidation, and media independence and objectivity) have progressed, if modestly. Improvement in the protection of women's rights has been attributed to better implementation of the Domestic Violence Prevention Law, and the promulgation of the Gender Equality Labor Law in 2002. The latter is aimed at eradicating sexual harassment and discrimination, requires employers to offer up to two years' paid maternity leave, and embodies principles of equal pay for equal work, and equal rights in places of employment. Taiwan also made progress in rights for children, elderly, and the handicapped.[41]

Political Reform in Taiwan

The Kuomintang maintained its political dominance until the turn of the century in part by opening up its membership to a broader segment of the population. It thereby allowed social diversity and political pluralism to be expressed *within* the KMT. The "Taiwanization" of both the KMT and governmental institutions after Chiang Kai-shek's death in 1975 actually permitted the KMT to ignore the demands of the Taiwanese for an independent opposition party until the late 1980s. The KMT also hijacked the most appealing issues in the platform of the Democratic Progressive Party—notably, the DPP's demand for more flexibility in relations with the P.R.C., environmental issues, and greater freedom of the press. By the time of the 1996 elections, the dominant wing of the KMT had even co-opted the DPP's platform for a more independent Taiwan. In short, as Taiwan became more socially and politically diverse, the KMT relinquished many of its authoritarian methods and adopted persuasion, conciliation, and open debate as the best means to maintain control.[42]

External pressures played a significant role in the democratization of Taiwan's institutions. American aid from the 1950s to the 1970s was accompanied by considerable American pressure for liberalizing Taiwan's economy, but the United States did little to force a change in Taiwan's political institutions during the Cold War, when its primary concern was to maintain a defense alliance with Taiwan against the Chinese Communists. Taiwan's efforts to bolster its integration into the international economy has allowed it to reap the benefits of internationalization. The government has also, after much prodding, responded positively to demands from its citizens for greater economic and cultural contact with China,[43] and for reform of the party and government. As a result, the KMT was able to claim responsibility for Taiwan's prosperity as well as for its eventual political liberalization; but as noted elsewhere, it must also take responsibility for the many problems it left on the platter for the incoming DPP administration in 2000.

The KMT's success in laying claim to key elements of the most popular opposition- party policies forced the opposition to struggle to provide a clear alternative to the KMT. Apart from the issue of Taiwan independence, when the DPP was acting as the opposition party it demanded more rapid political reforms and harshly criticized the KMT's corrupt practices. The DPP's exposure of the KMT's corruption, and of the infiltration into the political system by criminal organizations, brought public outrage. Over the decades of its rule, the KMT used money and other resources to help tie local politicians and factions to itself. The KMT's power at the grassroots level was lubricated through patronage, vote buying, and providing services to constituents.[44] The public demanded that the interweaving of political corruption, gangsterism, and business (referred to as "black and gold politics" in Taiwan) be brought under control, and that the KMT divest itself of corporate holdings that involve conflicts of interest and permit it to engage in corrupt money politics. (When it also controlled the government, the KMT *as a political party* possessed an estimated U.S.$2.6 billion of business holdings, a sizable percentage of corporate wealth in Taiwan.) According to statistics published in the *Taipei Times,* "two-thirds of gangs in Taiwan have lawmakers running on their behalf in the legislature, while one-quarter of elected public representatives have criminal records. . . . [T]hey are invulnerable because, as the KMT's legislative majorities have slowly declined, the ruling party needs the support of independent lawmakers—including those with organized crime backgrounds—to pass its legislative agenda."[45]

By the time of the first democratic elections for the president of Taiwan in 1996, much had changed in the platforms of both the KMT and the DPP. The KMT, which had by then developed a powerful faction within it demanding greater international recognition of Taiwan as an independent state, adopted what amounted to an "independent Taiwan" position. Although President Lee Teng-hui stated this was a "misinterpretation" by Beijing and the international community, and that Taiwan merely wanted more international "breathing space," his offer of U.S.$1 billion to the United Nations if it would give Taiwan a seat was hardly open to interpretation.

Angered by Lee's efforts to gain greater recognition for Taiwan as an independent state, China began missile "tests" in the waters close to Taiwan in the weeks leading up to the 1996 elections. Fortunately, none of the missiles accidentally hit Taiwan. As a result of Beijing's saber-rattling and pressures from the United States, the KMT had, by the time of the elections, retreated from its efforts to gain greater recognition as an independent state. Many members of the KMT regretted Lee's pushing for an independent Taiwan. By the 2000 election, moreover, many of those who did favor independence left the KMT to form a new party. In the 2004 legislative elections, the KMT ran on a platform rejecting independent statehood and supporting a positive and stable relationship with China to protect their business interests. It managed to keep the DPP and other parties sympathetic to declaring independence from winning a majority in the Legislative Yuan.

Taiwan's large middle class, with its diverse and complex social and economic interests arising from business interests and ownership of private property, has been a catalyst for political liberalization. Moreover, Taiwan has not suffered from vast economic disparities that breed economic and social discontent. The government's success in developing the economy meant at the least that economic issues did not provide fuel for political grievances. Thus, when martial law ended in 1987, the KMT could undertake political reform with some confidence. Its gradual introduction of democratic processes and values undercut much of its former authoritarian style of rule without its losing political power for more than a decade. Reform did generate tensions, but by the 1990s the KMT realized that street demonstrations would not bring down the government and that suppressing the opposition with harsh measures was unnecessary. This being the case, the KMT liberalized the political realm still further. Today, Taiwan's political system functions in most respects as a democracy; but as the KMT is the first to admit, it was so busy democratizing Taiwan that it neglected to democratize itself. Once it lost the presidency in the 2000 elections, and only narrowly remained in control of the Legislative Yuan, it rethought its political platform and tried to rid itself of the serious corruption and elitism that has alienated Taiwan's voters.[46] This may partially explain why in the 2004 legislative elections, the KMT, together with its political allies (the "Pan-Blue" alliance), was able to retain a narrow margin of control in the legislature.

Political Parties

Only in 1989 did the KMT pass laws legalizing opposition political parties. The Democratic Progressive Party, a largely Taiwanese-based opposition party, was for the first time recognized as a legal party. As with other political reforms, this decision was made in the context of a growing resistance to the KMT's continued restriction of democratic rights. Even after 1989, however, the KMT continued to regulate political parties strictly, in the name of maintaining political and social stability.

Angry factional disputes within both the DPP and the KMT have marred the ability of each party to project a unified electoral strategy. The KMT was particularly hurt by vitriolic disputes between pro-unification and pro-independence factions, and between progressive reformers who pushed for further liberalization of the economic and political systems, and conservative elements who resisted reform. These internal conflicts explain the KMT's inability to move forward on reform and its defeat in the presidential elections of 2000 and 2004.

In their first years in the Legislature, DPP legislators, no doubt frustrated by their role as a minority party that could not get through any of its own policies, sometimes engaged in physical brawls on the floor of the Legislature, ripped out microphones, and threw furniture. As the DPP steadily gained more power and influence over the legislative agenda, its behavior became more subdued, but its effectiveness was undermined by internal factionalism.[47] Poor performance, corruption, and internal power struggle contributed to the loss of the DPP in the 2008 presidential election.

Infighting became so serious in both parties that it led to the formation of three new breakaway parties, which competed for the first times in the 1998 elections. The Taiwan Independence Party, whose members had comprised the more radical faction within the DPP, refused to be intimidated by Beijing's possible military response to a public declaration of independence. Today, it has been renamed the Taiwan Solidarity Union. Within the KMT, members of the faction angered with the KMT leadership's slow-footedness in bringing about reunification with the mainland of China and its liberalizing reforms of the KMT, broke off to form the New Party, which first ran candidates in the 1994 elections. Its bitter disputes with former colleagues in the KMT made legislative consensus difficult. By the 2000 presidential elections, angry debates over who should lead the KMT led to the expulsion of James Soong, who then formed the People's First Party. Soong's effective campaign, which split the KMT vote, contributed to the victory of the DPP candidate, with Soong himself placing a close second and the KMT's candidate a distant third.[48] Today, the KMT, the New Party, and the People's First Party are in the "Pan-Blue" alliance in the Legislature, but are deeply divided on many issues .

Since the 1996 election, the most divisive issue has been whether or not to press for an independent Taiwan. Polls have indicated that although the Taiwanese people would like Taiwan to be independent, only a small minority has been willing to incur the risks of Beijing using force against Taiwan if the government were to endorse independence as a stated policy goal. The preference is for candidates who have promised a continuation of the status quo—namely, not openly challenging Beijing's stance that Taiwan is a province of China—but who favor Taiwan continuing to act as if it is an independent sovereign state.

The preconditions for reunification that the KMT set when it was in power are not likely to be met easily: democratization of the mainland to a (unspecified) level acceptable to Taiwan, and an (unspecified) level of economic development that would move the mainland closer to Taiwan's level of development. Symbolically, the most important step Chen Shui-bian made in advancing "the three links" (trade, postal, and transportation links) between mainland China and Taiwan was allowing direct flights to accommodate citizens at both ends to visit the other over the Chinese New Year's period. Although direct flights were already permitted in 2003, there has been a huge leap in the details: now commercial airliners from *both* sides (not just Taiwan) may take passengers across the Taiwan Strait; passengers may board in multiple cities on both sides; and China's planes only had to fly *through the air space,* not land in, either Hong Kong or Macao on their way to Taiwan, saving considerable time. Extremists condemned Chen even for this modest concession as selling out Taiwan's interests and taking further steps toward unification; but members of the KMT have taken far bolder steps to improve relations and economic integration with the Mainland. In an effort to promote cross-Strait relations, KMT chairman Lien Chan and People First Party chairman James Soong visited Chinese mainland in 2005. Both were received by CCP general secretary Hu Jintao.

Money politics, vote-buying practices, and general dishonesty have plagued all of Taiwan's parties. In fact, they have burgeoned over the years, in part because of the growing importance of the legislature; for now that the Legislative Yuan is no longer a body of officials who fled the mainland in 1949 but a genuinely elected legislature with real power to affect Taiwan's policies, who wins really matters. As a result, candidates throw lavish feasts, make deals with business people, and spread money around in order to get the vote. Equally disturbing has been election-related violence, and the influence of the "underworld" on the elections.[49] The Chen administration has been plagued with corruption scandals in its second term, starting with what many commentators allege was a staged assassination

THE U.S. SEVENTH FLEET HALTS INVASION

In 1950, in response to China's involvement in the Korean War, the United States sent its Seventh Fleet to the Taiwan Strait to protect Taiwan and the Offshore Islands of Quemoy and Matsu from an invasion by China. Because of improved Sino–American relations in the 1970s, the enhanced Chinese Nationalist capabilities to defend Taiwan and the Offshore Islands, and problems in the Middle East, the Seventh Fleet was eventually moved out of the area. The U.S.S. Ingersoll, a part of the Seventh Fleet, is shown at right. In 1996, however, part of the Seventh Fleet briefly returned to the Taiwan Strait when China threatened to use military force against Taiwan if its leaders sought independent statehood.

Courtesy of U.S. Navy (USN_DD-652)

USS Ingersoll DD 652.

attempt on the eve of the 2004 president election, to allegations throughout Chen's second term of family members engaging in insider trading and diverting public funds for private use. In 2006, there were two recall votes in the Legislative Yuan. Both failed to gain the two-thirds majority vote required to force Chen out of the presidency, but some opinion polls suggest that the majority of Taiwan's citizens think he should step down from the presidency before the end of his term in 2008.[50]

The positions of the KMT-led "pan-blue alliance," and the DPP-led "pan-green alliance" are far apart on the issue of Taiwan independence. The pan-blues do not support any policy that would risk a military confrontation with the PRC, and they are actively promoting "engagement" with China's officials. By contrast, the pan-greens have been highly confrontational, although there is considerable dissent about this strategy within its ranks. In part, this is because the people of Taiwan, regardless of how much they would like Taiwan to become an independent state, don't want to risk war. On social and economic issues, there is less difference between the two major parties. Both are also committed to democracy, advocate capitalism, and support an equitable distribution of wealth.

Finally, although Chinese Mainlanders are almost all within the KMT or the New Party, the KMT has become so thoroughly "Taiwanized" that the earlier clear divide between the DPP and KMT based on Mainlander or Taiwanese identity has eroded considerably. Even those who strongly favor reunification with the mainland have for many years identified themselves not as Mainlanders but as "new Taiwanese." They are, in short, "born-again Taiwanese."[51]

Interest Groups

As Taiwan has become more socially, economically, and politically complex, alternative sources of power have developed that are independent of the government. Economic interest groups comprised largely of Taiwanese, whose power is based on wealth, are the most important; but there are also public interest groups that challenge the government's policies in areas such as civil rights, the environment, women's rights, consumer protection, agricultural policy, aborigine rights, and nuclear power. Even before the lifting of martial law in 1987, these and other groups were organizing hundreds of demonstrations each year to protest government policy.

On average, every adult in Taiwan today belongs to at least one of the thousands of interest groups. They have been spawned by political liberalization and economic growth, and in turn add to the social pluralism in Taiwan. They are also important instruments for democratic change. Taiwan's government, has then, successfully harnessed dissent since the 1990s, in part by allowing an outlet for dissent through the formation of interest groups—and opposition parties.

Mass Media

With the official end to martial law, the police powers of the state were radically curtailed. The media abandoned former taboos and grew more willing to openly address social and political problems, including corruption and the abuse of power. A free press, strongly critical of the government and *all* the political parties, now flourishes. Taiwan, with 23 million people, boasts close to 4,000 magazines; about

100 newspapers, with a total daily circulation of 5 million; 150 news agencies, several with overseas branches; 29 television broadcasting stations, which are challenged by 75 cable stations that offer some 120 satellite channels; and more than 551 radio stations, which now include foreign broadcasts such as CNN, NHK (from Japan), and the BBC. More than 3,000 radio and 3,000 television production companies are registered in Taiwan. Although television and radio are still controlled by the government, they have become far more independent since 1988. About 75 percent of households buy a basic monthly package that gives them access to more than 70 satellite channels, many of which are operated by foreign companies. Programs from all over the world expose people to alternative ideas, values, and lifestyles, and contribute to social pluralism. Political magazines, which are privately financed and therefore not constrained by governmental financial controls, have played an important role in undercutting state censorship of the media and developing alternative perspectives on issues of public concern. New technology that defies national boundaries (including satellite broadcasts from Japan and mainland China), cable television, the Internet, and VCRs are diminishing the relevance of the state monopoly of television.[52]

THE TAIWAN–P.R.C.–U.S. TRIANGLE

From 1949 until the 1960s, Taiwan received significant economic, political, and military support from the United States. Even after it became abundantly clear that the Communists effectively controlled the China mainland and had legitimacy in the eyes of the people, the United States never wavered in its support of President

Chiang Kai-shek's position that the R.O.C. was the legitimate government of all of China. U.S. secretary of state Henry Kissinger's secret trip to China in 1971, followed by President Richard M. Nixon's historic visit in 1972, led to an abrupt change in the American position and to the final collapse of the R.O.C.'s diplomatic status as the government representing "China."

Allies of the United States, most of whom had loyally supported its diplomatic stance on China, soon severed diplomatic ties with Taipei, a necessary step before they could, in turn, establish diplomatic relations with Beijing. Only one government could claim to represent the Chinese people; and with the KMT in complete agreement with the Chinese Communist regime that there was no such thing as "two Chinas" or "one Taiwan and one China," the diplomatic community had to make a choice between the two contending governments. Given the reality of the Chinese Communist Party's control over one billion people and the vast continent of China, and, more cynically, given the desire of the business community throughout the world to have ties to China, Taipei has found itself increasingly isolated in the world of diplomacy. It should be noted, however, that even when the R.O.C. had represented "China" in the United Nations, and at the height of the diplomatic isolation of the People's Republic of China from 1950 to 1971, Taipei was never officially recognized by any of its neighbors in Southeast Asia (unless they were in a defense alliance with the United States)—even though they distrusted China. That this was the case even at the height of China's unpopularity in the region was a bad omen for Taipei's dream of obtaining international legitimacy."[53]

Eventually the United States made the painful decision to desert its loyal Cold War ally, a bastion against communism in Asia, if not exactly an oasis of democracy. The United States had, moreover, heavily invested in Taiwan's economy. But on January 1, 1979, President Jimmy Carter announced the severing of diplomatic relations with Taipei and the establishment of full diplomatic relations with Beijing.

Taiwan's disappointment and anger at the time cannot be overstated, in spite of the fact that an officially "unofficial" relationship took its place. American interests in Taiwan are overseen by a huge, quasi-official "American Institute in Taiwan"; while Taiwan is represented in the United States by multiple branches of the "Taipei Economic and Cultural Office." In fact, the staffs in these offices continue to be treated in most respects as if they are diplomatic personnel. Except for the 23 countries that

Republic of China (ROC) Taiwan Navy.

The ROC's naval exercise.

officially recognize the R.O.C. (primarily because they receive large amounts of aid from Taiwan), Taiwan's commercial, cultural, and political interests are represented abroad by these unofficial offices.

The United States's acceptance of the Chinese Communists' "principled stand" that Taiwan is a province of China and that the People's Republic of China is the sole legal government of all of China, made it impossible to continue to maintain a military alliance with one of China's provinces. Recognition of Beijing, therefore, required the United States to terminate its mutual defense treaty with the R.O.C. In the Taiwan Relations Act of 1979, the United States stated its concern for the island's future security, its hope for a peaceful resolution of the conflict between Taiwan's government and Beijing, and its decision to put a moratorium on the sale of new weapons to Taiwan.

Renewal of Arms Sales

In October 2008, the United States sold $6.5 billion worth of weapons to Taiwan, based on the Taiwan Relations Act. The Taiwan Relations Act was, however, largely ignored by the administration of President Ronald Reagan. Almost immediately upon taking office, it announced its intention to resume U.S. arms sales to Taiwan. The administration argued that Taiwan needed its weapons upgraded in order to defend itself. Irate, Beijing demanded that, in accordance with American agreements and implicit promises to China, the United States phase out the sale of

military arms over a specified period. The U.S. has never actually agreed to this, but because of the gridlock in Taiwan's Legislative Yuan, in effect, U.S. arms sales have come to a halt (see below). Nevertheless, the fact that the U.S. *wants* to sell arms to Taiwan is a constant source of tensions with China. Similarly, the U.S. Congress's proposed Taiwan Security Enhancement Act in 2000—which, had it passed, would have amounted to a military alliance with Taiwan—and the possibility that Congress may authorize "theater missile defense" for the island, have been major irritants to the U.S.–China relationship.

When it took office in January 2001, the George W. Bush administration immediately stated its intention to go forward with deepening military ties with Taiwan. Tensions with Beijing generated by the U.S. sales of military equipment to Taiwan are aggravated by China's own sales of military equipment, such as medium-range missiles to Saudi Arabia, Silkworm missiles to Iran (used against American ships), nuclear technology to Pakistan,[54] and massive sales of semiautomatic assault weapons to the United States (one of which was used to attack the White House in 1994). These sales have undercut the P.R.C.'s standing on the moral high ground to protest American sales of military equipment to Taiwan. But views even within Taiwan concerning the purchase of U.S. military weapons and equipment are complicated. The DPP has argued that they are necessary to protect Taiwan against an attack by China. The KMT is, however, firmly opposed to further purchases, considering them a waste of money; for in the event of an attack, its defense would depend almost entirely on the United States—assuming that the Americans decided to come to its defense. Even worse, the KMT argues, additional arming of Taiwan would accelerate the arms race with China, and further destabilize the Taiwan Straits. The KMT has even accused President Chen of wanting greater military power as part of an effort to lay the groundwork for declaring Taiwan's independence.

This is a bizarre twist to the issue of Taiwan's defense; for in the past, the United States and other countries have repeatedly backed out of proposed arms deals in the face of Beijing's threatened punitive measures. Now it is Taiwan that is backing out. U.S. policymakers are frustrated with Taiwan's falling military expenditures and the perception that Taiwan's defense readiness has declined as a result.[55] But most analysts agree that, with or without arms purchases from the U.S., Taiwan knows that its own defenses would be overwhelmed by a military onslaught from the mainland. As to the U.S. position on what it would do if Taiwan were attacked by China, it remains one of "strategic ambiguity"; for even though President Bush in 2001 stated the U.S. would come to Taiwan's aid if it were attacked, since that time, the administration has made it clear to Taiwan's president that the U.S. will not be pulled into a war with China to defend Taiwan if it declares independence. The U.S. also has to consider that, with more than 120,000 troops in Iraq, with others tied down in Afghanistan, and with no end in sight, the U.S. simply does not have the resources to participate in a conflict with China. This does not stop the U.S. military from portraying the Chinese buildup across the Taiwan Straits as a grave threat and, on this basis, requesting more of the budget for "defense."

The United States wants Beijing to agree to the "peaceful resolution of the Taiwan issue." Meanwhile, the PRC claims it will peacefully resolve the Taiwan issue under the "one country two systems" policy, but it will not rule out the use of force in case Taiwan declares formal independence. China insists that Taiwan is an "internal" affair, not an international matter over which other states might have some authority. From China's perspective, then, it has the right as a sovereign state to choose to use force to settle the Taiwan issue. There is general recognition, however, that the purpose of China's military buildup across from Taiwan is not as much to attack Taiwan as to prevent it from declaring independence as a sovereign state.[56] Indeed, apart from a mild statement from Japan protesting China's "testing" of missiles

over Taiwan in 1996, no Asian country has questioned China's right to display force when Taiwan pressed for independent statehood. Still, Beijing knows that American involvement may be critical to getting Taiwan to agree to unification with the mainland. One thing is certain: the day Beijing no longer threatens to use force against Taiwan if it declares independence, Taipei *will* declare independence. So we can expect Beijing to continue its bluster about using military force until Taiwan is reunified with the mainland.

Minimally, Taiwan wants the United States to insist that any solution to the China unification issue be *acceptable to the people of Taiwan.* One possible solution would be a confederation of Taiwan with the mainland: Taiwan would keep its "sovereignty" (that is to say, govern itself and formulate its own foreign policy), but China could say there was only one China. An interim solution bandied about by the KMT in 2006–2007 is that Taiwan would promise not to declare independence for 50 years, and Beijing would promise not to use force to gain control of Taiwan for 50 years. Then, in that context, both sides would go about their business of furthering the integration of the two economies and deepening cultural ties. Neither this proffered solution, or one that promotes the idea of a Chinese commonwealth for the relationship of Taiwan to China, will likely be adopted any time soon.[57]

CHINA'S "PEACE OFFENSIVE"

Since the early 1980s, Beijing has combined its threats and warnings about Taiwan's seeking independence with a "peace offensive." This strategy aims to draw Taiwan's leaders into negotiations about the future reunification of Taiwan with the mainland. Beijing has invited the people of Taiwan to visit their friends and relatives on the mainland and to witness the progress made under Communist rule. Many Taiwanese have traveled to the mainland. In turn, a mere trickle of Chinese from the mainland has been permitted by Taipei to visit Taiwan. The government did allow mainland Chinese students studying abroad to come for "study tours" of Taiwan. They have treated them as if they were visiting dignitaries, and the students usually returned to their universities full of praise for Taiwan. They also eventually loosened visa restrictions for those Mainland Chinese who had become residents of Hong Kong, Macao, or another country. By 2005, the number of Chinese visitors had increased to 5,000 per month. Taipei has said it is willing to increase that number to 30,000 per month, a decision motivated, it appears, by Taiwan's

economy, which could use an infusion of tourist dollars to get it moving.[58] Economic issues have, at long last, trumped Taipei's worries about tourists overstaying their visas to find work, as well as political and security concerns. More recent mainland measures include giving two pandas to Taiwan as gifts, recognizing Taiwan's college degrees, allowing Taiwanese medical professionals to practice on the mainland, and giving more preferential policies to southern Taiwan farmers to export their produce to the mainland.

China's "peace offensive" is based on a nine-point proposal originally made in 1981. Its major points include Beijing's willingness to negotiate a mutually agreeable re-integration of Taiwan under the mainland's government; encouragement of trade, cultural exchanges, travel, and communications between Taiwan and the mainland; the offer to give Taiwan "a high degree of autonomy as a special administrative region" within China after reunification (the status it offered to Hong Kong when it came under Beijing's rule in 1997); and promises that Taiwan could keep its own armed forces, continue its socioeconomic systems, maintain political control over local affairs, and allow its leaders to participate in the national leadership of a unified China. This far exceeds what China offered Hong Kong.

The KMT's original official response to the Beijing "peace offensive" was negative. The KMT's bitter history of war with the Chinese Communists, and what the KMT saw as a pattern of Communist duplicity, explained much of the government's hesitation. So did Beijing's refusal to treat Taiwan as an equal in negotiations. Nevertheless, since 1992, Taiwan has engaged in unofficial "track 2" and "track 3" discussions on topics of mutual interest, such as the protection of Taiwan's investments in the mainland, tourism, cross-Strait communication and transportation links, and the dumping of Taiwan's nuclear waste on the mainland.

Taipei remains sensitive, however, to the Taiwanese people's concern about the unification of Taiwan with the mainland. The Taiwanese have asserted that they will never accede to rule by yet another mainland Chinese government, especially a Communist one. When the DPP was in power, Taiwanese had fewer fears that the leadership would strike a deal with Beijing at their expense; for, as the long-time advocate of the interests of the Taiwanese people and an independent Taiwan, the DPP is trusted not to sell out their interests. To speak of the "Taiwanese" as a united whole is, however, misleading; for it must be remembered that the overwhelming majority of members in the KMT, which favors stronger integration with the mainland, are Taiwanese, and that Taiwanese who do business with the mainland are eager to see integration—if not necessarily political unification at this point in history—progress much more rapidly. In addition, the political influence of those age cohorts most opposed to improving cross-Strait ties is waning. For younger Taiwanese, "loving Taiwan does not mean hating China. If the PRC refrains from acting in ways that provoke negative reactions from young Taiwanese, current trends suggest that Taiwan's public will demand better relations between the two sides in the future."[59] An increasing Taiwanese identity does not, then, necessarily mean greater support for a pro-independence policy. Indeed, public opinion polls indicate that support for declaring independence, in spite of the fact that 80 percent of the population today was born on Taiwan, has rarely exceeded 10 percent of voters.[60]

With only a handful of countries recognizing the R.O.C., and with Beijing blocking membership for the R.O.C. in most international organizations, Taipei is under pressure to achieve some positive results in its evolving relationship with Beijing. The introduction of direct commercial flights from Taiwan to Shanghai over the 2003 Chinese New Year was one of the first steps toward direct air links.[61] On the other hand, "indirect" trade between mainland China and Taiwan by way of Hong Kong has continued to soar, although the opening of Taiwan's Offshore Islands (Quemoy and Matsu) to direct trade with the mainland in 2001 has somewhat undercut the need for the Hong Kong connection. On December 15, 2008, the "three links" were officially launched between mainland China and Taiwan, with direct flight, shipping and postal services across the Taiwan Strait after a hiatus of almost 60 years.

Although China has become Taiwan's largest export market and the single largest recipient of investment from Taiwan, Taipei still hesitates to move forward on many issues that would further bind Taiwan with the mainland. Its policy on mainland spouses is particularly stringent and clearly indicates a perception that China's citizens are potential enemies, not compatriots. In the 1990s, relatively few Taiwanese residents who married individuals from the mainland were permitted to live with them in Taiwan. By contrast, Beijing's policy was to welcome Taiwan spouses to come live on the mainland. Taiwan's government argued that the mainland spouses could be spies and that internal security forces were inadequate to follow them around. Over time, however, this policy has relaxed, and as of 2007, there were 240,000 Chinese

spouses of Taiwan citizens. This number, expected to grow by the time of the 2012 election to 300,000 to 400,000 eligible to vote (though they may only vote after 8 years of residency in Taiwan), is causing concern to the ever-paranoid Taiwanese that they might vote as a block for political unity with the mainland.[62] As Mainlanders are smuggled into Taiwan in ever-larger numbers (primarily to satisfy the needs of entrepreneurs in Taiwan for cheap labor), and the number of fake marriages (marriages of convenience) with Taiwan's citizens grows (more than 16,000 had been discovered as of 2005),[63] the issue of surveillance has become a growing concern. At the same time, Taiwan spying on the mainland has grown steadily as its contacts with the mainland have increased. The Military Intelligence Bureau recruits from its approximately one million citizens who work, live, and tour on the mainland. They in turn form Taiwan spy networks that recruit local Chinese with sex, money, and "democratic justice" (an appeal to their sense of injustice at the hands of the Chinese government).[64]

In the meantime, China continues to deepen and widen harbors to receive ships from Taiwan; wine and dine influential Taiwanese; give preferential treatment to Taiwan's entrepreneurs in trade and investment on the mainland; open direct telephone links between Taiwan and the mainland; rebuild some of the most important temples to local deities in Fujian Province where Taiwanese like to visit; establish special tourist organizations to care solely for people from Taiwan; and refurbish the birthplace of Chiang K'ai-shek, the greatest enemy of the Chinese Communists in their history.

Taiwan's businesspeople and scholars are eager for Taiwan's relationship with the mainland to move forward. They seek direct trade and personal contacts, and try to separate political concerns from economic interests and international scientific exchanges. The manufacturing and software sectors are particularly concerned with penetrating and, if possible, controlling the China market. Otherwise, they argue, businesspeople from other countries will do so.

The business community, faced with Taiwan's ever-higher labor cost and Taiwan's lack of cheap raw materials, has flocked to China. Whether they move outdated labor-intensive factories and machinery to the mainland, or invest in cutting-edge technology, Taiwan's businesspeople benefit from China's cheap, hard-working labor force.

Others are concerned, however, that, with more than 15 percent of its total foreign investment in the mainland, Taiwan could become "hostage" to Beijing. That is, if China were to refuse to release Taiwan's

assets or to reimburse investors for their assets on the mainland in case of a political or military conflict between Taipei and Beijing, Taiwan's enterprises would form a pressure point that would give the advantage to Beijing. Any military defensive capabilities either Taiwan or the U.S. could offer are useless to counter possible Mainland economic warfare, such as an economic blockade, when most of Taiwan's trade is with the mainland itself and 60 percent of its investments are in the mainland.[60] Furthermore, without diplomatic recognition in China, Taiwan's businesses on the mainland are vulnerable in case of a conflict with local businesses or the government. High-level members of the government have even denounced those who invest in the mainland as "traitors." And members of the pro-independence press have attempted to whip up fear among its citizens that with Beijing's new anti-secession law, Taiwanese visiting or living in China will be vulnerable to "shakedown artists."[65] So far, affairs have turned out quite the opposite: China has actually *favored* Taiwan's businesses over all others; and Taiwan's investors have tended to turn a quick profit, and to construct many safeguards, so that any seizure of assets would result in negligible losses. To wit, Beijing learned that its heavy-handed approach to Taiwan in passing an anti-secession law was counter-productive, and now relies more on "soft power" in its relations with Taipei.

PROSPECTS FOR THE REUNIFICATION OF TAIWAN WITH THE MAINLAND

The December 2004 legislative elections kept an anti-independence majority in the legislature, and the 2008 presidential election returned the KMT to power, but most Taiwanese remain opposed to reunification. Most agree that, given China's threats to use force if Taiwan were to declare independence, it would be foolish to do so; and that the government's policy toward China should be progressive, assertive, and forward-looking. Lacking a long-term plan and simply reacting to Beijing's initiatives puts the real power to determine the future relationship in China's hands.

For the last 20 years, reform-minded individuals in Taiwan's political parties have insisted that the government needs to actively structure how the cross-Straits relationship evolves. One of the most widely discussed policies favored by those who opposed a declaration of independence has been a "one country, two regions" model that would approximate the "one country, two systems" model China has with Hong Kong. The problem is determining who would govern in that "one China" after reunification with the mainland. To call that country the People's Republic of China would probably never find acceptance in Taiwan—a point understood by Beijing. As a result, it now frequently drops the "people's republic" part of the name in its pronouncements. Symbolically, this eliminates the issue of two different governments claiming to represent China, and whether that China would be called a "people's republic" or a "republic." It would be called neither. But, would Beijing be in charge of the new unified government? Would the government of the "Republic of China," even were free and democratic elections for all of the mainland and Taiwan to be held, be the winner? There is certainly no evidence to suggest that most people on the mainland would welcome being governed by Taiwan's leaders.

In spite of the negative rhetoric, changes in Taipei's policies toward the P.R.C. have been critical to improving cross-Strait ties. For example, Taiwan's government ended its 40-year-old policy of stamping "communist bandit" on all printed materials from China and prohibiting ordinary people from reading them; Taiwan's citizens, even if they are government officials, are now permitted to visit China; scholars from Taiwan may now attend international conferences in the P.R.C., and Taipei now permits a few P.R.C. scholars to attend conferences in Taiwan; and KMT retired veterans, who fought against the Communists and retreated to Taiwan in 1949, are actually encouraged to return to the mainland to live out their lives because their limited KMT government pensions would buy them a better life there! Certainly some members of Taiwan's upper class are acting as if the relationship will eventually be a harmonious one when they buy apartments for their mistresses and purchase large mansions in the former international sector of Shanghai and elsewhere. (It is estimated that there are more than one million individuals from Taiwan living in China.) One survey indicated, in fact, that after the United States and Canada, mainland China was the preferred place to emigrate for Taiwan's citizens![66] And, from the perspective of the Democratic Progressive Party, things are getting worse: hundreds of thousands more Taiwanese are relocating to the mainland, and they are taking with them venture capital estimated at well over U.S.$100 billion—money that might otherwise be pumped into Taiwan's economy.

Some Taiwanese share with Beijing a common interest in establishing a Chinese trading zone in East Asia. A "Chinese common market" would incorporate China, Taiwan, Hong Kong, Macau, and perhaps other places with large ethnic-Chinese communities such as Singapore and Malaysia. Economically integrating these Chinese areas through common policies on taxes, trade, and currencies would strengthen them vis-à-vis the Japanese economic powerhouse, which remains larger than all the other Far Eastern economies put together.

Yet, with an ever-smaller number of first-generation Mainlanders in top positions in the KMT and Taiwan's government, few are keen to push for reunification. Indeed, the majority of people in Taiwan are not interested in reunification under current conditions. They are particularly concerned about two issues. The first is the gap in living standards. Taiwan is fully aware of the high price that West Germany paid to reunify with East Germany. Obviously the price tag to close the wealth gap with mammoth China would be prohibitive for tiny Taiwan; and any plan that would allow Beijing to heavily tax Taiwan's citizens would be unacceptable. Yet China is developing so quickly, at least along the densely populated eastern coast that faces Taiwan, that this issue should disappear. In developed coastal areas, such as Shanghai and Shenzhen, living standards are comparable to that of Taipei.

The second issue is democracy. Fears that they might lose certain political freedoms and control over their own institutions have made the Taiwanese wary of reunification. Finally, whether or not "one country, two systems" succeeds in protecting Hong Kong from Beijing's intervention, Taiwanese reject a parallel being drawn between Hong Kong and Taiwan. Hong Kong was, they argue, a British colony, whereas Taiwan, even if only in the last dozen years, is a fledgling democracy. The KMT stated that once China had attained a certain (unspecified) level of development and democracy, China and Taiwan would be reunified; but the DPP has made no such statement. In any event, with so much left open to its own arbitrary interpretation as to what is sufficient development and democracy, even the KMT seems to have made no real commitment to reunification. For its part, the DPP-led government was pressured into accepting greater interdependency with China, yet had tried desperately to move toward the formal declaration of an independent state, to no avail.

China's significant progress in developing the economy and increasing the rights of the Chinese people in the last 30 years should make reunification more palatable to Taiwan. Greater contacts and exchanges between the two sides should in themselves help lay the basis for mutual trust and understanding.

Many members of Taiwan's political and intellectual elite, including the DPP and KMT party leaders, think tanks, and the Ministry of Foreign Affairs, seem to spend the better part of each day pondering the meaning of "one China." In general, they would like China to return to the agreement that they reached with Beijing in 1992: namely, that each side would keep its own interpretation of the "one China" concept: Beijing would continue to see "one China" as the government of the P.R.C. and would continue to deny that the R.O.C. government existed. Taipei would continue to hold that Taiwan and the mainland are separate but politically equivalent parts of one China. Beijing now also supports the so-called "1992 Consensus."

Today, it is estimated that China has more than 900 (non-nuclear) missiles pointed at Taiwan; but unless Taiwan again pushes seriously for recognition as an independent state, an attack is unlikely; for the mainland continues to benefit from Taiwan's trade and investments, remittances and tourism; and it is committed to rapid economic development, which could be seriously jeopardized by even a brief war—a war that it might not win if the United States were to intervene on behalf of Taiwan. In spite of the fact that the U.S. has repeatedly made it clear that it does not support Taiwan independence, Beijing could well worry that the U.S. might suddenly be persuaded to come to Taiwan's support.

It is in Taiwan's best interests for the relationship with China to develop in a careful and controlled manner, and to avoid public statements on the issue of reunification versus an independent Taiwan, even as that issue haunts every hour of the day in Taiwan. It is also in Taiwan's interest to wait and see how well China integrates Hong Kong under its formula of "one country, two systems." In the meantime, Taiwan's international strategy—agreeing that it is part of China, while acting like an independent state and conducting business and diplomacy with other states as usual—has proved remarkably successful. It has allowed Taiwan to get on with its own economic development without the diversion of a crippling amount of revenue to military security. A continuation of the status quo is clearly the preferred alternative for Taiwan, the United States, and mainland China; for it avoids any possibility of a military conflict, which none would welcome; and it does not interrupt the preferred strategy of both the DPP and the KMT—"closer economic ties, lower tensions, and more communication with the mainland."[67]

At the same time, this strategy allows time for the mainland to become increasingly democratic and developed, in a way that one day might make reunification palatable to Taiwan. Meanwhile, Beijing's leadership knows that Taiwan acts as a

Timeline: PAST

A.D. 1544
Portuguese sailors are the first Europeans to visit Taiwan

1700s
Taiwan becomes part of the Chinese Empire

1895
The Sino-Japanese War ends; China cedes Taiwan to Japan

1945
Japan is forced to return the colony of Taiwan to China when Japanese forces are defeated in World War II

1947–49
Nationalists, under Chiang Kai-shek, retreat to Taiwan

1950s
A de facto separation of Taiwan from China; The Chinese Communist Party is unable to bring its civil war with the KMT to an end because the U.S. interposes its 7th Fleet between the mainland and Taiwan in the Taiwan Straits

1971
The People's Republic of China replaces the Republic of China (Taiwan) in the United Nations as the legitimate government of "China"

1975
Chiang Kai-shek dies and is succeeded by his son, Chiang Ching-kuo

1980s
40 years of martial law end and opposition parties are permitted to campaign for office

1990s
Relations with China improve; the United States sells F-16 jets to Taiwan; China conducts military exercises to intimidate Taiwanese voters. Democratization develops. The Asian financial crisis deals a setback to Taiwan's economic growth.

PRESENT

2000
Chen Shui-bian is elected President, ending the KMT rule

2004
Chen Shui-bian is re-elected in a controversial election

2008
Ma Ying-jeou is elected president, returning the KMT to power

Chen Shui-bian under corruption investigation

Chen Yunlin, chairman of the Association for Relations Across the Taiwan Straits, visits Taiwan

de facto independent state, but it is willing to turn a blind eye as long as Taipei does not push too openly for recognition. Thus far, the reality has mattered less to Beijing than recognition of the symbolism of Taiwan being a province of China. Beijing's leadership is far more interested in putting resources into China's economic development than fighting a war with no known outcome. In part for this reason, and in part because of continuing efforts of the U.S. to sell armaments to Taiwan, Beijing has made it clear to Washington that China's own buildup of missiles targeted at Taiwan would be linked to American sales and efforts to install a theatre missile defense system around Taiwan.

Because China's sovereignty over Taiwan has been an emotional, historical, and nationalistic issue for the Chinese people, however, Beijing does not make a "rational" cost-benefit analysis of the use of force against a rebellious Taiwan. Taiwan does not like Beijing's militant rhetoric, but some mainland Chinese analysts believe that China's leadership is forced to sound more militant than it feels, thanks to the militant nationalism of ordinary Chinese people and the Chinese military. Indeed, some go so far as to say that, were China an electoral democracy, the people would have voted out the CCP leadership because it has done little to regain sovereignty over Taiwan.

As Taiwan's relationship with China deepens and broadens, it is possible that more arrangements could be made for the representation of both Taiwan and China in international organizations, without Beijing putting up countless roadblocks. Indeed, Beijing welcomed Taiwan's membership in the WTO, if for no other reason than that it allows it to pry open Taiwan's market. Further, Taiwan's WTO membership has led to even more investments in the mainland and further economic integration.

Taiwan eagerly embraced membership in the WTO, not because it would necessarily benefit from WTO trade rules, but so that it could become a player in a major international organization. But, the very trade practices that led to Taiwan's multibillion-dollar trade surplus will have to be abolished to gain compliance with WTO regulations. Still, had Taiwan not joined the WTO, it would have eventually lost its competitiveness in agriculture and the automobile industry anyway.

To conclude, the benefits of Taiwan declaring independence would be virtually nil. Already Beijing refuses to have diplomatic relations with any country that officially recognizes the Republic of China. Those countries that do recognize the R.O.C., or Taiwan, as a sovereign state also have difficulty trading with the P.R.C. Given the size of the China market, this is an unacceptable price for most countries to pay. Beijing would no doubt use this trump card to punish those that would dare to recognize Taiwan as an independent and sovereign state, just as it does now.

Taiwan is looking for a place for itself in the international system, and it can't seem to find it. But its government realizes that the island is a small place, and that if Taiwan ever were to stop demanding international status and attention, it might well discover that it had suddenly become, de facto, a province of China while the international community looked the other way. If only for this reason, it is in Taiwan's interest to continue to press its case for greater international recognition, and to continue to engage in pragmatic unofficial diplomacy and trade with states throughout the world. It may not buy Taiwan statehood, but it may well buy the government's continued independence of Beijing.

NOTES

1. Before it won its bid to host the 2008 Olympics, Beijing had said that it would not allow Taipei to co-host them unless it first accepted the "one China" principle. Taipei did not accept it, so Beijing is the sole host of the 2008 Olympics.

2. John F. Burns, "Quemoy (Remember?) Bristles with Readiness," *The New York Times* (April 5, 1986), p. 2.

3. Mainland Affairs Council, "Report on the Preliminary Impact Study of the 'Three Mini-links' Between the Two Sides of the Taiwan Strait" (October 2, 2000); and discussions at The National Security Council and Ministry of National Defense in Taiwan (January 2001)

4. Edwin A. Winckler, "Cultural Policy on Postwar Taiwan," in Steven Harrell and Chun-chieh Huang, eds., *Cultural Change in Postwar Taiwan* (Boulder, CO: Westview Press, 1994), p. 22.

5. *Ibid.,* p. 29.

6. Thomas B. Gold, "Civil Society and Taiwan's Quest for Identity," in Harrell and Huang, p. 60.

7. Thomas A. Shaw, "Are the Taiwanese Becoming More Individualistic as They Become More Modern?" Taiwan Studies Workshop, *Fairbank Center Working Papers,* No. 7 (August 1994), pp. 1–25.

8. "Premier Hau Bristling about Crime in Taiwan," *The Free China Journal* (September 13, 1990), p. 1; and Winckler, p. 41.

9. Paul Li, "Trash Transfigurations," *Taipei Review* (October 2000), pp. 46–53.

10. Central News Agency, Taipei, "Nearly 90% support new garbage classification policy, survey finds," *Taiwan News Online* (December 27, 2004). http://www.etaiwannews.com/Taiwan/Politics/2004/12/27/1104112881.htm.

11. U.S. Energy Information Administration. Report on Taiwan, available at http://www.eia.doe.gov/emeu/cabs/taiwanenv.html

12. A dormitory for employees of Tai Power is one of these buildings. Ninety percent of Taiwan's nuclear waste is stored on Orchid Island, where one of Taiwan's 9 aboriginal tribes lives. Christian Aspalter, *Understanding Modern Taiwan: Essays in Economics, Politics, and Social Policy*

(Burlington, Vt.: Ashgate Publishers, 2001), pp. 103–107.

13. U.S. Energy Information Administration. Report on Taiwan, op.cit.

14. http://www.settlement.org/cp/english/taiwan/holidays.html

15. Lee Fan-fang, "Ghosts' Arrival Bad for Business," *The Free China Journal* (August 7, 1992), p. 4.

16. Ibid.

17. Marc J. Cohen, *Taiwan at the Crossroads* (Washington, D.C.: Asian Resource Center, 1988), pp. 186–190. For further detail, see his chapter on "Religion and Religious Freedom," pp. 185–215. Also, see Gold, in Harrell and Huang, p. 53.

18. "Presbyterian Church in Taiwan Calls for Reform," (February 18, 2004). Posted on http://www.christiantoday.com/news/asip/42.htm

19. See *Free China Review,* Vol. 44, No. 9 (September 1994), which ran a series of articles on educational reform, pp. 1–37.

20. Brian Cheng, "Foreign Workers Seen as a Mixed Blessing," *Taipei Journal* (October 20, 2000), p. 7.

21. Election Study Center, National Chengchi University, *Taipei: Face-to-Face Surveys* (February 2000). Funded by the Mainland Affairs Council.

22. Cohen, p. 107.

23. *Ibid.,* p. 108. For more on women, see the chapter on "Women and Indigenous People," pp. 106–126.

24. Jim Hwang, "The Civil Service: Walking on Glue," *Taipei Review* (October 2000), pp. 22–29; and "Taiwan's Civil Service Makes Headway on Gender Equality," *Taiwan Update,* Vol. 5, No. 3 (March 30, 2004), p. 7).

25. Cher-jean Lee, "Political Participation by Women of Taiwan," *Taiwan Journal* (August 20, 2004), p. 7.

26. Lynn T. Whyte III, "Taiwan and Globalization," in Samuel S. Kim, ed., *East Asia and Globalization* (New York: Rowman & Littlefield, 2000), p. 163.

27. Robert P. Weller, "Environmental Protest in Taiwan: A Preliminary Sketch," Taiwan Studies Workshop, *Fairbank Center Working Papers,* No. 2 (1993), pp. 1, 4.

28. Taiwan's workers could not get higher wages through strikes, which were forbidden under martial law. The alternative was to try starting up one's own business. Gold, in Harrell and Huang, pp. 50, 53.

29. Kelly Her, "Not-So-Iron Rice Bowl," *Free China Review* (October 1998), pp. 28–35.

30. "Taiwan: In Praise of Paranoia," *The Economist* (November 7, 1998) pp. 8–15.

31. Since 2005, a steady stream of high level KMT political and economic leaders have gone to China to assure China that they do not support Taiwan independence and want to expand their economic relations with China.

32. Peter Morris, "Taiwan business in China supports opposition," *Asia Times Online* (Feb. 4, 2004). http://www.atimes.com/atimes/China/FB04Ad04.html

33. "Taiwan: In Praise of Paranoia," p. 17. For 2004, Taiwan had an overall trade surplus (with all countries) of well over US$7 billion.

34. Francis Li, "Taiwan to Set Up Free-Trade Zones," *Taipei Journal* (October 11, 2002), p. 3.

35. "Taiwan: In Praise of Paranoia," p. 16.

36. Editor, "Standard-bearers for the Future," *Taiwan Review* (February 2007), p. 1; and Zoe Cheng, "The Biggest Leap," *Taiwan Review* (February 2007), pp. 4–11.

37. Until the DPP came into power in 2000 and began to promote the concept of Taiwan as an independent state, Taiwan was always shown on the map as a part of China, as were Tibet, Inner Mongolia, and even Outer Mongolia, which is an independent state.

38. From 1950 to 1986, military courts tried more than 10,000 cases involving civilians. These were in violation of the Constitution's provision (Article 9) that prohibited civilians from being tried in a military court. Hung-mao Tien, *The Great Transition: Political and Social Change in the Republic of China* (Palo Alto, CA: Hoover Institution, Stanford University, 1989), p. 111.

39. The Kaohsiung rally, which was followed by street confrontations between the demonstrators and the police, is an instance of KMT repression of *dangwai* activities. These activities were seen as a challenge to the KMT's absolute power. The KMT interpreted the Kaohsiung Incident as "an illegal challenge to public security." For this reason, those arrested were given only semi-open hearings in a military, not civil, tribunal; and torture may have been used to extract confessions from the defendants. Tien, p. 97.

40. Bureau of Democracy, Human Rights, and Labor, U.S. Department of State, *China (Taiwan only): Country Report on Human Rights Practices (2003),* (Washington D.C. 2004). Available at: http://www.state.gov/g/drl/rls/hrrpt/2003/27767.htm; and Lin Fang-yan, "Rights Group Reports on ROC Progress," *Taipei Journal* (January 3, 2003), p. 1.

41. Lin Fangyan, Ibid.

42. Tien, p. 72.

43. A February 2000 poll conducted in Taiwan indicated that only 6.1 percent of the respondents opposed conditional or unconditional opening up of direct transportation links with the mainland. Election Study Center, National Chengchi University, Taipei. Face-to-face surveys. Funded by the Mainland Affairs Council, Executive Yuan (February 2000).

44. Shelley Rigger, "Taiwan: Finding Opportunity in Crisis," *Current History* (September 1999), p. 290.

45. Shelley Rigger, "Taiwan Rides the Democratic Dragon," *The Washington Quarterly* (Spring 2000), pp. 112–113. Reference is to the editor, *Taipei Times* (January 4, 2000).

46. Discussions with Shaw Yu-ming, deputy secretary-general of the KMT, at KMT headquarters, Taipei, 2001.

47. Myra Lu and Frank Chang, "Election Trends Indicate Future of Taiwan Politics," *Free China Journal* (November 27, 1998), p. 7.

48. According to Shaw Yu-ming, the KMT was defeated not because of its policies but because it was the KMT leadership who chose the candidates to run in the election. The implication was that if instead, the KMT membership had chosen candidates, they would have picked candidates who had a better chance of winning.

49. Cal Clark, "Taiwan in the 1990s: Moving Ahead or Back to the Future?" in William Joseph, *China Briefing: The Contradictions of Change* (Armonk, NY: M. E. Sharpe, 1997), p. 206; and Myra Lu, "Crack-down on Vote-Buying Continues," *Free China Journal* (November 27, 1998), p. 2.

50. One poll, conducted by *The China Times* (June 18, 2006) indicated that 53 percent of respondents thought Chen should resign. Referenced in Kerry Dumbaugh: *China-U.S. Relations: Current Issues and Implications for U.S. Policy* (Washington: Congressional Research Service Report for Congress (February 2007), p. 9. Available at http://fpc.state.gov/documents/organization/81340.pdf.

51. Lee Chang-kuei, "High-Speed Social Dynamics," *Free China Review* (October 1998), p. 6.

52. *Taiwan Yearbook, 2007,* (Government Information Office, Taipei, 2007). Available at http://english.www.gov.tw/Yearbook/index.jsp?categid=28&recordid=52736; and Chin-chuan Lee, "Sparking a Fire: The Press and the Ferment of Democratic Change in Taiwan," in Chin-chuan Lee, ed., *China's Media, Media China* (Boulder, CO: Westview Press, 1994), pp. 188–192.

53. Chen Jie, *Foreign Policy of the New Taiwan: Pragmatic Diplomacy in Southeast Asia* (Northampton, MA: Edward Elgar Publishing, 2002), pp. 63–64.

54. In 2000, however, China agreed to stop selling nuclear and missile technology to Pakistan.

55. Kerry Dumbaugh: *China-U.S. Relations: Current Issues and Implications for U.S. Policy* pp. 2, 9.

56. Thomas J. Christensen, "The Contemporary Security Dilemma: Deterring a Taiwan Conflict," *The Washington Quarterly* (Autumn 2002), pp. 7–21.

57. Patrick L. Smith, "For Many in Taiwan, Status Quo with China Sounds Fine," *International Herald Tribune,* December 11, 2006.

58. Jimmy Chuang, "A 'foreigner's point of view' can boost tourist numbers: [Premier] Su," *Taipei Times* (January 4, 2007), p.4; Kathrin Hille, "Taiwan May Allow More

Mainland Chinese Visitors," *Financial Times,* October 21, 2005.

59. Shelley Rigger, *Taiwan's Rising Rationalism: Generations, Politics, and "Taiwanese Nationalism,"* Policy Studies 26 (Washington D.C.: East-West Center Washington, 2006), p. 84.

60. Robert S. Ross, "Explaining Taiwan's Revisionist Diplomacy," *Journal of Contemporary China,* Vol. 15, no. 48 (August 2006), pp. 446–447, 450. Ross (2006), pp. 452–454. See the charts based on public opinion polls by the Mainland Affairs Council, done 3 to 4 times per year from May 2000 through December 2006, in which the highest percentage of those polled who wanted to declare independence immediately only reached more than

10 percent once (10.3 percent in November 2005). Charts available at http://www .mac.gov.tw/english/index1-e.htm.

61. Taiwan's own airlines are now permitted to continue on to Shanghai.

62. China News Agency (Taipei), "Chinese Spouses of Taiwan Citizens Wont Sway Elections: Official," *Taiwan Headlines* (January 5, 2007). Available at http://www.taiwanheadlines.gov .tw/ctasp?xItem=57629&CtNode=5

63. Yulin County Government, "Over 16,000 PRC Citizens Found in Fake Marriages with Taiwanese" (2005). Available at http:// en.yunlin.gov.tw/index3/en/03Bulletin/ 03Bulletin_01_01.asp?id=686. However, "fake marriages" are more likely to be

related to human trafficking and prostitution than spying. See Zoe Cheng (Feb. 2007), p. 9.

64. Wendell Minnick, "The Men in Black: How Taiwan Spies on China," *Asia Times Online Co.,* (http://www.atimes.com), 2004.

65. Editorial, "The Chinese Gulag Beckons," *Taipei Times,* (January 10, 2005). http:// www.taipeitimes.com/News/edit/archives/ 2005/01/10/2003218825

66. Chien-min Chao, "Introduction: The DPP in Power," *Journal of Contemporary China,* vol. 11, no. 33 (November 2002), p. 606.

67. "Taiwan Stands Up," *The Economist* (March 25, 2000), p. 24.

The Real China Threat

ROBERT J. SAMUELSON

Obsessed with rankings, Americans are bound to see the Beijing Olympics as a metaphor for a larger and more troubling question. Will China overtake the United States as the world's biggest economy? Well, stop worrying. It almost certainly will.

China's economy is now only a fourth the size of the $14 trillion U.S. economy, but given plausible growth rates in both countries, China's output will exceed America's in the 2020s, *Goldman Sachs* forecasts. But this is the wrong worry. By itself, a richer China does not make America poorer. Indeed, because there are so many more Chinese than Americans, average Chinese living standards may lag behind ours indefinitely. By Goldman's projections, average American incomes will still be twice Chinese incomes in 2050.

The real threat from China lies elsewhere. It is that China will destabilize the world economy. It will distort trade, foster huge financial imbalances and trigger a contentious competition for scarce raw materials. Symptoms of instability have already surfaced, and if they grow worse, everyone—including the Chinese—may suffer. China is now "challenging some of the fundamental tenets of the existing [global] economic system," says economist C. Fred Bergsten of the Peterson Institute.

This is no small matter. Growing trade and the cross-border transfers of technology and management skills contributed to history's greatest surge of prosperity. Living standards, as measured by per capita incomes, have skyrocketed since 1950: up 10 times in Japan, 16 times in South Korea, four times in France and three times in the United States. Significantly, these gains occurred without serious political conflict. With the exception of oil, world commerce expanded quietly. The chief sources of global strife have been ideology, nationalism, religion and ethnic conflict.

Economics could now join this list, because the balance of power is shifting. The United States was the old order's main architect, and China is a rising power of the new. Their approaches contrast dramatically.

Economically dominant after World War II, the United States defined its interests as promoting the prosperity of its allies. The aims were to combat communism and prevent another Great Depression. Countries would make mutual trade concessions. They would not manipulate their currencies to gain advantage. Raw materials would be available at nondiscriminatory prices. These norms were mostly honored, though some countries flouted them (Japan manipulated its currency for years).

China's political goals differ. High economic growth and job creation aim to raise living standards and absorb the huge rural migration to expanding cities. Economist Donald Straszheim of Roth Capital Partners estimates the urban inflow at about 17 million people annually. As he says, China sees export-led economic growth as a magnet for foreign investment that brings modern technology and management skills. Prosperity is considered essential to maintaining public order and the Communist Party's political monopoly.

At first, China pursued its ambitions within the existing global framework. Indeed, the United States supported China's membership in the *World Trade Organization* in 2001. But as it grows richer, China increasingly ignores old norms, Bergsten argues. It runs a predatory trade policy by keeping its currency, the renminbi, at artificially low levels. That stimulates export-led growth. From 2000 to 2007, China's current account surplus—a broad measure of trade flows—ballooned from 1.7 percent of gross domestic product to 11.1 percent. The biggest losers are not U.S. manufacturers but developing countries whose labor-intensive exports are most disadvantaged.

Next, China strives to lock up supplies of essential raw materials: oil, natural gas, copper. If other countries suffer, so what? Both the United States and China are self-interested. But the United States has seen a prosperous global economy as a means to expanding its power, while China sees the global economy—guaranteed markets for its exports and raw materials—as the means to promoting domestic stability.

The policies are increasingly on a collision course. China's undervalued currency and massive trade surpluses have produced $1.8 trillion in foreign exchange reserves (China in effect stockpiles the currencies it earns in trade).

Along with its artificial export advantage, China has the cash to buy big stakes in American and other foreign firms. Predictably, that has stirred a political backlash in the United States and elsewhere. The rigid renminbi has contributed to the euro's rise against the dollar, threatening Europe with recession. China has undermined world trade negotiations, and its appetite for raw materials leads it to support renegade regimes (Iran, Sudan).

The world economy faces other threats: catastrophic oil interruptions; disruptive money flows. But the Chinese-American schism poses a dilemma for the next president. If we do nothing, China's economic nationalism may weaken the world economy—but if we retaliate by becoming more nationalistic ourselves, we may do the same. Globalization means interdependence; major nations ignore that at their peril.

At the Gate to Greatness

China's myriad problems could threaten its ascendancy

JOHN POMFRET

Nikita Khrushchev said the Soviet Union would bury us, but these days, everybody seems to think that China is the one wielding the shovel. The People's Republic is on the march—economically, militarily, even ideologically. Economists expect its GDP to surpass America's by 2025; its submarine fleet is reportedly growing five times faster than Washington's; even its capitalist authoritarianism is called a real alternative to the West's liberal democracy. China, the drumbeat goes, is poised to become the 800-pound gorilla of the international system, ready to dominate the 21st century the way the United States dominated the 20th.

Except that it's not.

Ever since I returned to the United States in 2004 from my last posting to China, as the Washington Post's Beijing bureau chief, I've been struck by the breathless way we talk about that country. So often, our perceptions of the place have more to do with how we look at ourselves than with what's actually happening over there. Worried about the U.S. education system? China's becomes a model. Fretting about our military readiness? China's missiles pose a threat. Concerned about slipping U.S. global influence? China seems ready to take our place.

But is China really going to be another superpower? I doubt it.

It's not that I'm a China-basher, like those who predict its collapse because they despise its system and assume that it will go the way of the Soviet Union. I first went to China in 1980 as a student, and I've followed its remarkable transformation over the past 28 years. I met my wife there and call it a second home. I'm hardly expecting China to implode. But its dream of dominating the century isn't going to become a reality anytime soon.

Too many constraints are built into the country's social, economic and political systems. For four big reasons—dire demographics, an overrated economy, an environment under siege and an ideology that doesn't travel well—China is more likely to remain the muscle-bound adolescent of the international system than to become the master of the world.

In the West, China is known as "the factory to the world," the land of unlimited labor where millions are eager to leave the hardscrabble countryside for a chance to tighten screws in microwaves or assemble Apple's latest gizmo. If the country is going to rise to superpowerdom, says conventional wisdom, it will do so on the back of its massive workforce.

But there's a hitch: China's demographics stink. No country is aging faster than the People's Republic, which is on track to become the first nation in the world to get old before it gets rich. Because of the Communist Party's notorious one-child-per-family policy, the average number of children born to a Chinese woman has dropped from 5.8 in the 1970s to 1.8 today—below the rate of 2.1 that would keep the population stable. Meanwhile, life expectancy has shot up, from just 35 in 1949 to more than 73 today. Economists worry that as the working-age population shrinks, labor costs will rise, significantly eroding one of China's key competitive advantages.

Worse, Chinese demographers such as Li Jianmin of Nankai University now predict a crisis in dealing with China's elderly, a group that will balloon from 100 million people older than 60 today to 334 million by 2050, including a staggering 100 million age 80 or older. How will China care for them? With pensions? Fewer than 30 percent of China's urban dwellers have them, and none of the country's 700 million farmers do. And China's state-funded pension system makes Social Security look like Fort Knox. Nicholas Eberstadt, a demographer and economist at the American Enterprise Institute, calls China's demographic time bomb "a slow-motion humanitarian tragedy in the making" that will "probably require a rewrite of the narrative of the rising China."

I count myself lucky to have witnessed China's economic rise first-hand and seen its successes etched on the bodies of my Chinese classmates. When I first met them in the early 1980s, my fellow students were hard and thin as rails; when I found them again almost 20 years later, they proudly sported what the Chinese call the "boss belly." They now golfed and lolled around in swanky saunas.

But in our exuberance over these incredible economic changes, we seem to have forgotten that past performance doesn't guarantee future results. Not a month goes by without some Washington think tank crowing that China's economy is overtaking America's. The Carnegie Endowment for International Peace is the latest, predicting earlier this month that the

Chinese economy would be twice the size of ours by the middle of the century.

There are two problems with predictions like these. First, in the universe where these reports are generated, China's graphs always go up, never down. Second, while the documents may include some nuance, it vanishes when the studies are reported to the rest of us.

One important nuance we keep forgetting is the sheer size of China's population: about 1.3 billion, more than four times that of the United States. China should have a big economy. But on a per capita basis, the country isn't a dragon; it's a medium-size lizard, sitting in 109th place on the International Monetary Fund's World Economic Outlook Database, squarely between Swaziland and Morocco. China's economy is large, but its average living standard is low, and it will stay that way for a very long time, even assuming that the economy continues to grow at impressive rates.

The big number wheeled out to prove that China is eating our economic lunch is the U.S. trade deficit with China, which last year hit $256 billion. But again, where's the missing nuance? Nearly 60 percent of China's total exports are churned out by companies not owned by Chinese (including plenty of U.S. ones). When it comes to high-tech exports such as computers and electronic goods, 89 percent of China's exports come from non-Chinese-owned companies. China is part of the global system, but it's still the low-cost assembly and manufacturing part—and foreign, not Chinese, firms are reaping the lion's share of the profits.

When my family and I left China in 2004, we moved to Los Angeles, the smog capital of the United States. No sooner had we set foot in southern California than my son's asthma attacks and chronic chest infections—so worryingly frequent in Beijing—stopped. When people asked me why we'd moved to L.A., I started joking, "For the air."

China's environmental woes are no joke. This year, China will surpass the United States as the world's No. 1 emitter of greenhouse gases. It continues to be the largest depleter of the ozone layer. And it's the largest polluter of the Pacific Ocean. But in the accepted China narrative, the country's environmental problems will merely mean a few breathing complications for the odd sprinter at the Beijing games. In fact, they could block the country's rise.

The problem is huge: Sixteen of the world's 20 most polluted cities are in China, 70 percent of the country's lakes and rivers are polluted, and half the population lacks clean drinking water.

The constant smoggy haze over northern China diminishes crop yields. By 2030, the nation will face a water shortage equal to the amount it consumes today; factories in the northwest have already been forced out of business because there just isn't any water. Even Chinese government economists estimate that environmental troubles shave 10 percent off the country's gross domestic product each year. Somehow, though, the effect this calamity is having on China's rise doesn't quite register in the West.

And then there's "Kung Fu Panda." That Hollywood movie embodies the final reason why China won't be a superpower: Beijing's animating ideas just aren't that animating.

In recent years, we've been bombarded with articles and books about China's rising global ideological influence. (One typical title: "Charm Offensive: How China's Soft Power Is Transforming the World.") These works portray China's model—a one-party state with a juggernaut economy—as highly attractive to elites in many developing nations, although China's dreary current crop of acolytes (Zimbabwe, Burma and Sudan) don't amount to much of a threat.

But consider the case of the high-kicking panda who uses ancient Chinese teachings to turn himself into a kung fu warrior. That recent Hollywood smash broke Chinese box-office records—and caused no end of hand-wringing among the country's glitterati. "The film's protagonist is China's national treasure, and all the elements are Chinese, but why didn't we make such a film?" Wu Jiang, president of the China National Peking Opera Company, told the official New China News Agency.

The content may be Chinese, but the irreverence and creativity of "Kung Fu Panda" are 100 percent American. That highlights another weakness in the argument about China's inevitable rise: The place remains an authoritarian state run by a party that limits the free flow of information, stifles ingenuity and doesn't understand how to self-correct. Blockbusters don't grow out of the barrel of a gun. Neither do superpowers in the age of globalization.

And yet we seem to revel in overestimating China. One recent evening, I was at a party where a senior aide to a Democratic senator was discussing the business deal earlier this year in which a Chinese state-owned investment company had bought a big chunk of the Blackstone Group, a U.S. investment firm. The Chinese company has lost more than $1 billion, but the aide wouldn't believe that it was just a bum investment. "It's got to be part of a broader plan," she insisted. "It's China."

I tried to convince her otherwise. I don't think I succeeded.

Does China Have It Right?

Beijing is riding the wave of the future, argues a renowned internationalist.

MAURICE STRONG

The China as portrayed in much of the Western media is far from the China that those of us who live here as foreigners, sharing in the excitement and the progress of this remarkable and dynamic country, find so compellingly attractive. As one who has been coming to China for more than 40 years and who now spends most of his time here, I cannot help but contrast, with dismay, what I see and experience here with the negative image to which so many in the West are exposed. Even the outpouring of sympathy at the tragic earthquake that caused such severe death and suffering in Sichuan province is accompanied by attempts by some to blame this on the Chinese government. Yet, no government could have responded so efficiently and expeditiously to a disaster of such immense proportions, and few if any are better prepared to do so.

True, the devastating impact of this earthquake and its aftermath reveal weaknesses and inadequacies in governance at the local level. China has been making progress in building a vibrant, modern society, but inevitably it still has to cope with massive problems left by its turbulent past. Still, that progress is clearly remarkable by any standard. China has raised more people out of poverty than any nation has ever done, and it is deeply committed to its objective of ensuring that those who have been left behind are able to participate in the benefits of its dynamic economy.

The constraints that the Chinese and foreigners living here continue to experience are minimal and for the most part understandable, given that no nation has suffered from societal breakdown, internal conflict and foreign intervention more than China has in the past century. It is a small wonder that the Chinese place such emphasis on the need for internal stability and security. And both the Chinese and the foreigners who appreciate the benefits of this understand and are impressed by the advancements that continue to be made in the movement toward more democratic processes and respect for human rights. Indeed, we must realize that even in our own societies the standards we exhort China to adopt are those we have only recently, and not yet fully, lived up to ourselves. The Chinese will be much more influenced by our example than by the uninformed and hypocritical content of so much of our criticism.

Societies progress at different speeds, and in different ways, toward incorporation into their political and social systems of the highest principles and values to which they aspire. China has made immense progress toward meeting the goals and objectives articulated by its leaders of producing a harmonious society guided by science that will meet the needs and aspirations of all its people and contribute to a more sustainable and equitable world society. Indeed, it is embarking on a distinctive and unprecedented pathway to a new model of development based on utilizing the methods of capitalism to achieve the goals of socialism—a socialist market economy. The entire world has a great stake in the success of China in making this transformation. Following the example of the traditional industrialized countries would not be sustainable for China, or for the world. To be sure, this is a monumental challenge that is still a work in progress. But it is in all of our interests that China be successful in doing so, and that we lend it our understanding and support.

Hostile attitudes and policies aimed at undermining China's progress and discrediting its policies and intentions can only be counterproductive, and contrary to our own interests. For there is not a single major world issue that can be resolved without China's co-operation. It is not that we should forgo legitimate and constructive criticisms and differences, but that these be resolved by engagement with China as a full partner, rather than by the kind of entrenched hostility and bias we so often display.

We should continue to facilitate China's full participation in the policy and decision-making processes by which the future of all of us is being shaped. Climate change is an issue that is especially relevant. China realizes that it will be one of the most vulnerable victims of climate change and is already taking serious measures domestically to avert these risks. But it cannot be expected to transform these into binding commitments that are not matched by firm and enforceable commitments by the countries, notably the United States, whose accumulated emissions of greenhouse gases have caused the irreversible damage already inflicted on the world. The attempt to shift the onus for climate change to China, India and other rapidly industrializing developing countries is neither fair nor workable.

China's participation in the post-Kyoto agreements now being negotiated is necessary and will be forthcoming only on the basis of a fair sharing of responsibilities and obligations in which those who have contributed most to the problem of climate change must take the lead.

Similarly, the attempt to shift the onus for increases in food, oil and commodity prices to China, as well as India and others now competing for these imports, will be counterproductive. The needs of the poor and the newly developing countries cannot be subordinated to the wasteful and indulgent appetites of the rich and their pre-emption of a disproportion of the world's resources.

Co-operation and co-operative engagement, on a scale that is without precedent, are the only ways of resolving these matters, rather than allowing them to escalate into a new generation of conflict—a very real possibility. China's role will be indispensable. It will be a willing and constructive participant in this process, but not a subservient one. The decisions taken by the G8 and other organizations that reflect the geopolitical alignments of the past cannot be expected to dictate the positions of China and other newly developing countries that not only represent a majority of the world's people, but the largest share of its GNP and its continued economic growth. The countries that since the Second World War have dominated the institutions and dictated the terms of international co-operation must accommodate the reality that they are now a minority—a still influential one, but one that must make room for the new majority.

China's commitment to internal security and stability and to regional and world peace must also be taken seriously. Unlike Japan, which has invaded and sought to dominate each of its neighbours, ceasing only when it was defeated in the Second World War, China's territorial disputes with its neighbours have been confined to differences over their boundaries rather than attempts to occupy or annex them. It gives its own minorities a high degree of autonomy, including special rights such as exemption from the one-child policy, while rigorously resisting separatist tendencies, as most countries do.

Recent disturbances in Tibet were led by monks whose traditional privileges and control over the majority of the population has been severely curtailed, while the majority who live in poverty and serfdom are experiencing new opportunities as a result of the modernization of the Tibetan economy. To be sure, this process has been a difficult and even painful one for many, but both Chinese and Tibetans continue to learn and to accommodate the changes that will enable Tibet to retain its distinctive cultural and religious heritage while according its people new and growing opportunities for a better life. Even the Dalai Lama does not advocate or expect the independence of Tibet from China, and his differences are related to the degree and nature of the autonomy Tibet could be given within China.

Recent events that underscore continuing problems should not obscure the immense progress that has already been made.

Taiwan is the other main example of China's unshakable commitment to retaining the integrity of its territory while accommodating the important differences that exist between the two societies, as Beijing did with Hong Kong. China will continue to defend its own frontiers and territories while respecting the sovereignty of its neighbours and resolving differences with them peacefully. As for other frontier issues, like disputes with Japan over islands claimed by both, China is endeavouring to resolve them through peaceful negotiations.

The alternative, in all these issues and others, is an ominous and growing potential for conflict, at a time when what the world needs is a new and immensely increased degree of co-operation. This must be focused principally on those issues that affect the very survival of humankind, and must transcend the narrower and self-serving interests of individual nations. This requires a radical strengthening of the international agreements and institutions to foster extensive co-operation, particularly a revitalized United Nations and its agencies.

China must be, and is, truly prepared to play a constructive and leading role in this process. It is in no one's interest to continue to subject China to the uninformed, prejudiced and hostile attacks that can only serve to nourish its own nationalistic and unilateral tendencies. But China will not and cannot be expected to be subservient to the decisions and influences of the small number of more developed nations that continue to assert dominance in international policy, decision-making and institutions, which they have enjoyed for so long.

Uninformed and ideologically biased critics of China should ask themselves why it is that the majority of Chinese today are better off and better satisfied than ever, why more overseas Chinese are returning to China, and why more foreigners are enjoying conditions of life here that make them want to stay, even if it involves changing their employment to do so. Indeed, I am one of the many who enjoy and appreciate being in China, and being caught up in the excitement of the remarkable dynamism of the unprecedented transition that this great nation is experiencing. Indeed, I feel privileged to participate in it. The re-emergence of China as a world leader is one of the most important events of this period of history, and one that will have a profound and decisive impact on the future of the entire human community. This is the China we know and want the entire world to know. The Beijing Olympics, which will focus the world spotlight on the new China, will provide a unique opportunity for the world to view China as its people and friends do.

Think Again: China

It's often said that China is walking a tightrope: Its economy depends on foreign money, its leadership is set in its ways, and its military expansion threatens the world. But the Middle Kingdom's immediate dangers run deeper than you realize.

HARRY HARDING

"China's Biggest Risks Are Economic"

No. In fact, China's most severe risks are ecological—particularly its environmental problems and its vulnerability to communicable disease. Of course, this is not to say that China has no economic problems. No country is immune from the normal business cycle, and China today is subject to both inflationary and recessionary risks. But Beijing is developing the fiscal and monetary tools to regulate the economy so as to prevent these problems from becoming catastrophic once they emerge.

In contrast, China's ecological and health risks are far more serious than people realize. Air pollution in China is affecting the quality of life in cities like Beijing, Hong Kong, and Shanghai, among others. The risk of water shortages, both in agricultural areas and major cities, is high and growing; only 1 percent of the surface water available to Shanghai is safe to drink. In one harbinger of things to come, an explosion at a chemical plant in northeast China in November 2005 sent a benzene slick cascading down the Songhua River. Millions of people in the large, industrial city of Harbin were without water for a week. The probability of more acute environmental crises resulting from chemical spills or toxic emissions is high. The Chinese government is already warning that the country's emission of carbon dioxide and greenhouse gases will significantly damage China's agricultural production.

China is also experiencing epidemics of chronic disease. Reported cases of HIV increased by 30 percent to roughly 650,000 in 2006, and the United Nations projects that 10 million Chinese will be infected by 2010. Hepatitis infects 10 percent of the country's population. The probability of an outbreak of an acute communicable disease, such as the avian flu, remains high. The main issue is how virulent the virus will be, and whether its spread can be contained. The risk is exacerbated by the decay of the rural public health system due to lack of funding and by the reluctance of local officials to report new occurrences of the disease, making it more likely that an outbreak will become a deadly epidemic.

"A Second Tiananmen Crisis Is Inevitable"

Hardly. The Tiananmen Square crisis of 1989 involved mass protests in scores of cities across China—and the demonstrations in Beijing were so large that the government was able to suppress them only through the use of brutal military force. Though not inconceivable, another dramatic uprising on that scale is unlikely.

It is true, however, that China has many problems that are producing widespread popular discontent. These include environmental problems; gaps in the country's social safety net, particularly with regard to health insurance and old-age pensions; controversies over land and water rights; and chronic corruption among officials. These grievances have caused a sharp increase in grassroots protests. The Chinese government itself reported some 80,000 such incidents in 2005, some of which were quite large and even violent. In the most notorious uprising, in late 2005, riot police fired at protesting farmers in a rural Guangdong Province village. Witnesses claim as many as 20 villagers were killed.

But Chinese leaders are adopting policies to address the causes of rural grievance, such as increasing spending on rural projects, abolishing onerous agricultural taxes, and cracking down on local officials who squeeze villagers. When protests do occur, they arrest the leaders but often try to remedy the particular issues that caused the unrest. Six months after the fatal confrontation in Guangdong, a similar protest nearby ended with official promises to review the terms of the land confiscation that had provoked it. Above all, by controlling the media and suppressing independent political organization, Beijing is trying to ensure that protests remain localized. Moreover, in many quarters, particularly China's growing urban middle class, political support for the government appears to be quite high.

The real concern is whether bigger issues could foil these efforts. The emergence of serious and widespread economic problems (especially inflation and unemployment) or the government being blamed for a major domestic or international crisis (such as an environmental catastrophe or an incident during

101

the upcoming 2008 Olympics) could lead to nationwide discontent. It would be particularly dangerous if the dissatisfaction were so widespread that it overwhelmed the party's control over the media and the Internet, or produced a divided leadership unable to respond effectively. In such a circumstance, there could be large-scale protests in several major cities that might be difficult to control, as was the case in 1989.

"Chinese Elite Politics Are Stable"

Yes, but less than you might think. Chinese politics has become increasingly institutionalized, the elite are more pragmatic, and top leaders want to avoid a perception of internecine feuding. But President Hu Jintao has had to tread more softly than his predecessors. Although he has been able to secure the dismissals of a few central and provincial leaders by charging them with corruption, he has not yet been able to replace them with his own protégés.

Hu is nearing the end of his first five-year term. Past practice suggests that one or two potential successors should have been appointed to the Politburo by now. The president will have to identify his heirs apparent by the 17th Communist Party Congress this fall so they have enough time to win broader support before Hu retires in 2012. If his choices are not widely accepted, the result could be a decline in the party's legitimacy. Indeed, the uncertainties surrounding succession now constitute the biggest political risk facing China this year.

What is even more worrying is that the grid-locked succession may reflect a lack of agreement on China's policy decisions. True, Hu recently secured formal endorsement of his stance that China needs to address its most serious domestic problems and spread the benefits of economic growth in order to tamp down social conflict. But that doesn't preclude a debate over how to achieve that goal. For one thing, the party has defined one of its primary goals as creating a "harmonious socialist society," which implies that any policy option that isn't "socialist"—for example, protecting private property rights or moving toward pluralistic democracy—should be taken off the table. For another, although Hu talks about the need for sustainable development, the party leaders still assign priority to rapid economic growth. Those decisions give easy rhetorical openings to any of Hu's rivals who may want to challenge his political agenda going forward.

"China's Banks Will Collapse"

Doubtful. Until very recently, China's banking system was in big trouble. It was the main mechanism for financing the country's high levels of investment, which made up 45 percent of gross domestic product (GDP) in 2005. The banks faced considerable pressure to lend money to inefficient state-owned enterprises. As a result, the volume of the country's nonperforming loans rose to alarming levels. But the banks survived, largely because depositors had few other outlets for their savings. The banking system was not that solvent, but it remained liquid.

In more recent years, though, China's corporate sector has become a less risky customer for the banks. Investment is increasingly being financed by means other than bank loans, such as bond issues, corporate profits, or stock offerings. The latter have yielded recordbreaking sums, with the Industrial and Commercial Bank of China leading the way with a $22 billion initial public offering last fall. And a gradual process of mergers, acquisitions, and privatization is increasing the profitability of formerly state-owned enterprises.

At the same time, the solvency of the banks has also improved. China has been recapitalizing banks, transferring nonperforming loans to management companies, and inviting partial foreign ownership of major banks. In addition, the banks' portfolios are being broadened through greater reliance on home mortgages and fee-generating services.

China's financial system isn't entirely out of the woods. The banks' lending decisions are still subject to political pressures, because the party still chooses senior bank executives from its ranks. The health of smaller local banks, various investment brokerages, and insurance companies is not ideal. And with a growing range of investment opportunities—including the stock market, real estate, and even foreign mutual funds—Chinese banks now have to worry that financial insolvency could more easily generate liquidity problems.

Even so, China's low level of foreign indebtedness gives the government the tools to contain the economic consequences of a financial crisis.

"China Is Too Dependent on Foreign Money"

Not really. China is certainly highly integrated into today's international economy. By abandoning the economic autarchy of the Maoist period, it has become a major trading nation. It exports large volumes of textiles, machinery, and electronic equipment. In turn, it imports advanced technology, petroleum, and other natural resources. It is also a favored destination for foreign direct investment (FDI), not only because of its attractiveness as a manufacturing platform for exports, but because of the size and dynamism of its own domestic market. China now attracts twice the FDI it did 10 years ago.

The relatively large share of exports to China's GDP and the volumes of incoming FDI have generated concern that China is too dependent on the international economy and is acutely vulnerable to a slowdown. But these concerns are overblown. For one thing, with $1 trillion in foreign exchange reserves, and an extraordinarily high domestic savings rate of roughly 47 percent, China is hardly dependent on foreign capital. It has relied on the technology and marketing networks that accompany foreign investment to promote its exports, but it would most likely survive a reduction in new investment fairly easily.

The same is true with trade. China is a large continental economy, and at 64 percent of GDP, its trade dependence is far lower than of places such as Hong Kong or Singapore. Moreover, much of the value of Chinese exports is provided by imported components and raw materials, with local elements providing relatively less value. Computers bearing the tag "Made in China" may be assembled there, but their screens and microprocessors likely come from Taiwan or South Korea. Processing and assembly accounted for 55 percent of China's total exports in 2006. That means that the net contribution of trade to the Chinese economy is less than the gross figures imply. Sure, China would take a hit if there were a severe global recession or a terrorist attack that crippled international trade flows. But its economy could weather that challenge far better than most.

"Chinese Nationalism Is on the Rise"

Yes, but don't exaggerate its implications. Popular nationalism has been a part of China's fabric since the middle of the 19th century. It emerged as a reaction to invasion by nations more technologically advanced than China—first from Europe, then Japan. More recently, the Chinese Communist Party, whose ideological appeal began to erode in the 1980s, has been encouraging nationalism as a source of legitimacy.

But the party recognizes that nationalism is a double-edged sword. Although it can be a source of domestic legitimacy, it can also generate apprehension and mistrust abroad. That lesson was borne out by several anti-foreign protests, including those against the United States for the accidental bombing of the Chinese Embassy in Belgrade in 1999 and for the collision between an American reconnaissance aircraft and a Chinese fighter in 2001. Although these episodes did no lasting damage to China's relations with the United States, Beijing was alarmed by the fervor of the protests and the time it took to bring them to an end. China's leaders understand that nationalism can generate public criticism of leaders who "capitulate" to foreign governments just as easily as it generates support for those who are perceived as upholding Chinese interests.

Accordingly, the promotion of nationalism now plays a smaller role in the party's search for legitimacy. It has been replaced to a degree by the quest for a "harmonious socialist society." The media now repeatedly emphasize that China's rise should be peaceful, and officials try to keep nationalist sentiment in check.

The problem is that popular nationalism can have its own momentum, independent of the wishes of the party's leadership. But without further democratization, nationalistic public opinion isn't powerful enough to determine Chinese foreign policy. At the margins, however, it reduces the flexibility of Chinese foreign policymakers. It could be a source of political instability if the Chinese government were accused of failing to uphold the national interest in the event of an international crisis.

"China's Rise Will Lead to Military Conflict"

Highly unlikely, at least for the foreseeable future. Yes, China is modernizing its military, seeking not only a stronger nuclear deterrent but also a greater ability to project conventional force. And like any powerful country, China will use force if it believes its vital national interests are at stake, particularly concerning the disputes over islands and undersea resources in the East China Sea and the South China Sea, the possible collapse of

North Korea, and, above all, the possibility of a declaration of independence by Taiwan.

But China is no longer a revolutionary power. It does not have fundamental complaints about the international economic and political systems from which it has benefited so much over the past 25 years. Moreover, its economic interdependence with the rest of the world will deter Beijing from military adventures unless such core interests are threatened. The rise of Chinese power, in turn, will deter China's neighbors from threatening its core interests. Beijing has drawn its red line in the Taiwan Strait so narrowly—a de jure declaration of independence by Taiwan—that it is unlikely ever to be crossed.

The real challenges from China are, therefore, far more subtle than alarmists would suggest. First, though China is willing to join the existing international order, it wants to play a larger role—as a rule-maker, not just a rule-taker. Fortunately, Washington's current policy of encouraging China to become a "responsible stakeholder" in the international system is largely compatible with Beijing's desire for greater influence.

A second challenge stems from the desire that Chinese firms gain the greatest market share domestically and join the ranks of large, profitable multinationals. China is a poster child for globalization, but Beijing's objective is to see that Chinese firms, and not foreign firms, are the winners of that global competition. Indeed, economic nationalism may pose a greater challenge for the world than any other form of Chinese power.

China is simultaneously rising on several dimensions—military, economic, diplomatic, ideological, and cultural. In that regard, it more closely resembles the United States of the 1950s than, say, 1930s Japan or Stalinist Russia. The greatest risk is not that Beijing will use its military power to attack other countries, but rather that it will use its growing resources to shift the overall balance of power in China's favor, especially in Asia. It is a strategic shift that has already begun.

References

For a comprehensive overview of current trends in China and their implications for the rest of the world, read *China: The Balance Sheet: What the World Needs to Know Now About the Emerging Superpower* (New York: PublicAffairs, 2006) by C. Fred Bergsten, Bates Gill, Nicholas R. Lardy, and Derek Mitchell.

The best account of China's daunting environmental problems can be found in Elizabeth Economy's *The River Runs Black: The Environmental Challenge to China's Future* (Ithaca: Cornell University Press, 2004). For insights on the future economic prospects for the Middle Kingdom, read *The Chinese Economy: Transitions and Growth* (Cambridge: MIT Press, 2007) by Barry Naughton.

For FOREIGN POLICY's recent coverage of China, see "The Dark Side of China's Rise" (March/April 2006) by Minxin Pei, who argues that China's economic success has blinded the world to its weaknesses. In "The Virus Hunters" (March/April 2006), Karl Taro Greenfeld reveals how Beijing tried to cover up the 2003 SARS outbreak and asks whether China will be prepared to handle the next pandemic when it strikes.

China's Image Sullied by Tainted Milk

Putting profit and prestige over safety, China compounds the crisis with a cover-up.

The latest scandal involving tainted milk adds to the perception that the label "Made in China" covers layers of warnings: a potentially resentful work force, suffering low pay and abuse; managers who place profits over safety, striving for quantity over quality in production; minimal quality-inspection procedures and enforcement; and government authorities conditioned to hide rather than expose problems. More than 50,000 Chinese children have fallen ill after drinking milk products tainted with melamine, a chemical that mimics protein in testing. Global and Chinese consumers alike express outrage that company officials knew about the problem for eight months and took no action. Government officials who learned about the problem before the August Olympics also kept mum. "What the government appears to fear, in this case as with previous class-action attempts on property and pollution, is a snowballing effect that could lead to a national political movement," explains journalist Mary Kay Magistad. To earn trust, governments and traders, particularly in the area of food products, must provide full and immediate disclosures of any problem. Otherwise, citizens will seek out substitute products and lose faith in their leadership. —YaleGlobal

MARY KAY MAGISTAD

Beijing: The flag flew, the music surged, and state-run television was filled with triumphant images of the Beijing Olympics and the successful Shenzhou VII spacewalk, marking, on Oct. 1st, the Chinese Communist Party's 49th anniversary in power. But if the party had hoped to spend the day basking in the adulation of the Chinese people and the admiration of the world, it hadn't counted on the reverberations of a self-inflicted body blow to Brand China—the tainted milk scandal.

At last count, 53 brands of dairy products in China, plus foreign brands made with Chinese milk ingredients including Cadbury chocolate and Lipton milk tea powder, have been found to contain melamine, a binding agent used to make plastics and floor tiles. Chinese dairy producers found another use for the chemical—adding it to watered-down milk, because melamine's high nitrogen content makes the milk's protein levels appear higher than they are.

The tainted milk found its way into yogurt, ice cream, cakes, cookies, cereals—and, most unbelievably for many Chinese parents, who have been ordered by the state to have just one child, powdered baby formula.

"Some people are saying the presidents of those milk companies should be executed, and I think they're right," says grocery store owner Tian Yang Qing, as she glances through a government-supplied list of dozens of tainted products. "How could those businessmen do this to little babies? Think of how the children's development is affected. Think of how their lives are affected. It's terrible."

Some 54,000 Chinese children have ended up in the hospital after drinking melamine-tainted milk formula, and at least three have died. Other children have been hospitalized with kidney stones in Hong Kong and Taiwan. So far, Chinese authorities have arrested at least 27 people in connection with the crisis.

The global response since the scandal broke in mid-September has been swift. More than a dozen countries have banned some or all dairy products from the affected brands. The European Union slapped a ban on any baby food originating in China that has even a trace of milk. Some analysts estimate it could take until 2010 for the $20 billion Chinese dairy industry to regain what it's lost in credibility and sales—and that's assuming China's leaders get serious about enforcing a rigorous and transparent quality-inspection system, something they'd promised to do after the last year's food safety scandals.

China's leaders have been scrambling to send reassuring messages. "The problem shows that we should pay more attention to business ethics and social morality in the development process," Premier Wen Jiabao told a World Economic Forum meeting in Tianjin. "These are some of the growing pains of China's road to economic reforms. We will overcome them by facing the challenges truthfully."

But Wen himself sounded less than truthful in another remark he made in the same speech. "China did not intend to cover the truth when the incident happened."

The state-run media have reported a different story. It is a story about managers of a major Chinese brand, Sanlu, knowing as early as last December that its powdered baby formula had problems, but doing nothing. It's a story of a father, 40-year-old Wang Yuanping of Zhejiang province, worrying as far back as February about why Sanlu's powdered milk was making his daughter sick. He was persuaded to shut up with the free supply of four cases of the same.

It was not until early August that Sanlu informed local government authorities of the problem. By then, just days before the opening of the Beijing Olympics, local officials knew better than to spoil the celebration. Weeks went by. More children fell ill. Eventually, in mid-September, the New Zealand government intervened with Beijing on behalf of Fonterra, a New Zealand company, which owns a 43 percent share of Sanlu. The hushed-up story was finally blown wide open.

As an online editorial on Access Asia, a China and Asia consumer market analysis group concluded, "Fonterra knew something was wrong. They decided to try and deal with the problem internally, worried about the negative effect on Sanlu, on China during the Olympics and of course on themselves."

But this isn't a story about just one bad actor. It's about dozens of Chinese dairy producers and collectors, gaming the quality-inspection system over time, adding not just melamine but also, in the past, other chemicals, so they could water down their milk, pass cursory quality inspection tests and make more money. It's also about a state regulatory system that failed.

"In any (regulatory) system, you can't rely on testing alone," says Jorgen Schlundt, director of the World Health Organization's food-safety department. "That's the old-fashioned way. You have to have a system where you look at what are the risks and how do we prevent them, as close to the source as possible. You need to have a system where you have a culture of openness and quick reporting."

That's exactly what China does not have. Instead, it has a system where many businesses try to get away with what they can, and many local officials try to cover up problems that happen on their watch, either because they're profiting from the businesses in question, or because they fear that problems could cut into their chances for a raise or a promotion. That mentality has delayed reporting in recent years on SARS, bird flu, toxic chemical spills and food contamination. In each case, local officials preferred to risk other people's lives than their own careers. The central government's warnings that it would fire those who don't report promptly have failed to transform the old mentality.

Meanwhile, consumer protection mechanisms in China remain weak, and the government appears to want to keep them so. About 20 of the lawyers who have been trying to help families affected by the tainted milk scandal say they have received calls from local governmental legal authorities, warning that they could lose their licenses if they continue to help affected families.

What the government appears to fear, in this case as with previous class-action attempts on property and pollution, is a snowballing effect that could lead to a national political movement. It seems to prefer to keep victims isolated from one another, while stressing social harmony and promising to pay medical bills and fix the problems.

Premier Wen has now pledged to overhaul the quality-inspection system for food and dairy. One problem, says the WHO's Schlundt, is that up to 16 different authorities now split that responsibility: "It is always a problem when you have many separate authorities that may not have the same culture of reporting." He says it's a good first couple of steps that China has put the Food & Drug Administration under the Ministry of Health, and suspended a system that allowed some favored companies, including Sanlu, to do their own quality inspection. But a thorough reorganization will take years.

Meanwhile, there's urgent damage control to be done. Without swift and effective action to better protect its own consumers and citizens, China's leaders may find that the wave of goodwill they've been riding of late may dry up, and bring them down to earth with a thud.

MARY KAY Magistad covers Northeast Asia for The World.

Where Gas Guzzlers Convey Status

China's booming car culture is helping drive up the demand for oil.

ARIANA EUNJUNG CHA

Nodding his head to the disco music blaring out of his car's nine speakers, Zhang Linsen swings the shiny, black Hummer H2 out of his company's gates and on to the spacious four-lane road.

Running a hand over his closely shaved head, Zhang scans the expanse of high-end suburban offices and villas that a decade ago was just another patch of farmland outside of Shanghai. To his left is a royal blue sedan with a couple and a baby, in front of him a lone young woman being chauffeured in a van.

"In China, size matters," says Zhang, the 44-year-old founder of a media and graphic design company. "People want to have a car that shows off their status in society. No one wants to buy small."

Zhang grasps the wheels of his Hummer, called "hanma" or "fierce horse" in Chinese, and hits the accelerator.

Car ownership in China is exploding, and it's not only cars but also sport-utility vehicles, pickup trucks and other gas-guzzling rides. Elsewhere in the world, the popularity of these vehicles has tumbled as the cost of oil has soared. But in China, the number of SUVs sold rose 43 percent in May compared with the previous year, and full-size sedans were up 15 percent. Indeed, China's demand for gas is much of the reason for the dramatic run-up in global oil prices.

China alone accounts for about 40 percent of the world's recent increase in demand for oil, burning through twice as much now as it did a decade ago. Fifteen years ago, there were almost no private cars in the country. By the end of last year, the number had reached 15.2 million.

There are now more Buicks—the venerable, boat-like American luxury car of years past—sold in China than in the United States. Demand for Hummers has been so strong that starting this year, Chinese consumers can buy a similar military-style vehicle called the Predator at more than 25 new dealerships.

Yet strong demand for oil isn't limited to China and its automobiles. Ever since an investment group led by a New York lawyer and a New Haven, Conn., banker came up with the notion of using Pennsylvania oil for lighting in the 1880s, petroleum has been an essential component of the industrial age. It fuels ships, planes and cars, and goes into road asphalt, home heating fuel, lubricants, plastics and petrochemicals.

The United States is the world's single largest consumer of oil, burning through more than 20 million barrels per day last year. This year, U.S. usage is on track to decline the most in 25 years, the result of high fuel prices and a sluggish economy. Still, about one of every eight barrels of oil produced worldwide ultimately ends up in the fuel tank of an American car or truck.

Demand in many developing countries, in the meantime, is accelerating because of the spread of middle-class lifestyles and populist policies that subsidize fuel to keep it cheap.

India's government, for example, will spend $24.5 billion this year on oil subsidies. And that's after subsidies were scaled back in June, triggering riots over the cost of diesel, which fuels most of the country's vehicles, and other oil products. "The hike in fuel prices last month has done little to damp soaring diesel demand," says Seema Desai, an analyst at the Eurasia Group. Indians are paying about $3.60 a gallon for diesel, far below market rates, and demand is still growing at an annual rate of more than 20 percent.

Oil-producing countries are even more generous to their residents. In Venezuela, gasoline costs 12 cents a gallon. In Iran, it costs 41 cents. In Saudi Arabia, it costs 47 cents; in Russia, $3.90.

All this growth is more than offsetting the conservation measures taken in the United States, Europe and other industrialized nations. This year, the combined consumption of China, India, Russia and the Middle East will increase 4.4 percent and for the first time exceed that of the United States, according to the International Energy Agency.

For energy planners in the industrialized world, this is a cruel irony, coming after a concerted effort by consumers and lawmakers to steer consumption downward. If China continues to increase its use of oil at the average pace of 6 to 7 percent a year, as it has since 1990, it will consume as much as the United States in more than 20 years.

But China bristles at criticism of its growing oil use, noting that per capita it will remain a small fraction of U.S. consumption for decades to come. Moreover, industrialized nations all relied on heavy petroleum use as they developed. Why should we be penalized, the Chinese ask, for coming late to the game?

While a number of factors contribute to China's surging demand, including rapid industrial development and hoarding by the government to ensure adequate supplies for this summer's Olympic Games in Beijing, it is autos that are having the biggest impact.

Yet despite this dizzying increase in passenger cars, less than 4 percent of the country's 1.3 billion people have already bought one. That's where the United States was in 1915.

"The entire energy market of the world is being affected by this country already. Can you imagine when we get to 50 people out of every 1,000 in China owning cars?" asked Friedhelm Engler, design director for General Motors and Shanghai Automotive Industry's joint-venture engineering and design lab in China.

For the previous generation, owning a car was the province of a privileged few—those in government, heads of state-owned companies and others in positions of power.

But starting in 2000, China began to aggressively promote consumption to balance its export-driven, white-hot economy. Zeng Peiyan, who was then director of the national planning committee, created a list of things average citizens should be encouraged to buy. At the top of that list was cars.

Beijing has simplified procedures for buying cars, cut sales taxes and improved the availability of bank loans. It encouraged local governments to build more parking areas. It banned bicycles on some larger streets. And it laid thousands of miles of gleaming, multi-lane superhighways around the country.

In the meantime, gas has been kept artificially cheap. Even after subsidies were partly lifted last month, a gallon of gas in China costs only $3.40, well below market prices.

Some Chinese cities actually promote bigger, fancier cars to help foster the image of a more "wenming," or civilized, modern society.

The northern port city of Dalian: the Human provincial capital, Changsha; Shenzhen, across the border from Hong Kong: and many other cities ban cars with engines smaller than 1 liter from entering their downtowns on the grounds that those cars are old and dirty. Some other municipalities ban smaller cars from expressways, claiming the cars are so small they may endanger their owners when going at high speed. Other local governments single out owners of small cars for special charges—"traffic capacity expansion" or "road and bridge maintenance" fees—that can run $150 to $1,500.

In 2006, when China released its most recent "five-year plan," a national road map of priorities, a newly environmentally conscious central government began to encourage local governments to remove any disincentives for consumers to buy and for manufacturers to produce small cars. But legislation that would require local governments to revise their old practices is still pending, and change has been slow.

The impact of China's official car polices is perhaps most evident in the manufacturing center of Dongguan, a maze of motorways and parking lots close to the country's southern border in the heart of the Pearl River Delta. For every 1,000 residents in Dongguan, 520 have cars—the highest rate in the nation and nearly 15 times the average.

Spread out over 952 square miles of industrial parks and housing complexes, Dongguan may be the closest thing to a Washington-style suburb in China. With no local subway system, a shortage of taxis and buses with limited routes, Dongguan's 7 million inhabitants often have no way of getting around without a car.

To help residents purchase cars, the government has offered numerous financial incentives. In 2007, the city worked with local banks to allow consumers to put zero down and get a car loan. Civil servants receive generous subsidies for using their own cars for official business, which prompted a rush on automobile purchases by local government workers. Dongguan also ordered operators of parking garages to cap their monthly charges at half the market price in neighboring cities.

All this has been good news for Feng Jiangming, 28, who owns a small business that sells nails, screws, ball bearings and other hardware to stores. Last month in Dongguan, Feng was at the Zhicheng car dealership shopping for a new car to supplement the one he has had for five years.

In 1998 at the age of 17, Feng arrived here from Hunan Province to try his luck as a laborer at the many export-oriented factories that were opening. He remembers that the area was dotted with small villages and that the dirt streets were packed with bicycles. Back then, he says, no one he knew had a car. These days, few of his friends don't.

Feng ran his fingers along the shiny four-door, brown Buick Excelle sedan in front of him and nodded at the roughly $22,000 sticker price. He inspected the sunroof, extra large head-lights, all-leather interior.

When he first heard about the increase in fuel prices in China, Feng said he gave the idea of a smaller car a few seconds of thought—and ruled it out, "If you want to go golfing or fishing, it's not very convenient," he said.

Salesman Xie Bin elaborated: "A small car is for people with money problems or if they want it as an extra car to give to their wives, daughters or girlfriends to go buy food."

As recently as a few years ago, automakers were betting that the future of the Chinese car market was in small vehicles that could easily maneuver the narrow alleyways of its ancient cities. Then they discovered a quirk in Chinese consumers' tastes.

Many car owners, even those who are lower middle-class, want to appear wealthy enough to have a chauffeured automobile. That means extra room for the owners in the rear. As a result, even big cars in China tend to be a third of a foot or more longer than their American counterparts.

This helps explain why roomy cars, such as the Volkswagen Santana—a family sedan based on the Passat that is the country's top-selling car—the Audi A6, Honda Odyssey and various Buick models are doing so well in China.

In China, the roomy Buick is associated with Sun Yatsen, the father of the modern Chinese state, and Zhou Enlai, one China's most respected leaders. Both used to ride around in classic black Buicks. Buick's advertisements in China these days add a modern twist, depicting two tall businessmen in suits giving each other high-fives as if they have just closed a sweet business deal.

Another factor driving the sale of bigger cars in China is the rapid emergence of suburbs. Many of these satellite cities are romanticized versions of how the Chinese imagine the United States and other Western countries, rich with spacious villas and two-car garages, big-box chain stores, strip malls and office parks.

Zhai Yongping, an energy specialist with the Asian Development ment Bank, fears the Chinese are buying into the American lifestyle: "big houses, big air conditioning, big roads." Compared with the breakneck pace of road construction, public transit has developed slowly.

To encourage the Chinese to go green, General Motors, which has ranked first for passenger car sales in China in each of the past three years, is preparing to market hybrid vehicles or cars that run on alternative fuels.

But Zhang doesn't expect Chinese consumers to change their car-buying habits. "Fuel economy is probably the last thing Chinese look for," Zhang said as he drove around the Shanghai suburbs in his Hummer. He said he wasn't worried about filling up the tank even after the government trimmed oil subsidies last month, raising gas prices about 18 percent.

Zhang bought the Hummer in 2006, on special order from the United States. It cost him $220,000, including hefty shipping and import fees. "It feels like a man's car," he said.

In June, he and two friends set up a Web site announcing the formation of a Hummer club in Shanghai. Some 20 other owners e-mailed him within days. They included several other businessmen but also coal mine bosses from inland provinces and three women in their 30s who are friends and purchased identical Hummer H3s.

Zhang says he and other club members are talking about organizing off-road trips, perhaps to the mountainous parts of Sichuan Province to help with reconstruction efforts in areas hard hit by the recent earthquake. For now, however, Zhang says he's happy just using his car to visit friends, cruising along at 17 miles per gallon on China's ever-growing network of highways.

Washington Post staff writer Steven Mufson in Washington and researchers Wu Meng and Crissie Ding contributed to this report.

China's Complicit Capitalists

KELLEE S. TSAI

Until the late 1970s, China did not even keep official statistics on private enterprises because they were illegal and negligible in number. Today there are over 29 million private businesses, which employ over 200 million people and generate two-thirds of China's industrial output. The private sector's spectacular growth has led many observers to speculate that China is developing a capitalist class that will overthrow the Chinese Communist Party and demand democracy based on the principle of "no taxation without representation."

Inspired by the experience of a handful of Western countries, this expectation is based on a two misguided assumptions: first, that private entrepreneurs comprise a single, consistent class; and second, that these entrepreneurs would support a regime change. Although China's capitalists are not poised to demand democracy, they have had a structural impact on Chinese politics. In order to run their businesses in a transitional and a politically charged regulatory environment, private entrepreneurs have created a host of adaptive strategies at the grass-roots level. The popularity and relative success of these strategies have, in turn, enabled reform-oriented elites to justify significant changes in the country's most important governing institutions.

Entrepreneurs Divided

China's private entrepreneurs should not be regarded as a coherent "class" that shares similar identities and interests. Business owners come from all walks of life, and as such, they bring different resources to bear when they have operational or policy grievances. The private sector now includes people as varied as laid-off state workers running street stalls, factory owners producing exports for the global marketplace and rags-to-riches capitalists on the Forbes annual list of China's wealthiest individuals. The sociopolitical composition of private entrepreneurs is further complicated by the emergence of "privatized" (technically "corporatized") state-owned enterprises, frequently operated by their former managers. The proprietors of newly privatized state entities are much more likely than regular private entrepreneurs—who have built up their businesses *de novo*—to be local elites with well-established social and political networks.

At the same time, China's capitalists face different operating realities at the local level. Observers who focus on aggregate statistics showing private-sector growth tend to overlook the significant variation in local political and economic conditions. Governments in areas that opened to foreign capital earlier on in the reform era, for example, have discriminated against local private businesses by offering foreign investors favorable tax rates and privileged access to bank loans and land use. It has similarly been more difficult for private businesses to thrive in localities that inherited a large state-owned industrial base as local officials have been too preoccupied with the challenges of subsidizing local factories and maintaining social stability to address entrepreneurship.

Then there are areas such as Wenzhou in Zhejiang province where the local government looked the other way as private entrepreneurs engaged in capitalist practices before it was officially sanctioned and even collaborated with local entrepreneurs to allow vibrant underground financial markets to flourish. Given the vast differences among local governments in their orientation towards the private sector, it is overly simplistic to assume China's private entrepreneurs face similar business conditions and concerns.

One might counter that the predictive logic of capitalists pushing for democracy is only meant to apply to the highest economic tier of business owners, i.e., that we would only expect the most successful entrepreneurs (not street vendors) to have both the ability and the means to agitate for political change. However, even if we set aside small retail vendors, the fact is that the wealthiest capitalists remain divided by region, sector and most significantly, by their previous backgrounds. A prerequisite of class formation is class identity, and a prerequisite of class identity is a sense of shared values and interests. Real-estate tycoons born out of party-state patronage have little in common with the owners of manufacturing conglomerates who still remember what it was like to grow up hungry in mountainous areas with little arable land. Social and political identity in China is defined by more than ownership of private assets and net worth.

Further evidence of private entrepreneurs' limited desire for democracy can be seen in their nonconfrontational modes of dispute resolution. When private entrepreneurs are disgruntled with policy issues, they are much more likely to use informal channels for solving their problems than the legal system or political participation. Based on a national survey of private entrepreneurs and extensive fieldwork in 10 provinces, I found that only 5% of business owners regularly rely on more assertive modes of dispute resolution—such as "appealing to the local government or higher authorities" or "appealing through judicial courts." Moreover, among the entrepreneurs who believe that there is a need to strengthen rule of law in China, few associate legal reform with democratization. Instead of aspiring for a more liberal political system, most entrepreneurs fear that democratic reforms would lead to instability, which would jeopardize the prospects for continued economic growth.

Indirect Political Influence

Although china's capitalists have not politically organized themselves, the business environment for private firms and their owners has improved dramatically since the late 1970s. After the political crisis of 1989, capitalists were banned from joining the Communist Party and there were a few years of uncertainty about whether economic reforms would continue. But the fact is, once unthinkable changes have occurred in both party rhetoric and official governmental regulations. Capitalists are now *encouraged* to join the Communist Party and the constitution of the People's Republic of China now protects private property rights (at least in principle). In fact, according to official surveys, 33.9% of private entrepreneurs are now members of the CCP, and conversely, 2.86 million or 4% of party members work in the private sector. Yet the really remarkable part about these changes is that private entrepreneurs themselves never lobbied the state or party directly for these macro level changes. Instead, Beijing has been surprisingly responsive to the adaptive, informal strategies created by entrepreneurs to get things done in the context of a transitional socialist economy.

For example, before 1988 it was illegal for "individual businesses" to hire more than eight employees because Marx's *Das Kapital* indicated that businesses with more than eight employees were "exploitative capitalist producers." Private entrepreneurs found a way of getting around this restriction by simply registering their businesses as "collective enterprises." This adaptive strategy became commonly known as "wearing a red hat." By the time private enterprises with more than eight employees were permitted to operate, there were already over 500,000 red-hat enterprises. In effect, the center sanctioned, post hoc, what was already going on.

A similar dynamic occurred with the Communist Party's incorporation of private entrepreneurs. Wearing a red hat enabled party members to become red capitalists, which changed the occupational composition of the party from within. As employees of the state began running their own businesses, albeit disguised as collective ventures, the party's ban on private entrepreneurs became increasingly unrealistic, if not anachronistic. By the early 2000s, the spread of red capitalists presented the party with the critical dilemma of whether to condemn their economic activities or embrace them: 19.8% of entrepreneurs surveyed by official entities in 2000 indicated that they were already CCP members.

After consulting with provincial and subprovincial officials throughout the country, the party's core leadership decided that it was in the interest of economic growth, as well as party rejuvenation and survival, to legitimize the existing red capitalists and co-opt other private entrepreneurs. Within a relatively short period of time, the party line shifted from banning capitalists to welcoming them. Such a policy reversal would have been difficult to justify in the absence of pre-existing grass-roots deviations from the party line.

Private sector development has clearly had a structural effect on Chinese politics, but not in the manner expected. Economic growth during the reform era has been associated with urbanization, higher rates of literacy and the emergence of economic elites. Moreover, China's political system has become more inclusive and institutionalized. But the people driving the country's growth, private entrepreneurs, never mobilized as a class to pressure the regime for these changes, and it is unlikely that they would do so in the future. Instead, in the interest of staying in power, China's leaders have proven to be remarkably responsive, if not overtly attentive, to the unarticulated needs and interests of private capital. Neither capitalists nor communists are interested in disrupting the implicit pact that has emerged in the last two decades: continued growth for continued communism.

China's Living Laboratory in Urbanization

With millions of farmers each year moving to its burgeoning cities, China is searching for novel ways to expand urban areas while conserving natural resources.

DENNIS NORMILE

Standing in a sea of marsh grass at the eastern tip of Chongming Island, in the mouth of the Yangtze River, it's easy to forget that this wilderness lies within the boundaries of Shanghai municipality. Tidal mud flats, feeding grounds for migratory birds on the East Asian-Australasian Flyway, reach toward the East China Sea as far as the eye can see. A million shore birds pass through every year, including the endangered black-faced spoonbill. To the west, scattered sparsely across the 1041 square kilometers of Chongming, the world's largest alluvial island, are villages, paddies, and orchards.

Shanghai is about to burst another seam and spill onto this peaceful isle. A bridge-tunnel link scheduled for completion in 2009 will turn a torturous 3-hour car-and-ferry trip from downtown—just over the horizon to the south—into a 30-minute commute. And with well over 300,000 new residents each year swelling one of the world's biggest cities—Shanghai has more than 17 million inhabitants—development of Chongming's wide-open spaces is inevitable.

Shanghai is hoping to show that development can be environmentally responsible with the world's first "carbon neutral" city, in which carbon emissions would be completely offset by carbon absorption. Construction of Dongtan Eco-city will begin early this year on land adjacent to Chongming's wetlands. Dongtan's backers hope it will offer a new model that contrasts with China's haphazard urbanization of the past 2 decades. Some planners familiar with practices here, however, wonder if Dongtan's ambitious aims can be fully realized.

Dongtan is one of a half-dozen or so ecocities on the drawing boards as Chinese leaders cope with one of the fastest urbanization rates in the world. The leadership now realizes that unchecked urban sprawl threatens the country's environment and security, says Niu Wenyuan, chief scientist of China's sustainable development strategy program and a counselor of the State Council. As a result, he says, the country is striving for three "zero net-growth rates": the population by 2020, urban energy consumption by 2035, and urban ecological degradation by 2050. "We still have a long way to go," Niu said at the first Xiamen International Forum on Urban Environment in Xiamen, China, last November.

This may be China's last chance to get urbanization right, says Qiu Baoxing, vice minister of construction. "If China chooses the wrong [urbanization] model," he says, "it will [impact] the entire world."

Much of the developing world is urbanizing rapidly, but China's sheer numbers make the stakes here higher. China now has 670 cities, up from 69 in 1947 and 223 in 1980. According to United Nations statistics, China has 15 of the world's 100 fastest-growing cities with a population of a million or more (based on population growth between 1950 and 2000); India, next on the list, has eight. China has 89 cities with a population of a million or more. The United States has 37 and India 32.

The government estimates that 44% of China's population now lives in cities, but that figure does not include migrant workers registered as residing in rural areas. If they are included, "China's real urbanization rate is already around 50%," says Deng Wei, an urban economics specialist at Tsinghua University in Beijing. By 2020, some 60% of the population will live in cities, according to government estimates. Each year, about 12 million farmers move to cities, Niu says: "The biggest agrarian society in the world is becoming the biggest urban society in the world."

The implications are enormous. "Urbanization concerns the use of resources, human lifestyles and culture, economic efficiency, modernization, the welfare system, everything," says Qiu, an expert in economics and urban planning. According to Zhao Jinhua of the Massachusetts Institute of Technology in Cambridge, China's cities weren't designed to accommodate breakneck growth, which leads to chronic problems such as water and housing shortages.

Throughout the world—China is no exception—city dwellers are typically wealthier, consume more, and produce more waste, including green-house gases, than people in rural areas. If China has not already done so, it will soon surpass the United States as the largest emitter of carbon dioxide. A large share comes from coal-fired power plants, but tailpipe emissions are an increasing contributor, especially in cities, Qiu says.

A generation ago, China's urbanites overwhelmingly relied on bikes and public transportation, Zhao says. But starting in the 1980s, haphazard planning spawned economic zones tailored for manufacturing but with minimal housing or shopping areas and bedroom communities with few job opportunities—all of which encouraged commuting by car. Then in the 1990s, dozens of "new towns" sprang up on the outskirts of cities, most "designed with the car as the dominant mode of transportation," says Zhao, who is also executive commissioner of the China Planning Network, an organization of Chinese and overseas scholars who study China's urbanization.

Well-intentioned development has exacerbated the problem. Beijing's ring roads, for example, were supposed to ease cross-town traffic but instead have accelerated sprawl and private-car use, Qiu says. In some areas, bicycle lanes and the median strips that once separated them from traffic were sacrificed to make more room for cars.

Well-planned cities could ameliorate these problems. That means "dense and diverse" cities, Qiu says. Packing more people per square kilometer makes public transportation more feasible, he says. Apartments use resources, including energy, more efficiently than detached houses. Diversity entails what planners call mixed-use—an intermingling of residential, shopping, and office areas that creates opportunities for walking or biking to shops or work. The construction ministry and local governments are also encouraging a nascent "green building" movement that seeks to make better use of energy, water, and materials to minimize a building's environmental impact throughout its life cycle. These trends are converging in plans for several eco-cities, the most notable being Dongtan.

From the outset, the Shanghai government, which owns the site, has viewed Dongtan as an "eco demonstrator" of urban development existing in harmony with the environment—even on an ecological treasure like Chongming. "This is not just about saving energy or saving water," says Roger Wood, a partner in the engineering consulting firm Arup in London that is in charge of Dongtan's master planning. "It is about a holistic approach that goes right through the social, governance, education, transportation, wastewater issues—all the things that actually make a community."

Dongtan will rise on a portion of an 86-square-kilometer strip of Chongming owned by the municipal government's Shanghai Industrial Investment Corp. The city wants housing for 10,000 residents completed in time for Shanghai's 2010 World Expo, which, appropriately, will explore the theme "Better City, Better Life." The goal of the start-up phase, scheduled for completion by 2020, is a community of 80,000, businesses providing 50,000 jobs, and shops, entertainment, and cultural amenities that offer residents everything they need in Dongtan, although it's expected that some people will commute to Shanghai and some nonresidents will work in Dongtan. Eventually, the Eco-city could be extended to cover 30 square kilometers and house half a million people.

The investments corporation instructed Arup to minimize the project's ecological footprint: the land and water areas needed to provide Dongtan's resources and absorb waste. Using established technologies, the planned ecological footprint could be less than half that of a comparable conventional city, Wood says. Buildings will be properly insulated and rely on low-energy lighting and appliances. A double-piping system will provide drinking water and treated wastewater to flush toilets and irrigate vertical farms (see p.752). The initial target is that no more than 10% of Dongtan's trash will end up in a landfill; planners would like to eventually make it the world's first zero-waste city. Most Chinese cities dump about 90% of their waste and burn the rest.

A second requirement is that all energy consumed in Dongtan comes from renewable sources. Solar panels, wind turbines, and a biomass cogeneration plant, fueled by rice husks, will generate electricity for power, heating, and cooling. Husks, currently burned or dumped, will be collected from throughout the Yangtze delta.

The plan also calls for all vehicles in Dongtan to have zero tailpipe emissions. That will be a stretch technologically, and it will require a mind shift in middle-class aspirations. Dongtan planners hope to reduce dependence or private autos with apartment buildings laid out in clusters so that all residents are within a 10-minute walk of a shopping center and public transportation, which could be pollution-free fuel-cell buses or electric light rail.

Cars running on fossil fuels cannot achieve zero tailpipe emissions, so conventional cars would have to be parked outside city limits. Dongtan residents who wish to drive in town will have to use hydrogen fuel-cell or electric vehicles. However, such vehicles that match the performance and affordability of conventional cars are years if not decades away. Zhao wonders if enough people will be willing to give up the dream of owning a car and a detached home. One unresolved issue likely to affect car use is whether the rail line connecting Chongming to downtown Shanghai will extend to Dongtan. Deng says previous new towns lacking good public transportation links ended up encouraging private-car use.

There are other concerns. Zhu Dajian, an economist who studies sustainability at Tongji University in Shanghai, says it will be a challenge turning Dongtan's impressive plans into reality without compromises: "The key issue is that the implementation is often out of the control [of the designers]." Zhu adds that although some of Dongtan's concepts and technologies could be put to use in other projects, he thinks it will be difficult to copy the model wholly because of Shanghai's financial and institutional support for Dongtan. (Official at Arup say they are unable to disclose estimated costs or how the costs compare to those of a conventional new town.)

As they wait for Dongtan to materialize, planners welcome growing efforts to reduce energy and resource use a trend that

Qiu says will be furthered by several new national laws on planning and energy consumption. In addition, Shanghai, to alleviate traffic and promote mass transit, is considering a toll system on private cars entering downtown, similar to schemes in London and elsewhere (see p. 750).

China's urban planners realize that ecocities, redevelopment projects, and green building efforts must be scrutinized to determine how well they enhance livability and reduce environmental costs, Qiu says. With so many cities growing so rapidly, China is already a laboratory for urbanization. Now it is poised to become an experiment in innovative urban planning as well.

DENNIS NORMILE With reporting by Richard Stone in Xiamen.

When China Met Africa

It seemed a perfect match: A growing country looking for markets and influence meets a continent with plenty of resources but few investors. Now that China has moved in, though, its African partners are beginning to resent their aggressive new patron. What happens when the world's most ambitious developing power meets the poverty, corruption, and fragility of Africa? China is just beginning to find out.

SERGE MICHEL

"Ni hao, ni hao." I had been walking along a street in Brazzaville only 10 minutes when a merry band of Congolese kids interrupted their ballplaying to greet me. In Africa, white visitors usually hear greetings like "hello, mista" or "hey, whitey," but these smiling kids lined along the street have expanded their repertoire. They yell "hello" in Chinese, and then they start up their game again. To them, all foreigners are Chinese. And there's good reason for that.

In Brazzaville, everything new appears to have come from China: the stadium, the airport, the televisions, the roads, the apartment buildings, the fake Nikes, the telephones, even the aphrodisiacs. Walking through this poor capital city in West Africa, a visitor could be forgiven for assuming he was in some colonial Chinese outpost.

No one knows more about China's reach in Congo than Claude Alphonse N'Silou, the Congolese minister for construction and housing. In fact, in Brazzaville, the Chinese are building more than a thousand units of housing designed by N'Silou, who is also an architect. They are also building the minister's house, a Greco-Roman palace that makes the U.S. Embassy next door look like a small bunker. I meet the minister at nightfall in the habitable part of his construction site, while, outside, Chinese workers from the international construction company WIETC have turned on spotlights so they can keep making concrete and hammering in scaffolding.

"Have you seen how they work?" N'Silou says jovially, gripping the arms of his leather chair while a servant serving French sparkling water glides along the marble floor in slippers.

"They built the Alphonse Massamba Stadium for us, the foreign ministry, the television company's headquarters. Now they are building a dam in Imboulou. They have redone the entire water system of Brazzaville. They built us an airport. They are going to build the Pointe-Noire to Brazzaville highway. They

are constructing apartment buildings for us. They are going to build an amusement park on the river. All of it has been decided. Settled! It's win-win! Too bad for you, in the West, but the Chinese are fantastic."

The story of China's quick and spectacular conquest of Africa has captured the imagination of Europeans and Americans who long ago considered the continent more charity case than investment opportunity. From 2000 to 2007, trade between China and Africa jumped from $10 billion to $70 billion, and China has now surpassed Britain and France to become Africa's second-largest trading partner after the United States. By 2010, it will likely overtake the United States as well. The Export-Import Bank of China, the Chinese government's main source of foreign investment funds, is planning to spend $20 billion in Africa in the next three years—roughly equal to the amount the entire World Bank expects to spend there in the same period. For the Chinese and the Africans, the partnership does seem to be "win-win": China gains access to the oil, copper, uranium, cobalt, and wood that will fuel its booming industrial revolution at home, and Africa finally sees the completion of the roads, schools, and other keys to development it desperately needs. Most analysts think it is only the beginning. With its basic but reliable technology, its ability to mobilize thousands of workers to building sites anywhere, and its phenomenally large foreign-cash reserves, China has the opportunity to assume a leadership position in Africa and to transform the continent profoundly. And why not? The Chinese have created a true economic miracle at home, so they more than anyone should be able to pull off the same magic in a place where the rest of the world has failed.

And yet, there are cracks in the facade. China's profits and influence may be on the upswing in Africa, but China is beginning to run into the same obstacles the West has faced for years: financial and political corruption, political instability, lack of interest—even resistance—from the local population, and sometimes a simply miserable climate. Several of the head-spinning contracts the Chinese signed throughout the continent have been canceled. Those cheap sneakers the Chinese are sending in by the shipload are infuriating the local manufacturers and storeowners they undercut. And the Chinese, with their laissez-faire attitude toward workers' rights, may be earning themselves more enemies than they realize. What's more, China, unlike its Western counterparts, is attempting to operate in a region that is, by and large, more democratic than it is. What happens when the world's most enterprising business people run up against the hard truths of a continent that has known more poverty than profits? Might China be just another mortal investor, subject to the same problems, inefficiencies, and frustrations every other global power has faced in Africa? If so, it may mean that, for Africa, the Chinese "miracle" is nothing more than another lost opportunity.

Hollow Victories

It isn't hard to see why Chinese immigrants would be attracted to Africa. With wages rarely exceeding $150 a month on the farms and in the factories of China's remote provinces—and with the eastern cities becoming overrun with migrant labor—Africa looks like a promised land. According to Huang Zequan, vice chairman of the Chinese-African People's Friendship Association, there are now 550,000 Chinese nationals in Africa, compared with 100,000 French citizens, and 70,000 Americans. Beijing sent some of them to build dams, roads, and railroads. Other Chinese simply hope to get rich in some of the poorest countries on the planet.

For many African governments, China's interest in the continent is most welcome. African leaders have not hesitated to hand over the responsibilities of public office to China. It's China that these leaders turn to when they want schools, housing, or hospitals—often just before elections in order to gain as much profit as possible from these projects. They rely on the efficiency and ambition of the Chinese in hopes of having their own shortcomings forgotten.

"The Chinese are incredible," says Omar Oukil, an advisor to the Algerian Ministry of Public Works. "They work round the clock, seven days a week. It would be good for us if a little bit of their rigorous work culture rubbed off on us." I was politely shown the door when his workday came to a close at 4 p.m. The hallways of the ministry were empty when I left. At the same time, on the Mitija plain in southern Algeria, Chinese workers from the Chinese construction firms CITIC and CRCC were putting night crews in place. They would have a little more than 3 years to build a large portion of a 750-mile highway full of tunnels and viaducts. To do so, they had to bring 12,878 workers from China to Algeria.

But these immense projects also highlight the competing interests of Chinese-African cooperation. Take, for example, the dam being built at Imboulou in Congo. Officially, it's a huge success: It's expected to help double national electricity production by 2009. Ten years ago, the World Bank had deemed the country too indebted to warrant financing of the project. China,

however, dedicated $280 million to it in 2002. Congo plans to pay that sum back in oil.

"The Chinese drive me crazy," says an engineer from Fichtner, the German company that oversees the work. They are building the dam at a discount, and he worries it might not hold up very long. He claims that the quality of the cement being used is sub-standard, that the Congolese workers are so poorly paid that none of them stays longer than a few months, and, above all, that the drilling has been so poorly done that half of the dam sits on a huge pocket of water that continually floods the site and could cause it to collapse one day.

It's difficult for Wang Wei, the Chinese engineer in charge, to respond to these accusations, and not only because he's been knocked out by a bout of malaria. "It is my first trip to Africa," he says, his eyes shimmering with fever. It is also the first time that his company, CMEC, has built a dam. Its previous business had only involved importing and exporting construction vehicles. Wang blames the company's problems on the sub-Saharan climate. "The rainy season is too long here," he says. "We have gotten a little behind, but we will emerge victorious from our battle with nature." The Chinese boss is particularly angry with the workers he pays three to four dollars a day. "They treat the site like a school. They have hardly learned something before they go somewhere else to use it." He would like to ask the Congolese government to make some prisoners available to him so he could be sure his workers wouldn't flee.

Angola, long held up as China's most spectacular success in Africa, is also beginning to question China's commitment to the country. In 2002, after 27 years of civil war that brought the country to its knees, Western countries refused to organize a conference of donors, citing a lack of transparency and the disappearance of billions of dollars in oil revenues. The government turned to China, which offered between $8 billion and $12 billion of credit to rebuild the country (and to make Angola its main supplier of oil, ahead of Saudi Arabia and Iran). At least, that was the plan. But you have to expect some surprises when you attempt to rebuild a railway connecting the coastal city of Lobito with the inland border of the country formerly known as Zaire. This vital artery of colonial Angola was entirely destroyed during the war. The Chinese promised to rebuild it by September 2007. By November, however, they had abruptly dismantled their base camps along the line.

"The Chinese spent months getting their camp together and bringing in brand-new bulldozers," says a security guard at Alto Catumbela, an old industrial center in the Angolan plateau that was devastated by the war. "Then, instead of beginning to repair the line, they dismantled it all, ate their dogs, and left." You can still see the spot in the middle of the big field where the sheds used to be. The vegetable plots where the Chinese cooks grew cabbage and other vegetables are still visible. But, except for a few antimalarial tablets on the ground, everything has vanished.

In Lobito, the assistant director of the Benguela Railway Company confirms that 16 Chinese camps were dismantled and reveals that the $2 billion contract has been canceled. "I don't know anything else about it; the negotiations are taking place at a very high level," he says.

This very high level, on the Chinese side, is a mysterious holding company in Hong Kong called the China International Fund (CIF). Its job is to coordinate funds and projects in Angola, as well as deal with reimbursements in oil. Its Internet site boasts about 30 gigantic projects, none of which appears to have broken ground. On the Angolan side, the very high level is the National Reconstruction Office, headed by Gen. Manuel Helder Vieira Dias. He is considered a possible successor to the president. Neither side agreed to respond to questions, but there are numerous signs of a major crisis brewing between the two countries: A $3 billion contract for an oil refinery in Lobito was canceled by the Angolans, and $2 billion allegedly disappeared into Chinese accounts.

It all brings a smile to the faces of the 20 or so Western diplomats in Luanda who send cryptic messages to their capitals detailing the Chinese-Angolan dispute, even as they try to make up ground in a country thought to have been lost to China.

"The Chinese promised an awful lot, [and] the Angolans demanded an awful lot," says a Western diplomat. They were both "out of kilter with reality. " Says another: "The Chinese do not have enough experience in Africa. They did not realize that the kickbacks in Angola would be so high." A European diplomat sticks the knife in deeper: "We say to our Angolan friends, 'It's great that you're taking a little walk with the Chinese. Enjoy yourself. But when you're ready to play in the big leagues, pay your debts and come and see us.' "

The Backlash Begins

Despite the arrogance and condescension in such words, they do reflect some hard truths. China may be a willing partner to many of the regimes and countries the rest of the world won't touch, but that hardly means Africans are always satisfied with their arrangements. In a country like Angola, which has raked in $100 billion in five years and has posted one of the highest growth rates in the world since 2002, newfound economic success often means they can begin to dictate the terms of their own deals. And often, those new deals don't include the Chinese. Ironically, because of early help from the Chinese, Luanda may now have the means to avoid getting trapped in a relationship with a partner as voracious and demanding as China. The oil refinery in Lobito is expected to be awarded to the American firm KBR, and the regime of José Eduardo dos Santos has just reconciled with France after an eight-year tiff.

And Angola isn't the only country beginning to feel comfortable saying no to China. In Nigeria, an April 2006 agreement in which China would have paid $2 billion for first access to four oil blocks was canceled. A similar agreement that involved CNOOC, the state-owned Chinese oil company, fizzled out. In Guinea, a billion-dollar financial package involving a bauxite mine, an aluminum refinery, and a hydroelectric dam was called off.

In some cases, such contracts have been canceled or failed to materialize as a result of a deliberate strategy on the part of African rulers. Spectacular announcements of Chinese contracts have been made with the intention of frightening Western partners into offering better terms. In meeting after meeting

with African officials, I heard the following plea: "Write in your magazine that the Chinese do not have a monopoly here, and we would love to have the French or anybody else doing work here, if they make a competitive offer." Niger, for instance, dangled uranium rights in front of Chinese companies and even went so far as to expel an official from the French nuclear concern Areva in an apparent effort to persuade it to increase its bid for a mine in Imouraren, which has one of the world's largest untapped deposits of uranium in the world. Areva signed the contract in January 2008, and it was considered a triumph for the regime of President Mamadou Tandja.

When China feels betrayed by African governments, it can't easily fall back on public opinion. Despite all its talk of brotherhood and lack of a colonial past, China remains unpopular. From Congo to Angola, taxi drivers, street sellers, even locals working on Chinese construction sites complain about the influx of Chinese. "They are like the devil," "They do not respect us," "They are here to take everything from us" are the common refrains. Perhaps the relationship is too recent—and one that really only exists between officials—to have given personal ties the chance to form. It's rare to see Chinese and African workers at the same construction site go and drink a beer together at the end of the day.

Grass-roots resistance to the Chinese has sprung up. In 2004, in Dakar, Senegal, the powerful lobby of Senegalese and Lebanese shopkeepers' organized several protests against the Chinese boutiques, whose prices they said were undercutting them. Shops were set on fire. President Abdoulaye Wade was given an ultimatum by the shopkeepers union to kick all Chinese nationals out of the country. Although he didn't go that far, he forced through a near total moratorium on visas issued to Chinese citizens from his country's embassy in Beijing. He then finagled a more open policy toward visas from the Chinese Embassy in Dakar. This enabled Senegalese storeowners to establish connections in China and maximize their profit margin on Chinese imports to Senegal. In October 2007, China's state-owned news agency had to admit that "the Senegalese doing business in China far exceeds the number of Chinese doing business in Senegal."

Undoubtedly, though, the country with the most intense anti-Chinese sentiment is Zambia. When an April 2005 explosion in a Chambishi copper mine killed at least 50 people, the Chinese owners were accused of ignoring basic safety regulations. The miners demonstrated against their employer, and their protests struck a chord in the capital, Lusaka. Opposition leader Michael Sata made the Chinese the focal point of his presidential campaign in September 2006 by accusing them of destroying the country. He even charged the Chinese Embassy with supporting his opponent, incumbent President Levy Mwanawasa. Although he briefly led in the polls, his bid was unsuccessful (and likely the result of voter fraud). Five months later, while touring the continent, Chinese President Hu Jintao was forced to abandon plans to visit the "Copper Belt" due to fears that the workers would revolt again. Never before had a Chinese leader experienced such an affront in Africa.

Generally, China seems to have difficulty maneuvering in countries more democratic than itself. Zambia is not a perfect democracy, but, unlike in China, its press is relatively free, unions exist, and public opinion matters. During a major China-Africa summit in Beijing in November 2006, organizers at the Chinese press center distributed the short book, *China and Africa 1956-2006,* by historian Yuan Wu. It presents democracy as a scourge because it "exacerbates" tensions inside African countries. "Fortunately," the author concludes, "the wave of democratization has started weakening."

Out Of Africa?

For all the tensions between Africa's need for development and democracy and China's need for resources and riches, however, there is one sector where the interests of both Africa and China seem to be in sync: oil. It's the most important commodity that China wants from Africa, and the oil-producing countries in Africa also happen to be the ones that receive the most Chinese investment. So, many experts consider oil to be the principal indicator of whether China will have succeeded or failed on the continent. And it's not the African oil that China buys at market price, which makes up around 20 percent of its imports, that's so important, but the oil that it manages to produce there. Oil-producing African countries have lured most of the Chinese investment, which was supposed to create "goodwill." So far, the harvest has been thin.

It has been a major handicap for Chinese companies that they lack almost any expertise in deep offshore oil production. It has prevented them from participating in bidding on the most attractive fields in the Gulf of Guinea. These companies have used Africa's east coast as a fallback location, though deposits there have turned out to be much less abundant than those in the west. Because four of CNOOC's six oil blocks proved too difficult to explore, the company returned them to the Kenyan government, which graciously took them back last July.

As a result, the only real success that the Chinese have had with oil in Africa has come in Sudan. International companies had to leave Sudan in the 1980s because of civil war and U.S. sanctions. China took advantage of the situation and invested massively, building oil wells, a refinery, and a huge pipeline to Port Sudan. Thanks to China, Sudan has been able to export oil, and Khartoum is experiencing an economic boom that makes it seem like an African Dubai.

Of course, this situation captures perfectly the problems inherent in China's approach in Africa. On one hand, China has an interest in convincing Khartoum to put a definitive end to the massacres occurring in Darfur, so as not to sully its reputation as a peaceful power. On the other hand, China wants to keep political risks high enough to ensure that Chevron, Total, and Shell—companies that once had operations in Sudan—do not jump back in. All this is not quite a failure, but it's hardly a "miracle," either. It's proof that what's good for China may not be good for Africa, and what's good for Africa may be something no foreign power, even one as ambitious as China, is able to deliver.

References

Serge Michel, Michel Beuret, and Paolo Woods spent a year and a half watching China's influence expand in Africa and documented everything from logging in Congo to uranium mining in Niger. The result is *La Chinafrique: Pékin à la conquête du continent noir (ChinAfrica: On the Trail of Beijing's Expansion on the Dark Continent)* (Paris: Grasset, 2008).

Political economist Chris Alden explores the impact of China's presence in Africa in *China in Africa* (London: Zed Books, 2007). In "The Fact and Fiction of Sino-African Energy Relations" (*China Security,* Summer 2007), Erica S. Downs details the problems China has discovered in its quest to secure African oil. Vivienne Walt watches what happens when Chinese cash floods a poor African capital in "A Khartoum Boom, Courtesy of China" (*Fortune,* Aug. 6, 2007).

For African perspectives on the Chinese invasion, see *China's New Role in Africa and the South: A Search for a New Perspective* (Oxford: Fahamu and Focus on the Global South, 2008) by Dorothy-Grace Guerrero and Firoze Manji, eds. To understand what China's role means for Americans, read "China's Emerging Interests in Africa: Opportunities and Challenges for Africa and the United States" by Drew Thompson (*African Renaissance Journal,* July/August 2005).

In FOREIGN POLICY's special report "China Rising" (January/February 2005), several of the world's most prominent China experts debate the Middle Kingdom's ascent as a global power. In "Why China Won't Save Darfur" (ForeignPolicy.com, June 2007), Morton Abramowitz and Jonathan Kolieb explain how China's economic interests often interfere with prudent foreign policies.

China's Factory Blues

DEXTER ROBERTS

The days of ultra-cheap labor and little regulation are gone. As manufacturers' costs climb, export prices will follow.

Entrepreneur Tim Hsu first started making lamps more than 20 years ago in Taiwan. And like tens of thousands of other factory owners in Taiwan, Hong Kong, and Macau, he later moved operations to the Pearl River Delta region of Guangdong in South China, setting up his Shan Hsing Lighting in a sleepy hamlet of rice fields and duck farms called Dongguan. Since then the region has grown into the largest manufacturing base in the world for a host of industries, including electronics, shoes, toys, furniture, and lighting. The combination of low wages, minimal regulation, and a cheap currency was unbeatable. Hsu was so confident of Guangdong's future as the world's workshop that he spent $7 million on a much larger factory, which opened earlier this year.

Now many of China's manufacturers—including Shan Hsing—are undergoing the kind of restructuring that tore through America's heartland a generation ago. The U.S. housing market, which generated demand for everything from Chinese-made bedroom sets to bathroom fixtures, has plummeted. A new Chinese labor law that took effect on Jan. 1 has significantly raised costs in an already tight labor market. Soaring commodity and energy prices, as well as Beijing's cancellation of preferential policies for exporters, have hammered manufacturers. The appreciation of the Chinese currency has shrunk already razor-thin margins, pushed thousands of manufacturers to the edge of bankruptcy, and threatened China's role as the preeminent exporter of low-priced goods.

Hsu's new factory, it turns out, is running at just 60% of capacity, and he predicts that half of China's lighting factories—almost all based in Guangdong—will have to close their doors this year. "Shoe factories, clothing, toys, furniture, everyone is shutting down," he says. Hsu's not alone in his alarm. "We spent 20 years building up our industry from nothing to one of the biggest in the world," says Philip Cheng, chairman of Strategic Sports, which produces half the global supply of motorcycle, bicycle, and snowboarding helmets out of 17 plants in the Pearl River Delta. "Now we are dying." Cheng says he once earned 8% margins. His margins now? Almost zero.

Comprehensive statistics on shutdowns are hard to come by. But the Federation of Hong Kong Industries predicts that 10% of

China's Rocketing Production Costs	
Average one-year rise in 2007 among 66 companies surveyed	
Management compensation	9.1%
Support-staff wages	10.3
Blue-collar wages	7.6
Raw materials	7.1
Data: Booz Allen Hamilton, American Chamber of Commerce in Shanghai	

an estimated 60,000 to 70,000 Hong Kong-run factories in the Pearl River Delta will close this year. In the past 12 months, 150 factories making shoes or supplying shoemakers have closed in Dongguan, says the Asia Footwear Assn. More plants will disappear as demand slows: UBS analyst Jonathan Anderson expects overall export growth of just 5% or less for China this year.

Chinese policymakers so far profess little concern. The closures are mainly hitting lower-value, labor-intensive exporters that pollute heavily and use energy inefficiently. Beijing now wants cleaner industries that produce higher-quality items for the local market, from cars and planes to biotech products and software. That emphasis not only helps boost domestic consumption—a key national goal—but also reduces frictions internationally from the ever-swelling trade surplus. "We are not abandoning the [exporters]," said Guangdong Governor Huang Huahua on Mar. 8. "[But] selling domestically is good for the country, good for the collective, and good for the people."

Still, the shift in the manufacturing base is likely to hit harder and be felt more widely than officials expect. So far, most shutdowns have been in Guangdong, but the pain is hardly limited to the region. When more than a hundred South Korean-owned factories closed over the Chinese New Year in the eastern province of Shandong, 1,200 miles from the Pearl River Delta, thousands of workers were left without jobs—and with unpaid wages.

Losing Its Allure

The bigger multinationals may be having second thoughts, too. A report by the American Chamber of Commerce in Shanghai found that more than half of foreign manufacturers in China believe the mainland is losing its competitive advantage over countries like Vietnam and India. Almost a fifth of the companies surveyed are considering relocating out of China. "The big story here is that globalization is for real—and China is no longer what it was," says Ronald Haddock, a vice-president at consultant Booz Allen Hamilton, which wrote the report.

The rise of the yuan may be the biggest single factor driving companies to relocate. But other government policies are contributing to the crisis. Last year, Beijing decided to cut or cancel tax rebates on more than 2,000 items used to make exported goods. The impact has been huge. "The end of rebates has raised the cost of manufacturing many goods by 14% to 17% at the factory level," says Harley Seyedin, president of the Guangzhou-based American Chamber of Commerce in South China.

Now a tough new law requires companies to provide employee benefits including pensions; to guarantee collective-bargaining rights; and to hire for the long term. It's "wreaking havoc," says Ben Schwall, president of Aliya International, a Dongguan company that does quality inspections for China's lighting industry. The law is raising operating expenses by as much as 40% when you add spiraling wages in almost every sector. "We knew it was going to be a more difficult year, but no one foresaw 40% more in costs," says Willy Lin, vice-chairman of the Textile Council of Hong Kong. "So when everything exploded in our face, we started to ask: 'What can we do?'"

For many companies the answer lies outside China. In early March, Hebei Yong Jin Cable opened a factory in Vietnam's Tay Ninh province, near the Cambodian border. "In Hebei province in China, it costs more than 1,000 renminbi a month [to pay relatively unskilled workers]," says Qu Huijun, Vietnam project director at Hebei Yong Jin. "But in Vietnam, it is about 500 RMB. So the cost of labor is cheaper by half."

Rising costs are also affecting sourcing decisions by big apparel and footwear labels. Adidas has told its suppliers in Guangdong to look at lower-cost regions in China as well as abroad. So Taiwan-run Apache Footwear, which has 18,000 employees in Qingyuan, Guangdong, is considering setting up smaller plants on the Guangdong border with Hunan and Guangxi, where costs are lower. It recently opened a second factory in India. "We will reduce our percentage produced in China because of growth in other countries," says Bob Shorrock, Adidas' global director for sourcing.

Beijing says cleaner, higher-quality producers will replace the closed plants. But the shift may hit China harder than officials expect

The Middle Class Feels the Squeeze

Food and Fuel Prices Are Forcing Chinese Consumers to Scrimp

For the Wei family, times should be good. The 41-year-old Wei Bing makes $634 a month teaching computer science at a local university. His wife, 39, makes $986 working at the civil aviation agency, while her parents, who live with them, receive a combined monthly pension of $845. They have their own four-bedroom, 600-sq.-ft. apartment close to key Olympics facilities. From the balcony off their nine-year-old son's room, they can just make out the Bird's Nest stadium where the opening and closing ceremonies will be held.

Nevertheless, the family of five is feeling the squeeze like never before. Monthly living expenditures have doubled from a year ago, to $282. While last year consumer price inflation was 4.8%, it reached 7.1% in January and 8.7% in February—the highest in China in 11 years. "Oil, milk, [and meat]—the price of things that we can't do without—they have all gone up," laments Wei. Pork alone has doubled in price in the last year. Salary increases have not matched inflation, with Wei's wages up only 10% or so over the last three years.

So the Weis are economizing wherever they can. The family is eating less fried food (vegetable oil has more than doubled in price, to almost $10 a cask) and more boiled foods—which are healthier anyway, points out Wei. What about meat? Simple: "We put less inside our dumplings and add more vegetables," says Wei.

With gas prices up, too—they've more than doubled, to 75¢ a liter in the past six years since the family bought their Volkswagen Jetta—the Weis are trying to drive less. That means fewer trips to the giant Carrefour hypermart that require a 30-minute drive. Now eager to buy a new car (the family has planned this purchase for years), the Weis are considering what was once unthinkable—getting a Japanese model. (Japan's invasion of China in the 1930s has prejudiced some Chinese against Japanese products.) "Originally, I didn't like Japanese cars. But now I'll consider them because they are fuel-efficient," says Wei.

Higher prices for goods made from petroleum products—including toys, clothes, and running shoes—are having an impact. The Weis are wearing their clothing and shoes longer and holding off on new toy purchases. That creates some friction in the family, concedes Wei. "My son likes the brand-name soccer shoes. I keep telling him to wait. Nike shoes are pretty expensive—children's shoes are $70 to $85."

It's tough, yet 67-year-old grandfather Huo Bailing offers some perspective. "In the '60s, we weren't afraid of an increase in prices," he says. "There was nothing to buy!"

—Dexter Roberts and Chi-Chu Tschang

Shifting manufacturing abroad, though, takes time and money. Complicated logistics networks that have grown over more than a decade to support everything from computer makers to shoe factories will have to relocate as industries move. "We have more than 100 suppliers in the Dongguan area," says Shan Hsing's Hsu. "Moving is not easy."

Even in countries like Vietnam, labor costs are already rising, and shortages are emerging. Other costs may far outpace those in China. The bill for constructing Apache's India factory was almost three times what it would be in China, the company estimates, because the Indian government required that it be built to strict British specifications on the materials used. Frequent power and water shortages mean Apache has had to provide its own expensive backup systems for its Indian plant as well. "Adidas says we should move as fast as we can to India. But productivity in India is 65% to 70% the level of China," says Charles Yang, Apache's executive general manager. "If we ramp up too fast in India, we may shoot ourselves in the foot."

Kindergarten and Camp

Fear of stumbling abroad has led many manufacturers to seek even more productivity gains in China. "The most important thing we can do to cope is to raise our efficiency," says Li Dongsheng, chairman of top Chinese electronics maker TCL. Some are trying automation. Reducing employee turnover—which nears 75% annually at many Guangdong companies—is another way. That's why Apache offers perks like a kindergarten and even a summer camp for employees' children to learn English. It has just finished building 280 apartment units it will sell at below-market prices to its married employees. "We are trying to make it feel like home here," says Yang. "It stabilizes your workforce."

Will these efforts keep a lid on the prices of products coming out of China? Probably not. For years manufacturers have met the demands of U.S. retailers to lower their prices. But their backs are finally to the wall, says Charles Swindle, a senior vice-president at Hong Kong's Flora Forté, which uses 20-plus China factories to make home decor items for Bed Bath & Beyond, Wal-Mart, and major U.S. department stores. "I know factories are turning down millions of dollars in orders because they will lose money if they take them."

The next step is inevitable, says the American Chamber's Seyedin: "There will be a rise in the prices of shoes, textiles, and all kinds of household products." Geoffrey Greenberg, president of Creative Designs International, saw the cost of toys and costumes he acquires from Guangdong factories rise as much as

Links

Sell Local, Sell Global

China Manufacturing Competitiveness 2007-2008, a study prepared in March by Booz Allen Hamilton for the American Chamber of Commerce in Shanghai, details the state of manufacturing on the mainland and how it compares with global rivals. The big conclusion is that the most successful multinationals in China use their operations there both to export back home and to sell to local customers. This approach generates profitability two-thirds higher than that of companies focusing solely either on exports or the China market. Yet only one out of four companies surveyed uses this dual strategy.

25% last year. He recently passed on price hikes of up to 10% to his customers, including Wal-Mart and Kmart.

"There will be a rise in the prices of shoes, textiles, and all kinds of household products," says an American Chamber of Commerce Exec.

Some manufacturers will try to avoid those increases by finding cheaper locales deep inside China. "The answer to high prices in China is more China," says William Fung, Hong Kong-based group managing director at the world's biggest consumer-goods sourcing company, Li & Fung. "There are still places like Sichuan or Hunan that are cheaper."

But there are plenty of signs that labor costs are rising in cities such as Chengdu in Sichuan and Changsha in Hunan. And no matter where they relocate on the mainland, manufacturers face the same newly stringent labor law, high commodity prices, and pressure from the ever-climbing currency. That has major implications for the global economy. "Unlike in the last 20 years, when China exported deflation, from now on, China will export inflation, " says Peter Lau, CEO of Hong Kong retailer Giordano International, which has extensive operations in China. "Consumers will have no choice but to accept the new reality. They should get psychologically prepared."

With Chi-Chu Tschang in Beijing.

Bye Bye Cheap Labor

Guangdong Exodus

Higher taxes, a new labor law and the growing demands of China's increasingly sophisticated workers are forcing manufacturers either up the value chain or toward the exits.

ALEXANDRA HARNEY

Chinese factories, whose ultra-low prices have been blamed for millions of job losses and countless plant closures around the world, are falling on hard times. A confluence of unfavorable factors—rising energy, material and payroll costs, an appreciating currency, higher tax rates and tougher environmental and labor regulations—are driving thousands of factories in southern China's Guangdong province out of business. Some plants are reopening in cheaper areas in inland China; others are packing up and moving to countries like Vietnam and Cambodia. Still others are closing their doors for good.

The Federation of Hong Kong Industries estimates that 10% of the 60,000–70,000 factories Hong Kong-owned factories in Guangdong will close this year. In 2007, nearly 1,000 shoe factories left the region. In any other country, an exodus on this scale would be a national political issue. There would be angry pickets by laid-off employees and complaints from labor unions about how the government's trade policies were crippling manufacturing.

But in China, the popular response seems to have been relatively muted. "It won't be too big a problem for the workers," says Liu Kaiming, executive director of the Institute for Contemporary Observation, a labor advocacy and consultancy group in the southern city of Shenzhen.

How could this be? The short answer is that China's economy is growing at such a staggering pace that it can absorb the loss of even thousands of factories. While it is difficult to determine precisely how many factories have left Guangdong, those that have closed appear to be small by Chinese standards, employing hundreds, rather than thousands of workers each. It is likely they were not the region's most efficient or profitable plants.

The longer and more surprising answer is that there are plenty of people who actually wanted these factories to leave anyway. How Guangdong came to be weary of the same factories that

Western workers still fear says much about China today. The country's export manufacturing sector is in the midst of a historic transition as the government reins in preferential policies and costs spiral higher. While this shift is likely to cause some disruption, it is mostly good for China, if not the rest of the world.

In the late 1970s, as China began to reform its economy after decades of turmoil and relative isolation, Guangdong was among the first to see the opportunity. Beijing gave the province more freedom to manage its economy and to attract foreign investment. Chinese leaders also put three out of four of the first "special economic zones" in Guangdong. They hoped these zones, which offered preferential tax rates and exemptions on import duties, would serve as a kind of Venus fly trap for foreign technology and investment.

Their plans worked. Hong Kong investors, facing rising labor costs in the then-British colony, poured millions of dollars into the region, setting up factories and workshops near the border. Tens of millions of workers flooded out of the countryside and into Guangdong. By the mid-1990s, Guangdong was a booming light industrial center, producing a growing share of the world's consumer goods. Its success also persuaded Taiwanese businessmen like Terry Gou to invest. Today, Mr. Gou's Shenzhen factory, owned by Hon Hai Precision Industry, employs some 270,000 people and counts Apple, Hewlett-Packard and Nintendo among its customers.

The export-processing industry made Guangdong one of China's wealthiest regions. But it also brought serious social and environmental problems. With so many cities vying for foreign investment, local officials often looked the other way when factories violated labor and environmental laws to keep investors happy. The tens of millions of migrant workers, living for years at a time in factory-owned dormitories, tested the public infrastructure and the management skills of their employers.

Labor protests and strikes are now common in Guangdong. A yawning income gap and growing pool of disgruntled migrant workers have lifted crime rates. Factories in Guangdong have been struggling to find staff for five years, driving up wages at double-digit rates. Turnover is so high that some factories have to replace their entire workforce every year. The province's air and water are now filled with the noxious side-effects of its industrial success. And a generation of factory owners from Hong Kong and Taiwan is reaching an age and a standard of wealth that allows for weekday golf games. Many of their children see their future in finance, not factories.

It's hardly surprising, then, that Guangdong's leaders, like many senior leaders in Beijing, want to propel the economy up the value chain, away from polluting, resource-draining, labor-intensive light industry and towards innovative, high-technology and service businesses. Over the past two years, Beijing has rolled out a series of policies that effectively end the last three decades of preferential policies toward many export manufacturers. It has slashed export tax rebates, the lifeline of many otherwise unprofitable factories. And it has allowed the yuan to float higher. The Chinese currency rose almost 7% against the dollar in 2007.

And while China still has a long way to go to improve law enforcement, local governments have started monitoring factories' environmental impact more closely and creating new regulations to better protect workers' rights. On Jan. 1, Beijing introduced a new contract-labor law which tightened requirements for employers and gave more power to the state-backed union. Foreign investors in southern China say some local governments are now refusing to license highly polluting industries such as leather tanning. Soaring raw material prices have added to the pressure on factories. Even in labor-intensive industries, raw materials can account for 70% of production costs. For the first time in years, manufacturers of many consumer goods are raising their prices to foreign buyers, who are in turn raising retail prices.

None of this means that China will cease to be the workshop of the world. Its advantages—modern infrastructure, a large pool of relatively cheap labor compared to developed countries, and an ecosystem of raw material and parts suppliers—cannot be quickly replicated elsewhere. And the lure of producing for China's 1.3 billion customers in their own market remains.

The rising costs in Guangdong do mean that export manufacturing will be dispersed more evenly around the country. Kenneth Chan, whose company, Gates 2 China, manages design, supply chains and logistics for multinational companies, says he relies increasingly on factories in the northern city of Tianjin as well as the eastern cities of Ningbo, Wenzhou and Nanjing. Goods from factories in those areas are cheaper than Guangdong, Mr. Chan says, but only by 5% to 10%. As these areas develop, wages have started to rise. In Wuhan, in Hubei province, the urban minimum wage has nearly tripled since 1995.

Nor are workers in inland China pushovers. One of the pillars of Guangdong's success in export manufacturing has been its reliance on migrants. Because their *hukou* or household registration was in their rural hometowns, these farmer-workers had no access to state-subsidized health care, education or housing. Living far from their families, migrants have been willing to log long hours on the assembly line for low pay. Their 18-hour days have been one of China's key advantages in producing goods so cheaply. But factories that employ local laborers in inland China are less likely to work those hours. Their employees live at home, rather than in dormitories. They have children and parents to care for. Working conditions tend to be better in inland areas, says Mr. Chan, in part because both factory managers and employees are local. It's harder to crack the whip on somebody you grew up with.

At the same time, China's younger generation of workers is increasingly willing to stand up for itself. Born after Beijing introduced its one-child policy in 1979, China's Generation Y comes from smaller families and has grown up in a more prosperous economy. Factory managers and labor advocates say that workers born after 1980, in particular, tend to be more selective about where they work, more assertive and more interested in developing a career instead of just earning money as their parents did.

These workers, while undeniably harder to manage, augur well for working conditions in China's manufacturing sector because they are more willing to voice their opinions. Employees who care more about their workplace might be tomorrow's whistleblowers, raising the alarm about product-safety problems or labor and environmental violations.

The current transition should be good for China's factories in other ways. Many sectors still struggle with excess capacity, which holds prices—and margins—down for everyone. "In the household appliances industry, where I have 30 years' experience, I still can't count all of the brands in this sector," says Yu Yaochang, deputy vice president of Galanz, the world's largest microwave manufacturer. "But there are certainly hundreds, if not thousands." Knocking out the least profitable tier of manufacturers should help those left standing to survive. It might even help improve the quality of Chinese exports.

In short, the transition in China's manufacturing sector will make it seem less exceptional. The challenges facing China's manufacturing sector and industrialized areas will begin to more closely resemble those of more developed countries: How can we attract the best talent? How do we motivate these people to perform? How do we move from being a producer of commoditized consumer products to design and development, technology and services? What is our competitive advantage?

Guangdong province is already asking these questions. "We have been trying to put quality over quantity in economic development," the China Daily, the government's official mouthpiece, quoted Guangdong governor Huang Huahua as saying in February 2007. But innovation is hard to achieve by diktat. Guangdong could, however, do more to protect intellectual-property rights to persuade more high-tech firms to invest there. And to keep the factories it has, it will need to improve its image with migrant workers, who have been moving to other provinces in pursuit of better working conditions.

As Guangdong and other parts of China invest more in higher value-added industries, they will need more engineers, skilled technicians and managers. But China's labor shortage in this area is more severe than among semi-skilled factory hands in Guangdong. For China's economy is developing more quickly than its universities. In a 2005 report, McKinsey & Co. argued that though China had 1.6 million young engineers, their education's emphasis on theory rather than practice left only 160,000 who were suitable to work at a multinational company.

So far, China's size has been an asset to its progress. But it must balance the need to move into more sophisticated industries with the political and social imperative of keeping the masses gainfully employed.

Trying to Catch Its Breath

China struggles to keep up with Olympian expectations.

DAVID AIKMAN

From the 20th-floor window of a new apartment block in the Wangjing district of Beijing, over-looking Beijing's Fifth Ring Road, a cold, winter's afternoon looks especially bleak. The city's smog hangs in the air like a sooty and chilly shroud, obscuring the view of anything more than a few hundred yards away. It's unwise to open a window at night, because you'll be breathing pure soot. Only when the north wind blows in gustily from Mongolia does the shroud momentarily rise, and the Western Hills appear like a magic mirage of nature to your left.

With Beijing's Summer Olympics only months away, athletes from several participating nations have declared that they will delay their arrival in the Chinese capital until the last possible moment. No permanent lung damage has been predicted by physicians observing China's preparations for the Games, but that will be small consolation for marathon runners and participants in other long-distance events.

China knows that Beijing's poor air quality has brought it constantly critical attention, particularly because of its promises ever since being awarded the Games in 2001 to reduce Beijing's pollution. In the last lurch to reduce the amount of soot athletes will have to breathe, Beijing car drivers have been warned that they will have to limit their driving to alternate days—odd and even number license plates—once the Games are under way in August.

The centerpiece of Beijing's preparations has been the National Olympic Stadium, called by everyone "the bird's nest" because of its tangled steel design. According to the *London Times,* at least ten workers have fallen to their deaths during its construction, their deaths hushed up and their families quickly paid off by the authorities. In January 2008, Beijing officially admitted that six workers had died in various Olympic Games construction projects.

Chinese and foreigners alike have billed the games as China's "coming out" party, a sign that China has finally "arrived" in the world. But if the world is expecting significant improvements in the area of human rights, it may be disappointed. When China first competed for the Games in 1993, barely four years after the Tiananmen Massacre, billboards around Beijing sheepishly announced that a "more open China" was vying for the prize. By 2001, China quite specifically told the International Olympic Committee that the Games would help bring the country's human rights policies closer to parity with the world's free nations. But there have been few signs of any improvement. The *New York Times'* Nicholas Kristof has dubbed the Beijing Olympiad "The Genocide Games" because of China's stubborn support of Sudan, perpetrator of massacres in the Darfur region. China has provided Sudan with $83 million in arms sales, not a huge amount, but enough, in conjunction with its political support of Sudan's government, to prompt one Sudanese *janjaweed* militia leader to express gratitude for the useful killing tools supplied by China. Partly in protest against China's apparent complicity in the Darfur violence, U.S. film director Steven Spielberg has resigned as an "artistic consultant" to the Chinese Games.

The question of Sudan aside, China's own human rights performance remains curiously mixed. In February 2007 it released Singapore *Straits Times* journalist Ching Cheong, who'd spent 1,000 days in jail on allegations of spying for Taiwan. Yet in late December it unceremoniously arrested veteran environmental and human rights activist Hu Jia after he had tried to help families of AIDS sufferers cope better and Chinese farmers to resist more effectively the expropriation of their farmland by avaricious developers in league with local party bigwigs. Hu, according to one Beijing resident who came to know him well, is a slightly built, wholly inoffensive man, a Buddhist, devoted to environmental causes like the protection of rare Chinese antelopes. He angered the authorities because he exposed the bureaucratic snafus endured by the families of AIDS sufferers. How, then, does one measure if China is moving forward overall or backward on human rights?

The answer is that China is going in both directions at once. The general civic freedoms that ordinary Chinese enjoy today are as different—because they are so much more extensive—from freedoms available 30 years ago as China's economy is different. You can do almost anything in China today as long as it doesn't have political overtones: travel abroad, get married and divorced and have a mistress, start a new corporation, invest overseas, own your own car, and even have your own private helicopter. On Beijing's concentric circles of ring roads or on the freeways that lurch their way out of the city in all directions on giant concrete buttresses, 1,000 new cars every day are turning the Chinese capital into the Los Angeles of Asia. Road signs now abound in English (well, sort of English)—"keep distance," "do not drive tiredly"—and when traffic shudders to a halt at red lights inside the city, entrepreneurial young men flit from car to car pushing fliers through driver's seat windows for new residential villa estates on the outskirts of the city.

Beijing's skyline today is completely unrecognizable to anyone who has not been back for 15 years, and appears to be renewed every week by the appearance of multi-story residential buildings. Meanwhile, prestige Chinese corporations vie with each other for the most outlandish commercial skyscraper designs. It may not be beautiful, but Beijing is now a modern city.

In many ways, Beijing is actually the ultimate global consumer-friendly big city. Personal services range from home delivery of bottled water and dry-cleaning to escort services for foreign businessmen and culinary opportunities of enormous variety. Almost every franchise popular in the U.S. is here, from Hooters to KFC, but if you want to spend a lot of money on entertaining privately over food, you can do so in the hundreds of private dining rooms in the city's hotels. Minimum outlay for a private dining room in the Shangri-la Hotel: 10,000 Chinese yuan, or some $1,200.

It is this boutique quality of economic freedom that, in a strange way, is reflected in the progressively uneven treatment of the wide variety of philosophies and worldviews that have emerged in China along with economic freedom. In predominantly Muslim Xinjiang, far away in China's west, the authorities' biggest worry is that Islamic revivalism may morph into irredentist support for an Eastern Turkestan separate from China. Christianity poses no such separatist fears; China's Christians have made it abundantly clear they would not support either an independent Tibet or an independent Taiwan. But as the largest, and fastest-growing, religion in China. Christianity poses significant challenges for the authorities, especially as the Olympics draw near. Will "foreigners"—the favorite bugbear of the Communist Party—seek to use Christianity to destabilize Chinese politics and society?

In fact, foreign Christian missionary efforts to evangelize China are completely dwarfed by the rise of China's own indigenous churches. In the 1980s and 1990s, the rural church took center-stage. But now China's urban churches have come into their own and are starting to occupy a curious no-man's-land between legality and illegality. Arrests of Christian leaders in China's provinces have, if any-thing, intensified as the Olympics come closer. Last December the authorities raided a Christian house church leaders' conference in Shandong, arrested all 249 present, and then jailed the 21 most important leaders for

"Education through Labor" on sentences of one to three years. According to Chinese law. no trial or official sentencing is needed to throw someone in a labor camp if the period of detention is less than three years. In February, Zhang Mingxuan, the president of the Chinese House Church Alliance, wrote an appeal to the international community to be aware that, despite the Communist Party's official policy of trying to construct a "harmonious society," life for Christians who are not part of China's officially approved Protestant or Catholic organizations is extremely hazardous. Zhang said that he had been arrested or beaten or forced to vacate rented housing by police a total of 12 times since he became a Christian in 1986.

But when you visit Zion Church in the Asian Games district of Beijing, you certainly don't get the impression of persecution. On a Sunday afternoon, 200 people are packed into rooms rented from a Beijing sauna-manufacturing corporation. A choir in pink and black robes that would not be out of place in Peoria, Illinois, sings contemporary Chinese Christian songs. Newcomers are asked to provide names and e-mail contact points, and during the service to rise, identify themselves, and, if they want, provide a brief personal testimony. A young preacher, Wang Dong, on one winter Sunday quoted a poem by Chinese premier Wen Jiabao that was published in the *People's Daily* in September 2007:

As I look up into the starry expanse
It is so vast and so profound
That infinite truth
Makes me struggle to seek and follow it.

Wang Dong wondered aloud in the sermon if this was not the beginning of an openness to theistic longings on the part of a senior Chinese leader. After the service, he admitted in conversation that Zion Church was playing a new, and unpredictable, role in China's fast-changing urban society: a mission-minded urban house church that is only six months old, is not "underground," but is also not officially recognized as a legal entity. "The government is not very well prepared," Wang said. "They don't quite know how to cope with us." Zion, he said, was an independent house church, but it was not registered with the Protestant Three-Self Patriotic Movement, China's "official" Protestant body. "The Christian movement in China has now become an urban movement," he explained. "We believe that Beijing will provide the model for urban churches in the rest of China and we hope our church becomes the model for Beijing."

And the effect on China of the 2008 Games? "In 2008 because of the Olympics all kinds of foreign influences will be coming into China, both good and bad," he said. "Things will not be the same in China after 2008. Perhaps if the Chinese government had known what would come into the country, they wouldn't have competed so hard for the Olympics."

Perhaps. But it is now too late for China to retreat from the world.

China's Currency Crunch

Why China needs to adopt a floating exchange rate.

MARVIN GOODFRIEND AND ESWAR PRASAD

As the U.S. trade deficit continues to balloon, American politicians are back on the warpath against their favorite target: China. The rising bilateral trade deficit with Beijing, which could now top $250 billion, provides ammunition for those in Washington who argue that Chinese currency policies are at the root of the U.S. trade imbalance. China's surging foreign exchange reserves (now more than $1.5 trillion) and massive current account surplus (about 12 percent of its gross domestic product) fuel American accusations of Chinese currency manipulation: By maintaining a fixed exchange rate against the dollar, China keeps its currency cheap and therefore gains an unfair advantage selling its products overseas. Until Beijing lets the value of its currency appreciate, critics contend, there is no hope of a more level playing field.

Chinese leaders, of course, see it differently. They accept that their exchange rate will someday need to be determined by market forces. But, faced with the pressures of running the world's hottest economy, they view currency reform as a distraction. These days, they are more preoccupied with completing their country's dramatic transformation from an agricultural backwater to industrial powerhouse. For Beijing's bureaucrats, there is little reason to let their currency appreciate, even modestly; doing so could dampen exports, which might cool their ability to create jobs for the millions of migrants pouring into their cities each year. And then there is the matter of pride: Who wants to do anything a bunch of American politicians tell you to do?

But never mind what the Americans think. China has a better reason to adopt a more flexible exchange rate: It would be good for China. For all its economic success, Beijing is juggling a number of dangerous imbalances. For example, China's astonishing growth—now more than 11 percent a year—has been largely fueled by domestic investment and exports, while domestic consumption remains relatively stagnant. Most countries would envy the surge of money flowing into China from overseas. But so much, so fast has made capital very cheap. Tremendous sums are flowing into real estate and equity markets, raising the risk of asset price bubbles that could easily burst.

To avoid those dangers, Beijing should aim for an independent interest rate policy whose main objective is to keep inflation low and stable, rather than being preoccupied with tightly managing the level of the exchange rate. Trying to keep the

yuan from rising against the U.S. dollar means that China's central bank must print more money to keep interest rates low and the currency cheap. There's then a chance that too much money will end up chasing too few goods. Low inflation creates a healthier environment where people, companies, and governments are able to make sounder savings and investment decisions based on more certainty about prices. That doesn't mean that monetary policy should ignore other economic goals such as high and stable growth. But by focusing on low inflation, the economy is less likely to lurch forward recklessly, stumble, and fall.

Exchange rate flexibility, however, is hardly an end in itself. But it would make some of the other reforms that Beijing seeks easier to push forward. Take, for example, controlling bank-financed investment. Right now, China's central bankers target a particular exchange rate because they have no choice. That means there's little wiggle room to raise interest rates sufficiently to help deter reckless investment in overheated industries, such as China's auto industry, where manufacturing plants continue to pop up even as car prices fall. If China's central bankers had the ability to raise interest rates within a system of flexible exchange rates, it would reduce the risk of boom-bust cycles. But if they were to try and sharply raise domestic interest rates while the country is still maintaining its fixed exchange rate, more money could flow in to take advantage of these higher rates. That money would remain too cheap, fueling even more investment, eventually causing the economy to overheat. With a flexible exchange rate, China's central bankers could tackle these problems much more effectively.

Chinese officials often argue that their outdated and stodgy banking system must be fixed before they can even begin to think about currency reform. But they have it backward. As China has opened its markets during the past decade, the central bank has been trying to get banks to function like modern financial institutions that respond to interest rates, rather than just getting their marching orders from Beijing. But since the central bank has little control over interest rates, it has essentially reverted to its old practice of telling banks how much to lend and to whom. That doesn't encourage those banks to behave like normal, independent commercial entities carefully assessing and pricing risk. With a flexible exchange rate and the freedom to change interest rates, central bankers would be better able to encourage state-owned banks to become robust and efficient financial intermediaries that could in turn aid in the transformation of the economy by financing the more dynamic private sector.

Allowing the exchange rate to appreciate would also boost domestic consumption. China is a country of diligent savers, with about one quarter of after-tax personal income tucked away for a rainy day. But if Chinese households could get more dollars for their yuan, their purchasing power would go up and they would spend more, not only on items made at home but on global goods as well. And isn't that what economic welfare is all about—the ability to spend more?

After all, that is the ultimate goal of Chinese leaders: for its citizens to eventually enjoy the same kind of spending power that people in richer countries like the United States enjoy today. Beijing shouldn't dismiss currency reform simply because American politicians are using it as a rhetorical weapon back home. Chinese leaders should view a flexible exchange rate as a healthy step in their society's transition to a market economy. And doing so will have one other benefit: American politicians will have to find something else to complain about.

From *Foreign Policy,* Jan/Feb, 2008, pp. 84–85. Copyright © 2008 by the Carnegie Endowment for International Peace. Reprinted with permission. www.foreignpolicy.com.

The Middle Kingdom's Dilemma

Can China clean up its environment without cleaning up its politics?

CHRISTINA LARSON

In January 2007, a geologist named Yong Yang set out from his home in China's western Sichuan Province with four researchers, two sport utility vehicles, one set of clothes, and several trunks of equipment for measuring rainfall and water volume; a camping stove, a rice cooker, canned meat, and more than sixty bottles of Sichuan hot sauce; a digital camera, a deck of cards, and several CDs of Tibetan music; and as many canisters of fuel as his team could strap to the roofs of their SUVs. No roads cross the part of China to which Yong was traveling, so he also brought topographical charts and satellite photos of the region. His final destination, deep in China's wild western frontier, was the unmarked place on the Tibetan plateau from which the Yangtze River springs.

For several weeks the two vehicles followed the Yangtze west, as the river turned from running water to ice. The thermometer became useless when the temperature dipped below the lowest reading on its scale. Occasionally they spotted an antelope, and once wolves devoured their fresh yak meat. As they climbed in elevation, tracing the course the Yangtze had cut through the Dangla Mountains many millennia ago, the air grew thinner and the wind fiercer. When the ground rose too steeply into the surrounding peaks for the SUVs to maneuver along the river-banks, they drove on the frozen river itself, though this approach was not without its perils. About a month into their trip, on the auspicious first day of the Lunar New Year, Yong heard a great crunching sound as his front and then back tires slid through the ice, trapping his vehicle midstream. Fortunately, the vehicle wasn't too far submerged, and the backseat passengers managed to clamber out and signal to the second SUV. With a rope tied to the rear bumper, they dragged the vehicle from the frozen river, with Yong still in the driver's seat, transmission in reverse.

Yong and his companions made it safely out of the river. But since then he's continued to travel, in many senses, on thin ice. A vital question had propelled his journey up the Yangtze: the Chinese government is embarking on the most colossal water diversion project ever attempted, and Yong had taken it upon himself to discover whether it would work.

Water is an unevenly distributed resource in China. Traditionally, the south has been lush while the north has been a land of dry tundra and frozen desert. In 1952, Mao Zedong conjured

a solution to this inequity: "Southern water is plentiful, northern water scarce," he said. "Borrowing some water would be good." Ever since, China's leaders have dreamed of diverting water from one of the country's great rivers to the other—from the southern Yangtze River into the northern Yellow River. (To fathom the scale of this undertaking, imagine watering the American Southwest by diverting the Mississippi River into the Colorado.)

In recent years, this eccentric scheme has become increasingly appealing to Chinese authorities, as water shortages in northern cities have become more and more dire. In 2002, China's highest executive body, the State Council, converted Mao's grandiose notion into a plan known as the South-to-North Water Transfer Project. Construction on two sections of the project have already begun, but the most ambitious stage is scheduled to begin by 2010. This phase will divert water from the Yangtze in southwestern China to the north, across mountains that rise to 15,000 feet above sea level. The entire project will cost at least an estimated $60.4 billion, and has aroused intense opposition because it is expected to displace hundreds of thousands of people and devastate fragile ecosystems.

Between January and March, Yong's team traveled more than 16,000 miles in the Yangtze River basin, threading every bend in the western reaches of the river. The previous summer they had driven roughly the same route, so they could compare water levels in different seasons. On both trips they collected data on rainfall, geology, receding glaciers, and other trends that affect the volume of water in the river. Yong had learned from first-hand experience that for about four months each year the upper Yangtze is a ribbon of ice; only an engineering miracle could transport the frozen water north. After he spent the summer and fall compiling data and circulating it among several dozen peer-researchers for feedback, he found more reasons to be skeptical of the ability of the project to live up to the government's vision. The bounteous stream of Beijing's imagination became, in Yong's careful calculations, a trickle.

The fact that Yong is free to conduct such inquiries at all says much about the recent political evolution of China. Fifteen years ago, the government wouldn't have tolerated public questioning of large-scale infrastructure projects. But in recent years, criticism from independent scientists and environmental organizations has prompted the government to postpone two planned western dam projects. In September, officials even acknowledged (after the fact) that unsound planning for the controversial Three Gorges Dam project had created a potential "environmental catastrophe." This isn't a sign that China's Communist Party is throwing the country's political system open to full democratic participation. But China's leaders know that a rapidly deteriorating environment could stall the country's economic miracle and ignite political unrest, and so they're experimenting with limited openness to help avert these hazards. It remains an open question, however, just how much scrutiny the government will tolerate, and how much impact Yong will be permitted to have. His midwinter expedition was only the first stage of his odyssey into uncharted terrain.

On my first visit to Beijing, last spring, I wheezed all the way from the airport to my hotel. The thick smog hid any hint of direct sunlight, and for a week I didn't see my shadow. When I returned in mid-October, the city appeared to be a changed place. I was surprised to see clear blue skies. Skyscrapers were visible from a distance, not shrouded in haze. There were other changes, too—swept sidewalks, a sudden absence of bootleg DVD hawkers, more policemen on the streets.

A week later, the city looked, sounded, and smelled like her familiar self again. The street vendors were back, along with the curbside cobblers and the men waving *Bourne Identity 3* DVDs. The skies were gray, the sun obscured, and cigarette butts and orange peels once again speckled the sidewalks.

The temporary makeover had coincided—not accidentally—with the Seventeenth Communist Party Congress, the meeting of party bigwigs that happens once every five years and attracts numerous domestic and international visitors. During the congress, the central government, eager to punctuate its new talk of environmental protection with some proof of its commitment, had directed its might toward cleaning up a targeted area for a discrete period of time, reportedly putting regional factories and Beijing's public vehicles on a compulsory holiday. The results were eerily impressive. (Expect an encore for the 2008 Olympics.) But the greater significance of this fleeting transformation was that it exposed the limits of the party's power. The central government can clamp down abruptly and indomitably, but it can't do so everywhere, all the time.

As I wrote in these pages last summer ("The Green Leap Forward," July/August 2007), China's political leaders have in recent years embraced the environmental cause, not out of sentiment or idealism but as a matter of survival. China's environment is becoming so degraded that it risks choking off the country's booming economy: the West balks at buying mercury-contaminated grain, while water shortages threaten Chinese paper mills and petrochemical plants. Also at risk is the country's political stability: peasant riots over land seizures and polluted rivers are becoming increasingly common (see "Pollution Revolution," page 42). But while the central government has issued stern directives aimed at reducing air and water pollution, it lacks the means to enforce them. That's because, in order to promote economic growth over the last three decades, Beijing has gradually relinquished certain types of authority to provincial governments. The result has been dramatic gains in the country's gross domestic product, with new factories multiplying across the countryside. However, provincial autonomy has also enabled local officials to ignore cumbersome central directives, including regulations on matters ranging from food safety to environmental standards.

Understanding their diminished ability to enforce green statutes locally, China's leaders have turned cautiously to civil society for assistance. Since 1994, Beijing has empowered nongovernmental groups to expose polluting factories. Today there are more than 3,000 citizen green groups in China. In 2003 and 2004, the government enacted laws requiring environmental impact assessments and citizen input on major public works projects. (These measures took effect shortly after construction commenced on the first two phases of the water transfer project.) In 2005, China's first national public hearing—over the fate of the Old Summer Palace—was broadcast on national television. Progressive environmental officials are introducing the concepts of "public participation," "hearings," and "rights" to the public. Environmental lawyers are litigating China's first successful class-action lawsuits. Compared to a decade ago, the situation is remarkable.

Still, there are limits to the government's spirit of reform, and perhaps some in the party feel they've been moving too fast. Around the time of high-profile events like the Party Congress, the flashpoints become more apparent. For instance, the first promotion resulting from the congress was Li Yuanchao, former party secretary of Jiangsu Province, who was elevated to a seat on the Politburo, the inner circle of Chinese leadership. In announcing his ascent, newspapers extolled Li's "environmental" record. A few months earlier, however, his province had shut off water to 4 million people for a week because chemical pollution and algae blooms had turned the local water source, Lake Tai, a brilliant pea green. An environmental activist named Wu Lihong had tried to alert the authorities and the public to the problem. For his trouble, he was arrested on the orders of local officials and sentenced to three years in prison. (His case was recently written up in the *New York Times*.) To many observers, it seemed odd that Wu was silenced while more prominent environmentalists were allowed to operate freely. But Wen Bo, a veteran environmentalist in Beijing, decoded the message for me: Wu was thrown in jail for questioning the real record of Li's Jiangsu government. "Li is a protégé of Hu Jintao," Wen said. "Jiangsu Province is the stronghold of Hu Jintao. If that area is quiet, their power-hold is strong."

The government does want citizen groups to help combat pollution, and it has created an opening for them to do so. But political power in China is still wielded behind closed doors, and that opening can constrict without warning when an activist crosses the agenda of an influential official. It is within this unpredictable sphere that Yong Yang is attempting to operate.

This October, I spoke with the forty-nine-year-old Yong in Beijing. (We first met last spring in western Sichuan Province.) He had thick black hair and hadn't shaved for a day or two. He was dressed in a black jacket, a gray sweater, and black jeans. Despite his rugged appearance and the adventurous nature of his research, his eyes seemed more sad than rebellious. "I am not against the government," he explained, snuffing out what was likely his sixth or seventh cigarette of the evening. "What I want is to get the facts."

In Yong's hotel room, we hunched over his laptop to look at slides from his trip. There were photos of his SUV crashing through the ice; of someone pouring hot water from a teakettle to defrost the engine's water tank; of Tibetan herders who offered Yong and his colleagues meat and milk along the way.

Then Yong opened a spreadsheet. On one side was a series of estimates, based on Yong's research, of the volume of water in the Yangtze. On the other side were the official estimates prepared by the government's Yellow River Conservancy Commission. The government data was supposed to be secret, but Yong had obtained it from a network of friends and former colleagues inside the government.

Yong found that the official figures were often "way off." In one section of the river, the government's plans call for diverting between 8 and 9 billion cubic meters of water north each year. However, Yong's research—supported by thirty years' worth of reports from hydrology monitoring stations—indicates that the average annual water flow for that section includes a low estimate of 7 billion cubic meters. This means that when the river flow is low, the government would be hoping to divert an amount of water *greater* than the total volume in the river. Moreover, no sound engineering plan should call for redirecting all of the water in a river, since downstream communities, including Shanghai, will still depend upon the Yangtze for agriculture, industry, and hydropower.

Yong is not alone in doubting the feasibility of the final section of the South-to-North Water Transfer Project. More than fifty scientists in Sichuan contributed to a 2006 book, *South-to-North Water Transfer Project Western Route Memorandums*. The collection of scientific articles and reports raises serious concerns about construction at high altitudes, seismic stability, pollution in the Yangtze, climate change (the river's volume is expected to diminish as Tibet's glaciers melt), and the potential for reduced river flow to shut down hundreds of downstream hydropower stations, perhaps inflicting blackouts on millions. According to one former government researcher, there are even critics within the Ministry of Water Resources.

Why are the official projections so fantastically optimistic? Yong, who once worked as a government scientist in the Ministry of Coal Industry, thinks he has some idea of how the numbers were produced. "The government, they will make a goal," he explained. "Then their researchers think their job is just to say it works. Everybody will just say the good word, and try to find data to support it," he said, shrugging. "It's not a very scientific way of doing research."

Yong says he has asked the Yellow River Conservancy Commission how they arrived at their figures, but their staffers have refused to respond. "They just emphasize that there won't be much problem," he said. (My request for an interview with the commission was referred to the Water Ministry's Propaganda Department, where an official said that no one would be available for comment for at least two months.) No matter whose figures are correct, what worries Yong most is that there is no independent system in place to determine whether such a colossal and disruptive undertaking will work.

Yet informed sources say that the project has a champion in retired President Jiang Zemin—still a powerful force in Chinese politics—and a handful of influential retired army officers. And many entrenched interests have a reason to hope that construction proceeds. The steering committee that manages the water transfer project is led by Premier Wen Jiabao, and its members include high-ranking officials from the national government. A similar bureaucracy has been replicated in affected provinces, creating hundreds of titles and salaries dedicated to moving the project forward. Five state banks have major investments in the plan, and expect loans to be repaid when water user fees are assessed. The two companies with multibillion-dollar contracts to build the early phases of the project are hungry for more. Yet the environmental impact assessment required by the 2003 law has still not been released, and the real deliberative battle over the project remains invisible.

The perennial unreliability of information pervades all aspects of China's environmental protection system, from water management to pollution control. Dr. Zhao Jianping, sector coordinator for energy in the World Bank's China Office, for example, told me he was dubious of the government's ability to achieve its goal of having 15 percent of China's energy come from renewable sources by 2020. Having looked at the official plans, he told me that Beijing's characterization of the potential of wind energy was somewhat realistic, but the discussion of biomass potential was, in his judgment, wishful thinking. "In most other countries, you do the analysis first, then set goals," he said. "In China, you set the goal first, then you do the research and set the policy to try to achieve it."

Similarly, Yang Fuqiang, vice president of the Energy Foundation, a research center and partnership of major international donors, told me about Beijing's efforts to stem rising coal consumption. To monitor progress, the central government relies on local cadres to report the number of new mines, but these officials often give faulty estimates—either for lack of accurate information or out of a desire to please Beijing. "Collecting reliable data is a major challenge," Yang said. There are no independent watchdogs to verify official statistics, which, unsurprisingly, often turn out to be wrong. In 2003, Beijing went back to review prior estimates of annual coal consumption, and discovered that its estimates for 2000 had failed to account for 50 million tons of coal burned—"a rather large oversight," Yang remarked.

Optimists say that what China needs most is more technical training for its officials: to ensure that regional administrators are better equipped to count coal mines, and local lawyers and judges understand the nuances of new environmental laws. China does need those things. But others are beginning to think that further changes are needed, too.

One person who has helped fund Yong Yang's research is Dr. Yu Xiaogang, founder of the nonprofit organization Green Watershed. Yu is also the architect of the greatest success story of Chinese environmentalism to date. In 2004, he coordinated opposition to a proposed series of dam projects on China's last wild river, the Nu. (Activists and scientists presented convincing evidence that the dam would have had a ruinous effect on local communities and ecosystems.) After a sustained campaign, Premier Jiabao personally suspended the project, pending a new environmental impact assessment. When I visited Green Watershed's offices in western Yunnan Province, Yu surprised me when he said that his success was only temporary. "There will always be another dam proposal, another financier," he explained. He said he wants a reliable process for gathering public and expert input while plans are being drafted, not when the bulldozers are ready to roll.

"What we have got to do," Yu said, "is change the system." The veteran environmentalist Wen Bo also told me, "For China's environment to improve, I think the political system needs to change. I don't know exactly what the future needs to look like, but it needs to be *more* democratic, more free society, more free media."

I n America, the popular and political momentum for creating our modern environmental apparatus was inspired by the work of a scientist, Rachel Carson, who challenged conventional wisdom and official policies governing the use of pesticides. After Congress passed a series of landmark environmental laws in the 1970s, independent environmental lawyers ensured that those statutes were upheld by suing the government when it failed to enforce legislation such as the Clean Water Act and the Endangered Species Act. When Washington has dragged its feet, independent scientists and reporters have uncovered White House obfuscations and pushed for government action. Every industrialized country—apart from Singapore, a green authoritarian city-state—that has cleaned up its environment has done so with the help of civil society and a free press.

In countries where the government hasn't been able to control pollution, environmental crises have sometimes helped spur momentum for broader political change. Two decades ago, many in eastern Europe had grown resigned to life under a repressive government. That changed on April 26, 1986, when a nuclear reactor exploded at the Chernobyl power plant in the former Soviet Union, sending vastly more radiation into the air than an atomic bomb. In downwind Poland and Slovenia, uproar over nuclear reactors and official secrecy (the state presses initially refused to report on the disaster) provoked the first mass demonstrations against the government. "Chernobyl [alone] did not topple Communism," Padraic Kenney wrote in *A Carnival of Revolution,* a history of democracy movements in the former Soviet bloc. "But it became a popular symbol of government breakdown, a rallying cry for dissenters, a wake-up call for the population at large . . . and helped galvanize dissent in the years leading up to 1989."

Another case—closer to home for the Chinese—is Taiwan. The country was under martial law until 1986; any kind of open political opposition to the ruling Kuomintang Party was strictly forbidden. As long as the government was delivering security and economic growth, the middle class tolerated one-party rule.

Then the effects of environmental problems began to affect their daily lives. The dissident groups that later became the Democratic Progressive Party first coalesced around environmental issues, especially air pollution and opposition to nuclear power. One former U.S. embassy official told me, "Pollution was the one issue Taiwan's middle class couldn't tolerate."

China's leaders are aware of these historical parallels. David Lampton, the director of the China studies program at Johns Hopkins University's School of Advanced International Studies, explained Beijing's conundrum: "The Chinese are caught between the logic of what they know they need to effectively implement environmental policy, and the fear of whether these groups could become the opening wedge to political liberalization."

D uring my time in China I often found myself wondering whether Beijing's experiment could succeed. Can a limited form of public participation help avert environmental ruin? Or are independent oversight, the rule of law, and the ability to vote out bad officials essential components of effective environmental protection?

Perhaps China will, once again, elide the apparent contradictions of its environmental politics in the same way that it has somehow melded capitalism and communism. Or perhaps smoggy cities, dwindling water supplies, and peasant protests over pollution will force the party to accept greater political openness. Or perhaps the environmental activists themselves will call for it. Whatever happens, the consequences will be epic. If China continues on its current course, within twenty-five years it will emit twice the carbon dioxide of all the OECD countries combined. The Middle Kingdom's dilemma is ours, too.

For now, China's environmental politics have a slightly schizophrenic quality. This summer, for instance, Beijing police shut down a long-running national environmental Web site, China Development Brief, which had pages in both Chinese and English and was closely monitored by experts inside and outside the country. Observers speculate that authorities were worried about the site's role as a hub for green groups to network nationally without any kind of state supervision. In October, however, the State Environmental Protection Administration sanctioned a national conference of green NGOs, which gave environmentalists the opportunity to conduct their national networking in person.

I attended the conference in Beijing, and saw representatives of more than 300 citizen groups from across China behaving anything but furtively, exchanging business cards and debating President Hu's environmental theories in nearby restaurants. A few government officials showed up on the first morning to commend the work of notable attendees and encourage citizens toward greater "public participation" in environmental protection. The program of speakers had been approved by the government, but as one participant told me, "The most important thing is not the schedule, but the chance to meet other environmentalists from everywhere in China." Some of the activists I spoke to said they wanted to be a "bridge" between the government and the public, helping to disseminate information about green priorities, while others said they wanted a greater role in setting or overseeing policy. Nearly all of them mentioned "the line"—the boundary between safe and potentially punishable forms of advocacy—which is perceived differently by the government and the public and fluctuates with changing political tides.

Yong Yang was at the conference too. He debuted a new PowerPoint presentation of his research, sharing information and gathering feedback. Having failed to open a direct line of communication with the government, he is now trying to telegraph his concern about the South-to-North Water Transfer Project through informal networks. (Over the summer, he had spoken with a reporter for the *South China Morning Post,* but the article was never published because, he thinks, it was scheduled to appear right before the National Party Congress.)

Although Yong's activities appear to bring him into increasingly open conflict with the government, he insists that his aim is not political—he sees himself as a scientist first, an environmentalist second. ("Science," he told me, "is the most damning kind of criticism.") Still, he is aware that his work is, as he put it, "a direct challenge to the system—to the government's decision-making process, and to the interest groups that benefit from it."

Yong has walked the line before. Two years ago, while researching power stations along the Min River, local business interests attempted—unsuccessfully—to silence him with bribes and threats. I asked if he was ever nervous for his safety. "Once you make up your mind to do this," he told me, "you have to be prepared for everything that happens."

CHRISTINA LARSON is an editor of the *Washington Monthly.* She traveled to China in the spring and fall of 2007. Her research was supported by the International Reporting Project at the Johns Hopkins University School of Advanced International Studies in Washington, D.C. Photographs by Liu Yan. Research assistance provided by Yang Yang in Beijing.

The Good Neighbor
Why China Cooperates

LAKE WANG

For much of Communist China's existence, ideology and revolution were cornerstones of the country's domestic and foreign policies. While aid and support was given to radical groups in Africa, Southeast Asia, and Latin America, wars were fought against India in 1962 and against the Soviet Union in 1969 because of trivial land disputes. The People's Republic of China (PRC) thus gained the reputation of an unstable and chaotic neighbor. The unpredictability of pre-1976 Chinese foreign policy was epitomized by the Sino-Soviet split in the late 1960s and rapprochement with the "great capitalist devil," the United States, in the early 1970s. However, in 1976, the death of the PRC's first leader, Mao Zedong, led to the ascension of Deng Xiaoping, a visionary who aimed to lead China on a path of pragmatism and economic growth in which foreign policy became less confrontational.

The ascension of Deng Xiaoping in 1979-1980 meant that Chinese foreign and domestic policy was no longer dictated by political ideology but instead by practicality). Deng's "Four Modernizations," emphasized the growth of agriculture, industry, military might, and science over previous concerns regarding perpetual revolution and class struggle. This about-face meant that stability and economic growth would become the top priorities for the Chinese Communist Party (CCP), as the CCP could no longer rely on revolutionary ideology to legitimize government rule. More importantly, this pragmatic attitude led to economic liberalization and opened the Chinese economy to the global marketplace, permanently linking the fete of the CCP to its foreign policy. As the Chinese economy rapidly expanded, it became more dependent on international trade and began to prioritize stable diplomatic relations in order to ensure economic growth.

The importance of maintaining healthy and constructive relationships with other nations, especially the United States and China's neighbors, ensured that China has often had to adopt an accommodating and non-assertive stance on many international issues. For example, in a 2005 article published in *International Security* on China's compromises and territorial disputes, political scientist Taylor Fravel found that China "has offered substantial compromises in most of these settlements, usually receiving less than 50 percent of the contested land." Furthermore, China has tried hard to convince both its neighbors and the world that it is intent on rising peacefully by joining and encouraging multilateral organizations and also by working with the United States on issues such as terrorism and trade.

However, China's recent military modernization, as exemplified by the anti-satellite missile testing in January 2007, has led many observers to claim that China will become more assertive and aggressive in its foreign policy in the near future, especially with regard to Taiwan, Japan, and the United States. With a restless population that is often riled up by nationalistic propaganda, it is possible that the CCP will turn toward aggressive means in order to ensure survival. But even as it seems that China will begin to assert itself further in international arenas, it is easy to forget that the legitimacy and ultimate survival of the CCP rests on economic growth that is highly dependent on trade, foreign investments, and access to natural resources and foreign technology. As a result of these strong economic incentives, Chinese foreign policy will largely remain pragmatic and diplomatic.

Regional Multilateralism: Means to an End

With the Chinese economy growing at breakneck speed, the larger Asian economy has become intertwined with Chinese development. Raw materials and capital flow into China, and cheap manufactured goods from China propel the service sectors of the other Asian economies. In Northeast Asia, China recently became both Japan's and South Korea's primary trading partner, with commerce likely to pick up with the passage of a looming trade agreement between the Chinese and the South Koreans.

China has also utilized multilateral organizations in order to shore up its relations with Southeast Asia and Central Asia by participating in the Association of Southeast Asian Nations (ASEAN) Plus Three, and the relatively new and homegrown Shanghai Cooperation Organization (SCO). Furthermore, China has begun to use multilateral organizations and conferences to cozy up to resource-rich African countries, as clearly evidenced by the Beijing Summit of the Forum on China-Africa Cooperation that was held in late 2006. Multilateral organizations and agreements serve as the ultimate tool for informing developing nations that China is willing not only to cooperate with its fellow developing countries, but also to negotiate.

Nevertheless, ASEAN represents a potential challenge to Chinese economic growth if poor Sino-ASEAN relations result In a Southeast Asian alliance aimed at restricting Chinese access to ASEAN markets, resources, and investment. Additionally, many Southeast Asian nations distanced themselves from the PRC during the Maoist era because of Chinese support for radical insurgent groups. Fortunately, the rise of Deng brought about a spirit of pragmatism and diplomacy that has continued to define Chinese relations in the region.

However, the most important factor that has shaped China's current image in Southeast Asia as a responsible power has been China's use of multilateralism. In the mid 1990s, disputes over islands in the South China Sea intensified when China built structures on Mischief Reef, an islet claimed by the Philippines. Both ASEAN ministers and the US State Department responded angrily to this move. Realizing the potential dangers of unilateralism, the PRC made a complete about-face in the late 1990s as the state worked with ASEAN to establish a universally accepted code of conduct. This turnaround helped propel Sino-ASEAN relations to an all-time high. For instance, a 2005 poll found that 76 percent of Thai citizens regarded China as Thailand's closest friend, while only 9 percent characterized the United States in such terms.

The SCO has also become a vital multilateral institution for Chinese foreign policy. Comprised of China, Russia, Kazakhstan, Kyrgyzstan, Tajikistan, and Uzbekistan, the SCO gives China a unique opportunity to lead multilateral discussions on topics such as terrorism and natural resource scarcity. The oil- and gas-rich countries of the SCO will become more integral to Chinese development as their proximity and relative stability make them easy choices for Chinese investment. In fact, cooperation in the energy market is arguably the most important benefit of the SCO, as China has increased access to energy projects in SCO nations.

Increased market access is another reason for Chinese interest in the SCO. In late 2003, a plan for an eventual free trade area in the SCO was proposed by Chinese Premier Wen Jiabao and signed by all the members of the SCO, clearing the way for increased trade between SCO nations. The Chinese government also depends heavily on SCO members for their support regarding the separatist movement in the Chinese province of Xinjiang, as it shares borders with three SCO countries.

In order to maintain its current rate of economic growth, China has become increasingly dependent on its neighbors for resources, security, and support. Trade between China and ASEAN reached over US$130 billion in 2006, a 25 percent increase since 2005, and mounting Chinese demand for Middle Eastern and African oil has prioritized security in Southeast Asian shipping lanes. China's strong relationship with ASEAN nations has granted the PRC unobstructed access to a rapidly growing region that has a combined nominal GDP of over one trillion dollars and a population of over half a billion people.

Moreover, continued support for China by ASEAN nations on the issue of Taiwan is also vital. China cannot afford to lose the support of its neighbors when dealing with Taiwan because Taiwanese independence would result in a huge loss of prestige to Chinese leadership. While the ASEAN nations serve as vital trade partners, strong relationships with Central Asian countries also guarantee Chinese access to vast energy reserves, as well as continued support vis-à-vis Taiwan and Xinjiang. The current and future leadership of the CCP will not risk losing the political and economic support of the SCO and ASEAN. The main goal of Chinese foreign policy is and will continue to be the maintenance of a stable political and international environment that is conducive to domestic economic growth and diplomatic leverage on the Taiwan issue, and there is no better way to ensure this than through multilateralism.

Foreign Relations and its Impact on Domestic Policy

Since Deng Xiaoping's economic reforms in the late 1970s, rapid economic expansion, deterioration of the social welfare program, and the largest migration in human history have put an unbelievable amount of pressure on both urban centers and the countryside. Enormous groups of migrant workers strain the already poorly funded educational and health systems of cities, and poor working conditions, corruption, and nationalistic fervor are mobilizing the poor against factory bosses, local leaders, and occasionally the CCP.

In the eyes of the CCP leadership, the marginalization of the working and peasantry class poses the most immediate political threat. A recurring theme in Chinese history has been the overthrow of the central government by groups that are able to mobilize the largest and most commonly mistreated class: the peasantry. In today's China, the peasantry is rapidly morphing into a vast working class, causing significant anxiety for the CCP leadership. Officials in China claim that annual economic growth of at least seven percent is necessary in order to tame unemployment. This is because state industries that once guaranteed employment have been downsized by free trade and economic liberalization. Trade accounts for a vast percentage of China's economic growth—exceeding US$1.7 trillion dollars in 2006—making diplomatic instability a serious threat to China's economy. For this reason alone, it is easy to see why the CCP leadership is so keen on maintaining stable relationships with the rest of the world, if only to ensure that its populace is employed rather than restless.

Exceptions to Chinese Multilateralism

If China were to adopt an aggressive and unilateral approach to foreign policy, its economic growth would suffer, and the legitimacy of the CCP would diminish. For the most part, Chinese foreign policy has been accommodating and non-assertive throughout the reigns of Deng Xiaoping, Jiang Zemin, and Hu Jintao. But three problematic issues have and will continue to complicate foreign policymaking for the Chinese leadership: Taiwan, Japan, and the United States.

The Chinese leadership has a policy of "peaceful rise," which has been reiterated multiple times since its first use in 2003. However, political conflicts with Taiwan, Japan, and occasionally, the United States, create so much nationalistic fervor within the general populace that the CCP leadership has often felt compelled to act brashly. One intense situation involved the bombing of the Chinese embassy in Belgrade by NATO forces in May 1999. In this and other extreme cases, the CCP leadership often believes that it must explicitly or implicitly support the resulting nationalistic movement. Consequentially, the CCP allowed anti-US protests to occur and demanded and received a public apology from President Clinton in the aftermath of the accidental bombing. The Chinese government fears that signs of weakness within the Chinese leadership when confronting Taiwan, Japan, or the United States could trigger a strong and unified nationalistic backlash against the CCP, as was the case in the final years of the Qing Dynasty.

China has become increasingly dependent on its neighbors for resources, security, and support.

Ironically, issues concerning Taiwan, Japan, or the United States are particularly sensitive because of the way history was taught under previous generations of CCP leadership. Students have been taught that Taiwan is a renegade province with an illegitimate government, while Chinese historians emphasize Japanese atrocities when discussing Japanese history. The United States, on the other hand, invokes a nationalistic response not only because of its role in protecting Taiwan, but also because of its hegemonic stature in the global community. Displeasure with US foreign policy reached a climax when Lee Teng-Hui, Taiwan's first democratically elected president, was allowed to visit his alma mater, Cornell University, in 1995. The Chinese interpreted this as implicit US support for Taiwanese independence despite the fact that the United States claimed to support a one-China policy. An incident concerning one of these three sensitive topics, combined with an increasingly market-oriented and sensationalistic Chinese media, can create a volatile situation for the CCP leadership. On the one hand, a strong response may destroy the "peacefully rising" image that China has worked hard for years to acquire. On the other, the CCP fears that nationalistic fervor, combined with local unrest could easily translate into a national movement aimed at taking down the central government.

However, the CCP has generally demonstrated a commitment to the current course of pragmatism and rationality when conducting foreign policy. For example, after Hu Jintao's tumultuous 2006 visit to the United States in which Hu was incorrectly announced as the President of the Republic of China and a Falun Gong protestor managed to disrupt Hu's speech, the CCP further restricted the media and quickly squelched any online discussions on the subject. This quick reaction by the CCP allowed the issue to be settled diplomatically, and provocative protests similar to those that followed the Belgrade bombing were avoided. Efforts made by the CCP to control the flow of information on sensitive issues may seem tyrannical, but it is much too easy to forget that the Chinese populace is more nationalistic and reacts more emotionally than the CCP.

Conclusion

With the exception of extreme threats, such as Taiwanese antagonism, it is unlikely that the Chinese government will stray from its path of cooperation and accommodation. If Chinese relationships with the rest of the world diminish, the Chinese economy could diverge from its current economic trajectory of growth and stability. This, in turn, would unleash the restless and dispossessed workers, peasants, and students onto the central government. Thus, the CCP has and will continue to do what it can to ensure that there is both regional and global stability. Increased diplomacy and communication with neighbors through multilateral organizations will help to placate fears of an aggressive and expansionist China, while a conciliatory attitude toward territorial disputes shows that China values stable and cordial relations. Chinese foreign policy has proven to be extremely constructive and pragmatic and will continue to be so as long as growth is heavily dependent on foreign trade and investment. A stable, peaceful, and pragmatic China benefits the whole world, but, the "peaceful rise" of China faces many difficult challenges ahead as it struggles to balance the demands of an ever more nationalistic populace with the need to maintain rational foreign policies.

LAKE WANG is a senior editor of *Harvard International Review*.

China's Spiritual Awakening

Why a growing number of successful urban professionals are flocking to Buddhism.

DEXTER ROBERTS

In early December, Beijing's in-crowd converged on the central business district for the opening of the Kunlun gallery. Sipping Veuve Clicquot and Mumm champagne, the real estate tycoons, stock market warriors, and Prada-clad celebrities gawked at Ming Dynasty Buddhist statuary and 15th century scroll paintings.

Four Tibetan art works eventually fetched $3.4 million and, at a follow-up auction eight days later, 87 pieces of Buddhist art netted $10.4 million. For the gallery's proprietor, a half-Tibetan, half-Chinese entrepreneur named Yi Xi Ping Cuo, 35, the brisk business was another testament to the popularity of Buddhism in China. "Every year there are millions more Buddhists," says Yi. "Of course they want to put a Buddhist statue in their homes to make their hearts peaceful."

Buddhism is booming—quite a paradox given the Communist Party's official atheism and its troubled relationship with the Dalai Lama. The faith's growing popularity reflects a yearning for meaning among China's yuppies, who increasingly are attracted to Buddhism's rejection of materialism and emphasis on the transitory nature of life. "They have a BMW and a house in the countryside," says Lawrence Brahm, an American who runs three boutique hotels, including one in Tibet. "And they're bored. They're realizing there's more to life than collecting toys." Buddhism's trendiness has spawned a surge in faith-related business: Flights to the Tibetan capital, Lhasa, are booked solid, monasteries are building guesthouses, and Web sites offering free downloadable mantras are proliferating.

Buddhism arrived in China from India in the first century A.D. and flourished right up to the modern era. After the Communists seized power in 1949, they discouraged religion. But like Christianity, Buddhism never entirely disappeared. Some believers continued quietly to practice at altars set up in their homes. And not long after China embraced market forces in the late 1970s and '80s, the faith reemerged in the countryside, with peasants visiting refurbished temples, where they burned incense and prayed.

Despite opening up, China remains wary of religious groups. Its relations with Rome, while improved in recent years, are hardly friendly. And some seven years ago the authorities crushed the Falun Gong, which the government deemed an unacceptable threat after 10,000 sect members showed up in Beijing to protest their official ostracism. But the government is comfortable with Buddhism. "Buddhists seldom mess with politics," says Chan Koon Chung, a writer and Buddhist in Beijing. "So it's more palatable to the government." In a recent speech President Hu Jintao even suggested that religion, including Buddhism, could help to ease tensions between the haves and the have-nots.

In the past few years, the faith has been resonating with the white-collar class. As China clocks its fifth year of double-digit growth, working 12 hours a day and on weekends is *de rigueur.* Li Xinglu once typified the breed: hard-working, successful, unfulfilled. She ran an events-promotion firm and brought the likes of Ricky Martin, Boyz II Men, and the Dance Theater of Harlem to Beijing and Shanghai. She mixed with pop stars, diplomats, and entrepreneurs. But something was missing. "I was smoking, drinking, and spending all night in the clubs," says Li, who is 39 and married to an American fund manager. "I spent a lot of time chasing happiness."

A recurring dream about her grandmother's death and conversations with a spiritually inclined colleague got her thinking. Before long, Li was on a plane bound for the northwestern city of Xining. After a 21-hour Jeep ride across the Tibetan plateau, she arrived at the Tse-Reh monastery. There Li met her teacher, a 19-year-old monk who set her on a new path. Today, Li has put her career on hold and focuses instead on charitable acts, including raising money for an orphanage for Tibetan children. She credits her conversion for halting a downward spiral. "I didn't understand there was such a thing as a soul or spirit," says Li.

Not long ago, young upwardly mobile Chinese flew to places such as Thailand for the sun, sea, and sand. Now, like Li, many are heading to Buddhist retreats at home. Temples are being refurbished for the tourist hordes. Jade Buddha Temple in Shanghai is now one of China's top Buddhist destinations. The 126-year-old monastery runs its own 44-room hotel (double occupancy: $134) and sells lucky amulets, DVDs of monks reciting mantras, and other spiritual paraphernalia. (Monks hoping to maximize profits are even attending MBA programs that offer temple-management classes.)

Welcome Respite

In November, the chamber of commerce in coastal Xiamen sponsored the second annual Buddhist Items & Crafts fair. More than 40,000 entrepreneurs descended on the vast Xiamen International Conference & Exhibition Center and loaded up on statuary, prayer beads, incense burners, and other goods. "This is a huge commercial opportunity," says Xuan Fang, who teaches religious studies at the People's University in Beijing.

"A string of prayer beads that may be worth no more than one yuan could sell for dozens of yuan in a temple."

Some traditionalists fret that Buddhism is becoming too trendy. Exhibit A: pop diva Faye Wong, a convert whose videos sometimes feature Buddhist images. And some monasteries focus as much on attracting tourists as practicing the faith. "Commercialization," says professor Xuan, "is one of the most dangerous trends of Chinese Buddhism." Still, for stressed-out yuppies, Buddhism is a respite from the rat race. "Society brings so many headaches," says Nikki Xi, a convert who works for a Web ad agency. "I'm more relaxed. [Buddhism] makes the whole work process smoother."

Chasing the Chinese Dream
A Growing Number of Immigrants Head East

Ariana Eunjung Cha

For more than three years, Khaled Rasheed and his family spent the nights huddled in fear as bombs exploded near their home in Baghdad. Like generations of would-be emigrants before him, he dreamed of a better life elsewhere. But where?

Finding a place that was safe was Rasheed's top priority, but openness to Islam and bright business prospects were also important.

It wasn't long before he settled on a place that had everything he was looking for: China.

For a growing number of the world's emigrants, China—not the United States—is the land where opportunities are endless, individual enterprise is rewarded and tolerance is universal.

"In China, life is good for us. For the first time in a long time, my whole family is very happy," says Rasheed, 50, who in February moved with his wife and five children to Yiwu, a trading city about four hours south of Shanghai.

While China doesn't officially encourage immigration, it has made it increasingly easy—especially for businesspeople or those with entrepreneurial dreams and the cash to back them up—to get long-term visas. Usually, all it takes is getting an invitation letter from a local company or paying a broker $500 to write one for you.

There are now more than 450,000 people in China with one- to five-year renewable residence permits, almost double the 230,000 who had such permits in 2003. An additional 700 foreigners carry the highly coveted green cards introduced under a system that went into effect in 2004.

China's openness to foreigners is evident in the reemergence of ethnic enclaves, a phenomenon that hasn't been seen since the Communist Party came to power in 1949. Larger and more permanent than those frequented by expatriate businessmen on temporary assignment, the new enclaves evoke prerevolutionary China, where cities such as Shanghai bustled with concessions dominated by French, British and Japanese.

The Wangjing area of northern Beijing is a massive Korea-town, complete with groceries, schools, churches, karaoke bars and its own daily newspapers. A few miles away, in the city's Ritan Park, signs in Cyrillic script and vendors speaking Russian welcome people from the former Soviet republics. In Yiwu, a city in the eastern province of Zhejiang that is the home of the world's largest wholesale market, "Exotic Street" lights up at night with stands filled with smoking kebabs, colorful hookahs and strong sugared tea for the almost exclusively Arab clientele.

Communist China's first attempt to make friends with outsiders and encourage cultural exchange came during the 1960s and '70s, as part of a campaign for ideological leadership in the developing world. China sought to spread socialism and unite the farmers of the world.

Today, its efforts to woo developing countries are driven by more calculated, strategic goals, most notably its need to secure longterm contracts for oil, gas and minerals to fuel its booming economy.

As part of this campaign, China has sought to portray itself as more open to Islam than other non-Muslim nations.

Over the past 20 years, the government has gradually allowed its own Muslim minority to rebuild institutions that were devastated by state-sponsored attacks on Islam during the Cultural Revolution. Islamic schools have opened, and scholars of Islam are being encouraged to go abroad to pursue their studies. Unlike Christians, China's estimated 20 million Muslims are considered an ethnic minority, a status that confers certain protections and privileges.

"In America, for people with my religion there can be a lot of problems," says Adamou Salissou, 25, from Niger. "The image they have of Muslims is that they are terrorists. Chinese don't have a problem with religion. They think, 'It's your religion and it's okay.'"

With funds from a Chinese government scholarship, Salissou is pursuing a master's degree in biochemistry and molecular biology at Xiamen University in Fujian province, where a community of Arab traders thrived in the 7th and 8th centuries. Salissou's brother Nour Mahamane, 23, joined him this fall and is studying for a master's degree in petrochemistry in Shanghai.

Mosques in areas such as Yiwu, where foreigners are concentrated, have been given more freedom than some others, which are under strict state control. Officials at the mosque here estimate that more than 20,000 Muslim immigrants, about 1,000 of them from Iraq, have settled in the area over the past five years.

"The main feeling is that they are free here," says Ma Chunzhen, the imam. "People are buying apartments and cars. They want to live here for good."

When he first arrived in Yiwu from Beijing in 2001, Ma says, there were just over 100 people in his congregation. Services were held in a rented space in a hotel room. These days, up to 8,000 people attend the Friday prayer service in the shiny new mosque that was converted from a silk factory's warehouse with money from foreigners who had settled in the city.

One prong of China's efforts to strengthen ties with the developing world is scholarships, a program that began in 1949 when the People's Republic was founded but that has been ramped up aggressively in recent years. In 1996, China offered about 4,200 scholarships. Last year, the number was 8,500.

Among the recipients are children of the elites in countries where China hopes to forge friendships. Salissou's father, for instance, works in Niger's presidential protocol office; Niger is rich in uranium, which China needs for its nuclear plants.

Benjamim Amade, 21, who is pursuing a bachelor's degree in public administration at Xiamen University, heard about the scholarships through his uncle, an ambassador for Mozambique, where China buys timber it needs for construction.

The student's interest in China is fueled by the rags-to-riches stories of self-made entrepreneurs.

Moatasem Anwar's is typical. The youngest of 12 children, Anwar grew up in Iraq's Kurdish-populated north during Saddam Hussein's rule. His family made a meager living selling socks at a bazaar in Irbil.

After the U.S.-led invasion, one of his older brothers had the idea of trying to start a business by importing goods from China to Iraq. Anwar came to China in October 2003 to help out. When he arrived at the packed airport with its strange smells and sights, his immediate reaction was, "I think one week— quickly I go back."

"But doing business with China turned out to be better than anyone had imagined. With their first batch of profits, the family traded their stand at the market in Irbil for a store. Soon they expanded to 10 stores. Then they built a factory and five warehouses. "Now we have a building—six floors. We rent to other people," Anwar says. The family not only had a business but a company, al-Sabeel General Trading.

Anwar, 29, had enough money to move himself and his wife, Bala Barzam, 27, formerly a junior high school teacher, to China. He's planning to send his two children, 2-year-old Sava and 8-month-old Ahmad, to a Chinese school. His older brother, two cousins and their families have also joined him in Yiwu.

Rasheed, the former Baghdad resident, has had similar good fortune in China.

When he told his children they were moving to China, he says, everyone cried. They didn't want to leave their home. But in the past eight months, he says, life has become comfortable.

"I like the peace," Rasheed says. "I don't want to hear the bombs and the hatred."

But there are limits to China's welcome.

It's nearly impossible for foreigners who don't have Chinese ancestry to obtain citizenship, and like anywhere else, China has had its share of racial misunderstandings and clashes with foreigners.

The most infamous took place in the city of Nanjing in 1988, when a dispute between a campus security guard and two African students degenerated into a fistfight and ended with African students seeking refuge at their embassies after fleeing a mob that was shouting "Kill the black devils!"

Tensions within China's black community rose again recently after police arrested about 30 African and Caribbean men in an anti-drug operation in Beijing on Sept. 22. Some witnesses accused China of racial profiling and claimed that some men were beaten. Beijing's Public Security Bureau has denied race was a factor in the operation.

In Yiwu, there was anger in the Iraqi community after an Iraqi man, Mostafa Ahmed Alazawi, was found dead in his rented home on March 30. His family wanted him to be buried in China and applied to the city for a piece of land. The city ruled that foreigners could not be buried in China, forcing the family to ship the body back to Iraq. The decision fueled outrage among the Iraqis. Through a friend, the family declined to be interviewed.

Anwar says that despite the tensions he's happier to be in China than elsewhere in the world.

"My brother lived in the Netherlands for nine years," he says. "There, if you are a foreigner, you are below them. When he came to China, everything was different. Here, if you are a foreigner, you are treated better than Chinese."

Researcher Yang Weina contributed to this report.

The China Model

Economic freedom plus political repression. That's the sinister, sizzling-hot policy formulation that's displacing the 'Washington Consensus' and winning fans from regimes across Asia, Africa, the Middle East, and Latin America. But, Rowan Callick asks, for how long?

ROWAN CALLICK

From Vietnam to Syria, Burma to Venezuela, and all across Africa, leaders of developing countries are admiring and emulating what might be called the China Model. It has two components. The first is to copy successful elements of liberal economic policy by opening up much of the economy to foreign and domestic investment, allowing labor flexibility, keeping the tax and regulatory burden low, and creating a first-class infrastructure through a combination of private sector and state spending. The second part is to permit the ruling party to retain a firm grip on government, the courts, the army, the internal security apparatus, and the free flow of information. A shorthand way to describe the model is: economic freedom plus political repression.

The system's advantage over the standard authoritarian or totalitarian approach is obvious: it produces economic growth, which keeps people happy. Under communism and its variations on the right and left, highly centralized state-run economies have performed poorly. The China Model introduces, at least in significant part, the proven success of free-market economics. As citizens get richer, the expectation is that a nondemocratic regime can retain and even enhance its power and authority. There is no doubt that the model has worked in China and may work as well elsewhere, but can it be sustained over the long run?

The Communist Party of China, or CPC, rose to power in the mid-20th century after decades of civil war, starvation, and eventually the invasion of the Japanese. But under Mao, communism fell far short of its economic promise. Then, after the bitter chaos of the Cultural Revolution, which began in 1966 and culminated with the death of Mao in 1976, Deng Xiaoping carefully devised and implemented the formula through which the CPC today retains its legitimacy: the party ensures steadily improving living standards for all, and, in return, the Chinese people let the CPC rule as an authoritarian regime. This economic basis for the party's power gives it a credibility that is being projected well beyond its own borders, with all the more success because of the recent decline in the international standing of the United States, focused as it is on its tough and increasingly lonely task in the Middle East.

The economic portion of the model works like this: open up the doors—*kai fang*—and let in foreign capital, technology, and management skills, guiding the foreigners to use China initially as an export base. Engage with global markets. Let your manufacturing and distribution sectors compete with the best. Give farmers control over their own land, and support the prices of staples.

Do everything you can to lift living standards. Give your middle class an ownership stake in the newly emerging economy by privatizing most of the government housing stock for well below the market price. Corporatize as much of the state sector as you can, and then list minority stakes on the stock market to provide a new outlet for savings. But don't let the central bank off the leash; use it to maintain a hold over the currency exchange rate and other key policy levers. Keep ultimate control over the strategic sectors of the economy; in China's case, these include utilities, transportation, telecommunications, finance, and the media.

The leaders of the Deng and post-Deng years have mostly been engineers, people of a practical bent with a particular enthusiasm for pouring cement and building infrastructure. The salient features of China's economic system, which is still evolving, include increases in inputs, improvement in productivity, relatively low inflation (with the state maintaining a grip on some prices while others are gradually exposed to the market), and rising supply, especially of labor. The country has a large pool of surplus rural workers, as well as many millions more who were laid off as state-owned enterprises underwent rapid reform, emerging from welfare-focused loss centers to become market-focused profit centers.

As it became easy to import sophisticated components from elsewhere in Asia and assemble them in China, most of the Asian neighborhood has been earning bilateral trade surpluses, becoming intimately enmeshed in the Chinese economy. The services sector remains undeveloped, a massive field awaiting investment and exploitation. Huang Yiping, chief Asia economist of Citigroup, says, "The mutually enhancing effects of reform and growth were probably the secret of China's success." The regime has succeeded in one of its prime goals, to generate sufficient surplus value to finance the modernization of the economy. China holds $1.3 trillion worth of foreign reserves.

Even after 30 years of the *kai fang* strategy, however, the Chinese economy remains only selectively open. For instance, although the currency, the yuan, can be converted on the current account, chiefly for trade, its conversion on the capital account, for investment, remains strictly controlled. China is still substantially a cash economy, with little use made of Internet banking or even of credit cards or mortgages.

The People's Bank of China remains a tool of government rather than an autonomous institution, as most Western central banks now are. A large range of core industries are, by policy, fully or majority-owned by the government, and although the four "pillar banks" have attracted massive investments from Western corporations and from international shareholders, their boards and management are regularly shifted according to the needs of the party-state. Foreigners are free to establish fully owned firms in a fast-growing range of activities from manufacturing, processing, and assembly to banking and leasing, rather than being required, as before, to enter joint ventures with local partners. But the regulatory hurdles to register such companies usually take many months to negotiate. Indeed, much of China's business environment is negotiable. There appear to be few absolutes.

Nontariff barriers to trade are declining, but they remain legion, especially in the services sector. Still, more and more foreigners are successfully doing business in China "below the radar" with small operations, such as restaurants, art galleries, and marketing firms, while the latest American Chamber of Commerce survey says that 73 percent of American companies operating in China claim they are operating profitably, with 37 percent adding that their profits in China are higher than their average global profits.

This steady but cautious opening of the economy to foreigners and to domestic entrepreneurs to a defined degree has ensured that as global liquidity has soared, much of it has found its way to China. The country's very scale, with a population of 1.3 billion, is a lure in itself, but it is the nation's convulsive arrival as not merely a receptacle but a driver of globalization that best explains its attraction to international business.

Many of China's global partners require transparent governance, independent courts, enforceable property rights, and free information. None of these is present in China today, or will be unless the party surrenders a degree of political authority it has so far regarded as inconceivable. Won't pressure for these four requirements in itself apply sufficient pressure to force liberalization? Not necessarily—because China meets all four, plus a freely convertible currency and a free port, in its own city of Hong Kong, governed under

the "one country, two systems" format devised by Deng. Hong Kong is a valve to release pressures that might cause a rigid centralized economy to explode.

Nor does China seem especially vulnerable to outside shocks. Daniel Rosen, principal of China Strategic Advisory, says that at the time of the Asian financial crisis a decade ago, which China largely sailed through, "the country had not opened its capital account, relied on foreign debt, floated its currency, freed monetary policy from political control, or even relinquished the role of the state as a predominant force in financial flows. A decade later, with a new sort of financial crisis unfolding in the United States subprime mortgage market, many believe the factors that insulated China in the past still buffer it today." However, he concludes, this isn't the final word: "The macroeconomic outlook is strong not because China is immune from adjustment pressures amplified by global credit conditions, but because it has a demonstrated willingness to accept adjustment where necessary."

The China Model is demonstrating this cautious adaptability by shifting its focus from inward investment to outward investment—making its foreign reserves start to build the returns it will need as it faces the demographic jolt caused by the shift in policies from Mao's "populate or perish" to the one-child urban family. "In addition," says Italian journalist Francesco Sisci, "the party has shown itself adept at co-opting potentially troublesome private sector businesspeople by recruiting them into the National People's Congress and the Chinese People's Political Consultative Conference."

When previous leader Jiang Zemin opened the Communist Party to such people, many commentators saw capitalists taking over the party. The reverse has happened, with the party extending its controls into the thriving private sector, where growing numbers of party branches are being established. But, Sisci concludes, "it is very hard to believe that in 15 to 20 years, when the middle class could be asked to pay 30 percent or more of its income in taxes, and both Chinese society and the world at large have become more open, that this middle class will remain content to stay out of politics."

No one, however, is anticipating such a shift anytime soon. In the 1990s, a presumption grew that the crowds of well-connected young Chinese returning with their Ivy League MBAs would not acquiesce to the continued unaccountable rule of the cadres. But many of them instead joined the party with alacrity. A striking example is that of Li Qun, who studied in the U.S. and then served as assistant to the mayor of New Haven, writing a book in Chinese on his experiences. After his return to China, he became a mayor himself, of Linyi in Shandong Province in the Northeast. There, he swiftly became the nemesis of one of Chinas most famous human rights lawyers, the blind Chen Guangcheng. First, Chen was placed under house arrest and his lawyers and friends were beaten because of his campaign against forced sterilizations of village women. Then, Chen was charged, bizarrely, with conspiring to disrupt traffic when a trail of further arrests led to public protests. He was jailed for four years.

Thus, best of all, in the view of many of the international admirers of the China Model, is that the leaders, while opening the economy to foster consumption, retain full political control to silence "troublemakers" like Chen. Indeed, the big attractions of China to capital from overseas has been that the political setting is stable, that there will be no populist campaign to nationalize foreign assets, that the labor force is both flexible and disciplined, and that policy changes are rational and are signaled well ahead. Economic management is pragmatic, in line with Deng Xiaoping's encomium to "cross the river by feeling for stones," while political management is stern but increasingly collegiate, the personality cult having been jettisoned after Mao and factions having faded together with ideology.

The CPC is replacing old-style communist values with nationalism and a form of Confucianism, in a manner that echoes the "Asian values" espoused by the leaders who brought Southeast Asian countries through their rapid modernization process in Singapore, Malaysia, Thailand, and elsewhere. But at the same time, in its public rhetoric, the party is stressing continuity and is assiduously ensuring that its own version of history remains correct. Historian Xia Chun-tao, 43, vice director of the Deng Xiaoping Thought Research Center, one of China's core ideological think tanks, says, "It's very natural for historians to have different views on events. But there is only one correct and accurate interpretation, and only one explanation that is closest to the truth." The key issues, he says, are "quite clearly defined" and not susceptible to debate. "There is a pool of clear water and there's no need to stir up this water. Doing so can only cause disturbance in people's minds. . . . However much time passes, the party's general judgment" on such key events won't change.

The party, for example, required its 70 million members to view, late in 2006, a series of eight DVDs made by the country's top documentary producers about the fall of the Soviet Union. The videos denigrated the Khrushchev era because it ignored the crucial role of Joseph Stalin and thus "denied the history of the Soviet Union, which in turn triggered severe problems." Young Soviet party members who grew up in this atmosphere lacked familiarity with the party's traditions, and "it was they who went on to bury the party." According to the CPC version of history, Stalin was wrongly viewed in the Soviet Union as the source of all sins, "in spite of the glories of socialism."

But the documentary series ended on an upbeat note: the Russian people are rethinking what happened, and two-thirds of those surveyed now regret the fall of the Soviet Union. "When Vladimir Putin stepped in, he reestablished pride in the country," according to the videos. For Stalin, of course, read Mao. The CPC has no intention of taking Mao's vast portrait off the Tiananmen Gate, nor burying his waxed corpse, sporadically on view at the Soviet-style mausoleum whose construction destroyed the *feng shui*, the harmony, of Tiananmen Square that Mao himself created.

I n the May/June edition of the American, Kevin Hassett, director of economic policy studies at the American Enterprise Institute, explained that evidence is emerging that developing "countries that are economically and politically free are underperforming the countries that are economically but not politically free." China, of course, is in the lead of the economically free but politically unfree nations. Hassett wrote, "The unfree governments now understand that they have to provide a good economy to keep citizens happy, and they understand that free-market economies work best . . . . Being unfree may be an economic advantage. Dictatorships are not hamstrung by the preference of voters for, say, a pervasive welfare state. So the future may look something like the 20th century in reverse. The unfree nations will grow so quickly that they will overwhelm free nations with their economic might."

The kleptocrats who have ruled many developing countries in past decades have tended to come unstuck when Western aid dwindles, their own economies falter and then fall backward, and all too often rivals emerge within their armies. The China Model presents the possibility that such rulers can gain access to immense wealth through creaming off rents while at the same time their broader populations become content, and probably supportive, because their living standards also are leaping ahead. This formula also entails hard work, application, policy consistency, and administrative capacity spread through the country—hurdles where followers of China are likely to fall. But for now, they're lining up in hope and expectation.

Even some Westerners are impressed by the new China. American swimming superstar Michael Phelps said on a visit to Beijing, the host city of the Olympic Games next August, "Going to the hotel, we see Subway, 7-Eleven, Starbucks, Sizzler, McDonald's. It's like a big American city. They have everything we have in the States." In fact, they don't. They lack basic freedoms.

It is true that the Chinese people are free to consume whatever they can afford. That's novel. They have also gained in the last three decades the freedom to travel where they want, at home and abroad. They can now work for whom they want, where they want. They can buy their own home, and live where they choose (the *houkou* system of registration is breaking down). A Chinese woman can marry the man she loves, though in the cities the couple can still only have one child unless they can afford the fine for having more. The Chinese can study at any institution that will have them. They can meet anyone they like, but not in a suspiciously large group.

The emerging middle class also benefits from a "gray economy" that, a recent survey by the National Economic Research Institute led by Wang Xiaolu has discovered, is worth a breathtaking $500 billion a year, equivalent to 24 percent of China's GDP. That's why new graduates clamor for government jobs ahead of those with glamorous international corporations—because the opportunities to get rich quick during this transitional period of asset transference from the state, and to benefit hugely from rent-seeking, are so great.

But Chinese citizens can't form a political party, or any other organized group, without official permission. They can't choose their leaders. Even the ordinary CPC members have no say in their hierarchy. Sisci, Beijing correspondent of the Italian newspaper La Stampa, writes in the China Economic Quarterly that "there is something like a 75 percent avoidance rate on personal income tax" because few people anywhere choose to concede taxation without any representation. "There is a political pact," he writes. "The government allows tax evasion in return for political obedience. So far, the middle class has acquiesced: it prefers to pay less taxes and not vote, rather than buy its right to elect the government by paying more taxes."

Phone calls, text messages, and emails are likely to be screened, and many Internet sites—such as Wikipedia and BBC News—are blocked or filtered by the 30,000 "net police." Bloggers must give their real names and identity card numbers to their Internet service providers, which must in turn make them available to the authorities when asked. Tim Hancock, Amnesty International's campaign director in the UK, says, "The Chinese model of an Internet that allows economic growth but not free speech or privacy is growing in popularity, from a handful of countries five years ago to dozens of governments today who block sites and arrest bloggers."

All books published in China must bear a license code from a state-owned publishing house. Books under question are sent out to groups of retired cadres to censor. Before art exhibitions, says painter Yao Junzhong, who now sells most of his work over-seas, the local cultural bureau usually sends a list of taboos to the organizers, and through them to the artists: "You will be told not to attack communism, not to attack the party. Sex is sensitive. So is violence. But not as much as politics." He recently had to send three photos of a painting, ready for an exhibition, to a gallery owner, the cultural bureau, and the exhibition organizer. The picture showed his young son holding a gun, set in a renminbi coin. "I named it 'Qianjin,' which means advance, and also means money." A cadre couldn't put his finger on it, but felt "there must be a political element," so the organizer was told it was not appropriate.

All films must be vetted by the State Administration for Radio, Film, and Television. All print media are government- or party-owned. The party's propaganda department has recently introduced a penalty scheme for media outlets that deducts points for defying government guidance. Twelve points means closure. Every inch of public territory remains tightly defended, although warnings are usually not explicit, leaving maximum space for artists to choose to censor themselves. Leading new-wave filmmaker Jia Zhangke, winner of the top award, the Golden Lion, at last year's Venice Film Festival, says, "If we don't touch the taboo areas, we will have a lot of freedom. But then those areas grow larger. If your tactic is to guess what the censors are thinking, and try to avoid their concerns, you are ruined as an artist."

Chinese people do not expect to obtain justice from the courts, which are run by the party, the judges answerable to the local top cadres. Ordinary people, the *laobaixing,* have to negotiate their way out of any troubles if they can. They have grown accustomed to, but not accepting of, widespread corruption. They are meant to report to the neighborhood police whenever someone new comes to stay with them. A file is kept on Chinese citizens, which follows their work and home moves, but they cannot see it. There are only two legal churches that the Chinese can join, the Catholic and the Three Self (Protestant) organizations; the leaders of both are ultimately responsible to the party. Evangelism is not permitted. There are no church schools.

Freedom House, in its annual survey, gives China a ranking of "7" for political rights—the organization's lowest rating and the same as that of North Korea, Burma, and Cuba (Japan ranks "1"). China ranks only slightly higher, at "6," for civil liberties, the same as Iran, Saudi Arabia, and Zimbabwe.

In the 1980s, wishful thinking on the part of some Western observers, combined with a form of historical determinism that was, in its way, a tribute to the thinking of Hegel and Marx, had China inevitably becoming more free and democratic as it became more of a market economy. The Tiananmen massacre caused some head-scratching for a while, but Western business, in particular, tended to take the public view, when pressed, that a semicapitalist country was bound to evolve in time into a democracy, because the emerging middle class would demand it.

Now, such views have faded. Premier Wen Jiabao said during the last annual session of China's version of a parliament, the National People's Congress, that the country would remain at the present "primary stage of socialism," during which it would require continued guidance by the party, for at least another 100 years. This model of the state has power going from the top down, and accountability from the bottom up. It also leans heavily on the seductive story of China's ancient uniqueness, its serial defiance of foreign prescriptions.

This story of cultural heroism, even though it is bound up in the China Model, with its far warmer embrace of globalization than most other developing nations have conceded, has acquired a glossy appeal because of the sheer, palpable success of China's modernization drive. The nation's gross domestic product has grown at an average annual rate of more than 10 percent since 1990.

When 21 leaders controlling three-fifths of the world's economy met at the latest Asia Pacific Economic Cooperation summit in Sydney in September, The Nation newspaper in Thailand editorialized: "One could easily spot who the real mover and shaker among them was. It used to be that what the leader of the U.S. said was what would count the most. That is no longer." The new mover and shaker is China. The entire piece was reprinted by The Statesman, an influential English-language newspaper in India. Developing nations believe that, as an ideal, the China Model has replaced the American Model, especially as embodied in the "Washington Consensus," a set of 10 liberal democratic reforms the U.S. prescribed in 1989 for developing nations.

Last November, 41 African heads of state or government were flown by China to Beijing for a summit hosted by President Hu Jintao. The government ordered most cars to stay off the roads as the leaders sped to meetings and banquets. One million security forces were deployed for almost a week to ensure the summit went smoothly. Abundant affirming slogans such as "La Belle Afrique" and attention to ingratiating detail—hotel staff learning African greetings, rooms decorated with African motifs, magnificent gifts even for the thousands in the presidents' and prime ministers' retinues—marked a contrast with concerns about corruption, crime, and cruel civil war that comprise most Western encounters with Africa.

Premier Wen said that two-way trade between China and Africa would double to $110 billion by 2010, after soaring tenfold in the last decade, with fuels comprising more than half of China's imports from Africa. China is canceling its debts due from the least developed countries in Africa, setting up a $5.5 billion fund to subsidize Chinese companies' investments in the continent, and increasing from 190 to 440 the number of items that Africa's poorest countries can export to China tariff-free. Already, by a large margin, China is the biggest lender to Africa, providing $8.9 billion this year to Angola, Mozambique, and Nigeria alone. The World Bank, by contrast, is lending $2.6 billion to *all* of sub-Saharan Africa.

The Western requirement that good-governance medicine must be consumed in return for modest aid is now not only unwelcome but also, as far as many African leaders are concerned, outdated. They are no longer cornered without options. Now they've got China, which is offering trade and investment, big time, as well as aid. And more than that, they've got the China Model itself.

This is no longer the communist program that Mao Zedong tried to export with little success except in places like Peru and Nepal, where Maoists have survived long after they have vanished from China itself. It is, instead, the program that gives business room to grow and make profits, while ensuring it walks hand in hand with big, implacable government. And, of course, the China Model holds out the promise of providing the leaders of developing nations the lifestyles to which they would love to become accustomed.

This is the China Model: half liberal and international, half authoritarian and insular. Can it last?

A few writers have become mildly wealthier by forecasting doom. The best known is lawyer Gordon Chang, whose book, *The Coming Collapse of China,* published in 2001 by Random House, concluded, "Beijing has about five years to put things right." Chang made clear that he did not expect the party to pull it off. His litany of likely triggers of collapse included entry into the World Trade Organization (which happened in December 2001), within whose regulatory structure, he said, China could not remain competitive; the impossibility of reforming the 50,000 state-owned enterprises, which he said sucked up 70 percent of domestic loans while producing less than 30 percent of the economy's output; the failure of the reform of the banking system, with its huge burden of nonperforming loans and planned restructuring through inexperienced asset-management companies; the government's lack of revenues; corruption; and the rush of new global information and views made available on the Internet. Chang's critique was plausible at the time, but now, six years later, it merely underlines how dangerous it is to bet against China's pragmatic economic reform program.

Randall Peerenboom of UCLA describes in his new hook—*China Modernizes: Threat to the West or Model for the Rest?*—the country's "paradigm for developing states, a 21st-century, technologically leap-frogging variant of the East Asian developmental state that has resulted in such remarkable success for Japan, South Korea, Hong Kong, Singapore, and Taiwan." China resisted the advice of foreign experts to engage in shock therapy, he says, and has persisted in gradual reform. The state has played a key role in setting economic policy, establishing government institutions, regulating foreign investment, and mitigating the adverse effects of globalization in domestic constituencies. And the strategy has broadly worked: "Chinese citizens are generally better off" than in 1989. "Most live longer, more are able to read and write, most enjoy higher living standards. China outperforms the average country in its income class on most major indicators of human rights and well-being, with the notable exception of civil and political rights."

Where China fails to match up, however, is in creativity and innovation, without which it may have to resign itself to remaining a net importer of new technologies, and a manufacturer under license. It has failed to produce a single global brand to compare with its neighbors. Japan has its Sony, Toyota, Panasonic, Honda, and the rest. South Korea has its Samsung and Hyundai. Taiwan has its Acer, BenQ, and Giant bicycles. China's Haier white goods and Lenovo personal computers remain, for now, wannabes. The controls that China deploys on use of the Internet, the battles it wages with its artists in every field, the focus in its education system on rote learning, the continuing failure to implement its own intellectual property rules, and now the embracing of a new Confucianism—all of these inhibit lateral thinking and invention.

As Maoism and Marxism lose their grip, the dangers of nationalism as a defining value system become apparent, and religion remains under suspicion as a potentially powerful rival to the Communist Party and the authoritarian state, Chinas leaders are eagerly rediscovering the country's 2,500-year-old Confucian tradition.

Contemporary philosophers claim to be reengineering Confucianism to suit the needs of 21st-century China by, for instance, focusing on the ecological potential in its advocacy of "the unity of heaven and humanity" and on its requirement of self-discipline. But the reasons that early-20th-century modernizers and artists, including China's greatest writer, Lu Xun, rejected Confucianism as essentially authoritarian and inimical to modernization remain unaddressed.

Lee Yuan-tseh, the president of Taiwan's top research institute, Academia Sinica, describes how, after a traditional Confucian upbringing, he shifted for postgraduate opportunities to the United States, first at the University of California at Berkeley, then Harvard, then Chicago, and back to California. He says that the inquisitive academic climate there "made me think bad thoughts: that my teacher was wrong." In time, he took what he describes as the biggest step of his life—telling the teacher so. In 1986, he won the Nobel Prize for chemistry. In 2000, Gao Xingjian won the Nobel Prize for literature, but only after he had exiled himself and become a French citizen. No person has ever won a Nobel Prize for work in China; the U.S., by contrast, has won nearly 300 Nobel Prizes, winning or sharing four of the six 2006 awards.

Even in entrepreneurship and wealth creation, the CPC retains its grip. Carsten Holz, an economics professor at the Hong Kong University of Science and Technology, wrote in the Far Eastern Economic Review that "of the 3,220 Chinese citizens with a personal wealth of 100 million yuan ($13 million) or more, 2,932 are children of high-level cadres. Of the key positions in the five industrial sectors—finance, foreign trade, land development, large-scale engineering, and securities—85 percent to 90 percent are held by children of high-level cadres."

Attempts are being made to shift the economy higher up the value-added chain by creating and importing more capital-intensive companies. For instance, on a vast industrial estate southeast of Beijing, Richard Chang, a Taiwan-raised American citizen, has built a $1.5 billion microchip-making factory for his company. Semiconductor Manufacturing International Corporation. The factory employs 2,000 staff who work in "clean rooms" constantly tested for dust and humidity. The machines there cost up to $30 million each. About 55 percent of the staff have undergraduate degrees, and 10 percent are hired from overseas. All have three months of in-house training before they begin work.

In 2006, manufacturers in China bought $64 billion worth of chips, but much of that hardware was imported. Whether SMIC—which Chang founded only in 2000, after working for 20 years with Texas Instruments—can build the research capacity and the skills needed to compete will provide an important test of China's ability to move its model on to a higher plane. China, in typical fashion, threw a heap of incentives Chang's way to ensure he got up and running: free land, syndicated loans, R&D aid, zero tax.

Like most other East Asian states, China's route to development placed economic reforms before democratization. But the China Model differs markedly from most of the region in that it has resisted taking any serious steps down that road to democracy. There is talk of "intraparty democracy" within continued one-party rule, but unsurprisingly, no champions of it have any real influence. There were also some token village elections, but they have remained dominated by the CPC and its cadres. Commentator Shu Shengxiang wrote in July, on the influential website Baixing ("the common people"): "The democratically elected cadres are gouging the people [by corruption] too. They do not know that a democracy which only has elections but not supervision is at best a half-baked democracy, if not a fake democracy. Halt-baked democracy not only harms the villagers' personal interests, but even gives them the misconception that democracy is not good."

At the same time, however, the party is refining its contract with the Chinese people to reflect shifting popular concerns about living standards: the quality of growth as well as the quantum. Leading this new agenda is the environment, which surveys show tends to top, together with corruption and access to health and education services, the concerns of most Chinese. The World Bank says China contains 16 of the world's 20 most polluted cities in their air quality, and anxieties about both water and air have triggered a large proportion of China's "mass events"—demonstrations and protests—which even official figures estimated at 87,000 in 2005.

The central government has effectively opened the environment to media commentary and to the establishment of NGOs, and has pinned the blame for the worst environmental disasters on avaricious or neglectful local officials. Ambitious targets have been set, in the five-year plan that began in 2006, for reduction of carbon dioxide and sulfur emissions, and for the use of energy per unit of production. The goals are not being met, and the central government appears determined to impress the whole apparatus that its new green program is not just rhetoric, but that it means business.

This shift from quantity to quality of growth will form the core of the agenda in the second term of the current "fourth generation" of leaders around Hu Jintao and Wen Jiabao. At the party congress, which occurs every five years and started on October 15, their aim is to ensure that only people on board this quality-of-life program get promoted, both in the central institutions and in the provinces. The key principle for their decade in power is the Confucian concept of harmony—as in stability and avoidance of dissent.

This China offers a seductive model that is being eagerly taken up by the leaders of countries that have not yet settled into democratic structures: Vietnam; Burma; Laos; the Central Asian dictatorships that were part of the Soviet Union; a growing portion of the Middle East, starting with the United Arab Emirates, including its glossy new centers like Dubai; Cuba; most of Africa, including South Africa; and even to a degree the hereditary cult that is North Korea. Beijing sometimes gives more than it receives to cement its developing world leadership, according most-favored-nation status to Vietnam, Laos, and Cambodia even before they join the World Trade Organization. In an unsettling way, the China Model is attractive to the leaders of some countries that had already become democratic, such as Venezuela. The model is even inspiring democratic India to compete with its own adaptive version.

The China Model is, of course, admired in the West, too, with business leaders' words (at platforms such as Forbes magazine conferences and the World Economic Forum, which has just instituted an annual summer session in China) providing great reinforcement for Chinese leaders. The World Bank is just one of the international institutions that champion China (its greatest client and in some ways its boss) as a paradigm for the developing world. Also fascinating is the appeal of the China Model to Russia, which as Azar Gat, professor of national security at Tel Aviv University, writes in Foreign Affairs, "is retreating from its post-communist liberalism and assuming an increasingly authoritarian character as its economic clout grows." China is exporting scores of Confucian Institutes, most of them at first just language schools but in the future offering platforms for extending Chinese influence.

But back to our question: Is the China Model sustainable? Two recent books come up with opposite answers. The British center-left economist Will Hutton, author of *The Writing on the Wall*, says China must accede to Enlightenment values or start to fall back again. American journalist James Mann, author of *The China Fantasy*, argues, in contrast, that the Chinese middle class is thoroughly behind the China Model as its major beneficiary, ensuring that the usual source of confrontation with the power elite is not just docile, but eagerly applauding.

It may take a non-Sinologist like Hutton to see how very strange it is that a one-party state that pays lip service (at least) to the doctrines of Marx, Lenin, and Mao should not only survive into the 21st century after all its principal totalitarian and authoritarian peers have collapsed, fallen apart, or been beaten in world wars, but actually prosper, to the degree that its system is starting to gain such currency in the developing world.

"The party is facing a growing issue of legitimacy," he writes. "If it no longer rules as the democratic dictatorship of peasants and workers, because the class war is over, why does it not hold itself accountable to the people in competitive elections?" The answer is in the phrase Hutton himself frequently uses; "party-state." The party won power by force of arms. The People's Liberation Army answers to the party, not to the government or the nation, insofar as those concepts can be levered apart from the party any more. The party's legitimacy, as viewed by most Chinese, lies in its history and past leaders, in its contemporary success at bringing prosperity to a thankful nation, and in its unyielding grip on the trappings of nationalism.

The large gold star in China's flag, for instance, represents the CPC, the four smaller stars the workers, the peasants, the petty bourgeois, and capitalists sympathetic to the party. In the early 1980s, there was some vestigial discussion about separating party and state, but the idea was abandoned as both impractical and undesirable. The party rules today through four pillars—the army, the legal apparatus including the courts and police, the administration, and the state corporations that dominate the "strategic" sectors of the economy. Without cutting away these pillars, without separating the powers, any attempt at "competitive elections" would be hollow. But the pillars appear, to use an understatement, firmly entrenched.

Hutton reiterates the old contention that China's middle class, "more internationalist than its poor," will ultimately insist that the party loosen its political control. James Mann replies that the middle class is doing very nicely, thank you, within the structure as it is. Its members are substantially incorporated into the party and are the structure's biggest supporters, not its underminers.

Hutton's most convincing critique is that "China has no business tradition that understands the moral facet of capitalism, . . . whose 'soft' institutions (a common culture and shared purpose) are as integral to growth and sustainability as the 'hard' processes." The difficulty Chinese enterprise has in understanding, let alone absorbing and practicing, the morality and trust that are at the root of capitalism and of successful globalization is on display ever more luridly as food, drugs, toothpaste, toys, and a growing list of other products ring international alarm bells and cast a shadow over the "Made in China" brand credibility.

His core conclusion is this: "Welfare systems, freedom of association, representative government, and enforceable property rights are not simply pleasant options. They are central to the capacity of a capitalist economy to grow to maturity. . . . The party can relax its political control to allow the economic reform process to be completed. Or it can retain political control, watch the economic contradictions build, and so create the social tension that may force loss of political control."

Hutton is not the first commentator to draw up a balance sheet of economic and social pluses and minuses for China, and figure that something has to give politically. "The clock is ticking," he warns. But time keeps passing unremarkably, and one diligent and uncharismatic group of leaders quietly makes way for the next, and the party-state not only remains intact but also appears to flourish.

James Mann, however, says that if China does retain a repressive one-party political system for a long time, this "may indeed be just the China that the American or European business and government leaders who deal regularly" with the country want. The "fantasy" in his book's title is the notion that commerce will lead to democracy or liberalization. One of his scenarios is that the party is still in power 25 years from now, though perhaps called the "Reform Party." But if it is to change names, the CPC will probably find that the "China Party" is the easiest sell.

Leading Australian economist Ross Garnaut, a former ambassador to China, adds an important element of historical perspective—that first Britain, and then the United States, industrialized in a helter-skelter way, which was crucially moderated and channeled by institutional accountability that prevented the industrial-baron entrepreneurs from losing proportion, alienating the population, and misallocating capital disastrously. The institutions that developed to meet this challenge of a rampant new power elite included parliaments, legal structures, and independent regulatory agencies. Will China follow suit, or will its go-it-alone party steer its economy, after three decades of success, into difficult waters (or onto the reefs) because it lacks the true self-confidence to expose itself to other sources of power?

It is almost certain that China will push on with its present structure, but with the prospect of broadening democratic competitiveness for posts within the party, and institutionalizing consultations with more diverse groups in Chinese society, some outside the party. The "ample evidence" that Randall Peerenboom catalogs in his book, "that other countries are looking to China for inspiration," reinforces the CPC's determination to persevere. Laos is following China's lead in implementing market reforms and producing higher growth. Iran and other Middle East countries, including Syria, have invited experts on Chinese law, economics, and politics to lecture to senior officials and academics. They are all attracted by what they see as China's pragmatic approach to reform. The official newspaper China Daily recently hosted on its website a reader discussion on the theme: "China is a role model to all developing nations. After centuries of oppression and domination by Western nations, most developing nations are trying to pull themselves up from poverty. They look at China's rapid progress as an example. China also gives aid and technical help to these nations." The theme attracted a host of supportive responses, such as, "China has shown that you can be successful by expanding through commerce and diplomacy, not by the imperialism demonstrated by the U.S. and UK."

Vietnam, Cuba, Burma, and Venezuela provide good examples of the China Model's attraction. Vietnam, whose economic reform program, *doi moi,* began 20 years ago, has followed China closely, especially replicating its outward-looking foreign investment regime. As a result, strong links have been created between the two communist countries, which are also the fastest-growing economies in Asia. In 2006, China had 377 direct investments in Vietnam. Since China and Vietnam resumed official economic relations in 1991, after Vietnam had allied itself with the Soviet Union, bilateral Chinese-Vietnamese trade has grown at an annual average of 40 percent. Meanwhile, Vietnam maintains a political system as authoritarian as China's, with a ranking of "7" for political rights from Freedom House.

Vietnam's new prime minister, Nguyen Tan Dun, says he wants to ramp up economic cooperation with China, and that the countries "should increase their cooperation to accelerate trade promotion and investment, plus organize trade fairs and exhibitions, to help each other seek more trade and investment opportunities." In Vietnam's north, close to China's booming Guangdong Province, average wages and real estate are much cheaper than in coastal China. Vietnam is the most successful economically of the countries using the China Model, and its entrepreneurial talents suggest that in some areas it could in time even leapfrog it.

China's ability to honor Mao, even as it tears down the economy he set in place, could provide a model for Cuba, says William Ratliff, a research fellow at Stanford University's Hoover Institution who is an expert on both countries. "During the past 15 years, important members of the Cuban political, military, and business elite, including Fidel and Raúl Castro and two-thirds of the members of the Communist Party Politburo, have visited China and remarked with great interest on the Chinese reform experience," Ratliff says. After Raul's visit to China, Zhu Rongji, a leading architect of economic reforms who was then premier, sent one of his chief aides to Cuba, where he lectured hundreds of leaders, with substantial impact.

Ratliff cites a Cuban intelligence official as saying: "Once Fidel Castro is out of the game, other areas of the Chinese experience will most probably be implemented in Cuba rather quickly." Besides the economic model, the Chinese concept of an orderly succession of leaders within an authoritarian system also holds a deep attraction.

Former Chinese Foreign Minister Tang Jiaxuan, often sent as an emissary by President Hu to neighboring countries, said in September that "China wholeheartedly hopes that Burma will push forward a democracy process that is appropriate for the country." The statement underlines China's crucial support for the ruling military regime, which usurped the election won convincingly in 1990 by Aung San Suu Kyi's party, with 390 of 492 seats. But Tang adds a note of disquiet; China is no longer blasé about being viewed as the main backer of dictatorships, including Sudan and Zimbabwe, and would rather that Burma, like those other outcast countries, worked harder to establish better relations with the rest of the world. In his speech. Tang was supporting the Burmese rulers' plan to introduce a new constitution, and at the same time move toward a market economy, reinforcing the influence of China as their key model.

Since the start of 2007, there has been a surge in diplomatic and business visits by leaders between the countries, with the intention of strengthening economic and strategic ties. As in other countries committing themselves to the China Model, the exchanges entail Chinese businesspeople, technicians, and workers coming to live in Burma for lengthy periods. The South China Morning Post has described three Burmese cities—Lashio, Mandalay, and Muse—as "virtually Chinese cities now." China is building a tax-free export zone for its own industries next to the port of Rangoon.

Meanwhile, Venezuela's regime has become the leader of the hard left's opposition to Western-led globalization. In August 2006, President Hugo Chávez said on arriving in Beijing: "This will he my most important visit to China, with whom we will build a strategic alliance. Our plans are to create a multipolar world, and to challenge the hegemony of the United States." His attempts to enmesh China in his high-stakes campaign against the U.S. were deflected by courteous formalities, but China's economic support—chiefly through investment in energy projects and purchase of oil, despite Venezuela's heavy crude being costly to refine and expensive to transport across the globe—considerably aided Chávez's election campaign last December. Chávez praised China as an economic model for the world: "It's an example for Western leaders and governments who claim that capitalism is the only alternative. One of the greatest events of the 20th century was the Chinese revolution."

Joshua Kurlantzick, the author of *Charm Offensive: How China's Soft Power Is Transforming the World,* writes: "No one has experience with today's China as a global player. . . . In a short period of time, China appears to have created a systematic, coherent soft power strategy, and a set of soft power tools to implement it"—particularly public diplomacy, aid, and trade—"though it is still in a honeymoon period in which many nations have not recognized the downsides of Beijing's new power." Those downsides might include a cavalier approach to the environment—other people's as well as China's own—growing military clout, the migration of large numbers of Chinese workers and businesspeople accompanying its trade and investment, harsh labor standards on its projects, and in general a new variant on old colonialism.

Kurlantzick writes: "As China becomes more powerful, other nations will begin to see beyond its benign face to a more complicated reality. They will realize that despite Chinas promises of noninterference, when it comes to core interests, China—like any great power—will think of itself first.

"China could create blowback against itself in other ways, too. Still a developing country itself, China could overplay its hand, making the kind of promises on aid and investment that it cannot fulfill. And in the long run, if countries like Burma ever made the transition to freer governments, China could face a sizable backlash for its past support for their authoritarian rulers. 'We know who stands behind the [Burmese] government,' one Burmese businessman told me last year. 'We'll remember.' "

The U.S., Japan, and other countries have been urging China to become more transparent about the rapid development of its military capacity, underlined last January by its missile shot that successfully destroyed an aging satellite, and by the sudden surfacing of a submarine, earlier this year, within five miles of the American aircraft carrier *Kitty Hawk*. At least some of the increased military budget is intended to compensate the People's Liberation Army for its lost revenues when it was required, by forceful former Premier Zhu Rongji, to sell off most of its considerable business portfolio.

The principal foreign policy goals appear clear: preventing Taiwan from converting its de facto independence to de jure independence, maintaining a constant capacity to attempt an invasion, extending China's capacity to open up new forms of access to reliable sources of energy and other commodities, and helping safeguard such routes.

China's capacity to project adventurist military power far beyond its borders, or to offer significant help for other countries to do the same—for instance in Venezuela, unsettling the U.S.'s immediate neighborhood—is limited today both by its resources and by its reluctance to leave its heartland short of the muscle the party may need to quell domestic disturbances like those that swept the country in 1989.

To prevent a growing fear of China's economic power, Beijing wants to demonstrate, Kurlantzick points out, that as it grows, it will become a much larger consumer of other nations' goods, creating—in a favorite phrase of the current leadership—"win-win" economics. Chinese leaders constantly talk up the value of likely investments and trade, with total outward investment rising, according to official statistics, 1,000 percent in 2005, though this figure includes mere commitments and the total is only $7 billion, compared with $60 billion in foreign direct investment (excluding the finance sector) flowing to China.

China's soft power offensive and the lure of the China Model remain, however, entirely official government programs. Where soft power has worked durably and has permeated connections among nations and nationalities, it has also involved civil society and the media, the arts, cultural attraction—the broad range of informal human contacts. Beijing will not let such areas of life off the leash at home, let alone license them for export. Thus, its charm in the developing world remains that of the official with his jacket still on, the limousine with darkened windows waiting outside—fully paid for—and the critics regularly, clinically rounded up and removed beyond earshot.

ROWAN CALLICK is the Beijing-based China correspondent of *The Australian* newspaper.

China's Rebalancing Act

JAHANGIR AZIZ AND STEVEN DUNAWAY

In the past 20 years, China has added about $2 trillion to world GDP, created 120 million new jobs, and pulled 400 million people out of poverty. These are big numbers—equivalent to adding a country of the economic size of Portugal every year; creating as many new jobs each year as the total number of people employed in Australia; and eradicating poverty in Ethiopia, Nigeria, Tanzania, and Zambia combined. In recent years, China has grown more than 10 percent annually while keeping inflation below 3 percent. Today, it is the fourth largest economy in the world and the third largest trading nation.

Despite these remarkable achievements, there is growing unease within China and abroad about the state of its economy. At the National People's Congress this March, Premier Wen Jiabao cautioned, "the biggest problem with China's economy is that the growth is unstable, unbalanced, uncoordinated, and unsustainable." More generally, the question is whether the pace of growth is sustainable or whether the imbalances in the economy might slow growth, perhaps significantly. And this is why China's policymakers are looking to rebalance the economy to rely less on exports and investment and more on consumption as the source of growth.

What are the underlying causes of these imbalances and how should they be addressed? Those are critical questions not only for China but also for much of the rest of the world, whose prosperity is linked to China. For as China has grown, its economic impact on many countries has magnified, whether through its large trade imbalances, exchange rate issues, or its large and growing need for resources and food. There are many suggestions about the policies China should pursue to rebalance its economy—and some even argue that the rebalancing will occur "naturally" as a result of market forces. We believe that a rebalancing will not happen on its own and lean toward an effort that relies on monetary policy, price liberalization, financial market reform, and changes in government expenditure policies.

How It Began

China's liberalization is usually separated into three phases—the reforms of 1978, 1984, and 1994—each of which further opened the economy. The 1994 reforms had three prongs: the unification of the official and market exchange rates and the removal of restrictions on payments for trading goods, services, and income; the opening of the export sector to foreign direct investment; and the reform of the state-owned enterprises (SOEs). The first two changes turned the export sector into a powerful engine of growth, and the third unleashed domestic entrepreneurship.

Foreign enterprises, on their own and in joint ventures, used China's cheap but skilled labor to convert the coastline into the "world's workshop" and a critical node in the global supply chain. Meanwhile, domestic enterprises, relieved of costly social responsibilities and not required to share profits with the government, began to invest in new technologies, expand rapidly, and seek out new markets. Domestic private sector firms also developed. A plethora of incentives from both the central and the local governments—in the form of tax breaks, cheap land, and low utility prices—helped to keep production costs low and raise profits to be reinvested in further expansion.

With capital controls and an underdeveloped capital market limiting investment choices, China's large pool of savings provided these enterprises with a captive and cheap source of financing through a state-controlled banking system. And with this, China began an economic expansion of unprecedented pace driven by investment and exports. But consumption growth, in particular, could not keep pace with the capacity created by rapid investment. As a result, the share of investment in GDP rose, while that of consumption declined, with the difference picked up by a rising trade surplus.

Rising Growth, Mounting Imbalances

The concern is that China's rapid growth could slow, perhaps even sharply, if the continued expansion of capacity eventually leads to price declines that reduce profits, increase loan defaults, and undermine investor confidence. As the imbalances grow, so does the probability of such a development. If the global economy slows at the same time and competition from other countries rises, Chinese firms would find it that much more difficult to sell their products abroad without deep price cuts. Moreover, the risk of rising protectionism in China's trading partner countries could worsen the situation.

But didn't many of today's successful economies sustain such a development strategy for some time? Indeed, an export-based growth strategy backed by large domestic savings and investment was the right path for China in the early 1990s. And it has been remarkably successful. That said, much has changed since 1990, when China was a small economy just starting to open up, importing sophisticated inputs and assembling them into consumer goods for the West. Today this assembly-line business makes up less than 10 percent of China's $250 billion trade surplus. Instead, China's exports have branched into new and more sophisticated products with a growing proportion of domestically made inputs. China also has become a dominant player in many markets. While it was relatively easy to expand market share before, further expansion will likely require Chinese firms to cut prices. If the price cuts needed to sell the created capacity turn out to be deep, many of today's investments could become unviable, turning into tomorrow's loan defaults.

Why is investment high? There is no big mystery here. Profits of Chinese companies have risen sharply over the past several years, suggesting that returns on investment are very attractive. In part this is because key input costs are low—including energy, utilities, land prices, and pollution control. But perhaps most important is the low cost of capital. Investment accounts for nearly 45 percent of China's GDP, and 90 percent of that is financed domestically (the national saving rate is 55 percent of GDP). Foreign direct investment accounts for less than 5 percent of GDP. Domestic bank lending and reinvested earnings of firms share the bulk of the financing needs. Bank lending rates are low because of low deposit rates set by the government.

Since the enterprise reform, the government has not sought dividends from SOEs, not even from those that are listed on the stock exchange and pay dividends to their private shareholders. For these enterprises, profits either are reinvested or sit in low-earning deposit accounts. Rising corporate saving has been the main reason that China's overall savings have gone up. Corporate savings roughly equal household savings—at about 23–24 percent of GDP. Low bank lending rates and retained earnings have kept the cost of investment funds low. Whereas real GDP growth in China has averaged about 10 percent, the real cost of investment has hovered at about 1–2 percent. In advanced economies that gap is negligible. In most emerging market economies it is positive, but in none is it as wide as in China. It is not surprising then that investment growth is so much faster in China and that investment's share of GDP is one of the highest in the world.

The cost of capital is not just low; it has fallen relative to wages, despite China's abundant labor supply. As a result, as economic theory predicts, production has been skewed increasingly toward capital-intensive processes, and job creation has slowed. In most countries, 3–4 percent GDP growth is associated with 2–3 percent employment growth, but in China, 10 percent GDP growth is generating only about 1 percent employment growth. In addition, the undervalued exchange rate and widely held expectations among investors that the currency will appreciate only gradually have biased investment toward

exports and import substitution, adding to the rise in the trade surplus.

Why is consumption low? Although consumption has grown at a real rate of 8 percent since the early 1990s, it has lagged GDP growth. Personal consumption's share of GDP has fallen by more than 12 percentage points, to about 40 percent, one of the lowest levels in the world. While household savings in China are high and their rate has increased somewhat in recent years, this can explain only about 1 percentage point of the drop. Nearly all the decline is attributable to a falling share of national income going to households, including wages, investment income, and government transfers. Many countries have seen their wage share decline. But, in most countries, overall household income has held up reasonably well because rising dividend and interest income have offset the falling wage share. In China, though, household investment income has declined from more than 6 percent of GDP in the mid-1990s to less than 2 percent today, mainly because of low deposit rates and limited household equity ownership (directly or through institutional investors). Moreover, in most countries, profits of SOEs are transferred to the government, which uses them to provide consumption goods, such as health care and education, and income transfers to households. But in China the government receives no dividends, and transfers to households and public spending on health and education have declined.

Why Rebalancing Won't Happen on Its Own

The way to address these imbalances seems straightforward: switch from investment and exports as the main drivers of growth to consumption. Some analysts question whether there is a major problem and suggest that the normal business cycle will rebalance the economy. During upturns, firms invest and expand, increasing the demand for resources, such as capital and labor, these analysts say. That raises input costs, driving down profits and slowing investment. Less productive firms exit, economic growth slows, and prices stabilize.

In China's case, however, that argument is flawed. Business cycles usually occur in more advanced economies in which markets are well developed and prices provide early signals, allowing firms and households to adjust smoothly. In China, markets are not developed and prices do not provide a true reflection of underlying supply and demand conditions in key markets. Instead they are influenced, to varying degrees, by the government. Consequently, rebalancing requires active involvement by the government in the form of policy changes and reforms. What are those needed policy changes and reforms? There are four principal steps:

First, raise the cost of capital. In the immediate future, interest rates and the exchange rate hold the key to curbing rapid investment growth and the associated rise in bank lending. Curbing investment has been the main goal of macroeconomic policy over most of the past three years. The Chinese authorities have also tried to control investment directly using a combination of administrative measures and "guided" bank lending, but these have not provided a lasting solution. China must increase its reliance on monetary policy to curb investment and credit growth by raising the cost of capital, the main reason investment is growing so rapidly. But the authorities fear that if the currency is tightly managed, increases in interest rates will encourage capital inflows that will add liquidity to the banking system, requiring further interest rate hikes to absorb it. China's government not only imposes a ceiling on deposit rates, it also sets a floor on lending rates and tightly manages the exchange rate, even after the changes made to the exchange rate regime in 2005.

The obvious way out is to simultaneously raise the floor on lending rates, lift the ceiling on deposit rates, and allow the exchange rate to appreciate more quickly. This will provide the room monetary tightening needs to be effective. Not only will the financial cost of capital increase, but, over the medium term, a stronger currency will help curb investments in the export and import-substituting sectors, while raising household incomes. The objective for economic policy should be that both interest rates and the exchange rate are increasingly determined by the market, so that the right price signals are provided to investors and households.

Second, liberalize prices. Reducing investment growth will require more than just monetary tightening. Other key prices in the economy also need to reflect market conditions and the underlying resource costs. In the past few years, the government has begun to raise the price of industrial land, power, and gasoline, and, importantly, to introduce stricter environmental standards and better enforce pollution controls. The government's goal of cutting energy use per unit of GDP by 20 percent over the next five years should help not only improve energy efficiency and reduce pollution, but also curb investment growth by raising business costs.

On the tax front, the government is unifying the enterprise income tax rate but still must cut tax and other incentives for investment that have proliferated over the past two decades, particularly at the local level. Raising the cost of capital also requires the government to exercise better corporate governance over SOEs, including asking profitable firms to transfer dividends to the budget. A pilot program is planned in which some SOEs would pay dividends to the budget in 2008, the first time since 1994. This is a step in the right direction, but the program needs to be expanded, especially to cover listed companies, which should pay the government the same dividends they pay to their private shareholders.

Third, reform financial markets. While weak corporate governance by the government has allowed SOEs to accumulate large savings, private enterprises, especially the small and medium-scale ones, have done the same because poor financial intermediation has limited their access to bank credit (Aziz, 2006). In the early 2000s, China embarked on an ambitious bank reform program and has made substantial progress in cleaning up nonperforming loans, recapitalizing banks, and opening the sector to foreign participation and competition. But, as a result,

banks turned conservative—because of their weak internal risk-management and risk-pricing systems—and have continued to direct most credit to large cash-rich SOEs at the expense of private firms and households. Because capital markets—bond and equity—are also weak, they have not been an alternative source of financing for firms or savings for households. Firms have instead had to rely on internal savings for investment, and consumers have done the same for almost all large purchases—education, health care, pensions, housing, and durable goods (Aziz and Cui, 2007). Greater access to credit and a broader range of instruments to raise funds would reduce the incentives of firms to hold large savings, and better access to credit, insurance, and private pensions would diminish household saving and boost consumption.

Better financial intermediation has thus become the government's top priority. The authorities are pushing for further improvements in the banks' commercial operations, internal controls, and governance. They should also lift the cap on deposit rates, which would not only help push up the cost of capital but also allow smaller and more aggressive banks to compete better against large state-owned banks and provide an incentive for big banks to expand credit to small and medium-scale enterprises. China is also looking to expand its other financial markets, especially bond and equity markets. However, continued government control over bond and equity issuance is a serious impediment to these markets. Raising household consumption requires not only increasing the household share of national income but also reducing the uncertainties that have kept precautionary savings high. For the first, a key factor is increasing households' investment income—through higher deposit rates and greater participation in the equity market, and directly and indirectly through expanded mutual and pension funds. Equity market reforms of the past few years have revitalized a languishing stock market, but the supply of equities needs to be increased.

Fourth, shift government expenditures. The government has another important role in this rebalancing exercise: improving the provision of key social services, especially education, health care, and pensions. Reducing the uncertainties surrounding their provision will substantially diminish the strong precautionary saving motive and give households the confidence to raise their consumption. In the 1994 SOE reforms, the provision of health care, education, and pensions was transferred from companies to local governments. However, in general, local governments were not provided with adequate resources to discharge these new responsibilities. Consequently, households have had to bear an increasing portion of the costs of health care and education. Chinese households pay about 80 percent of health care costs out of their own pockets, one of the highest proportions in the world. They also face considerable uncertainty about pensions, because reforms in this area have not produced a new, viable pension system, although China's one-child policy has intensified the aging of the population and raised the need to save for old age. The government has increased spending for education and health care in recent budgets, but the increases have been limited. In essence, households have self-insured against uncertainties associated with pensions, health care, and education. As a result, they have saved significantly more than they would have were these risks pooled socially.

Rather than provide quick fixes, the government has rightly decided to rebalance the economy by implementing fundamental reforms along several dimensions to shift the economy's heavy reliance on investment and exports toward consumption. China has already made progress on many of them, and most analysts agree on the basic elements of the strategy. However, there is a concern that the current high growth and low inflation in China and a benign world economy may give the false impression that China has time on its side in implementing these reforms. The reality could be different. Unchecked, the imbalances will continue to grow and, with them, the rising probability of a large correction will become a major threat to the country's economic growth and stability.

JAHANGIR AZIZ is a Division Chief and Steven Dunaway is a Deputy Director in the IMF's Asia and Pacific Department.

From *Finance & Development,* September 2007, pp. 27–31. Copyright © 2007 by The International Monetary Fund and the World Bank. Reprinted by permission of The International Monetary Fund and the World Bank via the Copyright Clearance Center.

China and HIV—A Window of Opportunity

BATES GILL, PH.D., AND SUSAN OKIE, M.D.

Last December in Wuhan, China, two middle-aged rural women who had become infected with HIV in the 1990s struggled to describe to foreign visitors how China's new HIV-treatment program had changed their lives. Suddenly, one woman's 12-year-old daughter spoke up. Her mother, she said, had been too sick to get out of bed, and the girl had left school to help at home and on the farm. But when the woman began taking antiretroviral drugs, she improved quickly, returned to work in the fields, and sent her daughter back to the classroom.

Such stories are increasingly common in China, reflecting a striking shift in the government's approach to HIV. Although China's first AIDS cases were discovered in 1989, the government did not publicly acknowledge the existence of a major epidemic until 2001. Two years later, as international attention mounted after the outbreak of severe acute respiratory syndrome (SARS), the government abruptly changed course, launching aggressive measures against AIDS. An interagency committee was created to coordinate a government-wide response, and a national AIDS treatment program was established. The national budget for HIV–AIDS grew from approximately $12.5 million in 2002 to about $100 million in 2005 and about $185 million in 2006.[1] In January 2006, the Chinese Cabinet issued regulations for HIV–AIDS prevention and control, outlining the responsibilities of the central and local governments and stipulating the rights and responsibilities of infected persons. The law requires county-level jurisdictions to provide free antiretroviral drugs to poor citizens who need treatment and free consultations and treatment to prevent mother-to-child transmission. Infected persons must take steps to avoid knowingly spreading HIV, but the statute forbids discrimination against them in employment, education, marriage, and health care.

The government also announced a 5-year plan that sets ambitious targets for educating the public about HIV, reducing stigma, training health care workers and technicians, ramping up treatment, improving surveillance, and delivering counseling and interventions to at-risk populations. The government estimates that 650,000 Chinese people are infected with HIV and hopes to limit the total to 1.5 million by 2010.

"There's really been a sea change" in China's response, said Peter Piot, executive director of the Joint United Nations Program on HIV/AIDS (UNAIDS). "The central leadership and policies are nearly as good as they can be."

Chinese and international health officials express optimism about controlling the epidemic but emphasize the need to move quickly. The current estimate represents an HIV prevalence of approximately 0.05% of the general population, but by the end of October 2006, only 183,733 infected persons had been identified, according to the Ministry of Health. Although HIV has been reported in all 31 Chinese provinces, about three quarters of infected persons are believed to reside in 5 provinces: Guangdong, Guangxi, Henan, Xinjiang, and Yunnan.[2] Henan, along with several neighboring provinces in central China, was the site of a 1990s HIV outbreak among rural residents who became infected through contaminated equipment at commercial plasma-donation centers. The other four are border provinces, crisscrossed by heroin-trafficking routes, where HIV transmission is fueled by injection-drug use. The epidemic is "quite young," said Ray Yip, director of the Chinese office of the U.S. Centers for Disease Control and Prevention (CDC). "It's still concentrated very highly among the highest-risk group of people. It hasn't really gotten out of hand even among the sex-worker population."

But the situation could worsen rapidly. Among new HIV infections in China, 48.6% are caused by drug use, 49.8% by sexual transmission, and 1.6% by mother-to-child transmission, according to Connie Osborne, senior adviser to the World Health Organization (WHO) on HIV–AIDS care and treatment in Beijing. The country is undergoing rapid economic and social change, including migration from rural areas to cities and increases in prostitution and illegal drug use. "It's a free-for-all kind of place," said Yip. "If you don't control the epidemic in the next 5 years . . . the sheer increasing numbers of people who engage in high-risk behavior can fuel the fire." Given China's enormous population, even a small increase in prevalence could be devastating. "If it went up to 4%, we would have 52 million infected, more than the total global figure today," said Wu Zunyou, director of China's National Center for AIDS/STD Control and Prevention (NCAIDS).

China's determination to confront its epidemic has attracted major funding. As of late 2005, international assistance programs for HIV–AIDS had been implemented in 27 provinces, with contributions of approximately $229 million.[3] China has received approximately $134 million for HIV programs from the Global Fund to Fight AIDS, Tuberculosis, and Malaria, which will provide more than $14 million over the next 5 years to strengthen civil society organizations that can reach high-risk populations.[4] China also receives aid for HIV–AIDS control from numerous other international partners.

In Beijing, it is common to hear health officials declare that controlling HIV–AIDS is now simply a technical matter of implementing existing policies. Although the Chinese government has indeed made some tough choices—for example, supporting needle-exchange programs and setting up methadone-maintenance therapy sites for injection-drug users—other critical problems must still be addressed.

First, those who are HIV-positive or in high-risk groups still bear a stigma and experience discrimination, both of which are major obstacles to care. Health care workers have been known to refuse to treat persons suspected of having HIV. People from "HIV villages," such as those in Henan, where many plasma donors became infected, cannot find jobs, and agricultural produce from these locales cannot find markets.

Far greater stigma is attached to persons who contract HIV through behavior that is criminal or deemed immoral. Injection-drug users and commercial sex workers, who make up the largest population of HIV-positive persons, are also among the most difficult to reach with counseling and treatment, in part because stigma drives them underground. There is tension between public health authorities, responsible for preventing and treating HIV infection, and public security officials, responsible for punishing illegal activity. Although officials in leadership positions may acknowledge that injection-drug users are patients as well as criminals, says Piot of UNAIDS, this understanding "has not been internalized by every policeman and security person." The February 2007 detention of Gao Yaojie—an elderly doctor turned HIV–AIDS activist in Henan province—to prevent her from receiving an international award in the United States is just one recent case in which local authorities took action that was contrary to national policies. After international pressure was exerted, Gao was permitted to travel.

About half of China's HIV-positive population contracted the virus by sharing needles for drug use. In 2005, the government authorized the rapid establishment of methadone-maintenance therapy sites throughout the country. According to Wu of NCAIDS, by the end of 2006, China had opened 320 such clinics, each dispensing methadone to an average of 200 patients per day; the aim is to have 1500 clinics operating by 2008. Yip of the CDC believes this program offers the strongest evidence of the government's determination to stem the epidemic: "It signals that they understand the critical link between drug use and control of HIV–AIDS. It's a permission to engage the most marginalized people."

Currently, however, most sites do not offer more comprehensive services, such as needle and syringe exchange, peer counseling, testing, or employment counseling. In addition, the efforts of local authorities to set up such clinics are often met with resistance, ranging from complaints that the clinics attract "the wrong elements" to questions about why drug addicts should receive free or subsidized medical care when the average citizen does not. Although China has also implemented needle-exchange programs, Wu said that because these programs do not reduce injection-drug use, they will "only be used in places where methadone maintenance is not available."

Men who have sex with men are another at-risk population that until recently received little attention. There are strong taboos against homosexual behavior in China, where men are under enormous pressure to marry and produce male heirs. Estimates of the population of men who have sex with men range from 5 million to 10 million, and the number may well increase as social mores continue to change. Chinese health officials estimate that nationwide about 1% of men who have sex with men are HIV-positive.[5] They have established an advisory group including activists and behavioral specialists to formulate policies designed to reach this marginalized population, but China still has a long way to go in allowing nongovernmental and civil society organizations to contribute to the fight against HIV–AIDS.

China also faces the daunting task of locating the half-million or more people believed to be infected with HIV infection without knowing it. A massive testing program undertaken from 2004 through 2005 focused on identifying plasma donors infected during the 1990s outbreak and on conducting testing in drug-detoxification detention centers and prisons. This effort is the single largest factor in the recent dramatic increase in reported HIV–AIDS cases.

Still, an estimated 70% of infected persons remain unidentified. Outside the prison and drug-detoxification systems, HIV testing is voluntary. Mandatory premarital testing for sexually transmitted diseases was eliminated in October 2003, although some localities may reinstate it. Because of stigma, distrust regarding confidentiality, and the absence of effective counseling and referrals, most people are reluctant to be tested. Moreover, although screening tests are available free, patients usually must pay for confirmatory tests that cost $25 to $40—nearly a month's salary in parts of China. Reliance on confirmatory testing also increases loss to follow-up: many people never receive their results, according to Osborne, who says the WHO is promoting rapid testing.

China's epidemic, unlike that in most countries, is concentrated in rural areas, where poor residents have little access to health care. The hard work of stemming the epidemic will fall to county-level jurisdictions. With more than 3000 counties in China, the task of ensuring an effective and relatively standard response will be an enormous one. The implementation of the central government's mandates will vary widely, depending on local resources and priorities. HIV has hit hardest in the poorest, most remote areas that are hard-pressed to provide the money, training, and personnel needed. "With the introduction of the market economy, there has been a collapse of public health services and other services for the poor . . . particularly in rural areas," said Piot of UNAIDS. "Getting treatment to people is therefore not so easy, even if the will is there."

Since 2003, China has rapidly expanded the availability of first-line antiretroviral treatment. By the end of 2006, approximately 24,400 people were receiving therapy, up from about 20,450 in 2005, and the number is expected to reach 30,000 to 35,000 this year. But further increases are likely to be slower, since reaching marginalized groups will be more difficult than enrolling people infected through plasma donation. WHO authorities in Beijing fear that China's treatment program may not reach its goal of extending free treatment to 80% of those who need it by 2010. With 1 million to 1.5 million expected to be HIV-positive by then, 200,000 or more people may require treatment.

Relying almost entirely on generic drugs produced in China, the country's first-line therapy regimens—zidovudine, didanosine, and nevirapine or stavudine, didanosine, and nevirapine—have severe side effects, raising concerns about adherence and the emergence of drug resistance. Laboratory tests to monitor treatment are not paid for by the central government, and the costs are commonly passed along to patients. In early 2005, more effective and less toxic compounds such as efavirenz and lamivudine became available and were introduced into some first-line regimens. Chinese health authorities are negotiating with foreign pharmaceutical firms to purchase second-line drugs, which are not widely available.

In addition, despite some new training programs, most regions lack health care providers with sufficient expertise to properly diagnose and treat AIDS and to monitor patients' viral loads. With suboptimal treatment, drug-resistant virus will surely emerge, but a national drug-resistance surveillance system does not yet exist. The rate of resistance to first-line treatment was 18% in one small Chinese study but 45 to 80% in separate cohorts in another study.

International health experts remain cautiously hopeful about China's chances of controlling its epidemic. Success, however, will depend on how well the government handles challenges such as overcoming stigma, mounting aggressive outreach efforts for high-risk groups, and mobilizing funding, expertise, and commitment throughout the vast and diverse country to identify, counsel, and care for the people who are infected. Although a political corner has been turned in Beijing, there is still an enormous amount of work to be done on the ground.

"When you have a country where the prevalence of HIV is less than 1 per 1000 and the government has started to respond seriously, that's good news," noted Yip of the CDC, but China must now implement strategies aimed at the hardest-hit populations. "A good policy," he warns, "doesn't always translate into a sound program."

Notes

1. Spending on HIV/AIDS prevention set to double. China Daily (Beijing), December 28, 2005. (Accessed April 13, 2007, at http:// www.chinadaily.com.cn/english/doc/2005-12/28/ content_507212.htm.)

2. People's Republic of China Ministry of Health, Joint United Nations Program on HIV/AIDS, World Health Organization. 2005 Update on the HIV/AIDS epidemic and response in China. Beijing: National Center for AIDS/STD Prevention and Control, January 24, 2006. (Accessed April 13, 2007, at http://data.unaids.org/Publications/External-Documents/rp_ 2005chinaestimation_25jan06_en.pdf.)

3. New rules to combat AIDS spread. China Daily (Beijing), October 28, 2005. (Accessed April 13, 2007, at http://www. china.org.cn/english/government/146791.htm.)

4. Sixth call for proposals for grant funding. Geneva: The Global Fund to Fight AIDS, Tuberculosis, and Malaria, 2006. (Accessed April 13, 2007, at http://www.theglobalfund.org/ search/docs/6CHNH_1291_0_full.pdf.)

5. Chinese gay population announced for the first time. China Daily (Beijing), April 5, 2006. (Accessed April 13, 2007, at http://www.chinadaily.com.cn/hqylss/2006-04/05/content_ 560655.htm.)

DR. GILL is a China scholar at the Center for Strategic and International Studies, Washington, DC. Dr. Okie is a contributing editor of the *Journal*.

Dr. Gill reports receiving consulting fees from Merck and Abbott Laboratories and grant support from Merck and the Gates Foundation.

China's Coal Future

To prevent massive pollution and slow its growing contribution to global warming, China will need to make advanced coal technology work on an unprecedented scale.

PETER FAIRLEY

A visitor arriving in Shanghai immediately notices China's technological conundrum. Through the windows of the magnetically levitated train that covers the 30 kilometers from Pudong International Airport to Shanghai at up to 430 kilometers per hour, both the progress the country is making and the price it is paying for it are apparent. Most days, a yellow haze hangs over Shanghai's construction frenzy. Pollution is the leading cause of death in China, killing more than a million people a year. And the primary cause of pollution is also the source of the energy propelling the ultramodern train: coal.

To keep pace with the country's economic growth, China's local governments, utilities, and entrepreneurs are building, on average, one coal-fired power plant per week. The power plants emit a steady stream of soot, sulfur dioxide, and other toxic pollutants into the air; they also spew out millions of tons of carbon dioxide. In November, the International Energy Agency projected that China will become the world's largest source of carbon dioxide emissions in 2009, overtaking the United States nearly a decade earlier than previously anticipated. Coal is expected to be responsible for three-quarters of that carbon dioxide.

And the problem will get worse. Between now and 2020, China's energy consumption will more than double, according to expert estimates. Ratcheting up energy efficiency, tapping renewable resources with hydro dams and wind turbines, and building nuclear plants can help, but—at least in the coming two decades—only marginally. Since China has very little in the way of oil and gas reserves, its future depends on coal. With 13 percent of the world's proven reserves, China has enough coal to sustain its economic growth for a century or more. The good news is that China's leaders saw the coal rush coming in the 1990s and began exploring a range of advanced technologies. Chief among them is coal gasification. "It's the key for clean coal in China," says chemical engineer Li Wenhua, who directed advanced coal development for Beijing's national high-tech R&D program (better known in China as the "863" program) from 2001 through 2005.

Gasification transforms coal's complex mix of hydrocarbons into a hydrogen-rich gas known as synthesis gas, or "syngas."

Power plants can burn syngas as cleanly as they can natural gas. In addition, with the right catalysts and under the right conditions, the basic chemical building blocks in syngas combine to form the hydrocarbon ingredients of gasoline and diesel fuel. As a result, coal gasification has the potential both to squelch power plants' emission of soot and smog and to decrease China's growing dependence on imported oil. It could even help control emissions of carbon dioxide, which is more easily captured from syngas plants than from conventional coal-fired plants.

Despite China's early anticipation of the need for coal gasification, however, its implementation of the technology in power plants has lagged. The country's electricity producers lack the economic and political incentives to break from their traditional practices.

In contrast, large-scale efforts to produce liquid transportation fuels using coal gasification are well under way. China's largest coal firm, Shenhua Group, plans to start up the country's first coal-to-fuels plant in 2007 or early 2008, in the world's most ambitious application of coal liquefaction since World War II. Shenhua plans to operate eight liquefaction plants by 2020, producing, in total, more than 30 million tons of synthetic oil annually—enough to displace more than 10 percent of China's projected oil imports.

China's progress in constructing coal-conversion plants puts it far ahead of the United States, where coal gasification is still recovering from a damaged reputation. Gasification demonstration programs initiated in the U.S. after the energy crises of the 1970s were orphaned when oil and gas prices plummeted in the 1980s. That left many with the impression that the technology itself was unreliable (*see "Carbon Dioxide for Sale," July 2005*). In China, by contrast, oil never looked cheap, and coal has never lost its shine.

Coal and Cashmere

Northern China is fast becoming the epicenter of China's energy industry. The leading draw is the Shenfu Dongsheng coalfield, a 31,000-square-kilometer solid layer of shallow coal that stretches from the northern tip of China's Shaanxi Province to the southern edge of Nei Mongol, or Inner Mongolia. The Dongsheng field's estimated reserve of 223.6 billion tons of coal makes it the world's seventh largest; efforts to convert much of that coal to transportation fuels could make it the world's most profitable.

Until recently, Inner Mongolia's coal capital, Erdos, was largely untouched by the modern world, bounded by mountain ranges and the Great Wall to the south and by the Yellow River to the north. Its isolation is now over, thanks to freshly poured highways and new rail lines rolling over its fissured hills and steep valleys. An airport should open this year.

Erdos's GDP doubled between 2001 and 2004, largely because of coal, chemicals, and cashmere (Erdos supplies a quarter of the world's cashmere). To reach the coalfields, you drive 40 minutes south of the city, passing a 1950s-era mausoleum for Genghis Khan, the 13th-century warrior who conquered much of Asia. As you approach the dry floodplain of the Wulanmulun River, the imposing infrastructure of a dozen coal mines, including some of the world's largest and most mechanized, leaps out of the barren landscape. The region is also home to several hundred smaller, less modern mines (gases and cave-ins kill at least 6,000 Chinese coal miners a year). Miners on their day off zip by on mopeds, three or four to a vehicle, racing past 40-ton trucks heaped with coal. Along the highway, coal-sorting terminals load railcars destined for power plants and ports on the industrialized east coast.

None of that infrastructure and activity, however, prepares a visitor for Shenhua's coal-to-fuels complex, which rises from a plateau cut into the hills. It is an impressive site, with its own coal-fired power plant, gasification plants, and two massive reactors where coal will be liquefied, each weighing 2,250 metric tons (Shenhua claimed the world hoisting record when it lifted the reactors into place last June). Flush from a $2.95 billion IPO in 2005 and $5 billion in annual revenues from its integrated mines, railroads, and power plants, Shenhua is rapidly expanding its operations. It sold 113 million metric tons of coal in just the first half of 2006, nearly matching the previous year's total. If Shenhua maintains that pace this year, it may become the world's largest producer of coal.

China's government in Beijing created Shenhua a decade ago to bring economies of scale and modern technology to bear on the Dongsheng coalfields. The company's $1.5 billion coal-to-fuels plant is an expression of that strategy—a facility so technically ambitious that many experts, Chinese and Western alike, doubted it would ever be built.

The production of transportation fuels from coal dates to early-20th-century Germany, where chemists developed two approaches to converting coal's solid long-chain hydrocarbons into the shorter liquid hydrocarbons found in motor fuels. (Nazi Germany, with little access to oil, relied heavily on these processes to fuel its highly mechanized army and air force, producing gasoline, diesel, and aviation fuel from coal.) Franz Fischer and Hans Tropsch invented the better known of the two approaches in the 1920s. Fischer-Tropsch synthesis reduces coal to syngas, a mixture of hydrogen and carbon monoxide. A catalyst, often cobalt, then causes the carbon and hydrogen

atoms to reconnect into new compounds, such as alcohols and fuels. Fischer-Tropsch synthesis is conventional chemistry today: in South Africa, for example, Johannesburg-based Sasol built Fischer-Tropsch coal-to-oil plants to ensure the country's fuel supply during the trade boycotts of the apartheid years; and by swapping in different catalysts, China's coal-to-chemicals gasification plants have employed Fischer-Tropsch for decades to yield products such as synthetic fertilizers and methanol.

Shenhua's plant, in contrast, chose Fischer-Tropsch's lesser-known rival, invented by Friedrich Bergius a decade earlier. Though used extensively by the Nazis, Bergius's process was subsequently abandoned. The process has come to be known as direct liquefaction, because it bypasses the syngas step. In direct liquefaction, the bulk of the coal is pulverized and blended with some of the plant's synthetic oil, then treated with hydrogen and heated to 450°C in the presence of an iron catalyst, which breaks the hydro-carbon chains into the shorter chains suitable for refining into liquid fuels.

Direct liquefaction produces more fuel per ton of coal than Fischer-Tropsch synthesis. Experts at the Chinese Coal Research Institute in Beijing estimate that the process captures 55 to 56 percent of the energy in coal, compared to just 45 percent for Fischer-Tropsch. However, direct liquefaction is also far more complicated, requiring separate power and gasification plants to deliver heat and hydrogen and considerable recycling of oil, hydrogen, and coal sludge between separate sections of the plant. And breaking down hydrocarbons to just the right length requires exquisite control of the operating conditions and a consistent coal supply.

Shenhua redesigned the process over the last five years to boost efficiency and reduce waste but, at the same time, increased its complexity. And the company is taking a huge engineering and economic risk by pursuing so novel a technology on such a vast scale.

By the end of this year, Shenhua hopes to be pumping out 20,000 barrels of synthetic oil per day, nearly 500 times as much as its pilot plant in Shanghai produces. According to Jerald Fletcher, a natural-resource economist at West Virginia University in Morgantown, the Erdos plant constitutes a $1.5 billion experiment that could only take place in China. "It would be hard to get that kind of commitment of funds in the West without a more proven technology," says Fletcher. Eric Larson, an expert in energy technology and modeling at Princeton University, puts it more bluntly: "It doesn't make a lot of sense to build a huge plant like that, because it may not work."

But for the Chinese government, the rewards could be worth the risk. Despite its 2005 IPO of some assets, Shenhua remains a largely state-owned firm, and the direct-liquefaction plant serves a critical state interest: energy security. "No matter how big the cost, Shenhua will build it," says Zhou Zhijie, a gasification expert at East China University of Science and Technology's Institute of Clean Coal Technology in Shanghai. "China's government will support this project until the liquid flows."

Of course, if the new plant works, Shenhua stands to earn a substantial profit. The company predicts that its synthetic oil will turn a profit at roughly $30 a barrel, though many analysts say $45 is more realistic. (The U.S. Department of Energy's most recent price forecast predicts that crude oil will dip to $47 a barrel in 2014, then climb steadily to $57 a barrel in 2030.) Hedging its bets, Shenhua has also entered a preliminary agreement with partners Shell and Sasol concerning several similar-sized or bigger Fischer-Tropsch fuel plants in Northern China, which would start up in 2012.

Shenhua's Chinese coal competitors, too, are already breaking ground on their versions of coal-to-fuel plants. The Yankuang coal group, the second-largest coal producer in China, is planning a Fischer-Tropsch fuel plant near Erdos that will use a proprietary gasifier and catalyst.

Beyond the risks inherent in the large-scale deployment of unproven technology, the gasification building boom also is an environmental gamble. Indeed, what may ultimately check China's coal-to-oil ambitions is water. China's Coal Research Institute estimates that Shenhua's plant will consume 10 tons of water for every ton of synthetic oil produced (360 gallons of water per barrel of oil), and the ratio is even worse for Fischer-Tropsch plants. Last summer, China's National Development and Reform Commission, the powerful body charged with regulating China's economy and approving large capital projects, issued a warning about the environmental consequences of the "runaway development" of synthetic-oil and chemical plants, which it said will consume tens of millions of cubic meters of water annually.

That prediction sounds particularly ominous in northern China, where water is scarce. Erdos is a mix of scrub and desert whose meager water supplies are already overtaxed by population growth and existing power plants. Zhou Ji Sheng, who as vice manager of ZMMF, one of Shenhua's Erdos-based competitors, is seeking financing for a gasification project, acknowledges that water scarcity could put an end to coal gasification in the area. "Even though we have so much coal, if we have no water, we will just have to use the traditional way—to dig it out and transport it," he says. "Water is the key factor for us to develop this new industry." Zhou says his firm plans to supplement its water supply by building a 120-kilometer pipeline to the Yellow River. But evaporation from hydroelectric reservoirs, the increased demand of growing cities and industries, and the effects of climate change mean that in the summer, the Yellow River barely reaches the sea.

Carbon Power

While China's desire to end its dependence on foreign oil is helping to drive huge capital investments in liquefaction technology, the country's power producers are moving much more slowly to take advantage of coal gasification. What they, like their American counterparts, are missing is an incentive to upgrade from conventional pulverized-coal plants to the more expensive gasification plants. According to Li Wenhua, the former 863 program manager (who now directs gasification research in China for General Electric), Chinese industrialists perceive pulverized-coal plants as a license to print money. "People say you shouldn't call it a power plant; it's a money-making machine," says Li. As yet, no power company has been willing to be the first to hit the off switch.

Ironically, China's move to a more open economy has hampered efforts to deploy more innovative technologies. In the 1990s, it looked as if China's power sector was headed for its own gasification revolution. In 1993, China's leading power engineering firm, China Power Engineering Consulting in Beijing, began designing the country's first gasification power plant. The monopoly utility of the era, the State Power Corporation, planned to build the commercial-scale plant in Yantai, a thriving seaport not far from the Bohai Sea. The Yantai plant was to be the beginning of a transition to cleaner coal technology, says Zhao Jie, the plant's designer, now vice president of China Power Engineering. "China wanted to take a cleaner and more efficient way to produce power," says Zhao. Instead, the demonstration plant she designed went on a roller-coaster ride to nowhere. Design work was temporarily halted in 1994 when the cost of the technology was deemed unacceptably high, revived in the late 1990s, and then cut adrift after 2002 by the breakup of the State Power Corporation.

The Yantai power plant was based on integrated gasification combined cycle (IGCC) technology. IGCC plants resemble natural-gas-fired power plants—they use two turbines to capture mechanical and heat energy from expanding combustion gases—but are fueled with syngas from an integrated coal gasification plant. They're not emissions free, but their gas streams are more concentrated, so the sulfurous soot, carbon dioxide, and other pollutants they generate are easier to separate and capture. Of course, once the carbon dioxide—the main greenhouse gas—is captured, engineers still need to find a place to stow it. The most promising strategy is to sequester it deep within saline aquifers and oil reservoirs. In preliminary analyses, Chinese geologists have estimated that aging oil fields and aquifers could absorb more than a trillion tons of carbon dioxide—more than China's coal-fired plants would emit, at their current rate, for hundreds of years.

The Huaneng Group, a power producer based in Beijing, has pulled together a consortium of power and coal interests (Shenhua included) called GreenGen to build the first Chinese IGCC demo plant by 2010; like the related FutureGen project organized by the U.S. Department of Energy, Green-Gen is to start with power production, then add carbon capture and storage. China's vice premier, Zeng Peiyan, made an appearance at GreenGen's ceremonial debut last summer, indicating Beijing's support for the project.

The problem is that IGCC plants still cost about 10 percent to 20 percent more per megawatt than pulverized-coal-fired power plants. (And that's without carbon dioxide capture.) China's power producers—much like their counterparts in the United States and Europe—are waiting for a financial or political reason to make the switch. In part, what's been missing is regulation that penalizes conventional coal plants. And China's environmental agencies lack the resources and power to make companies comply even with regulations already on the books. Top officials in Beijing admit that their edicts are widely ignored, as new power plants are erected without environmental assessments and, according to some sources, without required equipment for pollution control.

Even advocates of IGCC technology expect that its widespread deployment in China will take at least another decade.

Indeed, Du Minghua, a director for coal chemistry at the Chinese Coal Research Institute, predicts that it will be 2020 before application of IGCC technology begins in earnest.

Waiting to Inhale

Despite such pessimistic predictions, China's vast experience with advanced coal technologies and its proven ability to implement new technologies at a startling pace provide ample room for optimism. When you're racing into Shanghai at one-third the speed of sound on a train supported by an electromagnetic force field, it's hard to believe that a country capable of such an engineering feat will continue to ignore the deadly pollution engulfing its cities.

To some analysts, the switch to clean-coal technology seems almost inevitable. "China has to rely on coal for future electricity and fuel needs, and it will eventually have to cap its CO_2 emissions," says Guodong Sun, a technology policy expert at New York's Stony Brook University who has advised the Chinese government on energy policy. "Gasification is one of a very few technologies that can reconcile those conflicting scenarios at reasonable cost."

Still, the timing of such a technology transition is very much in question. Will China really wait until 2020 to start the process of cleaning up its coal-fired power plants? The answer will depend, ultimately, on when China begins to feel that using coal gasification to generate electricity is as urgent as using it to produce transportation fuels—when the costs of air pollution become as worrisome as the costs of relying on foreign oil.

PETER FAIRLEY, a Technology Review contributing writer, traveled to China in October.

Tibet: Death by Consumerism

LINDSEY HILSUM

Smoke from incense burners scented the air as crowds of pilgrims laboured uphill in the dark. At dawn, four monks in maroon and saffron robes climbed on to the roof of the Drepung monastery overlooking Lhasa. They blew deep, reverberating horns, heralding the moment when some 50 monks and pilgrims would emerge bearing a rolled-up, 35-metre-square *thangka*—a painting of the Buddha on cloth—and start their slow trek to the hillside where it would be unfurled.

Buddhists say the annual Yoghurt Festival dates back to the 11th century. After the *thangka* is spread, the faithful give monks and nuns yoghurt as thanks for weeks spent in meditative retreat. A few hours later, in one of the Tibetan capital's less lovely suburbs, the Yoghurt Festival Real Estate Show conjured a rather different atmosphere. It opened with speeches, ticker tape and the unveiling of key messages in Chinese, Tibetan and English: "The value of the modern villas are very large in Tibet," read one. Young Han Chinese couples browsed leaflets and rickety scale models of proposed high-rise apartment blocks. "Rise abruptly, new area Dragon Spring," read one advertisement.

Traditional Tibetans may be as devoutly Buddhist as ever, but modern China worships Mammon. More than half a century after the Chinese invasion of Tibet, and 48 years after the Dalai Lama fled into exile in India, China's Communist rulers are hoping that an economic boom will help them consolidate control over the recalcitrant region. Last year, 2.5 million tourists and business people—some westerners, but most Han Chinese—visited Lhasa. Now the new railway from Beijing has reached the Tibetan capital, the number is expected to increase by 80 per cent this year alone. "It works on the principle of the market economy," says He Ben Yun, a smooth-talking, statistic-spouting official who serves as deputy director of the Tibetan Development and Reform Commission. Born in Hunan Province—"like Chairman Mao"—he has embraced China's post-Mao economic philosophy with enthusiasm. "More people mean more consumption. I think it's good. Nowhere can develop in isolation," he says.

According to government figures, Tibet's economy has grown by more than 12 per cent per year for the past five years. In its attempt to deter "splittists"—those who believe Tibet should be independent—the government is trying to knit the Tibetan economy into the fabric of China. Chinese companies are encouraged to "go west" to start mines, tourism companies and other businesses, while Chinese provinces sponsor development aid and town twinning projects. The Hong Kong-based Information Centre for Human Rights and Democracy says more than 50 ethnic Tibetan officials have recently been sidelined, while a further 850 reliable Communist cadres from across China have been offered incentives to join others spending three years in Tibet.

At midday in the main square, in front of the Dalai Lama's traditional seat, the red and white Potala Palace, a skinny Chinese girl in evening dress was miming Chinese pop songs for an audience of imported officials and military officers. To show that this was part of the Yoghurt Festival, a huge cardboard cut-out of what looked like a cup of shaving cream had been propped up on one side of the stage. The officials in the audience sported baseball caps from Amway, an American "multi-level marketing" company. They took pictures with their mobile phones, while police kept the public well back.

It's a common complaint that only the Han and other migrants, such as the Muslim Hui, are benefiting from the boom. "They take up a big part of the employment market. They settle and start their families here. Tibetans are slowly marginalised," says Woeser, a Tibetan dissident writer who was expelled from her government work unit in Lhasa for praising the Dalai Lama. (Like many Tibetans she uses just one name.) "They not only build houses and open restaurants in Tibet, but they're also taking over the traditional Tibetan industries. Tibetan food, Tibetan furniture, Tibetan costumes are all made by Han people now," she said. Such views are taboo in Tibet. Woeser's blogs have been blocked and her book, *Tibetan Journal,* banned. She now lives in Beijing, but still travels around provinces with Tibetan communities to gather information. When she visits her family in Lhasa, she is closely watched.

Tibet is more solidly under Chinese control than ever before, yet the government remains nervous of dissenting views. While Beijing-based foreign journalists travel without supervision in most of China, the government imposes a "minder" on all correspondents visiting Tibet officially. When asked why, Mr He says it is because of the high altitude. "Our main concern is that journalists should adapt physically," he says. Journalists who try to work after entering as tourists are frequently harassed or arrested.

Resettlement

Tibetans are cautious about talking politics to foreigners, but —although there are still political prisoners—these days the Chinese attitude tends to be more patronising than brutal. It is official policy to tolerate ethnic minorities and their religions, provided they are loyal to the party and the state. "The government pays full respect to ethnic customs," says Mr He. "Tibetan culture is an exotic flower among Chinese cultures. It has existed for more than 2,000 years. But we will help them remove bad or backward habits, and lead them to a more civilised life." As part of its civilising mission, and to integrate Tibetans into the modern economy, the government has resettled 25,000 nomadic and farming families into "new socialist villages". The plan is to settle 80 per cent of rural Tibetans in the next five years.

The countryside is being transformed, with small enclaves of white houses, many flying the red flag, along the roads. An hour's drive north of Lhasa, 260 families have been resettled in the village of Sangbasa. The railway runs past the new houses, each guarded by a ferocious, chained dog. There is no doubt that these houses are an improvement on the huts and tents in which nomadic herders used to stay, nor that settlements make it easier for older people to get medical help and children to go to school. Huang Qian Min, a half-Han half-Tibetan official, explained that it should be possible for Tibetans to continue their traditions while living in improved conditions. "They can live in the settlements in winter and herd animals in summer. Then they can go on herding and enjoy the modern life at the same time," she said. Asked whether the programme was designed so the party can control Tibetans better, she said such an idea was ridiculous. "When they were scattered they knew very little about the world. Through TV and radio, they become more knowledgeable and make more progress. By living together, they can exchange ideas and improve themselves," she said. TV and radio are controlled by the Chinese government; only those with access to the internet or shortwave can hear alternative views.

Suo Nang Zhuo Ma's grandchildren were herding yaks in front of her new house, which boasted glass windows and a comfortable sofa, as well as a television. At 58, she looked 20 years older, and appeared to have little nostalgia for the harsh life she had led, tending livestock and bringing up six children. "With help from the Communist Party of China, we have started a happier life, without many worries," she said. But those who have had to give up the nomadic life altogether are struggling. The train runs over the Tanggula Pass to Qinghai Province, which has a substantial Tibetan minority. Concerned that overgrazing is damaging the fragile grasslands, the government has instructed several thousand Tibetan nomads to sell their herds and move to newly built suburbs on the outskirts of Golmud, a bleak mining town.

The result is ghettos—more than a hundred years on, the process of deprivation and deracination experienced by Aborigines in Australia and Native Americans in the US is being repeated high on the Tibetan plateau. Young men play pool at tables laid out along the street, or kick a ball around the dusty wasteland.

Each family is given a house and the equivalent of £ 70 a month in welfare. "In the beginning, the Tibetan nomads are excited that the government is giving them free money to live in the cities, so they sign up to move, looking forward to living like the people they see on TV," says Woeser. "At first, they have money from selling their animals plus money given by the government, but over time, their money is used up. They learn to spend money like city people but they don't have the skills to make money like city people."

Power of Religion

Most of the former herders are enthusiastic about education, but frequently Tibetan children—who may have never been to school before—are in classes of younger children, learning in Mandarin, which is not their native language. They face discrimination, often being seen as backward or stupid. Outside school, they have little interaction with non-Tibetan children, and are rapidly becoming an underclass.

While the men start to drink, the women increasingly turn to religion. One afternoon in mid-August, dozens of Tibetans, mostly women dressed in traditional clothes, packed into a small room in a Qinghai town to hear a visiting lama. For more than four hours, they spun their prayer-wheels and chanted, as children scurried in and out. On a table at the front, carefully concealed behind Coke bottles, biscuits and a vase of plastic flowers, was a portrait of the Dalai Lama. Showing such images is banned, because the Chinese government demands that its citizens be loyal only to the party. Yet some children sported medallions bearing the Dalai Lama's image and a 25-year-old former herder had created a shrine in his house, including a photo of one of his relatives posing with the Dalai Lama in Dharamsala, where the Tibetan government-in-exile has its headquarters. "The Dalai Lama is not only a religious, but also a national leader," says Woeser. "His international influence makes Tibetans proud. They like to prove that they're not like the Communist propaganda, which says they're backward and dirty."

Jealous of the power of religion, the Chinese government announced in August that lamas must have official permission to reincarnate—a directive which may prove a little hard to implement. The real target is the Dalai Lama, who is now 72. The Chinese hope that when he dies, all thoughts of independence will die with him, but they fear a repetition of the furore over the reincarnation of the second most holy figure in Tibetan Buddhism, the Panchen Lama. When the 10th Panchen Lama died in 1989, the Chinese government not only dictated who should succeed him, but "disappeared" the boy identified by the Dalai Lama as the true reincarnation. He is still missing.

In early August, Runggye Adak, an ethnic Tibetan, leapt on stage at an annual horse festival in Sichuan and shouted that the Dalai Lama should return, the imprisoned Panchen Lama should be released and Tibet should have independence. He is now in Chinese custody. At this summer's horse fairs, thousands of Tibetans eschewed their traditional ceremonial fur garments after the Dalai Lama said killing animals for fur was bad. The government allegedly threatened to penalise civil servants who did not wear fur to the festivals, seeing it as an indication that they were following the Dalai Lama.

As the sun rose above Lhasa, shafts of light fell across the grassy hill where a grid had been placed so the giant Yoghurt Festival *thangka* could be spread. As Sakyamuni, the Buddha, was slowly revealed, a great sigh of joy rose from the crowd.

Monks and pilgrims threw white silk scarves known as *hadas* on to the image in a gesture of reverence.

The momentum towards modernity in Tibet is unstoppable. Physically, the Chinese Communist Party can dictate where people live and how they are governed. It can bring in millions of tourists and business people. But, after half a century, it still cannot control what Tibetans believe.

LINDSEY HILSUM is China correspondent for Channel 4 News.

Mao Now

China's transformation in the 30 years since the death of Mao Zedong has been breathtaking. But it will not be complete until the nation comes to terms with Mao's complex legacy.

Ross Terrill

In the early 1990s, a story circulated among chinese taxi drivers about an eight-car traffic accident in Guangzhou that resulted in injuries to seven of the drivers involved; the eighth, unscathed, had a Mao portrait attached to his windshield as a talisman. The story fueled Mao fever (*Mao re*) in China, with shopkeepers offering busts of Mao that glowed in the dark and alarm clocks with Red Guards waving Mao's little red book at each tick of the clock. Mao temples appeared in some villages, with a serene portrait of the Chairman on the altar. Transmuted uses of Mao continue today. Nightclub singers in Beijing croon songs that cite Mao's words. Youths dine in "Cultural Revolution-style" cafés off rough-hewn tables with Mao quotations on the wall, eating basic peasant fare as they answer their cell phones and chat about love or the stock market.

This nonpolitical treatment of Mao Zedong (1893–1976) is an escape that fits a Chinese tradition. When floods hit the Yangzi valley and farmers clutch Mao memorabilia to ward off the rushing waters, it is reminiscent of Chinese Buddhists over the centuries clutching images or statues of Guan Yin, the goddess of mercy, to keep them safe and make them prosperous. Following the eclectic nature of Chinese popular beliefs, Mao is added to the panoply of faith.

But where is Mao the totalitarian? Each of the major nations that experienced an authoritarian regime in the 20th century emerged in its own way from the trauma. Japan, Germany, Italy, even Russia departed politically from systems that brought massive war and repression. China, still ruled by a communist party, has been ambiguous about Mao. Although Mao's portrait and tomb dominate Tiananmen Square in the heart of Beijing, Mao himself—unlike Stalin in Russia or Hitler in Germany—has floated benignly into a nether zone as if somehow he was not a political figure at all, let alone the architect of China's communist state.

The cab drivers, farmers, pop singers, and shopkeepers are really only following the lead of the Chinese Communist Party, which does not quite know how to handle Mao's legacy. New history textbooks approved for initial use in Shanghai have largely brushed Mao out of Chinas 20th-century story. China

has abandoned Mao's policies but not faced the structural and philosophical issues involved in Maoism—and probably won't until the Party's monopoly on political power comes to an end. Yet unless China gets the Mao story correct, it may not have a happy political future.

The moral compass of the Mao era has gone, unregretted. But moneymaking, national glory, and a veil over the past in the name of "good feelings" are not enough to replace it. Can a society that lived by the ideas of Confucianism for two millennia, and later by Mao's political athleticism, be content with amnesia about the Mao era and the absence of a believed public philosophy?

In a recent biography, *Mao: The Unknown Story* (2006), Jung Chang and Jon Halliday pile up evidence that Mao was a monster to eclipse Stalin and probably Hitler and Lenin as well. "Absolute selfishness and irresponsibility lay at the heart of Mao's outlook" from his teens to his dotage, say the authors. In a second influential volume, *The Private Life of Chairman Mao* (1995), Mao's physician Li Zhisui portrays the Chairman as exceedingly selfish, jealous, and promiscuous. Soon after his book came out, Dr. Li came to speak at Harvard, and I showed him around the campus. "Three words did not exist for Mao," the gentle doctor remarked as we strolled. "Regret, love, mercy." These two books—both written from outside China—explain the Mao era in China as essentially the consequence of having an evil man at the helm.

Certainly Mao's rule was destructive. Tens of millions of Chinese died in the forced collectivization of the Great Leap Forward of 1958–59, victims of Mao's willful utopianism and cruelty. Millions more died, and tens of millions had their lives mined, during the Cultural Revolution of the 1960s. Practicing brinkmanship toward India, Taiwan, and the Soviet Union, Mao declared that a loss of hundreds of millions of Chinese in a nuclear war would be a setback China could readily digest.

Yet "bad man" does not adequately sum up Mao and his legacy. To believe so would be to embrace the moral absolutism of communism itself, with its quick verdicts ("enemy of the people," "hero of the proletariat"), and to repeat the manipulations of official Chinese imperial history, in which even a flood or earthquake "proved" the evil character of the emperor. Were the "good men" around bad man Mao blind to his failings for so many decades? Were the hundreds of millions of Chinese who bowed before Mao's portrait and wept at the sight of him out of their minds?

Mao made history; at the same time, history made Mao. In addition to looking at Mao's failings as a human being, we must look at the structures and pressures that turned whim into tyranny. At the ideas Mao wielded. At the evaporation—in Mao's case, as in that of several other dictators—of youthful idealism and exactitude. Above all, at the seduction of a "freedom" bestowed from above by a party-state that believed it knew what was best for the citizenry.

In a letter he wrote in 1915, Mao said, "Jesus was dismembered for speaking out. . . . He who speaks out does not necessarily transgress, and even if he does transgress, this is but a small matter to a wise man." Immediately we face a puzzle: Young Mao was an ardent individualist. In his years at the teachers' training college he attended in Changsha, the capital of Hunan Province, Mao's credo became the self-realization of the individual. "Wherever there is repression of the individual," he wrote in the margin of a translation of Friedrich Paulsen's *System of Ethics* (1889), "wherever there are acts contrary to the nature of the individual, there can be no greater crime" His first published newspaper work, written in 1919, was a plea for the liberation of women, a passionate nine-part commentary on the suicide of a young woman in Changsha moments before her arranged marriage.

Mao at 24 saw the Russian Revolution of 1917 as an outbreak of freedom for the individual that lit the way for China. A young female friend objected, "It's all very well to say establish communism, but lots of heads are going to fall." Mao, who had recently read Marx and Engel's *Communist Manifesto,* retorted, "Heads will fall, heads will be chopped off, of course. But just think how good communism is! The state won't bother us anymore, you women will be free, marriage problems won't plague you anymore." Although these words hint at Mao's later callousness about human life, it is striking that he viewed Lenin's revolution in terms of the "marriage problems" of individual women.

The anarchism of Peter Kropotkin, the author of *Mutual Aid* (1902), had a strong hold on Mao until he was nearly 30. A great virtue of the Russian anarchist, Mao felt, was that "he begins by understanding the common people." Anarchism in Mao's perception was linked with Prometheanism; Friedrich Nietzsche was also among his early enthusiasms. The Promethean individual would prepare for his heroic role by taking cold baths, running up mountains, and studying books in the noisiest possible places. This prefigures the fascism to come in Mao's Cultural Revolution, just as fascism in Europe owed a debt to Nietzsche. At the time, however, Mao's individualism was nurtured by the influence of a Chinese professor at Changsha who had imbibed

the idealist liberalism of T. H. Green, the late-19th-century British philosopher.

Mao was a rebel before becoming a communist. The psychological root of his rebelliousness was hostility to his father, and, by extension, to other authority figures. The political root was dismay at China's weakness and disarray in the face of foreign encroachment, shared by most informed Chinese of the period. Mao's chief use for the steeled individual was as a fighter for justice and China's salvation. "The principal aim of physical education," he wrote in 1917 in *New Youth* magazine, "is military heroism." The authoritarian strain in Mao's individualism was already present.

Eventually, Mao's respect for individual freedom collapsed. There were four causes. One was the powerful current of nationalism in early-20th-century China; the cry to rescue the nation eclipsed the cry for the self-realization of the individual. A second was the large role of war in China from the 1920s to the '40s. Pervasive violence made political debate a luxury and favored repression. A third was Mao's embrace of Marxist ideas of class, central economic planning, and communist party organization. Fourth was the hangover in Mao's mind and Chinese society generally of a paternalistic imperial mentality.

In the end, Mao Zedong, facilitated by Stalin, put the population of the world's largest nation under a regimen that combined Leninism, the paternalism of early Chinese sage-rulers, and, by the 1960s, a hysteria and military romanticism that amounted to fascism Chinese-style.

The imperative of national salvation was the first factor working against Mao's attraction to freedom. Mao was mildly attracted to a movement comparable in spirit to Europe's Enlightenment that sprang into existence in China in 1919. Named May Fourth (after the date of an initial student demonstration), it aimed at modernizing China by embracing quasi-Western ideas of individualism, democracy, and science. Liberated individuals would rescue China. But May Fourth soon split in two, a left wing jumping to Marxist collectivism and a right wing sticking with individualism. Leftists, including the 27-year-old Mao, founded the Chinese Communist Party (CCP) in 1921.

Bolshevism helped Mao be progressive and anti-Western at the same time. Opposition to the West was necessary to many young Chinese leftists, despite the appeal of Western ideas, because of British and other foreign bullying of China since the Opium War of 1839–42. From Lenin, Mao learned that social justice and national salvation could come as one package. Leninism—and to a lesser degree Marxism—joined anarchism, nationalism, and individualism in the ragbag of Mao's political ideas. It was Lenin who showed Mao his road to power. Anti-imperialism was going to be for Mao, as it was for Lenin, the framework for revolution. But this anti-imperialist—soon anti-Japanese—nationalism that Mao injected into the Chinese Revolution negated individual freedom.

In the 1930s, Mao argued to the semicriminal secret society Gelaohui (Elder Brother Club) that its principles and the CCP'S were "quite close—especially as regards our enemies and the road to salvation." Of course, the threat of enemies was the central point. In his appeal to non-Han "minority" peoples during the Long March of 1935–36, when Mao emerged as the CCP'S top leader as the Communists retreated before Chiang Kai-shek's Nationalist forces, Mao challenged Mongolians to "preserve the glory of the era of Genghis Khan" by cooperating with the Communists. Pressing the Muslims to support him, he told them that this would ensure the "national revival of the Turks." Of course, Chinese nationalism had turned Mao into a trickster. After the wars with Japan and Chiang Kai-shek were over, there would be no common cause with the Gelaohui, no freedom for the Mongolians or the Muslims of Xinjiang.

The violence that continually rippled through China was another force militating against individual freedom. After the death in 1925 of Sun Yat-sen, a leader in the overthrow of the Manchu dynasty in 1911 and a founder of the Nationalist movement, the gun was prominent in Chinese public life. Sun's wavering leadership gave way to warlordism, a violent rupture of the tenuous coalition of Nationalists and Communists in 1927, and growing incursions by Japan beginning in 1931. Guns were to freedom as a cat is to mice. From the time Mao used force to confiscate the holdings of Hunan landowners in 1925, when he was just one of many CCP leaders, his political life cannot be understood aside from violence, both the wars he waged and those waged against him. As he sought to organize farmers in a remote mountain region, he remarked, "The struggle in the border area is exclusively military. The Party and the masses have to be placed on a war footing." Mao spoke of "criticizing the Nationalists by means of a machine gun."

A third enemy of freedom was the class, organizational, and economic theory Mao drew from Marx and Lenin. Here Mao's story is similar to that of Stalin, Castro, and others. Class theory has intrinsic distortions; people often do not act as members of an economic class. Class labeling became especially inimical to freedom when Mao was forced to rely on farmers rather than workers as the key class in Chinas revolution. Anyone who pointed out this departure from Marx's theory of proletarian revolution was stamped out as a renegade.

Eventually, class became little more than a convenient way to demarcate friends and enemies of the moment. Hence, longtime colleague and expected successor Liu Shaoqi was "discovered" by Mao in the 1960s to be a "bourgeois" who had "sneaked into the Party." Never mind that Mao and Liu had worked together as leftist organizers on and off since 1922.

Within a year of the founding of the CCP in 1921, Mao also fatefully embraced Leninist authoritarianism, and with it Lenin's argument that an elite revolutionary vanguard must guide the rank and file. He accepted the secrecy, duplicity, and absolute party loyalty of communist discipline. Individual autonomy, honoring the troth, friendship, the long bond with Liu Shaoqi—they all meant little by comparison. With Leninism also came a cult of personality stemming from the vanguard theory; a logical further step was to posit a supreme leader who, in turn, would play a vanguard role for the party elite. Mao's cult began in the dusty

hills of remote Yanan, north of Xian, where he led a settled life following the Long March, and seriously studied Lenin's writings for the first time. The later defense minister Lin Biao spoke of Mao in 1938 as a "genius"; in 1941, former classmate Emi Xiao called him "our savior." Mao could have no further doubt that he was a "hero" in the May Fourth leftist mold, able (as he later put it) to "teach the sun and moon to change places."

By the 1960s, Chinese arriving at urban work units would bow three times before a blown up image of Mao's face, asking for guidance with the day's labors. Before going home, they would bow again before the portrait, reporting to the Chairman what they had accomplished since morning. The wisdom of Mao's thoughts made the blind see and the deaf hear, said the official media. On airplanes, the flight began with a hostess holding aloft a copy of *Quotations From Chairman Mao*, then reading a selected maxim to the passengers. (I recall, on a flight from Beijing to Xian, a shrill voice delivering the startling quote, "Fear not hardship, fear not death," just before the engines started up.) Leninism had again, in Mao's case as in Hitler's and Mussolini's, shown a certain hospitality to fascism.

Mao's commitment to the communist command economy was likewise antithetical to freedom. One thinker who saw the flaws of central planning clearly long ago was Friedrich von Hayek, who spoke in the 1940s of the "synoptic illusion." There simply is no one point, Hayek argued, where all the information bearing on an economy can be concentrated, observed, and effectively acted upon. Rather, it is dispersed, changes constantly, and only comes into play in the bids and offers of market participants. Freedom shriveled as Mao extended the command economy in the Great Leap Forward of the late 1950s. The demands made on the grassroots were irrational for the reasons Hayek named. The grassroots, in turn, falsified reports going up to Beijing, as local officials were afraid to tell Mao the truth about the bleak results of his social engineering. The next step was to punish the class enemies who, Mao concluded, must have sabotaged the beautiful socialist vision of the Great Leap Forward.

As an old man, Mao seemed to enjoy calling himself "emperor." He found influences from China's imperial history both appealing and useful for bolstering paternalistic rule. This was a fourth reason for Mao's weakening attachment to individual liberty.

Mao's eventual role as a supreme leader above even the Party gave expression to his father's impact. Mao in old age became everything his father had been—and found young Mao incapable of being. Mao Shunsheng did not like to see his son reading a book; Chairman Mao came to scoff at book learning. Mao's father made his son work in the fields against the boy's will; Chairman Mao sent tens of millions to the countryside to do just that. Mao's father had been in the army; Mao made military virtues the yardstick for the nation's values. People became props in Mao's collective pageant.

In the last two decades of his life, Mao became a changed leader, half modern Führer and half ancient Chinese sage-king. As the autocratic impulses of his father and other antifreedom forces shored each other up, the façade of his socialism decayed and his relationship to the CCP changed. Mao fought two phantoms he could never vanquish: the failure of socialism to take on the splendor he expected of it and the refusal of the CCP to be simply a Mao Party. These disappointments made him more arbitrary. "Revisionism" came to be the term Mao applied to the alleged betrayal that produced his disappointments. But Mao never clearly defined revisionism; hence, he never found a way to eliminate it. He knocked down many revisionists, but never revisionism.

One could say in Mao's defense that after 1949 he had priorities higher than freedom. These included organizing a vast country, stabilizing the currency, producing steel and machine tools, and balancing Soviet and American power. And as a practical matter, the dictatorial Soviet Union was willing to give him aid, whereas America was not.

Yet Mao's impulse toward freedom was crippled at its heart. What is freedom for the individual? One viable form is freedom to act as you please as long as you do not inhibit a like freedom for others. A second notion is that an individual is free to the degree she is able to realize herself. The mature Mao believed in neither of these two concepts of freedom, though he was closer to the second than to the first. He knew the kind of citizens he wanted in China. It was not for each person to realize himself, but for all to become suitable building blocks for Mao's Chinese update of Sparta. He egregiously confused the remolding impulse of Confucius with the functions of a modern state. "Can't you change a bit?" he once asked a roomful of intellectuals with "bourgeois" tendencies. But was it Mao the Confucian teacher talking or Mao the dictator of a police state?

"Opinions should not be allowed to become conclusions," Mao declared. In the abortive Hundred Flowers drive of 1956, he realized that some cut and thrust was necessary as a safety valve against the rigidity of his rule. But only Mao knew the difference between a flower and a weed. The blossoms were to swell and open according to a formula the gardener held in his pocket. Mao wanted the impossible: open debate to keep the system lively, yet with the outcome of the debate fixed in advance. "I told the rightists to criticize us in order to help the Party," Mao said pathetically to his doctor. "I never asked them to oppose the Party or try to seize power from the Party."

Mao's practical achievement was to unite China and demonstrate to Asia that China after 1949 was a force to be reckoned with. Other Chinese leaders in Beijing have built on that achievement. But Mao's social engineering efforts were largely canceled by Deng Xiaoping after Mao's death in 1976. In subsequent years, the totalitarian party-state became an authoritarian party-state. Under totalitarianism, it is said, many things are forbidden and the remaining things you must do; under authoritarianism, many things are forbidden and the remaining things you may do. Today, the retention of power and economic development, rather than the pursuit of ideological phantoms, is the drive around which the political process arranges itself. With Mao's "new" Chinese man gone, the "old" Chinese man of family values and entrepreneurial spirit seems alive and well.

The passing of totalitarianism has brought into view some tentative realms of freedom, including partial property rights and the beginnings of autonomy for lawyers, journalists, and other professionals. Above all, there now exists for most people the freedom to ignore politics. Yet the institutionalization of the new space opening up for Chinese citizens has barely begun.

As I write, Beijing has jailed three intellectuals on trumped-up charges behind which lie the sin of speaking indiscreet words. Ching Cheong, chief China correspondent of a Singapore newspaper, got five years for "spying," but really for getting a fee to speak at a seminar run by a think tank that Beijing dislikes. Zhao Yan, a researcher for *The New York Times* in Beijing, got three years for "fraud," but really for feeding the *Times* information on some mild political tensions within the Chinese government. Chen Guangchen, a blind self-taught lawyer, faces four years for "gathering a crowd to disrupt traffic," but really for annoying officials in Shandong Province by representing victims of sterilizations and forced abortions that were carried out contrary to Beijing's own regulations. The rule of law seems far off, and equally so a free press and much-needed federalism. The intended intimidation in these three cases is an all-too-clear residue of the Mao era, when citizens never knew where they stood in relation to authority.

One might have expected Deng's successor, Jiang Zemin, and the current president, Hu Jintao, to put in place structures that, following the Deng era, took account of the new relationship between politics and economic and cultural life. But this has not yet happened.

We return to the "solution" of having Mao float into folklore as a modern-day Yellow Emperor, whose photo on the windscreen will ward off traffic accidents, and who can serve as a fashion model for green silk pajamas, as I recently noticed in a Shanghai department store. Such "Maoism" is the twitching of a society whose post-Mao leaders have brought economic advancement but political stagnation. Mao's totalitarian leaps kn ocked illusions out of generations of Chinese, but also soured them on public-spiritedness. By the destruction entailed in his revolution, and particularly his Cultural Revolution, Mao took away China's past.

China has moved beyond Mao as a builder of socialism. But China should never move beyond the grim lesson of how Mao could begin in idealism yet become an oppressor. It is easier and safer, of course, to criticize Mao as an evil person, or simply to draw a veil over him, than to broach the problem of the political system he introduced to China.

Philosophically, a value to be retained from Mao is that a society does require shared moral values. He was correct to see a good society as more than gadgets and cars. Talking with the French writer André Malraux in 1965, Mao ridiculed Soviet premier Alexei Kosygin's statement at the 23rd congress of the Soviet Communist Party that "communism means the raising of living standards." Snorted Mao to the Frenchman, "And swimming is a way of putting on a pair of trunks!" But Mao's proposed moral compass was a high-minded fraud. The Chinese farmers were "poor and blank," he said. On the blank page of Chinese humanity, Mao the sage-king would sketch wonderful designs!

Today, young pro-market Chinese who devour Hayek's *Road to Serfdom* and books on American business are leaving Mao in the dust and embracing an antistate Chinese tradition (best known in the West through Daoism). They would like—but will not get—a China without politics. A new public philosophy, when it comes, as it must, will draw on China's humanistic traditions as well as the best of the experience of the People's Republic. Procedurally, a new moral compass will come from below as people express themselves politically, not, again, as a diktat from a father-figure above. "When societies first come to birth, it is the leader who produces the institutions," said Montesquieu. "Later it is the institutions which produce the leaders." Later still, in a democratic era, the voting public sustains the institutions that, in turn, frame those leaders who are given the short term authority to lead.

Ignoring the Past

Forty years on, the government still avoids discussion of the Cultural Revolution.

HONGSHENG AND ANREN

In the village of Hongsheng, Li Furong feared trouble when he was summoned one day in August 1966 to a meeting. He had been denounced as a "capitalist-roader" and thought fellow peasants had gathered to attack him. Instead he found himself press-ganged into helping with the murder of octogenarian former landlords in one of the bloodiest orgies of violence in or around China's capital, Beijing, during the Cultural Revolution. Even 40 years later, the authorities are trying to suppress news of what happened in Hongsheng and nearby villages of Beijing's Daxing district.

The Communist Party's unwillingness to confront the horrors of the Cultural Revolution, which was launched on May 16th 1966 and officially ended ten years later with the death of Mao Zedong and the fall of the Gang of Four, means that for Chinese historians as well as for millions of victims that entire period is, in effect, off-limits for debate. The passage of time does not appear to be helping. Chinese scholars say the government has been even more intent on stopping public commemoration of this week's anniversary than it was a decade ago. No mention of it has appeared in the state-controlled media. A group of scholars who held a private symposium in Beijing in March to discuss the Cultural Revolution avoided using e-mail to arrange it for fear their communications would be intercepted by officials.

Partly, it is embarrassment about the scale and brutality of the violence carried out in Mao's name. In Hongsheng, Mr Li, now 75, says village officials told the meeting that former landlords and rich peasants, stripped of their holdings after the Communists took power in 1949, planned to stage a revolt. No evidence was offered. The plan was to kill the alleged plotters and their entire families that night. Mr Li, worried that as a "capitalist-roader" he too would be killed, agreed to use his well-known skills with rope to bind the victims. Two former landlords in their 80s were the first to be dealt with. Mr Li had barely finished his work before the old men were dragged away and beaten to death.

It could have been worse. Mr Li says that, had he not asked the village party chief whether he had written authority for this, other members of the landlords' families would have been murdered that night too. In some neighbouring villages there was much greater bloodshed. The youngest victim was one month old. Bodies were thrown down wells or into pits. In the commune to which Hongsheng belonged, 110 people were slaughtered within 24 hours. This was only one of 13 communes in Daxing district involved in what has become known to locals as the "8/31 [August 31st] massacre". City officials called a halt to the violence after a couple of brave village officials travelled to the party's headquarters in central Beijing, 35 km (22 miles) away, to complain.

Even today, few in Beijing know anything about this, even though the official death toll, 324, exceeds the conservative government estimate of around 200 killed in the suppression of the Tiananmen Square protests of 1989. A brief mention of the massacre appeared in a book on the Cultural Revolution that was published in 1986 and quickly banned. A detailed government account was published only four years ago in an appendix to the "Daxing County Gazette", a hefty and little-read tome, but was not reported in any newspaper. Of those killed, the book says, 91 were women. Nineteen entire families were eliminated.

The Daxing killings were part of what some perpetrators boasted of as a "red terror" that gripped Beijing between August and October 1966. Wang Youqin of the University of Chicago says officials have never acknowledged the extent of the bloodshed in the capital. She says that Red Guard mobs, obeying Mao's exhortation to "be violent", killed some 2,000 Beijing residents in the space of two weeks.

One reason for the government's reticence is that, during this stage of the Cultural Revolution, many Red Guard leaders were the offspring of high-ranking officials who were subsequently purged but who became powerful again after Mao's death. Perpetrators of the violence were barred from influential positions after Deng Xiaoping took control in 1978. But Ms Wang says their family connections often protected them from punishment. The "Daxing County Gazette" says 348 people were "directly responsible" for the murders there, nearly two-thirds of them party members. Only 38 were jailed, the longest for 12 years. Pardons were granted to 246.

Officials fear that closer scrutiny of the Cultural Revolution could destabilise the country by inflaming long suppressed antagonisms. Many scholars now believe that well over 1m were killed or driven to suicide in political struggles between 1966 and 1976. The lives of almost all urban residents were profoundly disrupted. Schools and universities were closed. Educated people were forced to leave cities and work on farms. Family members turned on one another. Many of those now in their 50s belong to a "lost generation" whose education and careers were permanently blighted by the Cultural Revolution.

In 1981 the party leadership issued a long denunciation of the Cultural Revolution, as well as various other "mistakes" made by Mao, though these were portrayed as secondary to his contributions. The "Gang of Four" led by Mao's wife, Jiang Qing, who were deemed responsible for the Cultural Revolution's atrocities, were given lengthy prison terms (the last of the four died in December). Most of those persecuted were officially "rehabilitated" by the early 1980s.

There is, however, no official memorial to the victims. Appeals by some intellectuals for a museum dedicated to the events have gone unheeded. In recent months, private funds have started to remedy this. Last year, a privately run Cultural Revolution museum opened near the coastal city of Shantou in southern Guangdong province. In Anren township, near Chengdu, the capital of the south-western province of Sichuan, a wealthy real-estate developer, Fan Jianchuan, says he is preparing to open another later this month.

These ventures are still modest. The one in Shantou shows pictures of officials and other prominent figures being persecuted, but otherwise sticks to the government line. Mr Fan's will concentrate at first on porcelain artefacts from the period. His vast and lavishly designed complex, opened last year, is already home to a remarkable display of historical daring: a whole building of exhibits concerns the (positive) contribution of the Kuomintang, China's then ruling nationalist party, to the war against Japan. In Communist Party histories the Kuomintang is portrayed as having shirked the war.

But Mr Fan has no plans to display objects relating to the Cultural Revolution's factional warfare and other violence. "It's not just that I'm too cowardly and don't want trouble, but I also think it wouldn't be good for the peace of society," he says. He may perhaps do so in 20 years.

Paralympics Bring Forward Plight of China's Disabled

China's government only recently began addressing the needs of its 83 million disabled citizens.

Peter Ford

The Paralympic Games that opened here Saturday are drawing tens of thousands of spectators to venues across Beijing. Hardly any of them, though, are disabled.

Even at the premier global event celebrating handicapped peoples' achievements, China's 83 million disabled citizens remain almost invisible, victims of a society slow to change its attitudes and a government that only recently began addressing their needs.

Officials and activists for the disabled, however, hope the Games will give fresh momentum to changes they say have been under way for some time, giving disabled people more of a role in Chinese society.

The interest in the Paralympics shows that "society is starting to recognize the existence of blind people," says Zheng Xiaojie, who runs a small school in Beijing teaching radio broadcasting to blind students. "People's attitudes are changing a lot."

Few, however, expect the two weeks of athletic competition to spark dramatic change. "A single event cannot change people's attitudes," cautions Sun Xiande, deputy head of the government-backed Disabled Persons Federation. "It is a lengthy process."

China has embarked on that process from a low threshold. "Most of the time the Chinese don't even know there is such a thing as the disabled," says Keith Wyse, an American who cares for orphans diagnosed with brittle-bone syndrome at a foster home south of Beijing. "When we take the kids out people stare, because they have never seen anyone in a wheelchair."

Even highly educated youths are often ignorant of disabled people's needs. When Wang Xiao, a junior at Peking University, took the exam to be an Olympic volunteer, the two hardest questions, she admits, were how to deal with someone in a wheelchair and how to help those walking with a cane.

That is largely because disabled people rarely venture out of their homes or institutions, for both physical and psychological reasons.

"The facilities and access for disabled people are generally not very good—there is no barrier-free access to lots of public places," points out Zheng Gongcheng, head of the department of Disabilities Studies at Beijing's People's University and an adviser to the government.

Harder than getting around, complains Wang Tao, a young man confined to a wheelchair since a car accident seven years ago, "is getting out of the house. Lots of residential compounds didn't plan for barrier-free facilities in their design."

Living with his parents in the port city of Tianjin, 50 miles east of Beijing, Mr. Wang says he goes out only once every week or two because his parents cannot carry him up or down stairs.

Even in Beijing, people still stare, he says, and "a lot of disabled people don't feel as if they are members of society. They feel alienated."

In recent years, the government has passed a raft of legislation—more than 50 laws of one sort or another—designed to give disabled people equal chances at education and jobs and to counter prejudice and discrimination.

"The Chinese government deserves praise for enacting laws," says Sophie Richardson, Asia advocacy director at the New York-based Human Rights Watch. But a failure to fully implement these laws, she adds, means that "so far these protections have meant little."

On the physical front, the Paralympic Games have clearly sparked improvements in Beijing's cityscape for disabled people. Two thousand low-chassis buses have been brought into service, every subway station has a platform lift for wheelchair-bound passengers, and ramps have been built at many shopping malls and tourist spots such as the Forbidden City.

Such innovations, however, have barely spread beyond the capital, and there are few educational opportunities for disabled people outside big cities.

Zhang Jiong, for example, one of Ms. Zheng's students, had to leave his home province of Henan, where no high school could accommodate him, to study in another province.

That move changed the way people treated him, says Mr. Zhang. "When I was a kid people looked at me differently, they thought I had no future," he recalls. "Then I went to high school and people realized that I could learn a skill and I could survive."

Even so, Zhang says he does "not dare hope to get a job in a big radio station. I just want to fulfill my dream and show that blind people can do broadcasting."

He is a rare exception, however. Ninety-five percent of blind Chinese who find work are masseurs, Zhang says, and most of the rest are fortune tellers. Few other jobs are open to them.

The 20,000 disabled people in higher education, who represent only 0.5 percent of the disabled student-aged population, will rise, officials say. "We started late with education for the disabled, but in the last two decades we have been developing it fast," says Mr. Sun. "Still it will take some time to provide access to higher education to everyone who could benefit."

It is still unclear just how much lasting impact the Paralympics will have on Chinese policies and perceptions. Beijing's barrier-free facilities will last beyond the Games, organizing committee vice president Tang Xiaoquan told the state news agency Xinhua recently, "and we mean to get the city's nearly one million handicapped population more involved in public life."

"The Paralympics will focus the whole country's attention on the disabled, and they have pushed the government to invest more for the disabled" says Professor Zheng. "They will also show that people with a physical disability can contribute to society and be very useful citizens."

If that is a lesson that most Chinese still need to learn, Mr. Wyse says his experience caring for disabled children here has left him skeptical that the government will keep teaching it.

"The disabled parking slots you see at the airport were not there two months ago," he points out, "and I am not optimistic" they will still be there in two months' time. "When the Games are gone, everything will be gone with them," he says.

Wang Tao, is more sanguine. "People's attitudes to the disabled were improving anyway, but without the Paralympics they would not have improved so much," he says.

"It used to be that I would be in my wheelchair at the bottom of a flight of steps and nobody would offer to help," he remembers. "That doesn't happen any more."

CAROL HUANG contributed to this story.

China's New Prosperity Fuels Fitness Craze

Didi Tang

Several days a week, Wu Ruiyao hits the gym, where she sweats on a treadmill, tones her abs in a group exercise or stretches under the guidance of a personal trainer.

The 90-minute workout is routine to Wu, a 36-year-old ad sales representative. But the surroundings—a four-story fitness club catering to different fitness levels and needs—would have been unimaginable just a decade ago.

"When I thought of a gym in the 1990s, it would be bare with dumbbells and maybe running machines in a room," said Wu, a small woman with big, smiling eyes. "My mom thought doing house chores was working out, but that's not a truly aerobic sport."

Their lives transformed by breakneck economic growth, many Chinese are embracing creature comforts which would once have been denounced by their communist bosses as bourgeois indulgences.

Fitness is largely an urban, middle-class craze. Most Chinese still rely on farming for a living, and hard, physical exercise is not their idea of recreation, nor was it for urban Chinese just escaping Mao-era poverty 20 years ago.

Now they are free to shape and pamper their bodies, and fitness clubs are moving in.

"Once the people have more time and more money, they will think of fitness," said Gu Haoning, who monitors the health and fitness industry for the government's General Administration of Sports. "It would be impossible if they are still trying to eke out a living and don't have extra money for fitness."

The national fanfare surrounding the Beijing Olympics is adding to the momentum.

A generation ago, most people exercised in parks and side streets. In the 1980s, Jane Fonda's aerobics videos began circulating. Now, in a country long shadowed by famine, food has become plentiful and there are even signs of an obesity problem.

Matt Lewis is a pioneer in Beijing's fitness market. The New Zealander came to Beijing in 1997 to manage an elite country club and immediately saw opportunities in bringing fitness to the emerging middle class.

Gyms back then were "either very, very expensive, or very, very cheap," he said, but with an initial investment of $500,000, Evolution Fitness opened in 2001 as one of the first private gyms in Beijing.

The gym on most work nights heaves with young Chinese professionals spinning on bikes, making waves in the pool or striking a triangle pose in yoga classes. It is making money, said the 37-year-old Lewis, the managing director, though he wouldn't say how much.

With China's economy having grown at double digits in recent years, urban Chinese have extra money to spend. Investment in sports and other recreational equipment leaped 8.5 percent in the first seven months this year compared with the same period last year, to $1.5 billion, according to government figures.

Wu, the ad sales executive, said stress from work and hours spent in Beijing's clogged traffic drove her to sign up this year at the Alexander City Club, an airy gym in an up-market apartment complex in the business district.

"I feel energetic and buoyant after working out," Wu said. "Otherwise I would be dragging my tired body home."

Wu, who is single, makes about $30,000 a year. She paid $1,150 for two years of membership and $70 an hour for personal trainers.

"It is money well-spent," Wu said. "As you get older, you realize health is important, and having a private trainer is more effective and timesaving."

Her mother, back in southwestern Yunnan province, would have never gone for it. "Raising two children, my mother never had the time, and there was no money or gym either," she said.

"Those who were born in the 1960s and 1970s have been working so hard. They have been pursuing success at any cost," said Yin Yan, the former editor-in-chief for the fashion magazine *Elle* in China and founder of the Yogiyoga Center yoga studio in Beijing in 2003.

"Now they have it—money or social status—thanks to China's economic development, but they also find their health worsened and their lives in a mess."

The newly stressed can visit spas for full-body rubs, foot massages and aromatherapy. They range from hotel chains to mom-and-pop operations.

One sensation is the mega-bathing center. Though descended from bathhouses that operated before homes had water heaters, many have more in common with Las Vegas. Oriental Hawaii and Oriental Venice bathhouses in Beijing employ hundreds and are twice the size of an average Wal-Mart Supercenter.

The one-stop pampering offers foot rubs, massages, ping-pong, food, easy chairs and overnight stays.

Chinese families come there to spend time together, businessmen woo clients over a foot-soaking, and young people come to idle away a night.

"Whenever I am tired or drowsy, I go there to lie down," said Sun Desheng, 45, a businessman in the garment industry. "I like the ambiance created through background sound and lighting, and the services are great. I will relax and sometimes fall asleep."

Demand is so high that the Beijing Adult Massage Occupational Technical Training School, which opened in 1998 to train the blind as masseurs, has since had to admit sighted students. The school has trained more than 20,000 massage therapists, President Zhang Haiyan said.

Zhang estimates Beijing, with a population of 17 million, has at least 50,000 to 60,000 massage therapists, yet "Employers are calling for more students than we have."

Big cities like Beijing are far from saturated with gyms and spas while smaller cities are untapped, meaning the industry is sure to keep growing.

"Chinese people want to live forever, while Americans want to enjoy themselves, but it's all about being healthy," said Gu, the health official. "It's the kind of spending that comes from the heart of the people."

Confucius Makes a Comeback

You can't keep a good sage down.

"Study the past", Confucius said, "if you would define the future." Now he himself has become the object of that study.

Confucius was revered—indeed worshipped—in China for more than 2,000 years. But neither the Communist Party, nor the 20th century itself, has been kind to the sage. Modern China saw the end of the imperial civil-service examinations he inspired, the end of the imperial regime itself and the repudiation of the classical Chinese in which he wrote. Harsher still, during the Cultural Revolution Confucius and his followers were derided and humiliated by Mao Zedong in his zeal to build a "new China".

Now, Professor Kang Xiaoguang, an outspoken scholar at Beijing's Renmin University, argues that Confucianism should become China's state religion. Such proposals bring Confucius's rehabilitation into the open. It is another sign of the struggle within China for an alternative ideological underpinning to Communist Party rule in a country where enthusiasm for communism waned long ago and where, officials and social critics fret, anything goes if money is to be made.

Confucius's rehabilitation has been slow. Explicit attacks on him ended as long ago as 1976, when Mao died, but it is only now that his popularity has really started rising. On topics ranging from political philosophy to personal ethics, old Confucian ideas are gaining new currency.

With a recent book and television series on the Analects, the best-known collection of the sage's musings, Yu Dan has tried to make the teachings accessible to ordinary Chinese. Scholars have accused her of oversimplifying, but her treatment has clearly struck a chord: her book has sold nearly 4m copies, an enormous number even in China.

Further interest is evinced by the Confucian study programmes springing up all over the Chinese education system. These include kindergarten classes in which children recite the classics, Confucian programmes in philosophy departments at universities, and even Confucian-themed executive-education programmes offering sage guidance for business people.

But perhaps the most intriguing—albeit ambivalent—adopter of Confucianism is the Communist Party itself. Since becoming China's top leader in 2002, President Hu Jintao has promoted a succession of official slogans, including "Harmonious Society" and "*Xiaokang Shehui*" ("a moderately well off society"), which have Confucian undertones. On the other hand, says one scholar at the party's top think-tank, the Central Party School, official approval is tempered by suspicions about religion and by lingering concern over the mixture of Buddhism and other religious elements in Confucian thinking.

The relevance of Confucian ideas to modern China is obvious. Confucianism emphasises order, balance and harmony. It teaches respect for authority and concern for others.

For ordinary Chinese, such ideas must seem like an antidote to the downside of growth, such as widening regional disparities, wealth differentials, corruption and rising social tension. For the government, too, Confucianism seems like a blessing. The party is struggling to maintain its authority without much ideological underpinning (Deng Xiaoping questioned the utility of ideology itself when he said that it doesn't matter if a cat is black or white so long as it catches mice). Confucianism seems to provide a ready-made ideology that teaches people to accept their place and does not challenge party rule.

As an additional advantage, Confucianism is home-grown, unlike communism. It even provides the party with a tool for advancing soft power abroad. By calling China's overseas cultural and linguistic study centres "Confucius Institutes", the party can present itself as something more than just an ideologically bankrupt administrator of the world's workshop.

Yet despite this, Confucianism is not an easy fit for the party. It says those at the top must prove their worthiness to rule. This means Confucianism does not really address one of the government's main worries, that while all will be well so long as China continues to prosper, the party has little to fall back upon if growth falters.

Writing last year, Professor Kang argued that a marriage of Confucianism and communism could nevertheless be made to work. He argued that the party has in reality allied itself with China's urban elite. "It is", he wrote, "an alliance whereby the elites collude to pillage the masses," leading to "political corruption, social inequality, financial risks, rampant evil forces, and moral degeneration." The solution, he argued, was to "Confucianise the Chinese Communist Party at the top and society at the lower level."

But Stephen Angle, a Fulbright scholar at Peking University and a philosophy professor at Wesleyan University in America, argues that Confucianism may not be as useful to the party as it thinks. For a start it has little to say about one of the party's biggest worries, the tension in urban-rural relations. More important, a gap in Confucian political theory should alarm a government seeking to hold on to power in a fast-changing environment. "One big problem with Confucianism", says Mr Angle, "is that it offers no good model for political transition, except revolution."

From *The Economist*, May 19, 2007, p. 48. Copyright © 2007 by The Economist Newspaper Ltd. Reprinted by permission via Copyright Clearance Center.

The Beautiful and the Dammed in China

Matthew Knight

The Chinese have long dreamt about taming the Yangtze River.

As far back as 1919, Sun Yat-sen, founder of the Chinese Republic proposed the dam as a way of providing energy for China's industrial development and to stop the constant flooding which had claimed thousands of lives over the years.

Attempts to revive the project were tried throughout the 20th Century but it was only in 1993 that plans were approved and construction began at Yichang in the Hubei Province.

The scale of the project is breathtaking. When completed in 2009, at a total cost of $25 billion, the Three Gorges Dam will be the world's largest hydroelectric dam, generating almost a third more power than the Itaipu Dam—currently the largest in the world—on the Brazil-Paraguay border.

China's creation will churn out a massive 18,200 megawatts of power. That's as much power as 18 nuclear power plants.

To stem the flow of the Yangtze—measuring 6,245 kilometers, it is the world's third longest river after the Nile and the Amazon—engineers had to construct a barrier over 2,300 meters wide and 180 meters tall.

In all, over 27 million cubic meters of cement were used. To put that in perspective, when completed in 1936, the Hoover Dam required a mere 3.2 million cubic meters.

The resulting reservoir which stretches 600 kilometers upstream, will allow much larger commercial freighters (up to 10,000 tonnes) to penetrate deep into China's interior providing a further boost to trade.

But the monumental task of constructing the dam has come at a cost.

Ever since the reservoir began to fill up in 2003, the rising water levels have submerged more than 100 towns and thousands of acres of farming land along the Yangtze's banks leading to the displacement of over one million people.

New settlements have been provided by the Chinese Government but these have been beset by delays and criticized for being sub-standard.

As tens of thousands of home sink without trace, so to do more than 1,000 archaeological sites, including the homeland of the ancient Ba people.

The project had also been plagued by allegations of corruption and claims that the environmental impact on the area will be disastrous.

No attempt has been made to clear submerged industrial sites and their toxic materials, which has led to fears of water pollution. And when the water levels are lowered for five months each year, to accommodate the rainy season, it is feared that noxious fumes will consume the surrounding countryside.

Furthermore, Chinese meteorologists expect the dam will instigate a change in the climate, raising the local temperature by a third of a one degree Celsius.

American scientists have gone further, suggesting that it may even alter the climate as far away as Japan.

What cannot be denied though is that the Three Gorges Dam is a staggering engineering achievement and a potent symbol of Chinese ambitions to become the dominant economic superpower in the 21st Century.

Nearly 400 years after the Great Wall was completed, China has another wonder which is visible from space.

Privatisation Would Enrich China

Zhiwu Chen

China has a large untapped source of further growth: its vast state-owned assets, including enterprises, resources and land. Privatising these assets would unleash the wealth effect and boost domestic consumption. This reform would transform China's growth model from being investment and export-driven to being led by domestic consumption. It would reduce its over-dependence on industry and stimulate its service sector. At a time of a global slowdown, such reform is timely.

When reform started in 1978, almost all productive assets were state-owned in China. But reforms since then have not included privatisation. Today the government owns more than 70 per cent of China's productive wealth. During the first 20 years of reform, concentrating the country's assets in government hands served a good development purpose, allowing the creation of infrastructure and expansion of industrial capacity. If state assets had been privatised, it might have been difficult for China to mobilise resources during the rapid industrialisation of the 1980s and 1990s. To the government's credit, the initial marketisation-without-privatisation approach has paid off. A robust infrastructure has emerged and China is an industrialised economy.

But this industry-first, government-investment-driven and export-oriented growth model has run its course. The focus on industry not services has damaged China's environment. It has also been highly resource intensive. China has expanded export markets beyond developed countries to include Latin America, the Middle East and Africa. But this past success is limiting the potential for further export growth. The slowdown, coupled with rising protectionism in the US and the global economy is not making export growth easy. To transform its economy, China needs to shift towards growth driven by domestic demand, not exports, and one led by services not industry.

What can stimulate such a transformation? Given that industrial capacity is already too high, privatisation is the answer. A decision to continue to concentrate resources in government hands would do more harm than good.

China's gross domestic product has been growing at more than 10 per cent a year, but its domestic consumption has been slow to catch up. Why?

This becomes less puzzling once we examine how past income and wealth gain are split between the government and households. First, the government's share in China's income has been rising at the expense of private citizens. From 1995 to 2007, the inflation-adjusted annual growth rate was 16 per cent for government tax revenues (not including state enterprise profits or proceeds from selling land usage rights), and 8 percent and 6.2 percent, respectively, for urban and rural household disposable income. In 2007, government tax revenues increased by 31 per cent but urban and rural disposable income went up by just 12.2 percent and 9.5 percent respectively. As private households' share in China's income pool is shrinking fast, consumption growth can only be slow.

However, the split in asset ownership between the government and households is even more damaging to consumption growth. It is true that 30 years of fast growth has enlarged China's income pool and dramatically increased asset values. Thus one would have expected a significant wealth effect on private consumption. However, with 70 plus per cent of this gain going to the government, private citizens have not been able to feel much of a wealth effect.

A wealth effect on private consumption is not possible unless consumers own more wealth. It is no surprise that all state-owned economies, whether China's or the Soviet Union's, have one thing in common: growth driven by investment, not consumption.

Therefore wages from labour are the main, or even the only, source of disposable income for most Chinese consumers. Even this single source is growing more slowly than expected. That is why private consumption is slow to rise. State ownership depresses consumption demand.

In addition, depending on whether the government or private households control the country's wealth and income, the economy will have a different demand structure. If households control spending power they will favour consumer goods and services, which benefits the service sector. If the government controls spending power, it will favour infrastructure, industrial projects and industrial goods, boosting heavy industries and energy and natural resource consumption.

In the 1980s and 1990s, these consequences of state ownership were growth-enhancing. Now, the over-investment in industry is a negative. It is fundamental for China to distribute ownership rights of the remaining state assets equally among its citizens. This private ownership would return the missing wealth effect to millions of families. In the short run, it would help maintain growth during a global slowdown. In the long run, it would improve China's industry/service sector mix, reduce its dependence on exports and also create more employment.

Yes, privatisation has created short-term disappointments in eastern Europe. However, it ran into challenges because it occurred in former socialist countries that had no prior experience with capital markets, mutual funds and the associated legal and regulatory structures. China has nearly two decades of experience in these. Its mutual fund industry manages more than 100m accounts. China is operationally ready.

The writer is professor of finance at the Yale School of Management.

Chinese Muslims Join Global Islamic Market

They are forging economic ties with the Muslim world at a time when interest in Islam is also growing.

PETER FORD

Mohammed Yussuf picks up a giant onion and smiles as he admires it. The vegetable on display at a trade fair here pleases him not only because of its proportions; the onion's main virtue in his eyes is that it is halal, acceptable on Muslim dining tables.

Mr. Yussuf, a Malaysian businessman, makes a tidy profit importing halal foods from this remote corner of northwestern China. He's the type of foreign trader this Muslim region hopes to attract more of, in its bid to grab a slice of the multibillion dollar global Islamic food business.

"One-third of our population is Hui," says Ma Yingqiu, this city's deputy mayor, referring to the Muslim ethnic minority who live in the Autonomous Region of Ningxia. "They have the same habits as people in Islamic countries. They are this region's competitive advantage."

As the local government strives to forge new economic ties with Middle Eastern and other Muslim nations, citizens of this impoverished part of China bordering the Gobi Desert are rediscovering Islam. Emerging from centuries of religious isolation, Ningxia Muslims are developing "an international sense of community," says Ma Ping, head of the Institute of the Hui and Islam here.

While that might once have unnerved the Chinese government, always uneasy about divided loyalties, Ningxia's desperate economic straits—it is the country's third poorest province—have prompted a rethink, says Professor Ma.

"Stability used to be the top priority here, but now it is development," he says. "What the government wants most is money."

It was in search of money that the Ningxia government last week held the third annual International Halal Food and Muslim Commodities Trade Fair, which closed here over the weekend. "This fair is Ningxia's chance to march into the world," provincial governor Wang Zhengwei proclaimed at the opening ceremony.

For four days, local producers manned stands offering meats and vegetables, which Hui Muslims consider halal if they don't use manure made from human or animal excrement to grow them. Vendors also sold clothes, ceramics, and other goods aimed at Muslim consumers.

Yussuf was one of the few foreign buyers at the fair, however, and his supplier, Ma Shengke, seemed to be one of only a handful of success stories so far in Ningxia's efforts to break into the competitive Islamic food market.

Most producers are having difficulty carving out a niche, a challenge to all newcomers but one that is heightened for Ningxia's would-be exporters by the recent rise in the value of the Chinese currency, which makes their goods more expensive on world markets.

"We have lost our price advantage, so the solution is to produce better quality meat," says Zhang Hongen, a local sheep farmer. "We need to impose standards."

Ningxia's halal food industry is worth nearly $700 million a year, according to government statistics, but less than 3 percent of its output is sold abroad, Ma Yingqiu points out. "We are still at the beginning of this and we have to work on it," the deputy mayor acknowledges. "But since we are starting from such a small base, it should be easy to grow fast."

Connecting with Islam

Ningxia has, nonetheless, managed to attract some attention from the Arab world, whence came the Muslim traders who introduced Islam into China more than 1,000 years ago. Today's 10 million Hui people are descended from those merchants.

The Tunisian embassy, for example, sent a team to the fair in search of Muslim tourists, while the Saudi Arabian stand offered dates and Chinese versions of the Koran.

The Saudi-based Islamic Development Bank funded the construction of Ningxia's Islamic Scripture College and an Arabic language school, and China's policy of opening to the world has fostered other links. Ten thousand Chinese Muslims went on the hajj to Mecca last year, a record number. Others visit the Middle East for business or tourism, and some 250 religious students leave China each year to study in Egypt, Syria, Iran, and Saudi Arabia.

Interest in Islam is clearly rising in Ningxia. New mosques are under construction (there are now 3,700 licensed mosques in the province, twice the number of a few decades ago), but even so the Scripture College is turning out imams, known locally as *ahongs,* faster than mosques can employ them.

Ordinary Muslims are turning in greater numbers to traditional Islamic dress, say local residents. "More and more people are wearing headgear, and more and more people are taking religious practice seriously," says Shami Ahmed, an Indian Muslim who came here five years ago to teach English. "Maybe it's because more are going on the hajj and see Muslims outside."

Ningxia's closer links with the rest of the Islamic world are a blessing for Wali Younla, an *ahong* at Yinchuan's main mosque. "Thanks to these trade relations more and more people get to know Islam," he says. "That's a good thing for religion and for society."

The Chinese government keeps a close eye on these developments, though. Mosques must be licensed, foreign imams are not allowed to preach in them, and youngsters are not allowed to pray in mosques.

"The government supports economic links, which it hopes will increase, but has a cautious attitude to cultural and religious links," with the Middle East explains Professor Ma. For the sake of trade, however, "they have put their concerns on the back-burner," he believes. "The Ningxia authorities are confident they can minimize negative cultural influences and maximize economic influences."

Loose religious adherence

There are few signs that stricter strains of Islam, as practiced in parts of the Arab world, are having much impact on life in Ningxia at the moment. Female *ahongs* continue to flourish in a Hui tradition of women-only mosques where women lead the prayers, which would horrify mainstream Middle Eastern Muslims. Ramadan, the holy fasting month, does not appear to be widely observed.

Last Wednesday, as a few dozen men in white skullcaps filed out of the Xihuan mosque after noon prayers, the Jinxiuyuan Halal Sheep Entrails restaurant across the street was doing a roaring lunchtime trade in defiance of religious regulations.

"We Hui people keep our lifestyle and our religion and our beliefs, but we have to lead our normal lives," says Ms. Ma, the deputy mayor. "We practice our religion according to local conditions."

Forced Harmony: China's Olympic Rollercoaster

"The Chinese leadership is caught between the demands of populism and internationalism. Again and again, in order to win international approval, the government has had to buck public sentiments that the party propaganda machine itself has helped to foster."

DALI L. YANG

Seven years ago, when the International Olympic Committee chose Beijing as the host city for the 2008 Summer Olympics, Xinhua, the official Chinese news agency, declared that "Beijing can give the world the best Olympic Games in history." What better event than the Olympics to showcase China's growing prosperity and rising international status, which have resulted from 30 years of reform and opening up?

The Chinese leadership pulled out all the stops to ensure the success of the games. For all their avowed lack of interest in superstition, organizers scheduled the opening ceremony to begin at 8 minutes past 8 P.M. on 8/8/08. In the Cantonese dialect, the pronunciation of the number 8 sounds like "prosperity." One could hardly have found a more numerologically auspicious moment than this.

By all conventional accounts, China's leaders have every reason to be pleased with the success of their nation, which the games were meant to showcase. Between 2001 and 2008, the size of the Chinese economy has more than doubled yet again. Whereas in 2001 China was still in the throes of painful economic restructuring and its banking system was in tatters, today the country boasts the world's largest foreign exchange reserves (more than $1.8 trillion) and is a force to be reckoned with in global affairs.

By lavishing the nation's resources on Beijing, China's leaders made sure that the capital would be among the best prepared Olympic host cities ever and probably the most transformed in terms of landscape. Since winning its bid for the Olympics, Beijing has enjoyed a massive banquet of development, including the construction of world-class sports venues and huge investments in subway and airport expansion. The completion of these and other iconic projects, mostly designed by the world's leading architectural firms, suggests an intense drive for excellence. The smooth launch of Terminal 3 at the Beijing Capital Airport, for example, contrasts sharply with the mess at Heathrow's Terminal 5 and opens a window onto China's growing capacity to get things done and manage them well.

Growing Pains

Yet the Olympics were but one item on a long list of challenges that China's leaders have had to tackle. While the Chinese economy has continued to enjoy double-digit growth, consumer price inflation—at 7.9 percent in the first half of 2008—has risen to the highest levels in more than a decade in spite of administrative controls on energy and other prices. Once renowned for its egalitarianism, China today has one of the most unequal economies in Asia, with sharp divides persisting between rich and poor, urban and rural residents, and the coast and the interior. At the same time, official corruption, especially at the local level, remains rampant despite increased scrutiny.

This combination of rising inflation, income inequality, and perceptions of serious corruption makes a fertile ground for social discontent. In several Chinese cities, isolated incidents have touched off mass protests against local governments. Meanwhile, as the struggle to clean up the air for the Beijing Olympics showed, the country has finally had to reckon with the escalating costs of environmental degradation.

Even China's formidable export juggernaut has begun to show signs of vulnerability in the face of severe headwinds, including a slowing global economy, rising labor and land costs, stricter regulatory demands on quality, and soaring energy and raw materials prices. These factors have begun to shrink China's sizable trade surplus and put increasing pressure on labor-intensive sectors such as textiles.

One could go on. Suffice it to say that growth pains and development imbalances are taxing the ability of the party-state, riven by divergent interests, to deliver badly needed public goods, to redress injustices, to regulate growth, and to protect the interests of the Chinese public.

China Inc.'s Transition

Confronted with these challenges, the leadership in Beijing has placed great emphasis on protecting the corporate interests and enhancing the organizational integrity of the Chinese Communist Party (CCP). For any major organization, good leadership succession is essential to the institution's integrity and vitality. In the 1980s, during the era of Deng Xiaoping, all three men who served as chief of the Communist Party—Hua Guofeng, Hu Yaobang, and Zhao Ziyang—ended up demoted or sacked. Despite reports of differences among the current leaders (and elders) of the party, they appear determined to avoid a return to the succession uncertainties of the past.

In 2002, China witnessed the CCP's first orderly succession—from Jiang Zemin to Hu Jintao. In October 2007, the CCP's 17th Party Congress—whose 2,200 delegates represented about 73 million rank and file party members—reaffirmed, as expected, Hu's position as the top party leader for another five-year term. In the spring 2008 session of the National People's Congress, Hu was also chosen for a second term as China's president, while Wen Jiabao was reappointed prime minister.

In addition, the Party Congress selected a new contingent of the power elite, including a 204-member Party Central Committee headed by a 25-member Political Bureau. Nearly half of the 204 members of the Central Committee are new faces. Just under half come from the party's central administrative apparatus and the central government, along with roughly one-fifth from the armed forces and about one-third from the provinces.

Of special importance was the induction into the Political Bureau Standing Committee of Xi Jinping and Li Keqiang, both in their 50s and with doctorates earned while on the job. Xi and Li are now successors-in-waiting to Hu and Wen respectively. Xi's elevation occurred only a few months after he had been parachuted into the post of Shanghai Party Secretary and came as a surprise to most China watchers. Li on the other hand has long been seen as a loyal Hu follower and someone destined for high places. The dual succession scheme points to a drive to arrange the kind of smooth leadership transition that top corporations seek (though often do not achieve), and thus to have a seasoned team to lead the Communist Party and the country years down the road through new or existing storms. Given the challenges facing the party, there is no guarantee that the best-laid plans for succession will be successfully implemented, but one cannot fault the leadership for lack of trying.

China's leadership in the post-Deng years evolved into a collective mode, with the general secretary leading as *primus inter pares*. Nonetheless, the 17th Party Congress marked a milestone in the consolidation of General Secretary Hu's power and influence. The composition of the newly elected Party Central Committee reflects the increasing clout of Hu's supporters with a Youth League background. Hu also managed to enshrine into the party constitution his "scientific outlook on development"—a theory of Chinese socialism that incorporates sustainable development, social welfare, and ultimately the creation of a "harmonious society." While Hu's political report to the Congress left room for promoting modest political reforms at best and showed a continuing preoccupation with growth, it nonetheless offered greater attention to balance, efficiency, and equity.

Against a background of hyper-growth that depends in part on sweatshops and severe environmental degradation, Hu's call for human-centered development and ecological civilization is especially refreshing in the Chinese context. Equally significantly, in a move that harkens to the promotion of the Great Society by US President Lyndon Johnson in the 1960s, Hu has injected a much more expansive and ambitious policy agenda into the idea of a "well-off society" by enumerating a list of populist welfare goals with which the party hopes to continue harnessing public support and promoting a harmonious society.

The Politics of Protest

But challenges to harmony of course remain. Before the National People's Congress had voted this spring on second terms for Hu and Wen as president and prime minister, demonstrations erupted in Tibet. On the anniversary of the Dalai Lama's flight into exile (March 10), Tibetan monks in Lhasa, the capital of Tibet, protested peacefully against tight government controls on religious matters, especially forced denunciations of the Dalai Lama, the spiritual leader of the Tibetan people. Organizers of the protests apparently sought to bring pressure on the Chinese government, knowing that the world's attention was focused on China ahead of the Olympics. By March 14, however, the protests, into which ordinary Tibetans had joined, had turned into massive attacks on non-Tibetans, as well as on local governments in Lhasa and beyond.

What followed was no surprise. The Chinese government used the riots to justify a harsh crack-down and thus to impose law and order. As an element of emergency rule, the government largely ended foreign media access to Tibet and has since only permitted guided media tours.

Many questions may be asked about the turn to violence by Tibetans and the Chinese government in March 2008. The Chinese government quickly blamed the "Dalai clique" for orchestrating the protests and the violent attacks that, according to government spokesmen, were designed to split the motherland. Zhang Qingli, the party secretary of Tibet, denounced the Dalai Lama as "a wolf in monk's robes" and spoke of a "life-and-death struggle" with the "Dalai clique." The government filled the airwaves with footage of Tibetan violence.

But the eruption of protests against Chinese rule in Tibet highlights some of the deep fissures in that region. The protests point to the desire among many Tibetans for greater dignity, especially religious freedom, and reflect the discontent that many Tibetans feel about their marginalization in their own land. The protests also suggest that massive infusions of central government aid, designed to modernize Tibet and the Tibetans, have not been enough to win the hearts and minds of many Tibetans.

To be sure, Chinese policies have helped raise education standards and improve access to health care, but most Tibetans have suffered from relative deprivation and they resent the presence of many Han Chinese in critical positions in Tibet. In the eyes of many Tibetans, it is the outsiders, notably Han Chinese and Muslim traders, who have benefited most from the government's investments in Tibet. Chinese criticism of the Dalai Lama, especially when forced on Tibetan monks, has been a major source of insult and resentment. Most Han Chinese, however, appear to have bought into the government's view; they have rallied behind the regime and have tended to see the protesting Tibetans as ingrates.

While the government was able to quickly impose an austere calm in Tibetan areas, the forced harmony was soon strained by worldwide protests against the Olympic torch relay. These protests provoked sharply divergent perceptions in the West and in China. The Western media generally portrayed both the Tibetan and the Olympic torch relay protests with sympathy. China's leaders and the Chinese public, by contrast, mostly saw a diabolical anti-China alliance, which included the Dalai Lama and some Hollywood figures, intent on undermining the Olympics and hurting China. Many Chinese felt humiliated and were deeply angered by what they perceived as biased news coverage.

Such sentiments have fueled strong nationalist outbursts against nations, such as France, where the Olympic torch was not well received, as well as against some Western media organizations, especially CNN. Carrefour, the giant French retailer that has a big presence in Chinese cities, became the leading target for protesters.

Rising national pride has lent strong support to the Chinese government. Yet the xenophobia exhibited by Chinese protesters, including in the Han Chinese nationalist response to the Tibetans, also served to undercut China's official drive to soften its international image and to provide a favorable environment for the Olympics. Indeed, the xenophobia and strident nationalism raise profound questions about the nature of China's rise and its potential impact on the international system. Will China continue to be peaceful as it becomes ever more powerful economically and militarily? To what extent will it seek to rewrite the rules for the global economy and society?

As tensions rose in March 2008, both the Chinese government and the Dalai Lama stood to lose from further escalation of the conflict. By April, cooler heads had begun to prevail and both sides sought to de-escalate the confrontation. The Dalai Lama has again and again stated publicly that he no longer seeks outright independence for Tibet. He also said he supports the Beijing Olympics. Meanwhile, the government has subtly adjusted its stance. In early May and early July, government representatives met with the Dalai Lama's special envoys. It remains to be seen whether these talks will lead to more constructive dialogue, but they have helped stabilize the Tibetan situation for now, and they allowed the government to shift its attention to the Olympics.

The Earthquake of 2008

The Tibetan protests wrenched China's political machinery, but two major natural disasters have also served notice to the Chinese leaders that they must expect the unexpected. In early 2008, prolonged snowstorms in southern China wreaked havoc on the local economy and on the lives of millions. The mayhem underscored points of vulnerability in China's economy, in particular the national rail network and power grid. And on May 12, before the tensions in Tibet had eased, a massive earthquake struck, measuring 7.9 on the Richter scale. Centered on Wenchuan in Sichuan province, the quake reverberated across China and caused great devastation and massive loss of life, with 87,000 dead or missing and millions left homeless.

The Chinese government had reacted slowly to the snowstorm in southern China earlier in the year. But in this case Wen—a populist by political instinct and a geologist by training—was en route to the quake zone within hours after the earthquake struck. Wen, Hu, and other leaders mobilized the entire country to respond to the disaster. More than 100,000 soldiers, paramilitary police, medical personnel, and others were deployed to rescue survivors, bury the dead, and assist in the recovery.

By all accounts the Chinese government, unlike cyclone-devastated neighbor Myanmar, has responded effectively to the disaster. While the rebuilding will take Herculean efforts and is fraught with complications, it appears that the Chinese leadership has kept its focus and leveraged the authoritarian system to good effect. The central government has channeled vast resources into the quake-hit regions from its own well-cushioned budget and, in an important move, has ordered major cities and provinces to pair up with the quake-ravaged counties in Sichuan and provide reconstruction aid.

The initial instinct of the Communist Party Propaganda Department was to impose restrictions on reporting and issue guidelines to the media to toe the lines of Xinhua and CCTV, the official outlets. But China has changed in this age of the internet and text messaging. The internet, teeming with more than 200 million Chinese users, immediately buzzed to life. Also, knowing that this was China's worst natural disaster in more than three decades and a lifetime opportunity for reporting, some Chinese news organizations simply ignored the Propaganda Department and dispatched large numbers of reporters to the quake zone to provide their own extensive coverage.

In times of national disaster, greater freedom of the press has generally worked in the government's favor and allowed the country's leaders to rally the nation. Both the Chinese and international press devoted considerable attention to the leadership's role in organizing relief efforts and comforting the victims. As this openness won the government massive support and sympathy, the censors stayed away. In fact, in the initial aftermath of the earthquake, the usually feisty internet dialogue in China focused on saving lives and showed little tolerance for hard-nosed questions.

But the earthquake was nonetheless a watershed moment for China's "netizens," who used the internet to share information as well as grief, to form communities of support, and to organize relief activities, as well as to demand transparency and accountability. When the Chinese Red Cross failed to provide details on donations, Netease, a major internet service provider, declined to link its well-trafficked portal to the Chinese Red Cross and turned to organizations that were more transparent and accountable. When the government sought to manipulate public opinion by highlighting a blog by a well-known writer, Yu Qiuyu—who urged grieving parents to desist from protests—the blogosphere went live with debate and criticism. Although the censors have now tightened their leash on the media, including online news, the Chinese blogosphere continues to shine with public-spirited debate, and netizens have devised various strategies to get around the filtering and censorship.

Not since the death of Mao in 1976 had China been plunged into such collective grief as during the Sichuan earthquake. The massive coverage of the devastation and rescue operations tapped into a deep well of compassion and national solidarity. Impressive official rescue efforts were coupled with an equally magnificent outpouring of civic spirit. Indeed, the earthquake allowed Chinese society to rise above the crass materialism that has pervaded the nation; rich and poor joined hands in making donations of money, blood, and supplies. More than 100 non-governmental organizations formed a coordination office the day after the quake to cooperate in their relief activities. Thousands of civic organizations, singly or in association, served as critical links between donating communities and the disaster areas. As numerous volunteers rushed to the quake-stricken regions, donations too came pouring in from around the country and abroad. For several weeks in mid-2008, state and society worked in unison.

Under intense public scrutiny and in the context of the Chinese leadership's vow to promote "human-centered" development, the earthquake and its aftermath catalyzed a number of significant innovations. For instance, for the first time in China's history, authorities used helicopters to airlift ordinary civilians in large numbers to safety or treatment. In another first, the Chinese flag flew at half-staff on Tiananmen Square for three days to commemorate the victims of a natural disaster—rather than to mark the death of a national leader.

With billions of dollars in donations pouring in, public pressure has been exerted to ensure proper use of the donated funds and goods and to mitigate corruption and embezzlement. The public has also demanded improved transparency. For the country's leadership, major misuses of funds could severely dent the party's legitimacy. In response to this pressure, the leadership promptly established a dedicated group to monitor and supervise the distribution and use of earthquake relief funds and materials. Within days of the quake, the National Audit Office began to dispatch auditors—who eventually numbered over 10,000 nationwide—to monitor the use of donated funds and goods in real time.

In a departure from the past, the audit office has invited the public to report on possible cases of malfeasance. Especially interesting is an initiative by the Sichuan Provincial Discipline Inspection Commission to recruit more than 300 individuals to join the monitoring effort. Such measures of accountability have been vital in maintaining public support. So far, officials have punished dozens of employees for misuse of funds but have largely succeeded in preventing major misuse and corruption.

The Limits of Openness

Yet, even amid the tremendous outpouring of grief associated with the earthquake, the Chinese state has shown it prefers to place major initiatives under its own umbrella rather than let independent organizations occupy much space. Although some NGOs continue to work alongside government-sponsored civic organizations such as the Chinese Red Cross, those NGOs that did not make special efforts to collaborate with the state have had to curtail their activities in the quake areas.

The burst of openness and transparency after the quake also eventually proved to be too much for the censors. The domestic media were quite free to report as long as they offered paeans to survival and heroism. They were put on a short leash once hard questions began to be raised—regarding, for example, what the government could and should have done to prepare better for the earthquake (especially in the enforcement of building codes and construction quality) and whether the government's earthquake forecasting system, because of the leadership's preoccupation with stability ahead of the Olympics, failed in its mission of saving lives.

The uplifting story of Ye Zhiping, the principal of Sangzao Middle School, only served to underscore how much more could have been done in the years before the earthquake to save lives in an area well known as an earthquake zone. For more than a decade Ye had scraped together funds and materials to reinforce his once-rickety school building and had conducted emergency evacuation drills for his teachers and students. These measures produced a miracle: All the students at Sangzao survived the quake. Stories like this raise the painful question of why so many school buildings collapsed and more than 10,000 students died, while nearby government offices often remained standing.

So far, the regime has largely kept such questions away from public debate. For the many grieving and angry parents seeking justice, the local authorities have adopted a carrot-and-stick approach: They have offered condolences and some monetary compensation while pressuring parents to abandon demands for a full investigation and thus "not make trouble." Parents and volunteers who have questioned authorities have been threatened and even detained. Police invoked the charge of "inciting state subversion" against Zeng Hongling, a retired university lecturer, for writing three articles, posted on an overseas website, that criticized the construction of schools that collapsed in the quake.

Populism vs. Internationalism

The scope of the earthquake's devastation and China's heroic response have engendered much international sympathy and helped quiet many international critics. Meanwhile, the Chinese leadership has won praise for a variety of recent diplomatic initiatives. China has played an active role in multilateral efforts to end North Korea's nuclear activities—efforts that lately have produced some provisional successes. Beijing has modified its opposition to confronting the Sudanese government over its role in the violence in Darfur. China has also sought to improve relations with Japan, despite long-held grievances, and has reached out to archrival Taiwan. In this light, the talks with the Dalai Lama's envoys can be seen as part of a programmatic approach meant to create a favorable international environment—not just for the Olympics this year but for China's continued peaceful development.

Yet this turn to internationalism has occurred alongside bouts of populist nationalism within China. For observers, shifting public sentiment in China deserves careful analysis for what it reveals about the country's potentially volatile state-society relations. In particular, the overwhelming majority of Chinese, encouraged by the official media as well as the internet, appear to live in a world of almost pure black and white when it comes to the treatment of Tibetans, the protests surrounding the Olympic torch relay, and the response to the Sichuan earthquake.

In this moralistic universe, affronts to Chinese pride are not well received, and tolerance and forgiveness are not virtues. All too often, a take-no-prisoners approach has dominated the chatter in China's web-sphere. In the aftermath of the Sichuan earthquake, companies were graded on their generosity and miserliness, and huge pressure was exerted on individuals and businesses—whether it be basketball star Yao Ming, property mogul Wang Shi, or a multinational firm such as Intel—to increase their donations to relief efforts. Those who dare dissent from the prevailing view—regarding Tibet, for instance—must be prepared for a fusillade of verbal attacks.

National leaders such as Wen have tapped into this vein of populist sentiment and passion to win the party new legitimacy—and also used it as a tool in the earthquake relief effort. But at other times, such as during the anti-Japanese rallies in 2005 or the recent response to Tibetan protests, populist sentiment can be a severe constraint on the leadership's desire to take an internationalist approach abroad. It also can undercut China's efforts to increase its soft power in the world.

The Chinese leadership is caught between the demands of populism and internationalism. Again and again, in order to win international approval, the government has had to buck public sentiments that the party propaganda machine itself has helped to foster. The latest example is the leadership's agreeing to talk with the Dalai Lama's envoys even as the propaganda machine continues to lash out at the "Dalai clique." China's leaders, by adjusting their confrontational attitude toward the international community (especially Western countries) on the Tibet issue, were able to persuade leaders such as US President George W. Bush and French President Nicolas Sarkozy to attend the opening ceremony of the Olympics.

As the games drew near, it appeared the Chinese leadership had once again navigated the competing demands of populism and internationalism and thereby prepared the ground for a successful Olympics. However, following the rollercoaster events of the first half of the year, little remained of the jubilation that had seized China when the country originally won the right to host the games. Also gone was talk about staging the best Olympics in history. Instead, safety and technical execution became the foremost preoccupations. The Beijing Olympics have indeed defined 2008, but not in ways anticipated by the Chinese leadership.

As the Olympic rollercoaster comes to a stop, attention will again return to China's rapid growth and the pains associated with it. The leaders in Beijing will need all the public support and solidarity they can garner in order to cope with inflation, sagging stock prices, and increasing pressures on exporters who have been hurt by rising costs—as well as with the massive task of rebuilding earthquake-devastated areas where millions still live in temporary shelters. In the face of such challenges and rising public expectations, the Chinese leadership's quest for harmonious development will prove, like the pursuit of happiness, a never-ending task.

DALI L. YANG is a professor of political science and director of the Center for East Asian Studies at University of Chicago.

Taiwan's Liberation of China

RANDALL SCHRIVER AND MARK STOKES

On June 11 of this year, a handshake in Beijing marked a watershed moment in relations across the Taiwan Strait. With this handshake, senior-level dialogue between representatives of two semiofficial organizations authorized to negotiate on behalf of Taipei and Beijing was renewed after a decade's hiatus. The discussions came just after Taiwan, which once experienced decades of authoritarian rule, completed for the second time a peaceful, democratic transfer of power (with the first transfer coming in 2000).

Within days of the May 20 inauguration of new Taiwanese President Ma Ying-jeou, party-to-party talks had been held between Ma's Kuomintang (Nationalist Party, or KMT) and the Chinese Communist Party. When the June meeting took place between the two quasi-official cross-strait organizations, the specific agenda was to reach an agreement on increasing the frequency of direct passenger flights between Taiwan and the mainland, as well as to increase the number of Chinese tourists allowed to visit Taiwan.

But the event bore great significance beyond flights and tourism. It symbolized Taiwan's coming of age, the maturation of its ability to maneuver China toward recognizing the island as a legitimate political entity. The meeting also signified Taiwan's success in helping to steer China toward its recent moderation and its new role as a responsible stakeholder in the international community.

Taiwan, despite unfavorable odds, has played a central yet often unacknowledged part in China's liberalization since the leadership in Beijing initiated far-reaching economic reforms almost 30 years ago. China's reforms, aided by a massive infusion of Taiwanese capital and expertise, have increased Chinese standards of living, literacy levels, and personal freedoms. And Taiwan's influence, a manifestation of hidden but real "soft power," likely will continue to be felt well into the future. However embarrassing this fact may be to the Communist leadership, China needs Taiwan for the sake of its economic and political reform.

Leaders on both sides of Taiwan's political divide deserve credit for their role in this continuing narrative of Chinese liberalization. The Democratic Progressive Party (DPP) of former President Chen Shui-bian—though Beijing downgraded its political relationship with Taiwan during Chen's time in office—nonetheless built on the past successes of the conservative KMT. In fact, the June 2008 talks were a continuation of discussions conducted through private channels on cross-strait flights, tourism, and other issues begun in the early years of the Chen administration.

Under the newly elected KMT government, there is reason for guarded optimism that—as long as Taiwan's process of democratic consolidation continues—the island will continue to exert influence over China's peaceful transformation.

The Delicate Dance

The recent dialogue between the two cross-strait organizations—Taiwan's Straits Exchange Foundation (SEF) and China's Association for Relations Across the Taiwan Strait (ARATS)—represents the latest step in a long, delicate dance involving Beijing and Taipei. The dance got started in 1979, when China began its economic reforms and opening process and the United States shifted its diplomatic recognition from Taiwan to the People's Republic of China (PRC). At that time, the PRC made some conciliatory gestures toward Taiwan: for example, proposing direct flights, maritime shipping, family visits, and academic and tourist exchanges. In 1981 Ye Jianying, chairman of China's National People's Congress, proposed that the KMT and the Chinese Communist Party undertake negotiations that would lead toward Taiwan's integration into China as a special autonomous region.

The KMT rebuffed Beijing's overtures with a "three no's" policy—no contact, no negotiation, and no compromise. However, Taiwan's own political liberalization process eventually prompted President Chiang Ching-kuo and the ruling KMT to review their policies. When martial law on the island was lifted in 1987, and opposition political parties advocating formal independence were legalized, some interaction with the PRC was permitted. Restrictions on travel were relaxed, and investment and indirect trade were allowed. Many exchanges occurred through unofficial organizations like the Red Cross Society.

A new era in cross-strait relations began with the 1988 death of Chiang, the rise to power of President Lee Teng-hui during the KMT's 13th Party Congress in July 1988, and the PRC's setbacks in the wake of the 1989 Tiananmen Square massacre. As China's economic modernization progressed, Taiwanese business executives (backed by members of the legislature) advocated for greater protection of their investments in China, and formed an umbrella association to represent their interests. Some of Taiwan's most prominent corporate leaders visited China in 1990, and in July of that year a reported 600 Taiwanese businesspeople traveled to Beijing to attend a seminar on doing business in the mainland.

To help manage these growing exchanges, China and Taiwan established a quasi-governmental framework of organizations. In Taiwan, the Mainland Affairs Council was created to serve as the primary policy-making authority for cross-strait relations. In late 1990, Taipei and Beijing established the SEF and ARATS—which were authorized to negotiate on behalf of the governments to resolve practical issues. Also in 1990, Taiwan created the National Unification Council, which the next year promulgated guidelines specifying how democracy, freedom, equitable prosperity, and national unification were to be pursued through peaceful, democratic means.

In May of that year, President Lee announced the abolition of "temporary provisions" granting emergency powers to the president—provisions that had been in place since 1948. Lee, in essence acknowledging the existence of two separate political entities across the strait from one another, asserted that "the mainland is now under the jurisdiction of the Chinese Communists, and this is a fact that we must face." This statement ended the Taiwanese government's 40-year pretense of controlling the mainland.

Agreeing to Disagree

With a framework for exchanges now in place, the two sides moved with haste to intensify the relationship. Taiwanese media reports indicate that Lee, as early as December 1990, created a private window for direct communication between his office and senior leaders in Beijing. And an SEF delegation traveled to Beijing in May 1991.

In response to the PRC's insistence that Taiwan agree to a "one China" formulation as a prerequisite for more substantive negotiations, the National Unification Council in August 1992 passed a resolution that affirmed the formulation but highlighted differences between Taiwan's and the mainland's interpretations of the phrase "one China." (The meaning of this phrase is still in dispute, partly because of an absence of written records documenting the discussions that took place between the two sides in the early 1990s. Beijing argues that the "one China" principle establishes that there is only one China and Taiwan is a part of it. Some in Taiwan argue that, according to the principle, all sides are free to interpret "one China" as they wish. In any case, the two sides haggled over the definition of "one China" before finally agreeing to differ on interpretations and not pursue the issue further.) In April 1993, during meetings in Singapore, senior delegations representing the SEF and ARATS signed agreements that formalized certain aspects of the unofficial relationship.

A series of events that began in 1995 resulted in Beijing's suspending, in 1999, these senior-level, quasi-official contacts. Chinese President Jiang Zemin, concerned over Taiwan's perceived moves away from the ill-defined "one China" framework, in January 1995 publicly reaffirmed China's position on the "one China" principle and warned against any movement toward an independent Taiwan. Jiang's statement provided some specifics on the PRC's Taiwan policy, including the hope that unofficial exchanges would be further expanded; Jiang also proposed that "negotiations should be held and an agreement reached on officially ending the state of hostility between the two sides in accordance with the principle that there is only one China."

In April of that year, Lee in a speech before the National Unification Council responded that "we believe the mainland authorities should demonstrate their goodwill by publicly renouncing the use of force and refrain from making any military move that might arouse anxiety or suspicion on this side of the Taiwan Strait, thus paving the way for formal negotiations between both sides to put an end to the state of hostility."

The inauguration of independence-leaning President Chen in May 2000 did nothing to resurrect the quasi-official SEF-ARATS dialogue as a channel for working out differences. But despite the absence of senior government-sponsored talks, the eight years of the DPP administration saw exponential growth in economic, cultural, and other unofficial interactions. Arguably, this sharp rise in the scope and pace of exchanges—which were enabled partly through unilateral policy adjustments— was possible in large part because of Chen and the DPP's near-immunity from accusations of selling out the Taiwanese people or being weak on Taiwanese sovereignty.

Chen, faced with a Beijing that was attempting to undermine the DPP's authority and a US benefactor that was concerned about the DPP's seemingly pro-independence agenda, operated with caution. In the month before the March 2000 election, Beijing had issued a white paper outlining three conditions under which force might be used against Taiwan. One of these scenarios suggested that time was limited for reaching a negotiated unification settlement. And Beijing rejected Taiwan's calls to restart the SEF-ARATS talks.

Even so, the absence of official dialogue did not prevent an acceleration of economic, cultural, and other exchanges. Restrictions on Chinese tourism to Taiwan were relaxed in 2000. The three "mini-links"—special rules governing contacts between the outlying Taiwanese islands of Jinmen and Matsu and the Chinese city of Xiamen—were initiated on a trial basis in 2001. Restrictions on cross-strait economic activities were loosened; for example, Chinese investment in Taiwan's real estate market was permitted. Direct cross-strait charter flights were initiated during the Lunar New Year holiday in early 2003. The first Chinese tourists also began to flow into Taiwan, though they were capped at 1,000 a day.

In the Same Boat

Over the past quarter-century, while official exchanges have waxed and waned, Taiwan has become a hidden but major factor in China's economic reforms and its rapid, export-driven growth—which in turn have been essential for China's stability and modernization and its potential for gradual political liberalization. As economic ties have grown, Beijing's interests in Taiwan have become more complex." And economic interdependence has had the dual effect of discouraging moves toward de jure independence by Taiwan while also furthering the peaceful transformation of China.

Since Deng Xiaoping began opening China to the world in the late 1970s, investors and entrepreneurs from Taiwan have flocked to the mainland. While accurate statistics are elusive, Taiwanese business investment on the mainland reached at least $44 billion in 2007, according to Beijing's figures. Taiwanese government estimates—which presumably include investment funneled through Hong Kong, the British Virgin Islands, the Cayman Islands, and other offshore locations—put that figure closer to $150 billion. This accounts for almost half of Taiwan's total foreign direct investment.

Since 2003 the PRC has been Taiwan's largest trading partner, and more than 25 percent of Taiwan's exports go to the mainland. With bilateral trade growing by an average of 33 percent a year, Taiwan is China's fifth-largest trading partner. With the mainland's lower production costs, skilled labor force, and lenient tax and investment policies, an estimated 70 percent of China's exports in the information and communication technologies sector are believed to be manufactured in Taiwanese-owned factories in China. The mainland's top electronics exporters are predominately subsidiaries of Taiwanese firms. Thus, when one buys a computer-related or electronics product with a "Made in China" label, a more accurate representation might be: "Made in a Taiwanese Factory in China."

Taiwan's presence in China is subtle yet significant. An estimated 1 million Taiwanese live in China, concentrated in three or four areas around Shanghai and Guangzhou and in Fujian province. Taiwanese businesspeople operate an estimated 100,000 joint ventures or subsidiaries in China, and 63 of the 500 largest companies in China are Taiwanese-owned. Taiwan's presence in China provides employment to between 5 million and 20 million Chinese workers, depending on the estimate. One estimate claims that when indirect employment is added—for example, jobs associated with supplying Taiwan-owned manufacturing concerns—40 million Chinese workers owe their paychecks to Taiwan-based business executives.

Taiwanese managers have been invaluable in providing their counterparts in China with the skills needed to produce goods competitive in the international market. As Chinese labor costs increase and risks of financial and economic instability become apparent, Taiwanese are naturally beginning to seek diversification for their investments. With businesses from Taiwan providing jobs and income, directly or indirectly, to as many as 40 million workers, Taiwan has leverage over China. On the other hand, a collapse of the Chinese economy could have severe repercussions for Taiwan's own economic security.

This growing economic interdependence is affecting Taiwan's freedom of action. Chinese analysts are well aware of the coercive utility of luring Taiwan into China's economy—accepting a trade deficit with Taiwan while shutting it out of regional trade arrangements and deterring bilateral agreements. But the interdependence cuts both ways. Each side may find it increasingly risky to adopt policies that would be viewed as overly detrimental to the interests of the other. China's use of force to resolve differences with Taiwan could result in economic destruction on both sides of the Taiwan Strait. Since China's own economic success relies in part on Taiwan's investment and management skills, the damage resulting from any use of force likely would be exorbitant.

While the PRC has achieved impressive economic results over the past decade, challenges to further liberalization remain. Large state expenditures, geared at least in part toward securing the loyalty of key constituencies, could inhibit China from realizing its economic potential. The country's financial sector, partly because of state debt and nonperforming loans, is problematic. Without a free and open press that can expose malfeasance, corruption is difficult to stem.

Meanwhile, an increasing income gap between rich and poor may create social divisions, as might persistently high unemployment rates, particularly in rural areas. Ongoing deterioration of the country's public health infrastructure and education systems could increase social tensions, thus eroding the Communist Party's control and increasing its vulnerability to unforeseeable economic or political shocks.

Growing reliance on external sources of energy renders the Chinese economy vulnerable to supply disruptions. The PRC, because of its unprecedented economic growth and a rapid expansion in car ownership, passed Japan in 2004 to become the world's second largest consumer of oil; in 2007 it became the largest producer of the carbon emissions that are believed to have a major effect on climate change. About half of China's oil imports come from the Middle East, and this share is expected to grow in the future.

Slow Route to Reform

As China continues to open, optimists predict that state control will ease gradually. The hidden hand of free enterprise could eliminate inefficient industries and public pressure to reduce corruption will increase. Yet, while China was one of the earliest socialist economies to undertake serious reform, recent data on the country's regulatory environment, international trade practices, fiscal policy, and legal structure place China in the bottom third of countries in terms of economic freedom. It ranks behind India and Mexico, most Eastern European countries, and all of East Asia except for Myanmar and Vietnam.

Skeptics argue that the PRC's rapid growth, boosted by Taiwanese investment, has actually bolstered Beijing's legitimacy and thus reduced pressure on the ruling elites to liberalize. Indeed, China's economic growth could be viewed as a factor dampening enthusiasm for democracy—in that growth makes the ruling elite even more reluctant to part with power. Beijing's high levels of spending on internal security and defense make it less attractive for would-be reformers to press for a democracy agenda or to challenge authoritarian rule too aggressively. Even so, China's seemingly less strident position in dealing with Taiwan on such issues as direct flights, as well as a less shrill tone in forcing its "One Country, Two Systems" formulation, indicates a more liberal approach in resolving its differences with Taiwan.

Does Ma Know Best?

In light of China's continued economic reliance on Taiwan, the May 2008 election of Ma as Taiwan's president has provided the two sides of the strait with a pretext for restoring a quasi-governmental framework for dialogue so that the last decade's exponential growth in cross-strait interactions can be managed. The China policies of the Ma administration, based on the notion of "mutual non-denial" (according to which neither side of the Taiwan Strait denies the existence of the other) and a "three no's" policy ("no unification, no independence, and no use of force") appear to be a continuation of policies followed under the DPP.

Over the next four years, the Ma administration is likely to further advance financial and economic exchanges, exchanges that theoretically could lead to an agreement establishing a cross-strait common market. The Ma government likely will press Beijing to drop opposition to Taiwan's expansion of its international breathing space and participation in international forums. In line with Beijing's interest in good relations with the Ma administration, quasi-governmental entities likely will figure more prominently in the cross-strait dialogue. Exchanges in the cultural and educational arenas will continue to be advanced as well. Perhaps the greatest change in the offing is some decisive action to reduce the risk of military conflict arising in the Taiwan Strait because of miscalculation or accident.

The "one China" issue, in the meantime, remains unresolved. The meaning of the phrase is yet to be fixed—but a definition may not be necessary. Taiwan is a global paradox. It exists as a state but, because of the PRC's sovereignty claims, most of the international system does not recognize it as such. In a metaphysical sense, Taiwan shares a common heritage and culture with China and is part of China. However, in the same metaphysical spirit—and because of various historical legacies and interdependencies—Taiwan could also be viewed as part of Japan, the United States, and the broader international community. In any event, Beijing has argued that anything is possible as long as the Ma administration adheres to a "one China" principle, however "one China" may be conceived.

It remains to be seen whether the current agreement to put aside differences over the meaning of "one China" can be sustained. Over the next four years, it may prove difficult for the two sides to avoid the sovereignty issue and for Taiwan simultaneously to avoid sacrificing its territorial and administrative integrity. But the emphasis that Ma has placed on Taiwan's status as a "world citizen"—an approach that presents a third alternative to sinicization and localization—holds great promise. If one views the erosion of the Westphalian system of nation-states as being caused in significant measure by the emergence of information technology, then Taiwan can be seen, in light of its international dominance in this field, as on the cutting edge of globalization.

Indeed, if Taiwan manages to maintain its autonomy and unique culture, its future may lie more with its status as "a member of the global village" than with any status as part of "China"—depending on how "China" is defined.

The most prominent aspect of the new administration's agenda may be steps taken toward establishing a cross-strait common market. Such a market, initially proposed in 2001 by current Vice President Vincent Siew, would ostensibly be fashioned after the European model that eventually led to the formation of the European union. The Ma administration has expressed hope that a cross-strait common market arrangement could facilitate Taiwan's negotiation of free trade agreements with members of the Association of Southeast Asian Nations and other countries.

Finally, the Ma administration will likely press to end the state of hostilities between Taiwan and the mainland through some form of peace accord. While the prospective outlines of such an agreement are vague, an end to the state of hostilities would presumably involve Beijing's renunciation of force against Taiwan. Such negotiations would be laudable—assuming that no steps are taken to disrupt Taiwan's democratic consolidation and that all options regarding Taiwan's future international status remain open. The 23 million people of Taiwan deserve the right to determine their own future in an atmosphere free from coercion, and engaging the authorities in Beijing toward achieving this end is a positive agenda.

But talks leading toward renunciation of the use of force are not enough. An end to the state of hostility would also require a tangible decrease in the military threat that the Chinese authorities, and the military forces under their control, pose to the people of Taiwan. Beijing claims that its threats to use force are directed only against separatist elements. In Taiwan, however, it is becoming increasingly difficult to distinguish among separatists, unificationists, globalists, advocates of an elusive status quo, and other people. And, of course, in the event of any use of force against Taiwan, it would be difficult if not impossible to surgically target one group without affecting others.

The most widely recognized symbol of China's threat to Taiwan is the growing arsenal of increasingly accurate and lethal conventional ballistic missiles that the People's Liberation Army has assembled opposite Taiwan. Ma has called for removal of these missiles before formal negotiations with China begin.

When it comes to arms control or risk reduction measures, details and means of verification matter. Moving missiles back from the coast, or even closing one or two artillery brigades along the coast, may not make much difference in the nature of the threat. Given the scope and pace of China's force modernization, and taking into account Beijing's broad range of capabilities beyond ballistic missiles, a real threat reduction would require much more than removing the conventional ballistic missiles deployed opposite Taiwan. Nonetheless, removing them would be a good start.

Chaos and Order

Taiwan remains small and vulnerable, but its influence is out of proportion to its size and population. It is at the cutting edge of globalization and is a driving force behind the information technology revolution that is creating a flatter world order. The island's rapidly changing politics often appears to operate at the border between chaos and order. But this young democracy is growing stronger by creating an environment in which individuals have a greater voice in shaping the future.

Taiwan has influenced China's liberalization and has helped facilitate China's gradual emergence as a more responsible member of the international community. The continuation of this influence depends on how Taiwan manages its own house, but there is reason for cautious optimism regarding the island's future.

In March, voters gave Ma the opportunity to govern for four years. After that time, constituents will be able to evaluate his time in office and exercise their right to vote again. The KMT administration and Ma himself, depending on their performance, could go out as easily as they came in. But today, Ma has an opportunity to achieve greatness—and to improve the lives of the people in Taiwan who have entrusted him with leading the nation. He also has an opportunity to continue liberating China from its tradition of dealing with Taiwan as a subordinate entity. He can encourage China to treat cross-strait relations as a dialogue between equals.

RANDALL SCHRIVER, CEO of the Washington-based Project 2049, was US deputy assistant secretary of state for East Asisa from 2003 to 2005. **MARK STOKES,** country director for China and Taiwan at the US Department of Defense from 1997 to 2004, is executive director of the project 2049 Institute.

Beijing and Taiwan Try Their Hand at Détente

Beijing and Taipei are on a conciliatory path these days. The Communist Party in China has desisted with its military threats and the small island has stopped pushing as vociferously for independence. Direct flights have also been re-established between the mainland and Taiwan. Both sides seem to be experiencing change through rapprochement.

SANDRA SCHULZ

Fan Guishan's voice is booming. The sky above Taipei may be overcast, the Chinese man bellows, but his heart is full of sunshine. Fan sees no reason to keep his voice down right now. He's here leading an important delegation, and he wants to speak in great sentences on this great day. "We will fulfill our long-held dream," he cries to the others assembled in the ballroom. "Chinese tourists will come to Taiwan!" Everyone applauds.

Thirty-nine representatives of Chinese tour operators have gathered here in a Taipei luxury hotel. They're at the vanguard of the new business of Chinese tourism in Taiwan—and they're here to see what the island has to offer. One highlight, for example, is "the best tea in the world," according to an official at the tourism office. Another is a jade cabbage from the Qing Dynasty housed at the Taipei National Palace Museum—an entire vegetable carved from a single piece of white-green jade that is as famous as the Mona Lisa. And then there's Sun Moon Lake. Even as far back as the 1980's the lake was listed by the Chinese Communist Party's *People's Daily* newspaper as one of China's 10 most beautiful places—even though it lies in Taiwan, the "renegade province," as Beijing officially calls this island.

Massive China and little Taiwan are beginning to bridge their differences again. On July 4, they reintroduced direct weekend flights from the mainland to the Taiwanese island, and a maximum of 3,000 Chinese visitors are allowed to enter Taiwan each day. Until this month, the only way for Chinese citizens to reach Taiwan was by first passing through Hong Kong, Macau or a third country. Now they can come directly to Taiwan and explore, draw some comparisons and tell friends and family back home what they've seen. They talk about the clean subways—and about the political talk shows on TV. Chinese tourists, according to the Taiwanese tourism official, like to stay at their hotels in the evening and watch freedom of the press in action. "All that," he says, "is our gentle power."

A newly gentle era seems to be arriving in this part of the world with the Olympic Games, which begin in Beijing on August 8.

Though the Communist Party in Beijing is still standing firm on its "One China" policy, it has stopped provoking Taiwan with military maneuvers. Taiwan has also suspended its demonstrations for independence and seems satisfied with the status quo. China and Taiwan are both counting on their people, on winning their hearts and minds. Who knows, say the Taiwanese, perhaps people on the mainland will soon start wondering why the people of Taiwan are allowed to elect their government, while they are not?

"Beijing has realized that Taiwan will continue to drift away if China doesn't establish contact," says Lin Chong-pin, President of the Institute for International Studies. After nearly 60 years of separation, a generation has grown up in Taiwan seeing the People's Republic of China as a foreign country. Beijing now wants to draw the 23 million Taiwanese closer to the "motherland." The time is ripe, too: New Taiwanese President Ma Yingjeou got elected partly on a platform of wanting to improve relations with China, thus breaking with the policy course of his political predecessor. The main hope is that improved ties will translate into benefits for Taiwan's economy.

"The whole world wants to do business with China," says Tsai Eng-meng. "But Taiwan, though geographically closest to China, has been the only country to be shy about doing it. That's the big joke." Tsai himself, a successful Taiwanese entrepreneur, certainly couldn't be accused shyness. "If there's a mouth and some money to go with it, there's a market," he says. And with 1.3 billion mouths in China, Tsai has succeeded in making himself a very rich man—complete with a private jet and a corporate headquarters in Shanghai. He's chairman of Want Want Group, a food brand that markets rice crackers and other snacks in China. Tsai has more than 40,000 employees, including 38,000 on the mainland. Almost all of his staff are Chinese.

Tsai opened his first factory on the mainland 16 years ago, and today he has 110. When he got started, he recalls, the Chinese welcomed Taiwanese investors with open arms.

The interconnections between Taiwan and China have only grown in the intervening years. Around 1 million Taiwanese business people now live on the mainland, and there are more than 250,000 marriages between Chinese and Taiwanese. Chinese women in Taiwan have never had it easy, though. In the past, these women were often suspected of being spies. Today people shout insults at women like Cui Yon-mei, such as: "You just want money."

Cui used to believe all Taiwanese were rich, since they were always so generous with the tips they gave out at Chinese hotels. But then she landed in Taipei and somehow the airport struck her as cheap, dimly lit and small—hardly comparable to the glitzy new terminals in Beijing or Guangzhou.

Fighting for Loyalty

The wives, the businesspeople, they're all seeing to it that Taiwan gradually moves closer to China—too close, some fear. Critics argue the new president is getting too chummy with the Chinese. In the past, Ma used the anniversary of the June 4, 1989, Tiananmen Square Massacre—when several hundred protesters were killed by the military in Beijing—as a time to direct accusations at the Communist leadership in Beijing. This year, though, he flattered and praised. China has made "certain progress," he says, thanks to the country's reforms. The Taiwanese opposition, however, argued it would have been better if Ma had reminded the Chinese about the unrest in Tibet.

And when the president agreed, out of respect, to let a negotiator from China call him simply "Mr. Ma," the Taiwanese political opposition immediately criticized him for smudging the nation's honor by allowing himself to be humbled in such a way.

Taiwan's honor seems to be in constant danger as the island fights for "international space," the term used to refer to the island's international activities, like diplomatic ties with foreign countries. The size of this space is a matter determined by Beijing. Just 23 countries have diplomatic relations with Taiwan—states like Tuvalu and the Vatican. This January, Malawi also decided to join Beijing's side, and before that Costa Rica, Chad and Senegal shifted allegiance. Memory of the $30 million lost in an attempt to win over Papua New Guinea—a middleman

ultimately ran off with the money—still brings shame to the minds of the Taiwanese.

Taiwan has had the most success when it has been willing to be flexible about the name issue, making allowances for the "One China" policy. At the Olympic Games, Taiwan will compete as "Chinese Taipei," and within the World Trade Organization it is referred to as a "Separate Customs Territory." Those are the conditions under which Taiwan is allowed to participate.

An attraction that draws Taiwanese and Chinese both is the mausoleum of Chiang Kai-shek, Taiwan's national hero and a well-known figure in China as well. As the head of the Kuomintang (Nationalist Party) in China, Chiang agreed to an alliance with Mao's troops to fight against Japan during World War II. After subsequently fighting and losing to the Communists, he and his government fled to Taiwan in 1949. Mao's Communist Party gained control of mainland China, but Chiang Kai-shek ruled as dictator in Taiwan.

The path to the coffin of the "great leader," as he is called in the brochures for the tourists, passes through bamboo stands and palm trees. It leads past a small green lake, which the general loved because it reminded him of his home in mainland China. Guards stand at attention in the muggy heat, right hands to their rifles and left hands balled into fists, under attack by mosquitoes.

One Country, Two Systems?

Initially, Taiwan's military was none too happy about the prospect of mainland visitors coming to the general's provisional resting place. They feared the Chinese might not show enough respect—and that they might shuffle past the general's portrait in flipflops, or smoking cigarettes. But the Chinese visitors also bow to Chiang Kai-shek, just as a large sign nearby asks them to do. And when they come across the general's old soldiers, they're friendly and even exchange business cards.

Yang Jun-chi used to come here often, when his eyes were better. He's 83 now, a veteran, a small man in sweatpants and an undershirt. "I have nothing in Taiwan," he says. He lives in a small room with his songbird and his Thai wife, for whom he paid a marriage broker € 2,000 ($3,160). He left the cousin he loved behind on the mainland in 1949.

"Taiwan is a province of China," says Yang, and of course the politicians should be talking about reunification. It could be done the way it was in Hong Kong, where the "One Country, Two Systems" policy was established. Now in his twilight years, former soldier Yang, who once fought the Communists, has come to agree with the Communist Party.

In a couple months Yang will take one of the new direct flights to the mainland to attend a family celebration in his native village. While there, he'll also take a look at the urn he's ordered. Before he dies, Yang Jun-chi would like to finally leave Taiwan.

More than a Game for Taiwan

The island's pride is inextricably linked to baseball—and it just cannot lose to China today.

—Kathrin Hille

Fany Tsai is an agreeable woman. At her family's printing shop she treats visitors to food, drink and friendly words.

But when it comes to baseball, the petite housewife vents her fury. "No matter how far we get, we just cannot possibly lose against China," she says as Taiwan's baseball team faces China today in the Olympic competition. "After all, in baseball, Taiwan is somebody. And besides, the Chinese are the enemy, right?"

Few events contain the political undertones present in this encounter between the nationalistic host and the island it is obsessed with calling its own.

Baseball was brought to Taiwan by the Japanese, which ruled the island from 1895 to 1945. Besides building its modern infrastructure, such as an electricity grid and a rail network, the Japanese bequeathed cultural features that clearly distinguish Taiwan from China.

The Taiwanese lack the hatred many Chinese still harbour against Japan, and the island's art and design often show a Japanese influence. This heritage is clearest in a love for raw fish—and baseball.

Hence baseball crystallises feelings of national pride and dignity. Using baseball to overcome a sense of deprivation predates Taiwan's conflict with the mainland.

"From the beginning, the role of sports in general and baseball in particular in Taiwan has been very different from, say, football in British society," says Shieh Shih-yuan, a sports historian at the National Taiwan Museum of History. "In the UK, football developed because the industrial revolution created the working class. But baseball in Taiwan has always been linked to national pride and glory."

This link was created in 1931, when the Kano team, from the Agricultural College in Chiayi, travelled to Japan and stunned their hosts by coming second in the Koshien high school tournament, a rite of passage in Japanese baseball.

That team consisted of Japanese, Taiwanese aboriginal and ethnically Chinese players. "We proved that we can play baseball just as well as the Japanese," says Su Cheng-sheng, now 97 and a pitcher from that Kano team who recalls the game as the most glorious moment of his life. "On the field, everyone is equal."

This lesson is at the heart of Taiwan's love affair with baseball. After the Kuomintang (KMT) party, then in power in China, replaced the Japanese as Taiwan's rulers in 1945, the new authorities were reluctant to encourage baseball as they sought to make the island more Chinese.

But as the KMT-controlled state, the Republic of China, lost ground internationally to the People's Republic of China, the party rediscovered baseball to strengthen domestic morale.

In 1968, a school team from the remote village of Hungye beat a team from Japan, the country that had won the junior league world championships that year.

The next year, Taiwan won the championships itself. Such baseball triumphs gave the Taiwanese something to cling to as they lost their seat in the United Nations and descended into international isolation.

"For other countries that are strong in baseball, their own professional league may be more important than the Olympics," says Chen Chin-feng, who plays for Taiwan's La New Bears club, and is part of the Olympic team. "But this is an important moment to achieve something for our country."

China's Taiwan Dilemma

Beijing's obsession with Taiwan could damage its economic and diplomatic prospects, and even threaten Communist rule.

China's leadership believes strongly in the goal of a unified country—and for Beijing that means preventing Taiwan from declaring independence. For many Chinese, uniting with Taiwan is a matter of national pride. China scholar Michael Yahuda argues that pushing the issue politically or militarily would stimulate hostility abroad and cause an economic downturn at home, possibly leading to the demise of communist party rule. By keeping Taiwan low on its agenda, on the other hand, China could postpone dealing with the independence issue while soothing nationalist tensions on the mainland, especially within the military. Moreover, avoiding immediate confrontation with Taipei is key to preventing conflict with the US, which has pledged to intervene on Taiwan's behalf should the need arise. Constitutional reforms currently being proposed in Taiwan may threaten this passive course of action, Yahuda argues, but if China is to allay anxiety abroad and at home, it must focus more on appealing to Taiwan's people and less on coercion. —YaleGlobal

MICHAEL YAHUDA

Beijing has turned the Taiwan issue into a huge obstacle to China's rise as a great power. The higher Taiwan moves up Beijing's political and foreign policy agenda, the more Beijing raises tension in the region and in relations with the United States. That tension could endanger China's main goal of economic growth and development. Investors would become more nervous, neighbours would be more wary, and increasing American involvement would be to the detriment of China. Moreover, nationalist passions would be roused in China by promoting expectations of unification that could not be easily achieved, if at all. The result could lead to the worst of both worlds for Beijing by stimulating hostility abroad and an economic downturn at home, possibly causing the demise of communist party rule.

But if China can keep Taiwan low on its agenda, it could prolong the separation of the island from the Mainland and avert objections raised at home by the nationalistically minded and especially by the military.

Indeed, the military has a vested interest in keeping the Taiwan issue very much alive. Since China faces no immediate military threats, it is the Taiwan issue that justifies the military's abundant claims on the national budget and its imports of high tech weaponry; the potential for confrontation with the United States over Taiwan ensures that America remains an enemy (at least from the perspective of the military). Moreover, American military superiority over the Chinese has forced the PLA to devise various forms of costly asymmetric warfare that might give it a chance of deterring the US in the limited confines of the Taiwan Strait. The Taiwan issue also assures the military it has an important voice in determining the ultimate national priorities of the country.

Perhaps in recognition of the complexities and attendant risks in pursuing a policy of demanding rapid unification, Beijing's leaders in recent years have placed the emphasis on the less ambitious and less risky policy of opposing any moves that might lead to the separation of the island from the Mainland. However, Beijing cannot control the agenda on Taiwan. As Taiwan has democratized, Beijing has found that the people there have become increasingly less enamoured with the prospect for unification. Moreover, now that the island is a democracy, its politics have become less predictable. Given the history of discord between oppressive Mainlanders and the majority of Taiwan's inhabitants well into the 1980s, it is not surprising that issues of identity should figure prominently in this nascent, vibrant, but troubled democracy.

Beijing has found that its proposed unification on the basis of 'one country two systems' has increasingly less appeal to people in Taiwan. Consequently, it has had to employ coercion to prevent what it sees as a slide towards separation. But this is a threat not only to Taiwan, but also to the United States, which has pledged to help Taiwan should the need arise. Since neither Washington nor Beijing favors a military confrontation over Taiwan at this point, Beijing finds itself in the peculiar position of relying on the United States to stop Taiwan from being 'provocative'. Since the US is formally committed to a 'one China policy' that discourages Taiwan from publicly declaring its independence, the question as to what short of that may be considered to be 'provocative' or as to what might be said to change the 'status quo', is a matter of opinion, rather than something that can be defined by law.

Thus Beijing's current objection to the referendum proposed by Taiwan's President Chen Shui-bian is that it may lead to an attempt to change the constitution in accordance with the wishes of the electorate as opposed to the existing one, which is based on the principle of Taiwan being an integral part of China. Arguably, that would change the basis of sovereignty from the current one of the Republic of China, which at least conforms to the principle that Taiwan is politically part of China, to one in which the claim to sovereignty was based on the people of Taiwan alone. The process of democratization weakens Beijing's case, however, since it can be seen as an exercise of self-determination whereby legitimate political power is drawn from the people of Taiwan alone. Indeed, Beijing itself makes this very point in Hong Kong today by arguing that the democrats' claim for democracy is in fact a claim for full autonomy, i.e., for independence. Yet Beijing has been able to live, albeit uncomfortably, with the democratization of Taiwan without claiming that separation was at hand.

Beijing's belligerent course, coupled with its call to Washington to press Taiwan to desist, can hardly satisfy its own leaders. In effect, Beijing depends on the United States to prevent it from pursuing a policy it does not really want to pursue. The new leaders have indicated that they want to portray China's rise to great power status as a peaceful one, unlike that of Germany and Japan in an earlier period. But their stand over Taiwan threatens that goal. Regardless of the American response to China's continuing acquisition of advanced weaponry, the resulting power Bejing projects over Taiwan and adjoining waters will challenge China's neighbours too.

Beijing cannot be happy to be in a position where the political initiative is determined by the uncertainties of the Taiwanese electoral and democratic processes and mediated by Washington's sometimes inconsistent policies. Moreover, it is difficult to conceive of any government in Washington standing by if an authoritarian government in Beijing were to forcibly take over a democratic Taiwan—regardless of the assumed 'provocation.'

It would seem, therefore, that Beijing should be encouraged to reshape its Taiwan policy by paying more attention to making attractive offers to the people of Taiwan. If Beijing were to pay even half as much time and effort to that side of its policy as it does to the coercive side, it would ease much of the anxiety about China's future at home and abroad.

MICHAEL YAHUDA is Professor Emeritus of the London School of Economics and Visiting Scholar at the Sigur Center for Asian Studies of George Washington University.

Hong Kong Tests Art Buyers' Courage

Justine Lau

Sotheby's, the auction house, will test global investors' appetite for high-end works of art with a five-day sale of paintings, sculptures, jewels and watches starting today in Hong Kong, in the face of growing turmoil in the financial markets.

The auction house is still optimistic the sale will bring in $256m (€186m, £$145m), up from $200m last year. "I am not saying that the art market and the financial market go in opposite directions. But experience tells us that the art market usually survives a bit longer than the financial market," said Kevin Ching, chief executive officer at Sotheby's Asia.

Mr Ching said auction sales continued to thrive for about two years after the 1987 stock market crash and the 1998 Long-Term Capital Management collapse. World-wide auction sales at Sotheby's rose 5 per cent in 1998 and 16 per cent in 1999 before dropping more than 10 per cent in 2000.

Sotheby's sold 218 Damien Hirst items for £111m, hours after the collapse of Lehman Brothers investment bank last month.

"We were quite anxious [before the auction] but the results show how resilient the high-end art market is. Usually, the more high-end the pieces are, the less affected they get by a downturn," said Mr Ching.

Highlights of the Hong Kong sale include a 15.5-metre 18th-century scroll depicting Chinese Emperor Qianlong reviewing 16,000 troops, which is expected to fetch more than HK$80m ($10.3m, €7.5m, £5.8m) and *Flower Matango,* a fourmetre high sculpture by Takashi Murakami, the Japanese artist, which is estimated to go for HK$24m.

Sotheby's is hoping that an emerging class of buyer from more resilient economies and a rising number of Asian art lovers will keep auction prices high.

"The downturn has not really affected collectors from the Middle East and Russia, where a lot of wealth has been created in the past few years," said Patti Wong, Sotheby's Asian chairman. "Some collectors have been waiting for certain pieces to come to the market for 20 years. They know that art is not something that if they don't buy today, they can buy the day after."

Bonnie Engle, Hong Kong correspondent for the Asian Art newspaper, agreed that art market dips usually lag behind those in equity markets. "It doesn't mean that there won't be a slowdown. But many smart people are still buying art for passion," said Ms Engle.

Sotheby's is selling more than 1,700 items, mostly of ancient and contemporary Chinese art. Hong Kong is the world's third largest art market after New York and London in terms of auction turnover.

The auction will include Sotheby's first evening sale of modern and contemporary Asian art in Hong Kong.

The contemporary art market has experienced a dramatic boom in recent years and has so far resisted the effect of the credit crisis.

Sotheby's began holding its Hong Kong spring and autumn sales in 1974.

While the city has long been recognised as the world's leading centre for Chinese art trading, it is emerging as one of the biggest marketplaces for all Asian art.

Hong Kong does not impose any tax on art sale. China charges a 34 per cent import duty. Both Christie's and Sotheby's hold biannual sales in Hong Kong.

Hong Kong Poses Threat to City

BROOKE MASTERS

Hong Kong poses the greatest threat among Asian cities to the dominance of London and New York as the top world financial centres, according to research commissioned by the City of London Corporation.

The report, by Research Republic, looked at Singapore, Hong Kong and Tokyo, the three Asian centres ranked in the top 10 in the most recent Global Financial Centres Index, a biannual ranking by Z/Yen Group.

The study concluded that, in the near future, none of the three was likely to dominate Asia the way London and New York have done for European and US finance. However Hong Kong, currently ranked fourth, is the strongest contender because of its historic roots in finance and its ability to tap the Chinese market.

Singapore, which leapfrogged Hong Kong for third in last month's index, is fast becoming a world centre for asset management and private banking to rival Switzerland, but the current report concluded it will ultimately be limited by its small domestic market. Tokyo, ranked seventh, has stability but is hampered by a shrinking population, inward-looking policies and 15 years of slow growth.

For now, Asia is less integrated financially than it is in terms of trade. Though the continent holds more than 60 per cent of the world's foreign reserves, most of the savings and investment still flow through London and New York, the report said.

The onus, therefore, is on New York and London to keep capital flowing by avoiding protectionism and reacting to the financial crisis with sensible rather than intrusive regulation.

"It's for us to lose and for them to win," said Stuart Fraser, policy chairman of the City of London Corporation. "In difficult times, the strength of established centres will hold [New York and London] in good stead."

Glossary of Terms and Abbreviations

Ancestor Worship Ancient religious practices still followed in Taiwan, Hong Kong, and the People's Republic of China. Ancestor worship is based on the belief that the living can communicate with the dead and that the dead spirits to whom sacrifices are ritually made can bring about a better life for the living.

Brain Drain A migration of professional people (such as scientists, professors, and physicians) from one country to another, usually in search of higher salaries or better living conditions.

Buddhism A religion of East and Central Asia founded on the teachings of Siddhartha Gautama (the Buddha). Its followers believe that suffering is inherent in life and that one can be liberated from it by mental and moral self-purification.

Capitalist A person who has capital invested in business, or someone who favors an economic system characterized by private or corporate ownership of capital goods.

Chinese Communist Party (CCP) Founded in 1921 by a small Marxist study group, its members initially worked with the Kuomintang (KMT) under Chiang Kai-shek to unify China and, later, to fight off Japanese invaders. Despite Chiang's repeated efforts to destroy the CCP, it eventually ousted the KMT and took control of the Chinese mainland in 1949.

Cold War A conflict between the communist and anti-communist (democratic-capitalists) blocs, without direct military conflict.

Communism In theory, a system in which most goods are collectively owned and equally distributed. In practice, a system of governance in which a single authoritarian party controls the political, legal, educational, and economic systems in an effort to establish a more egalitarian society.

Confucianism Often referred to as a religion, actually a system of ethics for governing human relationships and for ruling. It was established during the fifth century B.C. by the Chinese philosopher Confucius.

Cultural Revolution Formally, the Great Proletarian Cultural Revolution. In an attempt to rid China of its repressive bureaucracy and to restore a revolutionary spirit to the Chinese people, Mao Zedong (Tse-tung) called on the youth of China to "challenge authority" and "make revolution" by rooting out the "reactionary" elements in Chinese society. The Cultural Revolution lasted from 1966 until 1969, but the term is often used to refer to the 10 year period from 1966 to 1976. It seriously undermined the Chinese people's faith in the Chinese Communist Party's ability to rule and led to major setbacks in the economy.

De-Maoification The rooting-out of the philosophies and programs of Mao Zedong in Chinese society.

Democratic Centralism The participation of the people in discussions of policy at lower levels. Their ideas are to be passed up to the central leadership; but once the central leadership makes a decision, it is to be implemented by the people.

ExCo The Executive Council of Hong Kong, consisting of top civil servants and civilian appointees chosen to represent the community. Except in times of emergency, the governor must consult with the ExCo before initiating any program.

Feudal In Chinese Communist parlance, a patriarchal bureaucratic system in which bureaucrats administer policy on the basis of personal relationships.

Four Cardinal Principles The Chinese Communists' term for their commitment to socialism, the leadership of the Chinese Communist Party, the dictatorship of the proletariat, and the ideologies of Karl Marx, Vladimir Lenin, and Mao Zedong.

Four Modernizations A program of reforms begun in 1978 in China that sought to modernize agriculture, industry, science and technology, and defense by the year 2000.

Gang of Four The label applied to the four "radicals" or "leftists" who dominated first the cultural and then the political events during the Cultural Revolution. The four members of the Gang were Jiang Qing, Mao's wife; Zhang Chunqiao, former deputy secretary of the Shanghai municipal committee and head of its propaganda department; Yao Wenyuan, former editor-in-chief of the *Shanghai Liberation Daily;* and Wang Hongwen, a worker in a textile factory in Shanghai.

Great Leap Forward Mao Zedong's alternative to the Soviet model of development, this was a plan calling for the establishment of communes and for an increase in industrial production in both the cities and the communes. The increased production was to come largely from greater human effort rather than from more investment or improved technology. This policy, begun in 1958, was abandoned by 1959.

Great Proletarian Cultural Revolution *See* Cultural Revolution.

Gross Domestic Product (GDP) A measure of the total flow of goods and services produced by the economy of a country over a certain period of time, normally a year. GDP equals gross national product (GNP) minus the income of the country's residents earned on investments abroad.

Guerrilla A member of a small force of "irregular" soldiers. Generally, guerrilla forces are used against numerically and technologically superior enemies in jungles or mountainous terrain.

Han Of "pure" Chinese extraction. Refers to the dominant ethnic group in the P.R.C.

Ideograph A character of Chinese writing. Originally, each ideograph represented a picture and/or a sound of a word.

Islam The religious faith founded by Muhammad in the sixth and seventh centuries A.D. Its followers believe that Allah is the sole deity and that Muhammad is his prophet.

Kuomintang (KMT) The Chinese Nationalist Party, founded by Sun Yat-Sen in 1912. *See also* Nationalists.

LegCo Hong Kong's Legislative Council, which reviews policies proposed by the governor and formulates legislation.

Long March The 1934–1935 retreat of the Chinese Communist Party, in which hundreds of thousands died while journeying to the plains of Yan'an in northern China in order to escape annihilation by the Kuomintang.

Mainlanders Those Chinese in Taiwan who emigrated from the Chinese mainland during the flight of the Nationalist Party in 1949.

Mandarin A northern Chinese dialect chosen by the Chinese Communist Party to be the official language of China.

Mao Thought In the post-1949 period, originally described as "the thoughts of Mao Zedong." Mao's "thoughts" were considered important because he took the theory of Marxism-Leninism and applied it to the concrete conditions existing in China. But since Mao's death in 1976 and the subsequent reevaluation of his policies, Mao Thought is no longer conceived of as the thoughts of Mao alone but as the "collective wisdom" of the party leadership.

May Fourth Period A period of intellectual ferment in China, which officially began on May 4, 1919, and concerned the Versailles Peace Conference. On that day, the Chinese protested what was considered an unfair secret settlement regarding German-held territory in China. The result was what was termed a "new cultural movement," which lasted into the mid-1920s.

Nationalists The Kuomintang (KMT). The ruling party of the Republic of China, but its army was defeated by 1949. Was the only political party in Taiwan until the 1990s.

Newly Industrialized Country (NIC) A term used to refer to those developing countries that have enjoyed rapid economic growth. Most commonly applied to the East Asian economies of South Korea, Taiwan, Hong Kong, and Singapore.

Offshore Islands The small islands in the Formosa Strait that are just a few miles off the Chinese mainland but are controlled by Taiwan, nearly 90 miles away.

Opium A bitter, addictive drug made from the dried juice of the opium poppy.

Opium War The 1839–1842 conflict between Britain and China, sparked by the British import of opium into China. After the British victory, Europeans were allowed into China and trading posts were established on the mainland. The Treaty of Nanking, which ended the Opium War, also gave Britain its first control over part of Hong Kong.

People's Procuracy The investigative branch of China's legal system. It determines whether an accused person is guilty and should be brought to trial.

People's Republic of China (P.R.C.) Established in 1949 by the Chinese Communists under the leadership of Mao Zedong after defeating Chiang Kai-shek and his Nationalist supporters.

Pinyin A newer system of spelling Chinese words and names, using the Latin alphabet of 26 letters, created by the Chinese Communist leadership.

Proletariat The industrial working class, which for Marx was the political force that would overthrow capitalism and lead the way in the building of socialism.

Republic of China (R.O.C.) The government established as a result of the 1911 Revolution. It was ousted by the Chinese Communist Party in 1949, when its leaders fled to Taiwan.

Second Convention of Peking The 1898 agreement leasing the New Territories of Hong Kong to the British until 1997.

Severe Acute Respiratory Syndrome (SARS) A grave respiratory illness that emerged in 2003 as an epidemic in Hong Kong and part of mainland China.

Shanghai Communique A joint statement of the Chinese and American viewpoints on a range of issues in which each has an interest. It was signed during U.S. President Richard Nixon's historic visit to China in 1971.

Socialism A transitional period between the fall of capitalism and the establishment of "true" communism. Socialism is characterized by the public ownership of the major means of production. Some private economic activity and private property are still allowed, but increased attention is given to a more equal distribution of wealth and income.

Special Administrative Region (SAR) A political subdivision of the People's Republic of China that is used to describe Hong Kong's status following Chinese sovereignty in 1997. The SAR has much greater political, economic, and cultural autonomy from the central government in Beijing than do the provinces of the P.R.C.

Special Economic Zone (SEZ) An area within China that has been allowed a great deal of freedom to experiment with different economic policies, especially efforts to attract foreign investment. Shenzhen, near Hong Kong, is the largest of China's Special Economic Zones.

Taiwan Relations Act (TRA) U.S. domestic law passed by Congress in 1979 to regulate unofficial relations between the U.S. and Taiwan.

Taiwanese Independence Movement An organization of native Taiwanese who wanted to declare Taiwan an independent state. Had to organize outside of Taiwan, as its leaders were persecuted in Taiwan by the KMT. Only with the recognition of the legitimacy of competing political parties in the 1990s could they adopt the goal of an independent Taiwan.

Taoism A Chinese mystical philosophy founded in the sixth century B.C. Its followers renounce the secular world and lead lives characterized by unassertiveness and simplicity.

United Nations (UN) An international organization established on June 26, 1945, through official approval of the charter by delegates of 50 nations at a conference in San Francisco. The charter went into effect on October 24, 1945.

Yuan Literally, "branch"; the different departments of the government of Taiwan, including the Executive, Legislative, Judicial, Control, and Examination Yuans.

Bibliography

SOURCES FOR STATISTICAL REPORTS

U.S. State Department *Background Notes* (2008)
C.I.A. *World Factbook* (2008)
World Bank *World Development Reports* (2008)
UN *Population and Vital Statistics Reports* (2008)
World Statistics in Brief (2008)
The Statesman's Yearbook (2008)
Population Reference Bureau *World Population Data Sheet* (2008)
The World Almanac (2008)
The Economist Intelligence Unit (2008)

PEOPLE'S REPUBLIC OF CHINA
Periodicals and Newspapers

The following periodicals and newspapers are excellent sources for coverage of Chinese affairs:

Asiaweek
Asian Survey
Asia Times Online
Beijing Review
China Business Review
China Daily
The China Journal
The China Quarterly
The Economist
Far Eastern Economic Review
Journal of Asian Studies
Journal of Chinese Political Science
Journal of Contemporary China
Modern China
Pacific Affairs
People's Daily
South China Morning Post

GENERAL AND BIOGRAPHIES

Jasper Becker, *The Chinese* (New York: Free Press, 2000).
Insightful portraits of peasants, entrepreneurs, corrupt businessmen and party members, smugglers, and ethnic minorities by a resident journalist. Reveals much about the effect of the government's policies on the lives of ordinary people.

Ma Bo, *Blood Red Sunset* (New York: Viking, 1995).
Perhaps the most compelling autobiographical account by a Red Guard during the Cultural Revolution. Responding to Mao Zedong's call to youth to "make revolution," the author captures the intense emotions of exhilaration, fear, despair, and loneliness. Takes place in the wilds of Inner Mongolia.

Jung Chang, *Wild Swans: Three Daughters of China* (New York: Simon and Schuster, 1992).
A superb autobiographical/biographical account that illuminates what China was like for one family for three generations.

Kwang-chih Chang, *The Archeology of China*, 4th ed. (New Haven, CT: Yale University Press, 1986).
_____*Shang Civilization* (New Haven, CT: Yale University Press, 1980).Two works by an eminent archaeologist on the origins of Chinese civilization.

Nien Cheng, *Life and Death in Shanghai* (New York: Grove Press, 1987).
A gripping autobiographical account of a woman persecuted during the Cultural Revolution because of her earlier connections with a Western company, her elitist attitudes, and her luxurious lifestyle in a period when the Chinese people thought the rich had been dispossessed.

B. Michael Frolic, *Mao's People: Sixteen Portraits of Life in Revolutionary China* (Cambridge, MA: Harvard University Press, 1980).
A must read. Through composite biographies of 16 different types of people in China, the author offers a humorous but penetrating view of "unofficial" Chinese society and politics. Biographical sketches reflect political life during the Maoist era, but the book has enduring value for understanding China.

Rob Gifford, *China Road: A Journey into the future of a rising power* (New York: Random House 2008).
Fascinating stories about China and Chinese people by a journalist as he traveled from Shanghai to Kazakhstan.

Peter Hessler, *River Town: Two Years on the Yangtze* (New York: HarperCollins, 2001).
Insights into Chinese culture by a Peace Corps volunteer who lived in a Yangtze River city from 1996 to 1998. The author gains considerable insights into the life of Fuling, a city that partly flooded when the Three Gorges Dam was completed.

Yarong Jiang and David Ashley, *Mao's Children and the New China* (New York: Routledge, 2000).
More than 20 ex-Red Guards who participated in the Cultural Revolution were interviewed in Shanghai in the mid-1990s. They reminisce about their lives then, revealing much about life in Shanghai during a critical period in China's political history.

Zhisui Li, *The Private Life of Chairman Mao* (New York: Random House, 1994).
A credible biography of the Chinese Communist Party's leader Mao Zedong, written by his physician, from the mid-1950s to his death in 1976. Fascinating details about Mao's daily life and his relationship to those around him.

Heng Liang and Judith Shapiro, *Son of the Revolution* (New York: Vintage, 1984).
A gripping first-person account of the Cultural Revolution by a Red Guard. Offers insights into the madness that gripped China during the period from 1966 to 1976.

Anchee Min, *Becoming Madame Mao* (Boston: Houghton Mifflin, 2000).
This novel vividly portrays Mao's wife, Jiang Qing, tracing her life from early childhood through her failed career as an actress, her courtship with Mao Zedong in the caves of Yenan, and her ultimate demise as a member of the notorious Gang of Four. A real page-turner.

Chihua Wen, *The Red Mirror: Children of China's Cultural Revolution* (Boulder, CO: Westview Press, 1995).
A former editor and reporter presents the heartrending stories of a dozen individuals who were children when the Cultural Revolution started. It shows how rapidly changing policies of the period shattered the lives of its participants and left them cynical adults 20 years later.

James and Ann Tyson, *Chinese Awakenings: Life Stories From the Unofficial China* (Boulder, CO: Westview Press, 1995).

Lively verbal portraits of Chinese people from diverse backgrounds (for example, "Muddy Legs: The Peasant Migrant"; "Turning Iron to Gold: The Entrepreneur"; "Bad Element: The Shanghai Cosmopolite").

HISTORY, LANGUAGE, AND PHILOSOPHY

Johan Bjorksten, *Learn to Write Chinese Characters* (New Haven, CT: Yale University Press, 1994).

A delightful introductory book about writing Chinese characters, with many anecdotes about calligraphy.

William Theodore De Bary, ed., *Sources of Chinese Tradition*, Vols. I and II (New York: Columbia University Press, 1960).

A compilation of the major writings (translated) of key Chinese figures from Confucius through Mao Zedong. Gives readers an excellent understanding of intellectual roots of development of Chinese history.

William Theodore De Bary and Weiming Tu, eds. *Confucianism and Human Rights* (New York: Columbia University Press, 1998).

Articles debate whether the writings of Confucius and Mencius (a Confucian scholar) are relevant to today's human rights doctrine (as defined by the United Nations).

John DeFrancis, *Visible Speech: The Diverse Oneness of Writing Systems* (Honolulu, HI: University of Hawaii Press, 1989).

Discusses the evolution of the Chinese written language and compares it with other languages that use "visible" speech.

Patricia Buckley Ebrey, *The Cambridge Illustrated History of China* (New York: Cambridge University Press, 1996).

A beautifully illustrated book on Chinese history from the Neolithic Period to the People's Republic of China. Includes photos of artifacts (such as bronze vessels) and art (from Buddhist art to modern Chinese paintings), which enrich the historical presentation.

John King Fairbank and Merle Goldman, *China: A New History*, 2nd Enlarged Edition (Cambridge, MA: Harvard University Press, 2006).

Examines forces in China's history that define it as a coherent culture from its earliest recorded history to the present. Examines why the ancient and sophisticated China had fallen behind other areas by the nineteenth century. The Chinese Communist Revolution and its aftermath are reviewed.

William Hinton, *Fanshen: A Documentary of Revolution in a Chinese Village* (New York: Random House, 1968).

A gripping story based on the author's eyewitness account of the process of land reform carried out by the CCP in the north China village of Long Bow, 1947 to 1949.

Edgar Snow, *Red Star Over China* (New York: Grove Press, 1973).

This classic, which first appeared in 1938, is a journalist's account of the months he spent with the Communists' Red Army in Yan'an in 1936, in the midst of the Chinese Civil War. It is a thrilling story about the Chinese Revolution in action and includes Mao's own story (as told to Snow) of his early life and his decision to become a Communist.

Jonathan D. Spence, *The Search for Modern China, 2nd edition* (New York: W. W. Norton & Co., 2000).

A lively and comprehensive history of China from the seventeenth century through the 1990s. Looks at the cyclical patterns of collapse and regeneration, revolution and consolidation, and growth and decay.

Song Mei Lee-Wong, *Politeness and Face in Chinese Culture* (New York: Peter Lang, 2000).

Part of a series on cross-cultural communication, this book discusses how politeness is portrayed in speech and how it relates to a central concept in Chinese culture: "face" and "losing face."

POLITICS, ECONOMICS, SOCIETY, AND CULTURE

Julia F. Andrews, *Painters and Politics in the People's Republic of China, 1949–1979* (Berkeley, CA: University of California Press, 1994).

A fascinating presentation of the relationship between politics and art from the beginning of the Communist period until the eve of major liberalization in 1979.

N. Susan D. Blum and Lionel. M. Jensen, eds., *China Off Center: Mapping the Margins of the Central Kingdom* (Honolulu, HI: University of Hawaii Press, 2002).

Arguing that there are many "Chinas," these articles offer new insights into the complexity and diversity of China. Interpretative essays on topics such as linguistic diversity, regionalism, homosexuality, gender and work, popular music, magic and science. Ethnographic reports on minorities.

Susan Brownell and Jeffrey Wasserstrom, eds., *Chinese Femininities and Chinese Masculinities: A Reader* (Berkeley, CA: University of California Press, 2002).

A reader that investigates various issues through the lens of feminist and gender theory.

Thomas Buoye, Kirk Denton, Bruce Dickson, Barry Naughton, and Martin K. Whyte, *China: Adapting the Past, Confronting the Future* (Ann Arbor, MI: The University of Michigan Center for Chinese Studies, 2002).

Articles on China's geography and pre-1949 history, including environmental history, Confucianism, and the Boxer Uprising. It also examines the last few decades, including homosexuality, the Internet, and culture; several short stories.

Guidi Chen and Chuntao Wu, *Will the Boat Sink the Water? The Life of China's Peasants* (New York: Public Affairs, Perseus Books, 2006).

An award-winning book of reportage. While most of the world focuses on China's rapid economic growth, these reporters present stories about the poor peasants in China's vast countryside. Theme challenges mainstream view that China's peasantry was the primary beneficiary of the Chinese Communist revolution, and argues that even under a Chinese-style market economy, the peasantry continues to suffer.

Deirdre Chetham, *Before the Deluge: The Vanishing World of the Yangtze's Three Gorges* (New York: Palgrave MacMillan, 2002).

A portrait of life along the Yangtze River just before it was flooded to fill up the Three Gorges Dam. Examines the policies that led to the dam, the criticisms of was, and the hopes and fears of what this dam might generate other than electricity.

Paul Close, David Askew and Xu Xin, *The Beijing Olympiad: The Political Economy of a Sporting Mega-Event* (New York: Routledge), 2007.

Looks at the motivations for Beijing to host the Olympics in 2008, and the opportunities and dangers for China embedded in this event. Chapters on the relationship of the individual, nationalism, and capitalism to the Olympics, as well as on how the Olympics can serve as a "coming out party" for an ambitious state.

Bibliography

Elisabeth Croll, *China's New Consumers: Social Development and Domestic Demand* (New York: Routledge), 2006.

Examines the expansion of the domestic market for Chinese-made goods, but challenges the conventional wisdom that there is an insatiable demand for goods among Chinese consumers. Looks at new expectations and social aspirations because of the consumer revolution, the livelihoods and lifestyles of various categories of Chinese consumers, and the government's policy of encouraging internal consumption. Includes chapters on consumption patterns of the rural poor, children, youth, and the elderly.

Deborah S. Davis, ed., *The Consumer Revolution in Urban China* (Berkeley, CA: University of California, 2000).

Articles cover the impact of China's consumer revolution on urban housing, purchases of toys, clothes, and leisure activities for children, and bridal consumerism.

Michael S. Duke, ed., *World of Modern Chinese Fiction: Short Stories & Novellas From the People's Republic, Taiwan & Hong Kong* (Armonk, NY: M. E. Sharpe, Inc., 1991).

A collection of short stories written by Chinese authors from China, Taiwan, and Hong Kong during the 1980s. The 25 stories are grouped by subject matter and narrative style.

Elizabeth Economy, *The River Runs Black: The Environmental Challenge to China's Future* (Ithaca: Cornell University Press), 2004.

The central government's inability to cope with the growing environmental crisis has led to serious social, economic, and health issues, as well as a steadily rising involvement of citizens in non-governmental organizations. Such civic participation may lead to greater democratization and the development of civil society.

Barbara Entwisle and Gail E. Henderson, eds., *Re-drawing Boundaries: Work, Households, and Gender in China* (Berkeley, CA: University of California Press, 2000).

Looks at how gender inequality affects types of work, wages, and economic success. Examines issues of work and gender in China's cities and countryside and among the "floating" population.

Merle Goldman and Elizabeth. J. Perry, eds., *Changing Meanings of Citizenship in Modern China* (Cambridge, MA: Harvard University Press, 2002).

Studies of citizenship in China over the last century. Focuses on the debate over the relationship of the individual to the state, the nation, the community, and culture.

Ellen Hertz, *The Trading Crowd: An Ethnography of the Shanghai Stock Market* (Cambridge, England: University of Cambridge Press, 1998).

An anthropologist examines the explosion of "stock fever" since the stock market opened in Shanghai in 1992. Looks at the dominant role of the state in controlling the market, resulting in a stock market quite different from those in the West.

Alan Hunter and Kim-kwong Chan, *Protestantism in Contemporary China* (New York: Cambridge University Press, 1993).

Examines historical and political conditions that have affected the development of Protestantism in China.

William R. Jankowiak, *Sex, Death, and Hierarchy in a Chinese City* (New York: Columbia University Press, 1993).

Written by an anthropologist with a discerning eye, this is one of the most fascinating accounts of daily life in China. Particularly strong on rituals of death, romantic life, and the on-site mediation of disputes by strangers (e.g., with bicycle accidents).

Maria Jaschok and Suzanne Miers, eds., *Women and Chinese Patriarchy: Submission, Servitude and Escape* (New York: Zen Books, 1994).

Examines Chinese women's roles, the sale of children, prostitution, Chinese patriarchy, Christianity, and feminism, as well as social remedies and avenues of escape for women. Based on interviews with Chinese women who grew up in China, Hong Kong, Singapore, and San Francisco.

Yarong Jiang and David Ashley, *Mao's children and the New China* (New York: Routledge, 2000).

More than 20 ex-Red Guards who participated in the Cultural Revolution were interviewed in Shanghai in the mid-1990s. They reminisce about their lives then, revealing much about life in Shanghai during the critical period in China's political history.

Ian Johnson, *Wild Grass: Three Stories of Change in Modern China* (New York: Pantheon Books, 2004).

The author portrays three ordinary citizens who, by testing the limits of reform, may cause China to become a more open country.

Lane Kelley and Yadong Luo, *China 2000: Emerging Business Issues* (Thousand Oaks, CA: Sage Publications, 1998).

Looks to the emerging business issues for Chinese domestic firms and foreign firms.

Conghua Li, *China: The Consumer Revolution* (New York: Wiley, 1998).

An impressive account of China's rapidly growing consumer society. Looks at the forces that are shaping consumption, China's cultural attitudes toward consumerism, consumer preferences of various age groups, and the rapid polarization of consumer purchasing power.

Jianhong Liu, Lening Zhang, and Steven F. Messner, eds., *Crime and Social Control in a Changing China* (Westport, CT: Greenwood Press, 2001).

Focuses on crime in the context of a rapidly modernizing China. Shows the deeply rooted cultural context for Chinese attitudes toward crime, criminals, and penology that might well interfere with reform.

Stanley B. Lubman, *Bird in a Cage: Legal Reform After Mao* (Stanford, CA: Stanford University Press, 1999).

Traces the victories and frustrations of legal reform since 1979, but is based on a thorough examination of the pre-reform judicial system.

Michael B. McElroy, Christopher P. Nielsen, and Peter Lydon, eds., *Energizing China: Reconciling Environmental Protection and Economic Growth* (Cambridge, MA: Harvard University Press, 1998).

Research reports address the dilemmas, successes, and problems in China's efforts to reconcile environmental protection with economic development. Addresses issues such as energy and emissions, the environment and public health, the domestic context for making policy on energy, and the international dimensions of China's environmental policy.

Joanna McMillan, *Sex, Science and Morality in China* (New York: Routledge), 2006.

Looks at the supposed "opening up" of the sexual world in China and discovers a world still defined by a deep conservatism, a propensity to judge sexual practices based on old-style morality, as well as intolerance of difference. Describes such topics as the coverage of sexual anatomy and sexual function by marriage manuals, transsexuals, homosexuals, masturbation,

Viagra, sexual dysfunction, sex shops, prostitution, and many other related topics as presented by China's sexologists and the media.

Gina Marchetti, *From Tian'an Men to Times Square: Transnational China and the Chinese Disaspora on Global Screens, 1989–1997* (Philadelphia: Temple University Press), 2006.
The portrayal of China in the media and in film since the crackdown on demonstrators in 1989. Interviews with Chinese and non-Chinese film makers provide basis for analysis of how global capitalism and other political and social forces have affected the aesthetics of film and presentation of China and the Chinese throughout the world's Chinese communities.

Katherine Morton, *International Aid and China's Environment: Taming the Yellow Dragon* (New York: Routledge), 2005.
Case studies on the three major donor approaches to giving environmental aid to China: helping to build the environmental infrastructure (Japan), introducing market measures and incentives (World Bank), and increasing stakeholder participation in order to improve decision-making (UNDP). Contrasts these with the Chinese emphasis on regulatory control. Examines impact of these three approaches to strengthening sustainable environmental capacity in China.

Andrew J. Nathan and Perry Link, eds., and Liang Zhang, compiler, *The Tiananmen Papers: The Chinese Leadership's Decision to Use Force Against Their Own People—In Their Own Words* (New York: Public Affairs, 2001).
Widely believed to be authentic documents that reveal what was said among China's top leaders behind closed doors during the Tiananmen crisis in 1989. These leaked documents lay out the thinking of China's leaders about the students and workers occupying Tiananmen Square for almost six weeks—and how they eventually decided to use force.

Kevin J. O'Brien and Lianjiang Li, *Rightful Resistance in Rural China* (New York: Cambridge University Press, 2006).
Examines question of how weak, unorganized groups go about resisting state control and articulating their demands. The focus is on resistance in rural China that relies on the use of officially-sanctioned policies, values, laws, and rhetoric to challenge political and economic elites who have abused their power, not implemented policies, or failed to live up to their professed ideals. Looks at how rightful resisters gain legitimacy by using approved channels and not resorting to illegal or criminal activity.

Suzanne Ogden, *Inklings of Democracy in China* (Cambridge, MA: Harvard University Asia Center and Harvard University Press, 2002).
Asks whether liberal democracy is possible or even appropriate in China, given its history, culture, and institutions. Looks at a broad array of indicators. Argues for fair and consistent standards for evaluating freedom and democracy in China and for comparing it with other states.

Suzanne Ogden, Kathleen Hartford, Lawrence Sullivan, and David Zweig, eds., *China's Search for Democracy: The Student and Mass Movement of 1989* (Armonk, NY: M. E. Sharpe, 1992).
A collection of wall posters, handbills, and speeches of the prodemocracy movement of 1989. These documents capture the passionate feelings of the student, intellectual, and worker participants.

Elizabeth J. Perry and Mark Selden, eds., *Chinese Society: Change, Conflict and Resistance,* 2nd edition (New York: Routledge, 2003).
A collection of articles on the resistance generated by economic reforms since 1979. Topics include suicide as resistance, resistance to the one-child campaign, and religious and ethnic resistance.

Paul G. Pickowicz and Yingjin Zhang, eds., *From Underground to Independent: Alternative Film Culture in Contemporary China* (Lanham, Md.: Rowman & Littlefield), 2006.
Examines the evolution beginning in the early 1990s from underground to quasi-independent film making in China: film making that is independent from the state-controlled system of film production, distribution, and showing, and which depends on private (including foreign) funding. Includes articles on diverse topics, such as independently-made documentaries, and film clubs in Beijing.

James Seymour and Richard Anderson, *New Ghosts, Old Ghosts: Prisons and Labor Reform Camps in China* (Armonk, NY: M. E. Sharpe, 1998).
A look inside labor camps in China's northwestern provinces, including details about prison conditions and management, the nature of the prison population, excesses perpetrated in prisons, and fate of released prisoners.

David Shambaugh and Richard H. Yang, *China's Military in Transition* (Oxford: Clarendon Press, 1997).
Collection of articles on China's military covers such topics as party–military relations, troop reduction, the financing of defense, military doctrine, training, and nuclear force modernization.

Susan L. Shirk, *China, Fragile Super Power* (New York: Oxford University Press, 2007).
China portrayed as very pragmatic in both its foreign and domestic policies because of a leadership motivated by fear of its own citizens. Chinese Communist Party leaders seen as insecure and afraid of losing power in spite of economic success and development.

Stockholm Environment Institute and United Nations Development Program (UNDP) China, *China Human Development Report 2002: Making Green Development a Choice* (New York: Oxford University Press, 2002).
Examines the key issues for sustainable development in China. Also looks at the government's response and the creation of environmental associations to address the issues.

United Nations Development Program, *China: Human Development Report* (New York: UNDP China Country Office, Annual report).
Provides measurements of the effect of China's economic development on human capabilities to lead a decent life. Areas examined include health care, education, housing, treatment and status of women, and the environment.

Jianying Zha, *China Pop: How Soap Operas, Tabloids, and Bestsellers Are Transforming a Culture* (New York: W. W. Norton, 1995).
Examines the impact of television, film, weekend tabloids, and best-selling novels on today's culture. Some of the material is based on remarkably revealing interviews with China's leading film directors, singers, novelists, artists, and cultural moguls.

Yuezhi Zhao, *Media, Market, and Democracy in China: Between the Party Line and the Bottom Line* (Urbana, IL: University of Illinois Press, 1998).
Raises the basic question of whether the expected value of a "free press" will be realized in China if the party-controlled press is replaced by private entrepreneurs, and a state-managed press is required to make a profit.

TIBET AND MINORITY POLICIES

Robert Barnett, *Lhasa: Streets with Memories* (New York: Columbia University Press, 2006).

Examines the interplay of forces from Tibetan history and culture, Chinese control, and modernization to create the streets and life of Tibet's capital today.

Melvyn C. Goldstein, *The Snow Lion and the Dragon: China, Tibet, and the Dalai Lama* (Berkeley, CA: University of California Press, 1997).

The best book on issues surrounding a "free" Tibet and the role of the Dalai Lama. Objective presentation of both Tibetan and Chinese viewpoints.

Melvyn C. Goldstein and Matthew T. Kapstein, eds., *Buddhism in Contemporary Tibet: Religious Revival and Cultural Identity* (Hong Kong: Hong Kong University Press, 1997).

An excellent, nonpolemical collection of articles by cultural anthropologists on Buddhism in Tibet today. Studies of revival of monastic life and new Buddhist practices in the last 20 years are included.

Hette Halskov Hansen, *Lessons in Being Chinese: Minority Education and Ethnic Identity in Southwest China* (Seattle, WA: University of Washington Press, 1999).

Examines Chinese efforts to achieve cultural and political integration through education of a minority population in Chinese cultural values and communist ideology.

Donald S. Lopez, *Prisoners of Shangri-la: Tibetan Buddhism and the West* (Chicago, IL: University of Chicago Press, 1998).

Explodes myths about Tibetan Buddhism created by the West. Shows how these myths have led to distortions that do not serve well the cause of greater autonomy for Tibet.

Orville Schell, *Virtual Tibet: Search for Shangri-la from the Himalayas to Hollywood* (New York: Henry Holt and Co., 2000).

Examines the journals of those hoping to find a spiritual kingdom in Tibet. Notes the perilous journeys undertaken for the last 200 years in pursuit of this quest, and the disappointment of almost all in what they found.

FOREIGN POLICY: CHINA AND THE INTERNATIONAL SYSTEM

Gerald Chan, *China's Compliance in Global Affairs: Trade, Arms Control, Environmental Protection, Human Rights* (Hackensack, NJ: World Scientific Publishing Co., 2006).

Assesses China's compliance with international rules and norms in the four areas of the title. Asks whether China has acted "responsibly" from the perspective of US-China relations. First looks at how China sees its "responsibility" to the world community, given its own history, culture, ethics, and level of economic development. Case studies of compliance with WTO rules, with the norms and regulations of the arms control and disarmament regime, with newly formed international environmental norms, and with Western notions of human rights, which are at odds with China's primary definition of human rights.

Jian Chen and Shujie Yao, eds. *Globalization, Competition and Growth in China* (New York: Routledge, 2006).

Chapters look at reforms in the financial sector, foreign direct investment, globalization, and China's strategies for development. Considerable technical analysis as well.

Alastair Iain Johnston and Robert S. Ross, eds., *Engaging China: The Management of an Emerging Power* (New York: Routledge, 1999).

A collection of articles on how various governments, including Korea, Singapore, Indonesia, Japan, Taiwan, the United States, and Malaysia, have tried to "engage" an increasingly powerful China.

Samuel S. Kim, ed., *China and the World, Chinese Foreign Policy Faces the New Millennium (4th edition)* (Boulder, CO: Westview Press, 2001).

Examines theory and practice of Chinese foreign policy with the United States, Russia, Japan, Europe, and the developing world as China enters the new millennium. Looks at such issues as the use of force, China's growing interdependence with other countries, human rights, the environment, and China's relationship with multilateral economic institutions.

Joshua Kurlantzick, *Charm Offensive: How China's Soft Power Is Transforming the World* (New Haven, CT, Yale University Press 2008). Looks at how China is using soft power to appeal to its neighbors and to distant countries alike.

Richard Madsen, *China and the American Dream: A Moral Inquiry* (Berkeley, CA: University of California Press, 1995).

Looks at the emotional and unpredictable relationship that the United States has had with China from the nineteenth century to the present.

James Mann, *About Face: A History of America's Curious Relationship With China, From Nixon to Clinton* (New York: Alfred A. Knopf, 1999).

A journalist's account of the history of U.S.–China relations from Nixon to Clinton. Through examination of newly uncovered government documents and interviews, gives account of development of the relationship, with all its problems and promises.

Ramon H. Myers, Michel C. Oksenberg, and David Sham-baugh, eds., *Making China Policy: Lessons From the Bush and Clinton Administrations* (New York: Rowman and Littlefield, 2002).

Examines the policy of the United States toward China during the George Bush and Bill Clinton administrations (1989–2000). Includes an account of China's perception and response to America's China policies.

Michael D. Swaine and Zhang Tuosheng, eds., *Managing Sino-American Crises: Case Studies and Analysis* (Washington D.C.: Carnegie Endowment for International Peace, 2006).

Looks at the pattern of management during crises between the U.S. and China. Case studies of wars in Korea, Vietnam, and conflicts over Taiwan, as well as incidents such as the U.S. bombing of the Chinese Embassy in Belgrade and the U.S.–China aircraft collision.

Ian Taylor, *China and Africa: Engagement and Compromise* (New York: Routledge, 2006).

China's policies toward African states reflect its stated foreign policy imperative of opposing the spread of "hegemonism" while trying to find a place for the expansion of its own economic interests. Need for China to fulfill aspirations as a great power complicated by an international system that has been hostile to its ambitions, in part by shutting China out from access to natural resources in many places. Chapters on the history of China's relationship with Africa, and its present relationship with specific African countries.

David Zweig, *Internationalizing China: Domestic Interests and Global Linkages* (Ithaca, NY: Cornell University Press, 2002).

Case studies on issues that connect domestic interests to China's foreign policy and international linkages, and the diminished role of bureaucrats in regulating the internationalization of China.

HONG KONG
Periodicals and Newspapers
Asia Times Online
Hong Kong Commercial Daily
Hong Kong News Online
The Standard
South China Morning Post

POLITICS, ECONOMICS, SOCIETY, AND CULTURE

Robert Ash, Peter Ferdinand, Brian Hook, and Robin Porter, *Hong Kong in Transition: One Country, Two Systems* (New York: Routledge Curzon, 2003).

Investigates changes since the 1997 handover in Hong Kong's business environment, including the role of public opinion and government intervention, and the evolving political culture.

Ming K. Chan and Alvin Y. So, eds., *Crisis and Transformation in China's Hong Kong* (Armonk, NY: M. E. Sharpe, 2002).

Examines political and social changes in Hong Kong since it was returned to China's sovereignty in 1997.

Robert Cottrell, *The End of Hong Kong: The Secret Diplomacy of Imperial Retreat* (London: John Murray, 1993).

Exposes the secret diplomacy that led to the signing of the "Joint Declaration on Question of Hong Kong" in 1984, the agreement that ended 150 years of British colonial rule over Hong Kong. Thesis is that Britain was reluctant to introduce democracy into Hong Kong before this point because it thought it would ruin Hong Kong's economy and lead to social and political instability.

Michael J. Enright, Edith E. Scott, and David Dodwell, *The Hong Kong Advantage* (Oxford: Oxford University Press, 1997).

Examines the special relationship between the growth of Hong Kong's and mainland China's economies, such topics as the role of the overseas Chinese community in Hong Kong and the competition Hong Kong faces from Taipei, Singapore, Seoul, and Sydney as well as from such up-and-coming Chinese cities as Shanghai.

Wai-man Lam, *Understanding the Political Culture of Hong Kong: The Paradox of Activism and Depoliticization* (Armonk, N.Y.: M. E. Sharpe), 2004.

Through case studies of protest, Lam challenges the view of a politically apathetic Hong Kong populace. Looks at role of ideology, nationalism, gender, civil rights, and economic justice as motivating political participation in Hong Kong.

C. K. Lau, *Hong Kong's Colonial Legacy: A Hong Kong Chinese's View of the British Heritage* (Hong Kong: Chinese University Press, 1997).

Engaging overview of the British roots of today's Hong Kong. Special attention is given to such problems as the "identity" of Hong Kong people as British or Chinese, the problems in speaking English, English common law in a Chinese setting, and the strictly controlled but rowdy Hong Kong "free press."

Jan Morris, *Hong Kong: Epilogue to an Empire* (New York: Vintage, 1997).

Witty and detailed first-hand portrait of Hong Kong by one of its long-term residents. Gives the reader the sense of actually being on the scene in a vibrant Hong Kong.

Christopher Patten, *East and West: China, Power, and the Future of Asia* (New York: Random House), 1998.

The controversial last governor of Hong Kong gives a lively insider's view of the British colony in the last 5 years before it was returned to China's sovereignty. Focuses on China's refusal to radically change Hong Kong's political processes on the eve of the British exit. Argues against the idea that "Asian values" are opposed to democratic governance, and suggests that "Western values" have already been realized in Hong Kong.

Mark Roberti, *The Fall of Hong Kong: China's Triumph and Britain's Betrayal* (New York: John Wiley & Sons, Inc., 1994).

A fast-paced, drama-filled account of the decisions Britain and China made about Hong Kong's fate beginning in the early 1980s. Based on interviews with 150 key players in the secret negotiations between China and Great Britain.

Ming Sing, *Hong Kong's Tortuous Democratization: A Comparative Analysis* (New York: Routledge Curzon), 2004.

An examination of the governance in Hong Kong since the 1940s, and the constraints to democratization. Looks beyond the limits imposed by Beijing to other forces, including lack of public support and weak pro-democracy forces, to explain why democracy has not yet emerged.

Alvin Y. So, *Hong Kong's Embattled Democracy: A Societal Analysis* (Baltimore: Johns Hopkins University Press, 1999).

Traces Hong Kong's development of democracy.

Steven Tsang, *A Modern History of Hong Kong* (New York: I.B. Tauris), 2004.

History of British colonial rule from before the Opium Wars. Examines problems in creating the rule of law and an independent judiciary in Hong Kong, and the impact of trade with China on Hong Kong's society and economy.

Frank Welsh, *A Borrowed Place: The History of Hong Kong* (New York: Kodansha International, 1996).

Best book on Hong Kong's history from the time of the British East India Company in the eighteenth century through the Opium Wars of the nineteenth century to the present.

TAIWAN
Periodicals and Newspapers
China Post
Taipei Journal
Taipei Review
Taipei Times

POLITICS, ECONOMICS, SOCIETY, AND CULTURE

Bonnie Adrian, *Framing the Bride: Globalizing Beauty and Romance in Taiwan's Bridal Industry* (Berkeley, CA: University of California Press), 2003.

A fascinating ethnographic study of Taipei's bridal photography as a narrative on contemporary marriages, intergenerational tensions, how the local culture industry and brides use global images of romance and beauty, and the enduring importance of family and gender.

Muthiah Alagappa, ed., *Taiwan's Presidential Politics: Democratization and Cross-Strait Relations in the Twenty-first Century* (Armonk, NY: M. E. Sharpe, 2001).

Focuses on Taiwan's presidential elections in March 2000 and the impact of those elections one year later on the democratic transition from a one-party-dominant system to a multiparty system. Also examines the degree to which Taiwan under the leadership of Chen Shui-bian was able to consolidate democracy.

Robert Ash and J. Megan Greene, eds., *Taiwan in the 21st Century: Aspects and Limitations of a Development Model* (New York: Routledge, 2007).

Examines what is unique, or at least special to Taiwan's economic and political development that makes taking Taiwan as a model for China or other Asian countries questionable. Also notes those aspects of Taiwan's development model that might be replicable.

Christian Aspalter, *Understanding Modern Taiwan: Essays in Economics, Politics, and Social Policy* (Burlington, VT: Ashgate, 2001).

A collection of articles on Taiwan's "economic miracle" and such topics as Taiwan's "identity," democratization, policies on building nuclear-power plants and the growing antinuclear movement, labor and social-welfare policies, and the role of political parties in developing a welfare state.

Melissa J. Brown, *Is Taiwan Chinese? The Impact of Culture, Power, and Migration on Changing Identities* (Berkeley: University of California Press, 2004).

Author explores the meaning of identity in Taiwan. From 1945–1991, Taiwan's government claimed that Taiwanese were ethnically and nationally Chinese. Since 1991, the government has, in a political effort to claim national and cultural distance from the mainland, moved to a position asserting that their identity has been shaped by a mix of aboriginal ancestry and culture, Japanese cultural influence, and Han Chinese cultural influence and ancestry. Examines cultural markers of identity, such as folk religion, footbinding and ancestor worship as well as how identities change.

Richard C. Bush, *At Cross Purposes: U.S.-Taiwan Relations* (Armonk, N.Y.: M. E. Sharpe, 2004).

The former head of the American Institute in Taiwan (1997–2002) examines why President Roosevelt decided that Taiwan ought to be returned to China after World War II, the U.S. position on the Kuomintang's repressive government rule, the nature of the U.S. "2-China" policy from 1950 to 1972, and the basis for U.S. military and political relations with Taiwan.

Fen-ling Chen, *Working Women and State Policies in Taiwan: A Study in Political Economy* (New York: Palgrave, 2000).

A study of the impact of social welfare and state policies on the relationships between men and women since 1960. "Gender ideology" has changed and, with it, women's views of the workplace and their role in society. Examines related issues of childcare, wages, the women's movement, and women in policy-making system.

Ko-lin Chin, *Heijin: Organized Crime, Business, and Politics in Taiwan* (Armonk, N.Y.: M. E. Sharpe), 2003.

An examination of the connection between Taiwan's underworld (*hei*—black) and business/money (*jin*—gold) to politics that has accompanied Taiwan's efforts to democratize since emerging from martial law after 1987. Looks at ways in which black-gold politics have undercut democratization through vote buying, political violence, bid rigging, insider trading, and violence.

Bernard D. Cole, *Taiwan's Security: History and Prospects* (New York: Routledge, 2006).

An objective, well-written, and interesting account of Taiwan's complex security issues by a faculty member at the National War College. Full of valuable insights concerning the strategic issues of Taiwan's defense that only someone with military training and academic research capabilities can offer. The perfect starting point for understanding the strategic standoff that continues in the triangular relationship among the U.S., the P.R.C., and Taiwan.

Bruce J. Dickson and Chien-min Chao, eds., *Assessing the Lee Teng-hui Legacy in Taiwan's Politics: Democratic Consolidation and External Relations* (Armonk, NY: M. E. Sharpe, 2002).

Focuses on the impact of Lee Teng-hui presidency (1996–2000) on democratic consolidation, the role (and demise) of the Nationalist Party and the rise of the Democratic Progressive Party, and the economy. Also examines President Lee's impact on security issues.

A-Chin Hsiau, *Contemporary Taiwanese Cultural Nationalism* (New York: Routledge, 2000).

Traces the development of Taiwanese cultural nationalism. Includes the impact of Japanese colonialism, post–World War II literary development, and the spawning of a national literature and national culture.

Chen Jie, *Foreign Policy of the New Taiwan: Pragmatic Diplomacy in Southeast Asia* (Northampton, MA: Edward Elgar, 2002).

Outstanding book on Taiwan's foreign policy (1949–2000). Shows patterns in Taiwan's diplomacy and provides basis for theories and insights about Taiwan's policies, frustrations, sensitivities, and motivations in international affairs. Also covers Taiwan's policy toward the millions of "overseas Chinese."

David K. Jordan, *Gods, Ghosts, and Ancestors: The Folk Religion of a Taiwanese Village* (Berkeley, CA: University of California Press, 1972).

A fascinating analysis of folk religion in Taiwan by an anthropologist, based on field study. Essential work for understanding how folk religion affects the everyday life of people in Taiwan.

Robert M. Marsh, *The Great Transformation: Social Change in Taipei, Taiwan, Since the 1960s* (Armonk, NY: M. E. Sharpe, 1996).

An investigation of how Taiwan's society has changed since the 1960s when its economic transformation began.

Shelley Rigger, *Taiwan's Rising Rationalism: Generations, Politics, and "Taiwanese Nationalism,"* Policy Studies 26. (Washington D.C.: East-West Center Washington, 2006).

Challenges conventional assumptions that identifying as a Taiwanese equates to a pro-independence stance or to opposition to improved ties with the China Mainland. Looks at generational differences in attitudes among Taiwanese.

Denny Roy, *Taiwan: A Political History* (Ithaca, NY: Cornell University Press, 2003).

A comprehensive narrative of the island's history from the first Chinese settlements to the Chen Shui-bian presidency.

Murray A. Rubinstein, ed., *Taiwan: A New History (expanded edition)* (Armonk, NY: M. E. Sharpe, 2007).

A collection of articles on a wide range of topics, from aborigines and the historical development of Taiwan during the Ming Dynasty, to topics in Taiwan's more recent history. These include such topics as Taiwanese new literature, identity and social change in Taiwanese religion, socioeconomic modernization, and aboriginal self-government.

Scott Simon, *Sweet and Sour: Life-Worlds of Taipei Women Entrepreneurs* (Lanham, Maryland: Rowman & Littlefield Publishers), 2003.

Examines the contradictions and tensions that characterize the lives of Taiwan's female entrepreneurs, who spear-headed Taiwan's economic "miracle." Presents portraits of these women, including street vendors, a hairdresser, a café owner, a fashion designer, and more. Sheds light on urban life and on impact of patriarchal culture on male-female relations.

John Q. Tian, *Government, Business, and the Politics of Interdependence and Conflict across the Taiwan Strait* (New York: Palgrave MacMillan, 2006).
Examines the complexities of the Taiwan-China mainland relationship generated by the many situations in which both sides must compromise in order to advance their interests.

Looks at the specifics of cross-strait trade and investment, how industrial organization and the financial system affect economic interactions, and how local governments in Mainland China attract Taiwanese investors.

Alan Wachman, *Why Taiwan? Geostrategic Rationales for China's Territorial Integrity* (Stanford University Press, 2007).
Traces the evolution, explains the appeal, and suggests implications of the strategic calculations that pervade PRC strategic considerations of Taiwan.

Index

Index

Index